D1192324

DATE DUE

Legal Orientalism

Legal Orientalism

CHINA, THE UNITED STATES, AND MODERN LAW

Teemu Ruskola

HARVARD UNIVERSITY PRESS

Cambridge, Massachusetts, and London, England

2013

Library of Congress Cataloging-in-Publication Data

Ruskola, Teemu.

  Legal orientalism : China, the United States,
and modern law / by Teemu Ruskola.

    p. cm.

  Includes bibliographical references and index.

  ISBN 978-0-674-07306-7 (hardcover : alk. paper)

  1. Law—China—Philosophy—History. 2. Rule of law—China—
History. 3. Rule of law—China—Public opinion. 4. Sociological
jurisprudence—China. 5. Law—United States—Philosophy—
History. 6. Rule of law—United States—History. 7. Rule of
law—United States—Public opinion. 8. Orientalism. 9. China—
Foreign public opinion, Western. I. Title.

  K237.R87 2013

  340'.11—dc23   2012038024

For my mother, Liisa Sjöstedt.

As there is a literary canon that establishes what is and what is not literature, there is also a legal canon that establishes what is and what is not law.

Boaventura de Sousa Santos,
"Law: A Map of Misreading"

Contents

Legal Orientalism

Introduction: Legal Orientalism

"Law" . . . is part of a distinctive manner of imagining the real.

—Clifford Geertz, "Local Knowledge: Fact and Law in
Comparative Perspective"

With the Chinese law . . . we are carried back to a position
whence we can survey, so to speak, a living past, and converse
with fossil men.

—Edward Harper Parker, "Comparative Chinese Family Law"

LAW'S ORIENT CONSTITUTES a wide and uneven terrain. This book describes the itinerary of one particular journey across that terrain, with a focus on China and the United States. Law is a key aspect of the political ontology of the modern world. It is exceedingly difficult, if not impossible, for us to think of politics outside of the framework of states, and of states outside of law. At the same time, no understanding of the world today is complete without consideration of China's place in it. The difficulties begin when we seek to combine the inquiries into law and China. Where is China in law's world? And why is the United States an important part of the answer to that question?

If there is one image of China that is seared in the collective consciousness of the West, it is that of a solitary man facing a tank in Tiananmen Square on June 4, 1989. Indeed, after the end of the Cold War and the roughly contemporaneous massacre by the Chinese government of its own citizens, China has come to occupy the role of the leading human rights violator in the East—a position left vacant by the collapse of the USSR. While the People's Republic of China (PRC) has by now secured itself a solid reputation

Tank Man, Tiananmen Square, June 4, 1989.
Screen capture, CNN. Courtesy of Getty Images.

as a law breaker in chief, the United States has emerged as the world's chief law enforcer as well as its leading law exporter, administering programs for the promotion of rule-of-law everywhere—and perhaps nowhere as vigorously as in China.

This book starts from the premise that the complex and unstable relationship among China, the United States, and legal modernity is of utmost global significance. To map that relationship, it analyzes law as a fundamental element in the modern worldview that conceives the individual— the singular human being—as the paradigmatic existential, political, and legal subject and the state as the privileged medium for the instantiation of its universal values, through law. More than just a set of rules for regulating behavior, law in this larger sense is a structure of the political imagination— "a distinctive manner of imagining the real," in Clifford Geertz's words. One of its most important imagined Others is the Orient, and legal Orientalism is the discourse in which it is imagined.

The remainder of this book sets out to map key elements of that discourse and a historical itinerary of its global development. It is a comparative and historical study about ideas of Chinese and U.S. law, and of how those ideas have produced distinctive subjectivities, articulated social relations, and shaped geopolitical conditions. In terms of its historical narrative, the heart of this book is the extraordinary and virtually forgotten story of how over the course of the nineteenth century a diffuse set of European prejudices about Chinese law developed into an American ideology and practice of empire, entailing the extraterritorial application of a floating body of U.S. law in an otherwise lawless Orient. It is only from a perspective that is both theoretical and historical that we can understand the effect that Orientalism has had on the development of both Chinese law and U.S. law, as well as on international law and Sino-U.S. relations more generally.

GLOBAL CIRCULATIONS OF LEGAL ORIENTALISM

The map of law's Orient here is a particular one, as is every map. Perhaps most importantly, the scale in the following chapters varies considerably, reflecting changes in the legal topographies they traverse and in the time periods they cover. To name only some of its concerns, this volume explores representations of Oriental despotism in the imagination of Euro-American Enlightenment thinkers; it reinterprets Confucian family law in late imperial China as a kind of corporation law; it examines the so-called United States Court for China, which sought to apply, among other things, pre-Revolutionary common law in early-twentieth-century Shanghai; it investigates the comparative standing of the United States and China in international law by examining the Boston Tea Party and the Opium War; it studies the enduring damage wrought on the U.S. Constitution by the enactment of Chinese Exclusion Laws near the end of the nineteenth century; and it links these historic studies with the legal geography of today's world by considering the political and phenomenological significance of the post–1978 legal reforms of the People's Republic of China.

This book brings these varied phenomena together under the compound rubric announced by its subtitle: China, the United States, and modern law. Rather than taking any one of these three categories as a pregiven object of knowledge, or adopting a single disciplinary approach, this book examines how China, the United States, and law are related to each other—historically, conceptually, culturally, and geopolitically. At the outset it is important to recognize that it is by no means obvious to all observers that the three notions are in fact related in any particularly meaningful way. Indeed, the genesis of this book lies precisely in an examination of the widely shared assumption that law and China exist in an antithetical relationship. Originally this study began with the more modest goal of producing "just" a historical and theoretical analysis of Chinese law—an undertaking that would certainly have been demanding enough on its own. However, as I started my inquiry, I had no choice but to confront the fact that one of the defining cultural and political characteristics of China is law's putative absence there. In fact, when I am asked what I do for a living and I respond that I study Chinese law, with remarkable frequency my interlocutors inform me that there is no such thing, thereby suggesting politely (and sometimes not so politely) that I have made a category mistake in choosing my academic vocation.

At first such reactions simply irked me, and my responses were not particularly considered. ("People who study French or German law don't have to convince others that their subject matter exists!" I protested to colleagues.) However, given the consistency and manifest sincerity with which this "truth" about China was being offered, it became evident that it could not be simply ignored. Approaching the notion of Chinese law ethnographically, I decided to examine what motivates the belief in its nonexistence and what makes that belief so intuitively appealing to so many. Pursuing that inquiry has turned out to be both more fascinating and more complicated than I originally anticipated. On the one hand, it has become a study of China's ambiguous place in legal modernity. On the other hand, the notion of rule-of-law—of which China is seen as the antithesis—is claimed today most insistently by the United States. Hence, a genuinely global understanding of China's place in law's world demands a consideration of the United States' role in the legal production of modernity.

My main framework for exploring the relationship among China, the United States, and modern law is a complex of ideas I call "legal Orientalism." In his path-breaking monograph, Edward Said uses the term Orientalism to refer to discourses that structure Western understandings of the East. He emphasizes the extent to which the identity of the colonial and postcolonial West is a rhetorical achievement. In a series of imperial gestures, we have reduced "the Orient" to a passive object, to be known by a cognitively privileged subject—ourselves, "the West." As Said puts it,

"Without examining Orientalism as a discourse one cannot possibly understand the enormously systematic discipline by which European culture was able to manage—and even produce—the Orient politically, sociologically, militarily, ideologically, scientifically, and imaginatively during the post-Enlightenment period."[1]

By now there are scores of studies of different varieties of Orientalisms. Remarkably, the study of specifically *legal* forms of Orientalism remains largely unexplored—the ways in which "the Orient," as well as the Euro-American "West," have been produced through discourses of law.[2] Given the centrality of law to the political modernity of the West and the fundamental way in which Said's analysis destabilizes the epistemological status of East–West distinctions, a global study of law's world cannot afford to ignore Said's challenge.

By the term legal Orientalism, then, I refer on the most general level to a set of interlocking narratives about what is and is not law, and who are and are not its proper subjects. This book focuses largely on one particular instantiation of legal Orientalism, and the remaining chapters illustrate how its narratives enjoy global circulation and how they have performed a variety of functions in various historical contexts, up to and including the present. Each of the chapters is concerned with defining an *Other* through its relationship to *law*. Of course, the West—to use the purposely imprecise term—has many Others, and the Orient is only one of them. At the same time, the Orient itself is a radically determinate category, denoting an entity of the European imagination that extends from Morocco in North Africa to Japan on the eastern edge of Asia. In this book the cultural world of China represents only one instance of Orientalism. It is not exemplary, but it is a historically and politically important case.

Focusing on Chinese law, then, I use the framework of legal Orientalism to ask a number of related, overarching questions: Who has law? Who gets to decide who has law? And, perhaps most importantly, what is at stake in asking the question? A statement that someone has or does not have law is not only a descriptive claim but also a normative assessment of a particular society. Inevitably, not having law implies missing something that one *should* have. In considering these questions, I examine the ways in which law has been a foundational element in the constitution of the modern Western subject and the nation-state. How, I ask, have ideas of the lack of Chinese legal subjectivity served to mark the conceptual outside of Euro-American law, and the cultural and political outside of a Euro-American "Family of Nations"?

To reiterate, there is indeed a strong cultural tendency to associate the United States with law (even if excessively so at times), and a corresponding historic tendency to associate China with an absence of law (whether that absence be considered a vice or a virtue). The distinction is crucial because the emergence of law, in the sense of rule-of-law, is one of the signal markers of modernity. This rough cultural mapping of the triangulated relationship among China, the United States, and law generates a number of assumptions that provide the framework for scores of comparative studies of China. These include, most notably, the notion that China is traditional—or worse, primitive—while the United States is modern, as is the law that embodies its essential values. From these fundamental oppositions much else ensues, historically and conceptually, as this book aims to show.

It is important to acknowledge at the outset that ever since Said's classic analysis the term Orientalism has acquired a distinctly pejorative connotation. Calling someone an Orientalist is often regarded as akin to calling someone a racist, and usually it elicits a similar reaction. By designating certain understandings of law and China as Orientalist, I do not mean to level an accusation but simply to open an avenue of inquiry into the field of knowledge in which Chinese law is studied and understood. As I suggest in Chapter 2, in the modern world in which we live there is no pure, un-Orientalist knowledge to be had. More modestly, but vitally importantly, what we *can* do is understand the history and conceptual parameters of Orientalism and how they structure what can be said, and known, about China and Chinese law—and indeed about the United States and U.S. law as well.

It is vital to emphasize that the discourse of Chinese law is not, and cannot be, a self-contained universe. It is never *only* about Chinese law, or lack thereof. Chinese law is a concept with a global circulation and with global effects. Although it may be heuristically helpful to begin from a contrast between an (idealized) American law and a (caricatured) Chinese lawlessness, such a juxtaposition is ultimately too simplistic and too static. The ostensibly heterogeneous subject matter of the following pages reflects the dynamic, uneven, and worldwide traffic in ideas of Chinese law, and of Chinese legal perversity.

The point is not necessarily obvious, so it may be useful to support it with an introductory example that also illustrates the development of this book. In the early stages of my research, when I still envisioned the project as essentially a historical and theoretical study of Chinese law, I learned that in 1906 the U.S. Congress passed a law entitled "An Act Creating a United States Court for China and prescribing the jurisdiction thereof."[3] The new court, equivalent to a federal district court, assumed civil and criminal jurisdiction over American citizens within the "District of China," which in turn was coincident with the Qing Empire. The court sat in the semicolonial port city of Shanghai, and appeals from its judgments were taken to the Ninth Judicial Circuit in San Francisco, with further appeals to the United States Supreme Court in Washington, D.C. Expanding its original mandate, the court eventually construed its jurisdiction to include not only American citizens in the so-called District of China but also American "subjects" from the newly colonized Philippines, and in some cases American citizens who had never set foot in China.

As I studied the court further, I was stunned not only by the improbable fact that it had existed and the vast jurisdiction that it exercised, but also by the plain weirdness of the body of law that it applied in China. That body included English common law as it existed prior to American independence, general congressional acts, the municipal code of the District of Columbia, and the territorial code of Alaska, parts of which continued being applied in China even after they were repealed in Alaska, to mention only some of the main sources of the court's jurisprudence. The court had only one sitting judge at any one time, and when he was away (either riding circuit in the cities of Hangzhou, Tianjin, or Canton, or being investigated for official misconduct in Washington, D.C.), prisoners sometimes had to wait for months for a trial. Indeed, virtually the only federal law that did *not* apply in the District of China was the United States Constitution. Hence, there was no right to a jury trial nor to constitutional due process, among other legal niceties.

In sum, all of this struck me as something rather like from *Alice in Wonderland,* the kind of befuddled jurisprudence one might expect to emerge from the courtroom of the Queen of Hearts, not from a court of the United States—which should not even be sitting in China in the first place.[4] Yet the tribunal operated for several decades and its jurisdiction was not formally abolished until 1943. As I became increasingly fascinated with the extraterritorial operation of American law in China, I pursued the topic as a discrete project. However, as I also continued my prior research into the

historical and cultural representations of Chinese lawlessness, it soon became impossible not to recognize just how oddly disjunctive, yet related,
the two projects were. While the District of China may have been full of
American law, the way in which the United States Court for China exercised jurisdiction over it was hardly law*ful* in a more fundamental sense.
Paradoxically, that erratic jurisdiction was justified precisely, and perversely,
by the United States' claims of alleged *Chinese* lawlessness.

In order to understand this paradox, I concluded that an examination of
how U.S. law operated in China must proceed simultaneously with a study
of how Chinese law has been represented in the United States, which in turn
is linked further to global discourses about the nature of Chinese law and
justice, or lack thereof. As it turns out, and as Chapter 4 elaborates, those
discourses have historic, and enduring, effects even on the *domestic* structure
of U.S. law, not merely on its extraterritorial operation. Notably, a belief in
the incapacity of the Chinese to understand, let alone embody, the virtues of
individual rights and rule-of-law came to provide a crucial justification for
anti-Chinese immigration laws passed by Congress beginning in 1882. When
Chinese would-be immigrants contested the laws, the U.S. Supreme Court
upheld them on the basis of an extraordinary theory. It held that in certain
areas, including immigration, the federal government possesses "plenary
powers": a discretionary authority unconstrained by the Constitution. Ironically, a desire to banish subjects of Oriental despotism outside the borders of
the United States resulted in the institutionalization of a kind of legal despotism *inside* the United States. It is in this sense that ideas of Chinese law
constitute, indeed, a transnational discourse with global effects. As Chapter 4
insists, those effects were significant and far-reaching: it is precisely the laws
at the margins of a liberal democratic state that define its center.

EXCEPTIONAL EMPIRES OF THE UNIVERSAL
AND THE PARTICULAR

Both China and the United States are, or view themselves as, exceptional in
many regards. Perhaps most importantly, they are the last two major empires
that remain standing in the beginning of the millennium. The achievement is
remarkable, considering the violent collapse of several other empires with
whom they shared the global stage at the dawn of the twentieth century,

barely a hundred years ago: the Russian (and subsequently Soviet) Empire, the British Empire, the Ottoman Empire, the Austro-Hungarian Empire, the French Empire, and the German Empire—all are long gone. To be sure, the more or less contiguous nature of the continental territories of the PRC and the United States may make it slightly more difficult to recognize them *as* empires than, say, the far-flung possessions of the erstwhile British Empire. Nevertheless, the vast territorial footprint of both states is an unmistakably imperial achievement, enabled by a not dissimilar process of continental expansion, whether in the name of a Manifest Destiny or a Confucian civilizing mission.[5]

In the discourse of legal Orientalism, too, both empires occupy an exceptional status, albeit in highly distinctive ways. One way to analyze that distinction is to consider the differential relationship of the United States and China to the universal and the particular—key categories by which Western thought has classified and evaluated knowledges, civilizations, polities, persons, and literally everything else for at least two millennia. For moderns, the state is the primary medium for the articulation of the universal, and law is the privileged language in which that universality is expressed. To put it in phenomenological terms, in the juridified world in which we live our lives, freedom means *rights*. That is precisely why to embody lawlessness is to be lacking something that is, or ought to be, universal, and, consequently, why both the United States and China occupy an exceptional status in the ontology of modern law.

The United States has from its founding regarded its political values as exemplary, not just reflecting the emancipatory values of the Enlightenment on the European model but embodying them even *better* than Europe does, or once did. The American system of government is thus not merely one expression among others of the universal values of democratic rule-of-law but their paradigmatic instance—a model for others to emulate. In short, the political values of the United States are *particularly universal*. At the same time, insofar as China's legal tradition grows out of an enduring Oriental despotism, its political values are inherently suspect. Worse than simply unlegal, they are in effect antilegal. Hence, while the United States' legal values are particularly universal, those of China appear as *universally particular*—categorically undemocratic.

It is one of the key contemporary effects of this discursive framework that it sets up the United States as a global enforcer of human rights and

China as one of their preeminent violators. Restated most broadly, then, this book is a global mapping of discourses of world-making and self-making through law. There is no discourse of rule-of-law that is not at the same time a discourse of legal Orientalism—a set of usually unarticulated cultural assumptions about that which is not law, and about those who do not have it. Whether we choose to recognize it or not, there is no world of legal modernity without an unlegal, despotic Orient to summon it into existence.

To avoid a possible misreading of the term Orientalism, it is important to note that I use it to refer both to ideational and material practices, which are ultimately indissociable from each other. While the world always and necessarily exceeds discourse, discourse always has a worldly existence and material effects. At the same time, all material practices take place within, and are mediated by, discourses. In terms of the structure of this volume, Chapters 2 and 3 focus on a predominantly discursive analysis of legal Orientalism. What are some of its key assumptions, and how do they permit us to know certain things about China, the United States, and law, while making other things unknowable or unintelligible? That is, these chapters analyze legal Orientalism primarily as an *epistemological practice,* examining how Western observers of Chinese law—especially but not exclusively within the academic field of comparative legal scholarship—have viewed the object of their study. Their central focus is the construction of China as an object of legal knowledge.

Chapters 4 and 5 of the book turn to legal Orientalism as a *material practice,* investigating some of the uneven effects produced by the global circulation of ideas of perverse Chinese legality. Of course, even epistemologies do not arise ex nihilo; knowledge, too, is produced in institutions with material support. However, the institutions analyzed in these chapters are primarily legal and judicial institutions rather than academic ones. The main vehicle for translating the knowledge produced by the academic discipline of comparative law into political institutions was the emerging profession of modern international law in the mid-to-late nineteenth century. As self-proclaimed carriers of the universal values of Western civilization, international lawyers developed institutionalized jurisdictional practices to restrict the particularistic operation of Chinese law.[6]

Needless to say, as knowledge of Chinese law was translated into international legal institutions, those institutions both reflected and continued to transform the epistemologies that supported them. In the end, it is part of the wondrous efficacy of legal discourse that it constructs its own reality. The empirical basis of legal Orientalism is, and always has been, ultimately beside the point. It is a discourse of legal reason rather than of factual truth. Once China's lawlessness was established as a *legal* rather than veridical fact, that fact came to justify its exclusion as a state from the privileges of international law. And similarly, as noted earlier, it permitted U.S. constitutional lawyers to justify a series of exclusion laws that for nearly sixty years denied Chinese persons admission to the United States (analyzed further in Chapter 4).

Viewed from a wide angle, this book might be described as a global history of China—a history of China and its place in the world, as seen from the point of view of law, epitomized by the U.S. legal order.[7] At the same time, despite the breadth of its subject matter, the book's main concern is still the analysis of Chinese law—the original project with which it began—as long as we understand the term in its broadest, most global sense. In such a usage, it refers not only to the legal mechanisms by which China has been regulated but also to ideas about Chinese legality, constructed in relation to ideas about Euro-American law; the global traffic in those ideas; and the effects they had both inside and outside of China, for Chinese and others.

Admittedly, a literally global analysis would ultimately entail a study of ideas of Chinese law and their effects far beyond North America and Europe, from South to North Africa, from Peru to Persia, and throughout East Asia.[8] Such a comprehensive investigation would take up several volumes. This book can therefore only begin the task of drawing a global map of Chinese law, by focusing primarily on two outsized and exceptional hemispheric actors, China and the United States. As Jonas Grimheden observes, for better or worse contemporary discourses of Chinese law are "dominated by Americans studying China and by Chinese studying the U.S. legal system."[9] What, then, does the cultural geography of modernity look like when analyzed through the lens of law, American as well as Chinese?

RULE-OF-LAW, RULE-OF-MEN, AND ORIENTAL DESPOTISM

The idea that China suffers from a lack of law was not invented by the global press on June 4, 1989. In 1899, the English consul Ernest Alabaster observed, melancholically, "To all intents and purposes foreigners are completely in the dark as to what and how law exists in China. Some persons whose reputation for scholarship stands high would deny the right of the Chinese to any law whatsoever—incredible but, to my knowledge, a fact."[10] Marcel Granet announced in 1934, "The Chinese notion of Order excludes, in all aspects, the idea of Law."[11] In his critical review of the status of law in studies of Chinese society, William Alford concludes that things have not improved markedly—indeed, the very title of Alford's essay is "Law, Law, What Law?"[12]

Just what do such oft-repeated claims mean, whether referring to law's absence in China or its near-total social and political insignificance? Only the most negligent observer could miss the fact that imperial China boasted dynastic legal codes going back to the Tang dynasty (618–907 c.e.), and earlier. The point is indeed usually a subtler one: whatever law China has known is of a particular kind that falls short of "real" law. This view is implicit in the frequently made claim that Chinese law has been historically exclusively penal and associated with criminal sanctions. Especially in the civil law systems of continental Europe, civil law stands at the heart of jurisprudence, and its absence therefore signifies a gaping hole at the center of the Chinese legal tradition. Sometimes the implicit yardstick for authentic law is formal legal rationality in the sense in which Max Weber uses the term.[13] Perhaps most commonly, the law that China lacks refers to a liberal legal order that constrains the state in a particular way—a configuration often referred to as the rule-of-law. Legal historian Thomas Stephens argues that Chinese law is not even worthy of the term jurisprudence. As a more descriptive term for the study of Chinese non-law, Stephens offers the neologism "obsequiiprudence"—presumably signifying the scholarly study of obsequious submission to authority and hierarchy.[14] (Stephens's problematic analysis is considered in greater detail in Chapter 5.)

If what China ultimately lacks is rule-of-law, we must begin by asking what we mean by rule-of-law. Although the discourse of rule-of-law has a long history, its current vogue dates from the early 1990s.[15] With the end of the Cold War, rule-of-law is not only shorthand for a system of restrictions on state power but has become a ubiquitous by-word for the promotion of freedom, democracy, and market economies more generally. For many, the apparent triumph of neoliberal capitalism over state socialism has constituted nothing less than the End of History.[16] Even though most of the same triumphalists recognize the emergence of a new East–West division, defined by the United States and the People's Republic of China, that cleavage is often understood as *cultural*—in contrast to the former rivalry between the United States and the Soviet Union, which is viewed in primarily *political* terms. In this new East–West discourse, it is no longer politics but civilizations that clash. The promoters of rule-of-law in turn view law as a fundamental element of a democratic culture. When understood in terms of legal Orientalism, this post–Cold War turn to culture is better understood not as the end of politics—let alone History—but as a displacement of what are often political differences onto the terrain of culture. From that perspective, legal Orientalism is the concept that names the cultural distance between East and West, as law reigns as the predominant universal of the post–Cold War world and culture is viewed, increasingly, as a particular difference standing in its way.

Although there is a global consensus on law's desirability, there is surprisingly little agreement on just what constitutes rule-of-law, culturally or otherwise. Legal theorists have proposed multiple definitions ranging from "thick" to "thin," from "instrumental" to "substantive."[17] Such conceptual indeterminacy may be bad for the development of legal theory, but it is precisely the ambiguity of rule-of-law that makes it so appealing politically. Like human rights, to which even human rights violators—including China—pay lip service, rhetorically the rule-of-law is just the kind of "unqualified human good" to which no sane person can object, whether liberal or conservative.[18] At the same time, the term's ambiguity covers differing, even inconsistent, agendas. In China, for example, the state's keenness for the rule-of-law seems often driven by a desire for foreign investment and the construction of (state-dominated) markets. In contrast, when political activists call for the establishment of rule-of-law, they typically associate it with the creation of the political institutions of democracy. (Democracy, in turn, is just as elusive of definition, both in China and the West, even while all agree on its standing as the highest political desideratum of modernity.)[19]

Moreover, not only does the rule-of-law hold the promise to cure all manner of social ills from economic corruption to political tyranny, but it promises to do so in a nonpartisan manner. On this popularly held view,

the rule-of-law is a *thing*, the rule of *rules*: a system of neutrally administered legal sanctions and incentives that provide the basis for an orderly
modern society.[20] This is far too modest a view. Rules do not exist apart
from the social context that gives them meaning. Whatever else it may be,
the rule-of-law is a social practice. At an even deeper level, the rule-of-law
constitutes also the political epistemology in which those social practices are
grounded. Indeed, it is "a way of being in the world," with its own particular
structure of beliefs.[21] Stated in Heideggerian parlance, law plays a key role in
worlding the modern world.[22] The world in which we live is a fundamentally
legal one.

While there is a rather stunning lack of agreement on what the rule-of-
law is, there is an equally overwhelming consensus on what it is *not:* the
rule-of-men. As Chief Justice John Marshall stated in *Marbury v. Madison,*
the Supreme Court case that opens numerous textbooks on U.S. constitutional law, "The government of the United States has been emphatically
termed a government of laws, and not of men."[23] The idea that the rule-of-
law means precisely *not* the rule-of-men is so fundamental that the two
terms are in fact best understood as forming a singular expression, rule-of-
law-and-not-of-men, whether or not the two phrases are tagged together.
This negative contrast is constitutive of law itself: "Law *is* not the rule of
men."[24]

Putting aside the fact that the contrast is exaggerated and oversimplified
even in terms of the American political self-understanding, it has ruinous
analytic consequences for the study of Chinese law. Historically, the Chinese political self-understanding has been premised on the very *ideal* of the
rule-of-men (人治), a kind of moral utopia where those in power derive their
authority to govern from their superior virtue—either Confucian virtue, in
the case of traditional China, or Communist virtue, in the case of socialist
China. This self-understanding is no less mythical and self-congratulatory
than the American one, but insofar as it provides the traditional normative
justification for the Chinese political order, it also means that, from a comparative perspective, any law that we find in that order will not qualify as
real, true, universal law. If the rule-of-law means *not*-the-rule-of-men, any
would-be Chinese law is an oxymoron, a transparent alibi for law's corruption under Oriental despotism.[25]

In short, despite their formally symmetrical relationship to each other,
the categories rule-of-law and rule-of-men are neither historically neutral

nor culturally equivalent. One is always pre-identified as Western, and hence modern, and the other as non-Western, and hence premodern or traditional. While we in the cultural West are often bemused to learn of Sinocentrism—the Chinese word for China (中国) means the Middle Kingdom, or in a more literal and somewhat less romantic translation, the Central State—we nevertheless accept with utmost unself-consciousness the notion that we are the First World, twice removed from the *soi-disant* Third World. Admittedly, the distances among the worlds are shrinking, as the Second World has all but disappeared, and even as a new Fourth World, comprised of indigenous peoples, has emerged on the political and legal landscape. (Remarkably, the peoples who claim the longest chain of title to the earth's surface have been placed at the end of the queue, after the three modern worlds.[26]) But our occidental solipsism aside, cultures and nations do not come labeled with ordinal numbers, ranked by their capacity to embody universal values. The division of Earth into economically and racially segregated worlds denies the essential coevalness of everyone who lives on this planet.

To recognize that European analytic categories are not universal, even while many European practices have become more or less globalized as an ongoing legacy of European imperialism, is a historical conundrum that has no simple exit. As Dipesh Chakrabarty puts it, European categories are "both indispensable and inadequate in helping us to think through the experiences of political modernity in non-Western nations."[27] Chakrabarty's response to this predicament is to "provincialize" Europe: to put Europe in its place by decentering Western analytic categories and subjecting them and their particular histories to critical scrutiny.

Provincializing the binary and moralistic rule-of-law versus rule-of-men distinction will not be easy, given how deeply it structures our political vision. At a minimum, we must learn to inhabit its contradictions more candidly. U.S. legal scholars have known how to recognize law's contradictions and live with them at least since the rise of Legal Realism in the first half of the twentieth century. On the most basic level, one need not be a trained lawyer to recognize that the person of the judge makes a great deal of difference. Otherwise, judicial elections for state and local courts would hardly matter, and confirmation battles over presidential nominees for the Supreme Court would be incomprehensible. Indeed, it is one of the risks inherent in rule-of-law that it is always at risk of becoming rule-by-judges, a kind of juristocracy.[28] But although the critique of the naïve view of the rule-of-law has been made domestically over and over—epitomized by the Realist aphorism that what the law is depends on what the judge had for breakfast—this critical self-awareness dissipates all too quickly when we turn to analyzing Chinese law. While we can understand, or at least gloss over, the contradictions and shortcomings of the rule-of-law at home, we become far more uncompromising in evaluating traditions elsewhere.[29]

In effect, as this book argues, law's contradictions cannot be resolved, only managed. One way of managing them is projecting them elsewhere. Peter Fitzpatrick calls this self-congratulatory worldview the "mythology of modern law."[30] The strategy is far from new. One of its ablest practitioners was Montesquieu, who has likely done more than anyone else to oppose "despotism" to "law" and then exile the former into the Orient. (This is not to say that he did not have important Greek and Roman predecessors who likewise associated the East with despotism.) In *The Spirit of the Laws,* one of the eighteenth century's most important works of political theory, Montesquieu elaborates a comparative theory of despotism on a global scale. He associates monarchies and republics with Europe (the former being the most desirable political system of all), whereas despotism as a form of government is native to Africa, America, and Asia. Monarchies and despotisms are structurally similar in that they are both ruled by a single person, but in monarchies a spirit of honor ensures rule by means of law, while despotisms are governed solely by a spirit of fear.[31] Although despotism is a generic extra-European form of government, Montesquieu locates its natural home in Asia, with China as one of its Asiatic prototypes.

To be sure, few invoke outright Montesquieu's disparaging language of Oriental despotism in managing law's contradictions today. However, those contradictions are likely inevitable, perhaps even productive. In any event, as the remainder of this book argues, they are inherent in the very notion of legality. Legal Orientalism is a discourse and a material practice that manages those contradictions.

DISCIPLINARY ORIENTATIONS

The following pages are aimed at multiple audiences. As its subtitle alone makes evident—*China, the United States, and Modern Law*—this book addresses Chinese studies, American studies, and legal scholarship. More generally, the investigations in this book owe an enormous debt to postcolonial studies. Collectively, they are driven by a set of questions they ask, not by a commitment to a specific method, a particular geographic scope, or even a single historical period. This interdisciplinary orientation is a corollary of the nature of legal Orientalism as a pervasive form of knowledge across numerous fields.

With this caveat, it may nevertheless be helpful to locate the study of legal Orientalism among institutionally organized areas of knowledge. First, where does the book fit in Chinese and American studies? In both fields, as in other fields of area studies, there has been an increasing turn to transnational and comparative approaches. In Chinese studies the transnational turn has been most notable in scholarship on emigration and studies of the Chinese diaspora—areas of inquiry that evidently lend themselves to, and indeed demand, a geographic perspective that extends beyond the boundaries of a single nation-state.[32]

Simultaneously, Chinese law itself has emerged as an increasingly important subject among historians of China. An earlier generation of scholarship on the Chinese legal tradition focused predominantly on orthodox Confucian representations of law. As Alford observes, those are generally negative, given Confucianism's ideological preference for rule-of-morality over rule-of-law.[33] However, with growing access to judicial archives in the PRC, the last few decades have allowed historians to study not only cultural attitudes and officially promulgated codes but also the mundane adjudications undertaken by county magistrates in the late imperial period.[34] These studies provide a far richer and more complex picture of the operation of Chinese law. Yet their perspective remains typically "China-centered," to use historian Paul Cohen's term, in contrast to the turn to transnational approaches in many other areas of Chinese studies. This book seeks to complement existing studies of Chinese law by doing just that, and asking what is at stake globally when we invoke the *idea* of Chinese law as an object of analysis.[35]

In American studies, too, the turn to the transnational is most evident in analyses of immigration, as a way of overcoming the intellectual tyranny that national borders impose on knowledge. In addition to studies of Latin America, the Caribbean, and elsewhere, these investigations include prominently histories of Chinese immigration. Unsurprisingly, while the movement of persons from China to the United States has historically appeared as a story of *emigration* in Chinese studies, in American studies it has been narrated as one of *immigration*.[36] Both kinds of histories have certainly been useful, but today we have also genuinely *transnational* studies that employ the two modes of analysis concurrently.[37] In a similar spirit, this book examines the United States' call for an Open Door policy in China and its contemporaneous enactment of anti-Chinese immigration laws in a single frame, despite their conventional segregation into separate fields of study.[38]

In terms of the projection of American power outward, there is a robust tradition of studies of American empire, in both its formal and informal aspects. Studies of formal empire date their subject matter from the Spanish-American War in 1898, in which the United States acquired the remains of the Spanish empire—Cuba, Puerto Rico, and the Philippines, or what came to be known in constitutional jurisprudence as the nation's "Insular Possessions." The study of informal U.S. imperialism in turn is focused largely on Latin America, from the establishment of the Monroe Doctrine to filibustering expeditions to liberal and neoliberal forms of economic imperialism today. Although the study of semicolonialism is an established part of Chinese studies, there is surprisingly little emphasis on the role played by the United States in that history.[39]

As I elaborate in Chapter 4, in Chinese studies the United States is conventionally cast as a "special friend" of China that historically defended it against depredations by Great Britain and other European imperial powers—evidently part of a larger narrative of American exceptionalism. Recently there has been a surge of interest in American studies in the Cold War, with a new focus on U.S. imperial actions in Asia in the post–World War II era, especially in Korea and Southeast Asia.[40] However, as this book insists, there is a far longer history of U.S. empire in Asia, dating back to the cultivation of legal Orientalism as an American ideology of extraterritorial empire in the mid-nineteenth century. There are multiple reasons why this history remains largely unexplored, but certainly one of them is the way in which it straddles both geographic and disciplinary boundaries. In addition to Chinese and American studies, it is a story of international law, comparative law, and U.S. constitutional law. Yet despite its pervasiveness it is easy to miss, for it does not come into full view from the perspective of any one of them. Precisely because of its seemingly peculiar nature, conventional disciplinary lenses render it all but invisible.

Indeed, legal Orientalism belongs under the purview not only of Chinese and American studies but that of legal scholarship as well. In the U.S. legal academy, the study of Chinese law is generally classified under the study of comparative law—an umbrella category that refers to the academic study of foreign legal systems. The historic focus of comparative law has been the comparison between Anglo-American common law tradition, on the one hand, and the civil law tradition of continental Europe, on the other, although the study of non-Western law—to use an inelegant qualifier—has always maintained a small but important presence in the field.[41] Until the end of the Cold War socialist legal systems remained another lesser, yet notable, area of study.[42] Because of its approach to Chinese law as a concept that circulates transnationally rather than as simply a practice localized in China, the analytic method of the following chapters extends beyond comparative law as such (even broadly defined) into the study of the significance of Chinese law from the additional perspectives of both international law and even U.S. domestic law. As I argue later, it has played constitutive roles in both.

As the thematic opposition between the universal and the particular is one that unfolds through all classificatory schemas of Western thought, it is possible to map it also in terms of the conventional division of labor between comparative law and international law. While comparative law is a purely academic study of "other" legal systems, international law refers to the body of law that regulates relations among states and protects the human rights of individuals irrespective of their national identity. At least according to some conventional wisdom, international law tends to focus on the universal, the supranational, while comparativists tend to focus on the local, the particular. As noted above, this study too began as a comparative study of Chinese law. However, over time I have come to recognize that a truly comparative understanding of China must in fact account for it in terms of international law as well. No comparative study of China is complete until it considers China *itself* as a legal subject—how, when, and why China was recognized, or not, as a full member of international society. To tell this story is, indeed, a way to provincialize the study of both international law and comparative law, by locating them within a particular history of the universal.

As I have already suggested, this book's concern with the geopolitical and historical determination of what counts as universal and particular is greatly indebted to postcolonial theory. At its heart lies a concern with the constitution of modernity and its universal subjects: citizens within nation-states. Postcolonial scholars have challenged the ways in which we imagine both. Approaching legal Orientalism as a geopolitics of knowledge—a study in the unequal global distribution of universality and particularity, achieved by and reflected in law—is thus a fundamentally postcolonial approach.

This book seeks also to contribute to, not only benefit from, postcolonial studies. There is already an impressive body of work that examines the legal and disciplinary structures of colonialism as well as the colonial history of international law.[43] What is still largely missing is a recognition and study of the role of law even in the operation of *informal* imperialism—imperial practices that fall short of formal territorial colonialism. The notion of informal empire itself is of course not new. However, in American studies, most notably, the vocabulary for analyzing U.S. power overseas is primarily military and economic, evidenced by the very terms in which it is commonly described, such as "gunboat diplomacy" and "dollar diplomacy." Nevertheless, the exercise of American power has never been based solely on the assertion of sheer military and economic might. From the beginning, it has been mediated through the language of law, as a matter of *right*. Hence, we witness the putatively exceptional character of American imperialism, often cast as an imperialism in the service of anti-imperialism (as in the United States' "liberation" of Spain's colonies in 1898).

It may strike some as odd to turn to the field of postcolonial studies to understand China, given that the country as a whole was never reduced to the status of a formal colony. Yet the very fact that China was *not* colonized formally may be considered an important *event* within the larger field of colonialism and can be analyzed as such.[44] The question becomes: How was China not-colonized? The United States' invocation of extraterritorial jurisdiction in China and throughout the Orient constitutes a prime example of the kind of nonterritorial colonialism that law can become—a form of jurisdictional imperialism this book characterizes as *extraterritorial empire*. An understanding of this empire of U.S. law enhances not only our understanding of China's semicolonial past but also rewrites the history of American empire. Although the beginning of U.S. imperialism in Asia is conventionally dated from the United States' acquisition of the Philippines in 1898 (followed shortly by the United States' colonization of Hawaii), it is a central argument of this book that the history of American *legal* imperialism in the Orient begins more than half a century before the Spanish-American War.

It is important to emphasize that a postcolonial perspective on law's history in the Orient unsettles not only our view of Chinese law but the study of U.S. law as well. The nature and extent of U.S. extraterritorial jurisdiction in the Orient are woefully unknown not only among scholars of American empire but also among students of American law. This is hardly surprising, as American law is, by definition, associated with the territory of the United States (even while the emancipatory appeal of its ideals is routinely regarded as universal). To be sure, there is an important emerging body of scholarship on the adoption, and adaptation, of American law in the U.S. colonial possessions from the Philippines to Hawaii to Puerto Rico.[45] However, the diasporic travels of American law in non-U.S. territories remain all but unknown.[46] Chapter 4 sets out for the first time a detailed jurisprudential analysis of the extraterritorial operation of U.S. law in the Orient—an empire that ranged from China to Japan, from Korea to Siam, from Borneo to Tonga, and beyond, and reached its most highly articulated expression in the jurisprudence of the United States Court for China.

Finally, before proceeding to chapter descriptions, it may be useful to state what this book is *not* saying. First, while I do insist that law's world is indeed not any more or less universal than other regimes of the political—and while I admit to harboring a certain utopian longing for recovering some of law's alternatives—this book is in the end not an argument *against* law, only a historical and conceptual study of it. That law is neither particularly universal nor universally particular does not make it either useful or useless as such, for the simple reason that there is no such thing as "law as such." Law only exists in concrete historical and political conjunctures and cannot be evaluated apart from them.

To be sure, in the particular world we have created—that of modern centralized states with unprecedented power at their disposal—it may be that life without rights would be literally unlivable. As the concluding chapter suggests, this constrained modern notion of politics recognizes ultimately only two authentic subjects, as it were: the state and the individual. However, whatever the critical limitations of rule-of-law as a meta-discourse of global governance may be, I want to emphasize at the outset that I am certainly not opposed to law reform in China. There is no doubt that in a legal order that at least officially still prioritizes (the ideological fiction of) "the people" over (the ideological fiction of) the "individual," the language of individual rights retains a progressive potential—especially as the PRC has modernized itself on the model of the centralized Euro-American state and exercises far greater power than the imperial state ever did. Today there are numerous sensitive and sensible advocates of specific law reform initiatives who are in fact aware of their roles as "assisting Chinese reformers in doing their work, not coming in as a great savior."[47] Nevertheless, my goal in this book is neither to prescribe nor to evaluate specific legal policies but, rather, to understand the nature, history, and political and cultural significance of Chinese law reform more generally.

Concomitantly, the point of analyzing legal Orientalism as a discourse is emphatically neither to prove nor disprove either the historical or theoretical existence of Chinese law. To be sure, one is inclined to agree with Mirjan Damaška who observes that a definition of law so narrow as to exclude China from the legal universe "smacks of the dogmatism of the untraveled."[48] Ultimately, however, the answer to the question of whether there is, or has been, law in China is always already embedded in the premises of the questioner. It necessarily depends on the observer's definition of law.

The second caveat is equally significant. Although this study situates its subject matter expressly within a global frame, it does not, and indeed cannot, fill in that frame in its entirety. Because of its specific comparative focus, the bulk of this book analyzes China's legal interactions with Europe and, especially, with the United States, in the nineteenth and twentieth centuries. Within that context, Euro-American law indeed typically functions in imperial modes. However, none of that is to suggest that China is today, always has been, and always will be only a victim. A world that consisted solely of victims and victimizers, victors and losers, would be wonderfully easy to navigate morally, but it is simply not the world in which we live. (Admittedly, it is often the world that law imagines—but that is part of the story that follows.)

To state the obvious, it is an incontrovertible historical fact that China is an empire in its own right, with territorial and political ambitions that have been realized to varying degrees at various times, especially in China's relationships with its own neighbors. While this book focuses on the circulation of ideas of Chinese law in Europe and especially the United States, there is an entire other circuit of uneven imperial legal exchange: the Confucian world of East Asia, consisting most notably of China, Korea, Japan, and Vietnam. Within that world, the classical Chinese language of statecraft and Chinese legal codes enjoyed widespread cultural and political hegemony. Indeed, just as the putatively universal foundations of Euro-American international law in fact reflect the particular values of its progenitors, so Chinese political and cultural values pretended to a universal status in East Asia—prescribing a normative standard of civilization in the form of a set of constitutional norms for a properly administered polity, and guidelines for interactions among such polities. We might call this an East Asian law of nations, roughly similar to the European tradition of *ius gentium*. Both traditions claimed universality, while each in fact embodied a particular set of imperial norms—Roman and Chinese, respectively.[49]

Evidently the universal and the particular are little more than functions of one's historic, cultural, and geopolitical viewpoint. As Gayatri Chakravorty Spivak remarks, "There is something Eurocentric about assuming that imperialism began with Europe."[50]

MAP OF *LEGAL ORIENTALISM*

Chapters 2 and 3 of this book approach Orientalism as a structure of legal knowledge, especially in terms of scholarly representations of Chinese law. Chapter 2 begins the mapping of Orientalist epistemologies by considering the role of law in the construction of modern subjects and their unlegal Others. To be a modern subject—a person who *owns* one's body, is *entitled* to the fruits of one's labor, and has the *right* to political representation—is to be a *legal* subject. The chapter first maps briefly a series of Orientalisms of the classical European variety, analyzing them as a discourse that produces both legal and unlegal subjects, legal and unlegal histories. It then turns to a comparative analysis of the U.S. legal subject and the Chinese nonlegal nonsubject. In the discourse of legal Orientalism, individuals in the American style are the universal subjects of history, while undifferentiated Chinese masses are its objects—witless myrmidons living under the tyranny of tradition, waiting to be emancipated and swept into the global mainstream of political and economic development.

How should a comparative inquiry confront the quandary posed by this logic, writing some of us into universal, progressive legal histories and others into particular, unlegal pasts that are never truly past? Rather than proposing an impossible morality of anti-Orientalism—a hopeless search for universal, pure knowledge—the chapter proposes an ethics of Orientalism. It is a fundamental effect of acts of comparison that they produce the objects that are being compared. Through those acts we create others as well as ourselves. We thus ought to wield that power responsibly, in ways that enable different kinds of subjects to emerge, rather than fix and classify historical subjects on the basis of their universality or particularity.

Representations of Chinese law examined in Chapter 2 inevitably tell us more about Euro-American ideas of law and legality than they tell us about China. It is vital to start with them, as there is no unmediated access to Chinese law as such, no direct route that simply bypasses the history of legal Orientalism. Chapter 3 moves us beyond Euro-American representations of Chinese law. It puts the ethics of comparison into practice in a specific legal field, the history of corporation law in China.

According to a long-standing Western—and indeed also Chinese—scholarly tradition, China has no genuine native predecessors to the modern business corporation. Purportedly, in the absence of corporate legal forms most Chinese enterprises have been family businesses. This is typically offered as a key explanation why capitalism "failed" to develop indigenously in China—as if the emergence of capitalism were simply part of history's natural unfolding. Importantly, the story about the socioeconomic predominance of the family is also a story about lawlessness. Part of a larger regime of particularism and of attachment to tradition, the family as a home for business organization necessarily impedes the development of economic relations on the universal basis of the market, structured by the laws of contract and property rather than those of kinship. Chapter 3 reinterprets this Orientalist narrative in which China is always a story about the dominance of the collective, and the history of the West becomes a just-so story about the emergence of the individual. It argues that in late imperial China many extended families constituted "clan corporations" in which Confucian family law functioned as a *kind* of corporation law. In fact, much as the idea of the modern corporation as a legal person, analogous to an individual, is a well-recognized fiction, so it turns out that in Chinese clan corporations too kinship was often little more than a legal fiction, serving to legitimate business enterprise in a polity where Confucianism was the official legal and economic ideology.

Placing the analysis in an expressly comparative framework, the chapter suggests a different story of U.S. law as well. There are many aspects of contemporary United States corporation law that may be better analogized to the norms of family law than to those of contract law, which has been recently a favored paradigm for theorizing corporation law. In short, the chapter destabilizes the logic of legal Orientalism by offering an antifoundationalist model of comparison, based on reversible analogies—in this instance, reading Chinese family law as a kind of corporation law and analyzing key elements of U.S. corporation law as a kind of family law. Rather than simply re-narrating a universal history of corporation law in a way that would fold China into it—"China, too, has corporation law"—it refuses the priority of either the universal or the particular, contesting instead the Orientalist logic by which the (Western) corporation and (Chinese) family are constructed as oppositional to each other in the first place.

Chapters 4 and 5 of the book examine the processes by which legal Orientalism as a regime of comparative knowledge about China has been transformed historically into a regime of legal institutions. With the expansion of Western imperial adventures in the nineteenth century, legal Orientalism moved beyond its academic home in the North Atlantic, starting to shape the Orient itself. As epistemological imperialism was transformed into imperialism as such, it began literally—and legally—to remake the world. Once comparative scholarship had characterized the Chinese legal order as essentially particular, it became the ground for a variety of institutions seeking to subordinate China to the universal order of legal modernity. Key among them was a system of so-called Unequal Treaties accompanied by extraterritorial courts.

Chapter 4 tells the little-known story of the beginnings of Sino-American legal relations, while also mapping the changing global distribution of claims to universality among Europe, the United States, and China over the course of the nineteenth century. Although the United States began its international legal career in 1776 as an outlaw, a rebel against the European legal order, it soon established itself as a juridical equal among the so-called Family of Nations, consisting of "civilized" European states. Yet it is a remarkable historical fact that when the British launched the Opium War in 1839, most Americans in fact sided *with the Chinese,* against the British.

With confiscated British opium being flushed into the Canton harbor, the events echoed the still not-so-distant Boston Tea Party—two heroic acts of struggle against British imperial interventions in trade, in China and America, respectively.

Over the course of the nineteenth century the identification of the United States changed, however, from that of an earlier victim of European imperialism to its avowed practitioner. As noted earlier, the transition occurred formally in 1898 when the United States became the custodian of the remains of the Spanish Empire. Chapter 4 argues that this shift was in fact prefigured by the 1844 Treaty of Wanghia—the United States' first treaty with China—which gave Americans in China the right of extraterritorial jurisdiction. Long before the Spanish-American War, the United States became a global leader in the institutionalization of legal imperialism in the Orient.

Yet the institutional consequences of the global travels of legal Orientalism were not limited to the Orient. As noted above, it provided a justification for the promulgation of anti-Chinese immigration laws in the United States, resulting in a regime of domestic judicial despotism in order to keep the Oriental kind out—a paradox with all too evident contemporary implications, as we witness the daily erosion of constitutional rights in the name of protecting them in a never-ending War against Terrorism.

Chapter 5 turns from the origins of America's extraterritorial empire in the international legal order of the nineteenth century to its actual operation in China in the early twentieth century. In the end the export of U.S. law to China did not become part of a universal history of law's unfolding in China but, rather, yet another chapter in a global story of legal Orientalism. In the historic encounter between Chinese and Western legal institutions—as opposed to their divergent depictions in Euro-American legal epistemologies—the purity of their elemental contrast became impossible to maintain.

The bulk of Chapter 5 consists of a close reading of the jurisprudence of the U.S. Court for China and of the contradictions that haunted it. Although the court purported to offer a model of law's rule for China, what it in fact provided was a despotism of law. Formally, the court was directed to apply the laws of the United States—to treat China as if it were literally part of the continental United States. No judge could bridge the gulf opened up by this massive legal fiction. As noted earlier, among the main bodies of law the court chose to apply were the codes of the District of Columbia and the Territory of Alaska. Lacking correctional facilities, it also sent American prisoners to the U.S.-occupied Philippines, while bringing back judges and law from the Philippines to China. Effectively, the court turned to the law and institutions of America's internal and external colonies to provide order in China. Simultaneously, it divested Americans in China even of its ostensibly most universal ideal, the constitutional rights of U.S. citizens. In the end, the leading American court in the Orient overcame the impossible contradictions entailed in its extraterritorial jurisdiction by fabricating a jurisprudence that had no coherent territorial or constitutional referent—an ultimately placeless law justified by the axiom that China itself was a lawless place. In the very institution that was designed to police the boundary between the rule-of-law and Oriental despotism, the distinction collapsed—a process that had already started when the United States denied entry to Chinese persons inside U.S. territory but admitted Oriental despotism inside the U.S. Constitution.

In addition, Chapter 5 examines the International Mixed Court, one of the sister courts of the U.S. Court for China in Shanghai's International Settlement. The Mixed Court was originally a Chinese court with a Chinese judge, with the authority to apply Chinese law to the Chinese population of the Settlement—a logical corollary of the fact that none of the Unequal Treaties gave foreigners jurisdiction in cases that involved Chinese parties only. However, over time the foreign consular body of Shanghai simply took over the court's administration. In the International Mixed Court, legal Orientalism thus did not claim merely an epistemological monopoly on how to *represent* Chinese law to a global audience. It became a political institution with the power to *produce* Chinese law itself, and to enforce it directly on a Chinese population in China. Any distinction between legal Orientalism as a system of representation and Chinese law as that which it represented simply vanished, as the former became the latter.

From a historical perspective, the story told in Chapters 2 through 5 is a genealogy of the universal. It is a (partial) account of how one particular idea of law has become a global standard for constituting free individual subjects as well as democratic states. In the process, it has remade the world, and human beings' relationship to it. In a sense, law has clearly won the day. Today, it *is* universal, at least in the geographic sense of having colonized the entire planet. Remarkably, while China had to be coerced to join the Western system of "free trade" in the Opium War, at the end of the twentieth century it staged a prolonged struggle to gain *admission* into the World Trade Organization. But although law has become a privileged contemporary medium for the universal, what remains contested is who has the authority, and power, to speak in its name. As long as global politics continue to be negotiated in legal terms, the Orientalist history of those terms will inform that negotiation.

Chapter 6 is an epilogue. It starts from the premise that if extraterritorial legal imperialism was a kind of colonialism without colonies, today's neoliberal economic and legal order can be analyzed as a colonialism without even colonizers. The chapter begins by considering the afterlife of America's extraterritorial empire and its replacement by a range of multilateral institutions after World War II. Today these new organizations—especially the World Trade Organization—have transformed not only China but the entire world in profound ways, legal and otherwise. One consequence of the globalization of liberal and neoliberal political institutions is that discourses of legal Orientalism are embraced as commonly in China as in the United States.

The bulk of the epilogue focuses on legal reforms in the PRC after 1978, examining how law has reconfigured notions of political and legal subjectivity and, indeed, thereby colonized much of the modern Chinese lifeworld. Nevertheless, even the colonized modern Chinese subject is not merely a replica of a legal subject made in the U.S.A. The analysis turns to two sites where *different* subjects—old and new, legal and nonlegal—continue to live: the "real" world of Chinese business organization and the imaginative world of legal theory.

Finally, the chapter returns to the contemporary status of legal Orientalism in the United States. Remarkably, the U.S. Supreme Court has never overruled the *Chinese Exclusion Case,* in which it upheld the constitutionality of Chinese Exclusion Laws. In effect, the far-reaching exception the case and its progeny carve to the seemingly universal values of due process remains good law to this very day. This book concludes by speculating on the future of both China and the United States in the world that legal Orientalism has made. Perhaps China can provide not only a target for U.S.-led law reforms but also a source of different visions, legal and otherwise. To stay with the case of economic enterprise, what *is* a corporation? Is it best likened to an abstract individual, a kinship group, a mode of government, or something else altogether? Although the answers to such questions about the nature of society and politics need not be found in law, they may well be found in the Orient—as long as we keep in mind, as this book insists throughout, that the Orient itself is a traveling concept, and that whatever else it may be law is, above all, a category of the human imagination.

CHAPTER TWO

Making Legal and Unlegal Subjects in History

> [In China,] animals are divided into: (a) belonging to the Emperor, (b) embalmed, (c) tame, (d) sucking pigs, (e) sirens, (f) fabulous, (g) stray dogs, (h) included in the present classification, (i) frenzied, (j) innumerable, (k) drawn with a very fine camelhair brush, (l) et cetera, (m) having just broken the water pitcher, (n) that from a long way off look like flies.
>
> —Michel Foucault, *The Order of Things*

A CITATION TO Michel Foucault's citation of a Chinese encyclopedia in the preface to *The Order of Things* is by now de rigueur in comparative studies of Chinese culture.[1] The shortcomings of Chinese law, like much else in China, are often blamed on a cultural confusion of categories. Perhaps most notably, Montesquieu's *Spirit of the Laws* finds in China a fatal conflation of religion, mores, manners, and laws, all of which are said to find expression in the all-purpose Confucian category of rites.[2] Such claims have great intuitive appeal. Like the brilliantly patronizing encyclopedia entry described by Foucault, they accord with expectations of Chinese taxonomical madness and essential cultural difference. The logic that organizes Chinese knowledge is evidently an extraordinarily particular one—in contrast to the universal reason that informs the organization of knowledge in the West, exemplified by the orthodox categories we have inherited from the Enlightenment *encyclopédistes*.

What many readers of Foucault ignore is that the amusing entry he quotes is not a real encyclopedia entry at all. It is a quotation from a fable by Jorge Luis Borges ("The Analytical Language of John Wilkins") that Foucault uses artfully to set up an epistemological foil for European systems of knowledge.[3] One assumes—though one cannot be quite sure—that Foucault is acting self-consciously in doing so.[4] Yet what is certain is that many enduring Western notions of Chinese law are based on Orientalist fables and betray little self-awareness of this fact. That fabulous jurisprudence is the chief object of analysis in this chapter.

An introductory caveat for the Sinological reader is in order here. Although this book is, indeed, a comparative study of the United States and China, China "itself" will not appear until the next chapter. The reason for this delay is precisely the comparative nature of the analysis. Insofar as Chinese law is defined negatively, in relation to Euro-American law, it is critical to begin by outlining the basic outlines of the latter. Although the very point of analyzing legal Orientalism as a discourse is *not* to reduce Chinese law to its Western representations—those representations tell us more about Western ideas of law than anything else—it is also not possible for us to examine the Chinese legal tradition apart from those representations.

At the same time, examining legal Orientalism as a discourse cannot mean simply decrying Orientalist distortions, whatever critical pleasure that might yield. Rather, the aim is to understand how history has shaped the field of knowledge in which the analysis of Chinese law unfolds today. The enterprise in this chapter is ultimately hermeneutical in Hans-Georg Gadamer's sense: its goal is "not to develop a procedure" for understanding Chinese law, "but to clarify the conditions in which [such] understanding takes place."[5] It is only by considering legal Orientalism as part of an ongoing historical tradition that we can understand why even today claims about the nature of Chinese law are so insistently normative.

Much of the introductory analysis in Chapter 1 refers to popular and journalistic accounts of China. It is notable that, despite vigorous efforts to debunk it, the notion of Chinese lawlessness continues to prevail, not only in the popular opinion and among policy makers but even among legal scholars who do not specialize in China and students of China who do not specialize in law.[6] Chinese ideas of civil law, for example, have been discovered and rediscovered periodically in the West. What are the preconceptions that make it possible for them to be discovered and forgotten again so quickly, leaving them to wait for yet another round of "discovery"? To answer such questions, this chapter canvasses a range of historical sources, including Orientalist scholarship in comparative law, comparative philosophy, and comparative politics. Inevitably, that scholarship constitutes one important tradition from which our modern understandings of Chinese law emerge.[7]

Stated differently, we must begin by taking account of the historical and cross-cultural context in which the study of Chinese law necessarily unfolds, and to understand the historicity of contemporary views of Chinese law. What are the historical processes by which claims of the absence of law in China have become part of the observers' cultural identity and, in turn, contribute to the contents of the observations themselves? What can we learn from the history of comparative legal scholarship and, indeed, from the history of Chinese legal history?

The analysis that follows opens by considering the *legal* aspect of legal Orientalism. It first examines some of the predominant scholarly methods by which Chinese law has been known, and unknown, and then proposes a discursive analysis of law as a site of subject-formation—a cultural medium through which subjects are made and unmade, placed in history and outside of it. Next, the chapter turns to the *Orientalist* aspect of legal Orientalism by sketching a preliminary genealogy of culturally embedded views of the American and Chinese political and ethical subject—the former taking the universal form of a progressive, historical individual, the latter that of a particular, stagnant object of history. From the law's point of view, Americans constitute legal subjects and the Chinese nonlegal nonsubjects. Finally, the chapter asks, what are the ethics of comparison in the postcolonial world of the twenty-first century? How should we live in the world that legal Orientalism has made?

HOW (NOT) TO COMPARE

Chapter 1 already began to unpack the naïve but popular vision of the rule-of-law as the rule of legal rules, pure and simple. Few serious legal scholars adhere to that view. Whether or not expressly avowed by its practitioners, the dominant methodology in the cross-cultural study of law is functionalism: analyzing legal rules as part of structural-functional systematic wholes. Functionalism in and of itself is not necessarily either good or bad—it can be practiced responsibly and with care, or poorly and irresponsibly. But like all methods, it has notable limitations, allowing us to know some things and making other things unknowable.[8]

The basic idea of functionalism—originally imported into comparative legal study from sociology—is powerfully simple.[9] The functionalist's task is to identify some type of more or less universal problem shared by several societies and then analyze how different legal systems solve the same problem. The legal solutions, by definition, will be functionally equivalent and hence comparable. For instance, scholars of Chinese law have frequently observed that many of the dispute resolution functions of the American legal system were performed in traditional China by extra-judicial mechanisms, such as the family.[10] Likewise, prominent observers have argued that Confucian ritual (禮) constituted the Chinese equivalent of natural law in the early modern West.[11]

In the social sciences, functionalism largely exhausted itself by the 1980s, after a very long run and with increasingly mixed results. However, it has retained a surprisingly tenacious hold on the imagination of comparative legal scholars. Despite its apparent value neutrality, it is premised on the identification of a problem that the law then solves. However, it is hardly self-evident what constitutes a "problem" for law to solve. What is a problem for one society may simply not be a problem for another. Furthermore, functionalists often make implicit assumptions about which problems *should* be resolved by legal, rather than some other, means. At its worst, functionalism leads to a kind of epistemological imperialism: either we find in foreign legal cultures confirmation of the (projected) universality of our own legal categories, or, equally troublingly, we find "proof" of the fact that other legal cultures lack some aspect or other of our law.

Before turning to the case of Chinese law, it is useful to consider the colonial administration of British India, a truly classic example of the first kind of conceptual colonialism. Describing the attempt of Sir William Jones to discover the principles of indigenous Hindu law, Bernard Cohn explains that what started "as a search for the 'Ancient Indian Constitution,' ended with what [Jones] had so much wanted to avoid—with English law as the law of India."[12] The reason was simple. As Jones set out to find "a Hindu civil law," his focus was on subjects that he, "a Whig in political and legal philosophy, was centrally concerned with—those rights, public and private, that affected the ownership and transmission of property."[13] Unsurprisingly,

Jones found precisely what he set out to find, which is indeed the hallmark of an enterprising functionalist.

As a perhaps trivial, yet telling, example of the opposite danger—the failure to find equivalents of one's own categories—consider an anecdote from the classroom. In her syllabus for a seminar on Chinese law, Janet Ainsworth included a scholarly article on ancient Chinese "contract law" in the Han dynasty (206 B.C.E.–220 C.E.).[14] Although the highly contextualized scholarly analysis of the piece makes quite evident the need for scare quotes, a student in the class queried her teacher urgently, "Tell me . . . had the ancient Chinese developed promissory estoppel by [the Han], too?" As Ainsworth observes tartly, with her reference to a specific doctrine of Anglo-American contract law, the student "apparently regarded the development of the concept of promissory estoppel as a natural evolutionary outgrowth of the law of contracts, such that any civilization possessed of a jurisprudence of contract doctrine would eventually produce the functional equivalent of Section 90 of the *Restatement of Contracts*."[15] At its extreme, a relentless insistence on exact equivalence can indeed lead a functionalist to conclude that China lacks not just Section 90 of the *Restatement of Contracts* but even the very category of law.

In functionalism's favor, one should note that there is nothing about it as a methodology that compels one to find either a presence or an absence in (place of) the object of comparison. Historically, the more contemporary variants of functionalism—unlike, say, nineteenth-century evolutionary functionalisms—have in fact tended to find even "primitive" legal systems more rather than less functional. In fact, insofar as functionalism is premised on the existence of certain universally shared conditions, it embodies the potential to make the exotic Other seem ultimately rational rather than merely primitive. As Max Gluckman insisted in his classic 1955 ethnography of tribal law, "it is unfortunately still necessary to demonstrate that Africans . . . use processes of inductive and deductive reasoning which are in essence similar to those of the West, even if the premises be different."[16]

If comparison is such an inherently risky enterprise, is there any way to talk about Chinese law without implicating oneself in the perilous act of comparison? Comparative legal scholars in fact often insist on a distinction between the study of "foreign law" and the discipline of "comparative law" in a proper sense. The latter consists of the express comparison of two legal systems rather than a mere description of foreign legal systems.[17] However, it seems inescapable that the description of foreign law—including Chinese law—is always an instance of comparative law. Even in "mere description," the implicit point of reference is always one's own system, against which one compares the object culture. This is precisely why the analysis in this chapter considers both American and Chinese legal subjects.

Moreover, the distinction throughout the remaining chapters between law in its epistemological form, as a system of representation, and law in its material form, as an institutional practice, is only heuristic, as noted in Chapter 1. To invoke Robert Cover's succinct formulation, law is defined by both "word" and "violence," and the two are inextricably connected.[18] In this chapter both "Chinese law" and "Western" or "American law" are considered primarily as cultural representations, while recognizing that how we imagine ourselves through law certainly affects also how we act, and our actions in turn affect the material conditions that support and give rise to legal representations and legal ideologies. These complicated historical interactions are considered in greater detail in Chapters 4 and 5.

Even as a matter of comparative method, it is vital to keep in mind that neither Western nor Chinese law exists in isolation of the other. It is a critical methodological premise of this book that *both* form part of a global discourse of legal modernity.[19] To be sure, the positions occupied by China and the United States in that discourse are hardly symmetrical, but neither of them is outside of it. How the West imagines China and Chinese law has colored its encounters with Chinese legal thought and legal practices. These encounters in turn have further influenced—through interpretation and misinterpretation—the status of China and Chinese law in Western minds. Likewise, the Chinese have brought their own views of the West to these encounters, and their understandings and misunderstandings of Western law have changed correspondingly. In fact, since the earliest Sino-European contacts, the Chinese too have used Western "barbarians" (to use the contested translation of a range of Chinese terms for foreigners) for their own instrumental purposes, to confirm their own self-understandings of what it means to be Chinese.[20]

Moreover, American and European observers do not have a monopoly on Orientalist understandings of Chinese law. Today the idea of Western superiority enjoys global currency, and it has resulted in Chinese legal and cultural responses that can best be described as a kind of self-Orientalism (as analyzed later in this chapter and in Chapter 6).[21] Put simply, both

Chinese and Western law exist in both Chinese and Western imaginations and are intersubjectively linked. Boaventura de Sousa Santos refers to this kind of legal intersubjectivity aptly as interlegality—the legal equivalent of intertextuality in literary theory. Santos defines interlegality as "not the legal pluralism of traditional legal anthropology, in which the different legal orders are conceived as separate entities coexisting in the same political space, but rather, the conception of different legal spaces superimposed, interpenetrated and mixed in our minds, as much as in our actions."[22] Thus, to the extent that we necessarily live our legal lives in the intersection of different legal orders, even as systems of representation Chinese and Western legal orders are not discrete.

Precisely because of this interlegality, the baggage that Westerners have brought to their understandings of Chinese law includes not only their "own" biases but often those of the Chinese as well. That is, the rhetoric of China's official Confucian ideology systematically privileged morality over law as a means of social control, even while in practice the state relied on a sophisticated legal system to govern the empire. However, in a process of "Confucianization," the law eventually came to embody the values of official Confucian morality, which in a sense allowed this Confucianized law to hide in plain sight.[23] As William Alford points out, Euro-American scholars in turn have failed to appreciate the role of law in China precisely because of their tendency to take official Confucian platitudes at face value.[24]

MAKING LAW'S SUBJECTS

Before considering further how to analyze a Chinese political preference for morality over law, it is important to consider just *how* it is that some of us become law's subjects, while others do not. Drawing on critical legal theories and postcolonial theory, I suggest a thicker notion of law as a social technology that produces in part the world in which it exists and the subjects whom it disciplines. This will in turn give us a method for a discursive analysis of legal Orientalism.

Deconstructing the binary opposition that legal scholars as well as social scientists posit conventionally between "law" and "society," Robert Gordon argues that law is in fact "omnipresent in the very marrow of society" and that law-making institutions are among "the primary sources of the pictures of order and disorder, virtue and vice, reasonableness and craziness."[25] In Gordon's legal epistemology, "the power exerted by a legal regime consists less in the force that it can bring to bear against violators of its rules than in its capacity to persuade people that the world described in its images and categories is the only attainable world in which a sane person would want to live."[26] This view that law is an inextricable part of the social world—often dubbed the constitutive view of law—accords law much power, but it is not the statist power of positive law.[27] Law matters, even terribly, but not always in officially sanctioned ways, and it certainly does not occupy a privileged place in the regulation of the world.

The more different the cultural and historical context, the easier it is to see law's constitutive nature and the limits of functionalism. As an example of legal proceedings that hardly lend themselves to a functionalist analysis, consider the practice in medieval Europe of prosecuting animals. Explaining in a functionalist framework why the early modern French chose to try rats, for example, would require considerable ingenuity. How would one even begin to frame the inquiry? ("How did the French deal with the problem of criminal rodents in the sixteenth century?" Or, "How did French law address cross-species disputes?") A more culturally specific analysis is required. What were the assumptions that supported these trials? What makes them conceivable in certain places at certain times but not others? As Joseph Needham observes, Chinese cultural assumptions, in contrast to those of medieval Europe, provided little support to the idea of trying animals: "The Chinese were not so presumptuous as to suppose that they knew the laws laid down by God for non-human beings so well that they could proceed to indict an animal at law for transgressing them."[28]

To be sure, observing connections between law and cultural practices is not news even to the comparative legal scholar. From the Enlightenment until the arrival of functionalism and its promise of a neutral social scientific paradigm, such observations in fact provided the main theoretical grounding for comparative legal study. Put simply, in this view each nation is defined by a unique cultural essence of which its laws are merely a reflection. It is a version of this view that continues to underwrite even today both American exceptionalism and Chinese exceptionalism: law as a key expression of the genius of the political order of the United States, and lawlessness as a constitutive feature of the Chinese cultural makeup. Indeed, Montesquieu's *Spirit of the Laws* is the *locus classicus* not only for the notion of Oriental despotism as an inherent aspect of the Chinese state but also for a culturalist mode of analysis more generally. As Montesquieu puts it, "the political and civil laws of each nation. . . . should be so appropriate to the people for whom they are made that it is very unlikely that the laws of one nation can suit another."[29]

To a critical contemporary observer, this sounds like cultural essentialism pure and simple. However, combining a postcolonial analysis with the constitutive view of law radicalizes the received culturalist approach. For when the constitutive view is extended beyond law's role in the construction of our social worlds to include its role in the construction of our *selves,* as subjects, then law does not simply mirror "our" pregiven national identity but *enacts* that identity. That is, the legal subject's consciousness is constituted in part by the categories enshrined in law. Therefore, no subject stands outside the law, and interpreting legal categories is not just something that we do to law. In the process, law also aids—and limits—us in our process of "self"-understanding.[30]

Today there are many analyses of the discursive production of racial, gender, and sexual identities, for example. Summarized crudely, the insight most critical to the comparative study of law is that our seemingly fixed, real, and ontological selves are neither fixed nor ontologically stable but, rather, a complex of socially and historically contingent identities, defined today most notably by discourses of race, gender, sexuality, and class. Those discourses consist partly of law, and, in this, law "subjects" us—defines us in part as subjects. In the argot of critical theory, law is *performative.*[31] Indeed, some of the most important accounts of subject formation emphasize how the social subject is produced through the language and practices of the law. For Foucault, for example, law is an important discourse that creates the modern subject as its effect.[32]

The French philosopher Louis Althusser similarly insists that the fundamental achievement of legal ideology is the notion that "man is by nature a subject," or, as he elaborates, law is one of the "rituals of ideological recognition, which guarantee for us that we are indeed concrete, individual, distinguishable and (naturally) irreplaceable subjects."[33] As an illustration of law's recognition of individuals as its subjects, Althusser provides his famous example of what he describes as "the most commonplace everyday police (or other) hailing: 'Hey, you there!'" He elaborates: "Assuming that the theoretical scene I have imagined takes place in the street, the hailed individual will turn round. By this mere one-hundred-and-eighty-degree physical conversion, he becomes a *subject*. Why? Because he has recognized that the hail was 'really' addressed to him, and that 'it was *really him* who was hailed' (and not someone else). Experience shows that the practical telecommunication of hailings is such that they hardly ever miss their man: verbal call or whistle, the one hailed always recognizes that it is really him who is being hailed."[34]

In this scene the subject is occasioned "through language, as the effect of the authoritative voice that hails the individual."[35] While law is not the only means of hailing, it provides a paradigmatic example of a modern apparatus of subjectification. Of course, the scene of a policeman hailing a pedestrian in the street is ultimately allegorical. A "concrete individual" does not, one day, magically turn into a socio-legal subject upon an accidental encounter with a policeman in the street. Rather, everyone is "always-already a subject, appointed as a subject in and by the specific familial ideological configuration in which [he or she] is 'expected' once [he or she] has been conceived."[36] Even before we are born, the law is waiting for us, with birth certificates as well as sets of social security numbers ready to go the moment we enter the world—not to mention family law and the kinship structures it defines for us.[37]

It is an axiom of poststructuralist thought that however social subjects are produced—legally or otherwise—they are never fully achieved. For one thing, we are all subjects of many discourses. The criminal is perhaps the clearest example of a (partially) failed legal interpellation, a subject who has not internalized all of law's interdictions. Yet no criminal can—or would even want to—flout all laws, as law is simply so pervasive in our social worlds that it can be violated only at chosen points at chosen times; to exist in complete, continuous violation of all law would be to be mad. Consider also Oliver Wendell Holmes's notoriously amoral "bad man"—the unethical person who cares about law only insofar as he is likely to be fined or locked up.[38] He is no criminal, nor is he insane, but his cost-benefit approach to law ("How much can I get away with?") certainly manifests a fractured legal subjectivity, a configuration where *homo juridicus* meets *homo economicus*. Being a legal subject does not imply being a perfect legal subject or being *only* law's subject.

If we accept that law defines in part who and what we are as subjects, then laws are part of a people's identity as a people. It is a commonplace of postcolonial theory that nations and peoples do not exist as inert facts of nature any more than our ostensibly individual selves do. Nations are, in Benedict Anderson's famous conceptualization, imagined communities.[39] Legal discourses have played an important role in the process of creating and maintaining the identity of both the United States and China as states, and that of their national subjects.

IMAGINING THE AMERICAN LEGAL SUBJECT

Structurally, Orientalism as a discourse entails the projection onto the Oriental Other of the kinds of things that we are not, including lawlessness. An analysis of representations of Chinese law must be preceded by considering first how we view *ourselves*. How do Americans imagine themselves as law's subjects?

To observe that Americans are a very legal, even legalistic, people is among the most time-worn clichés. In the classic words of Alexis de Tocqueville, Americans "borrow, in their daily controversies, the ideas, and even the language, peculiar to judicial proceedings." As the French observer concluded, "Scarcely any political question arises in the United States that is not resolved, sooner or later, into a judicial question."[40] This will hardly surprise us, considering that America's foundational myths are also peculiarly legal. As a political idea, the United States embodies the ambitions of the Enlightenment, which also gave birth to "modern" law: the first French civil code, the first Declaration of the Rights of Man, and, finally, the United States Constitution—the closest thing to a people's effort to negotiate a real-life Social Contract.

Even ordinary Americans' faith in law's redemptive power often rivals that of the Enlightenment *philosophes*. Perhaps the most extraordinary example of such faith is Frederick Douglass. Faced with a "state legal order no more likely to hold slavery unconstitutional than to declare the imminent kingship of Jesus Christ on Earth," a man born as a slave in antebellum America nevertheless believed in the ultimate unconstitutionality of slavery.[41] To an outsider today, it is almost equally remarkable to observe how Americans habitually invoke their constitutional rights. That they do so in seemingly trivial contexts makes it only more extraordinary. "You can't do that to me; it's unconstitutional," ordinary people protest in varied everyday situations, whether they are being bumped off an overbooked flight or stopped for a traffic violation. The Constitution and the rights it guarantees—in the popular imagination if not in the courtroom—are evidently part of what it means to identify as an American.

As an unusually powerful historical example of Americans' attachment to law, consider the clash of legal traditions in Mexican California prior to its annexation to the United States in 1848. Anglo-American expatriate traders were dismayed at the Mexican legal institutions, based on Spanish civil law, which they deemed inadequate for the purposes of contract enforcement. Paradoxically, in their dealings among themselves the traders nevertheless continued using fastidiously drafted "legal" contracts (based on laymen's recollections) even when there was no prospect of their enforcement.[42] What was the point of going through such quasi-legal motions?

David Langum suggests an answer in the Anglo-American expatriates' shared mercantile culture: "To a significant extent that culture included law. The law was a reality they believed in. It was for that reason that in the face of potential breakdown of contractual relations, these men could make technical legal claims on one another, claims of which they had no subjective hope of enforcement in the local courts, but with every hope that they could convince their opponent of the rightfulness of their positions."[43] De Tocqueville could hardly have asked for a better example of Americans who "borrow, in their daily controversies, the ideas and even the language, peculiar to judicial proceedings." Apparently unable to imagine commercial exchange apart from the legal form of contract, even in an extralegal setting these expatriate traders continued to conceptualize their commercial relations in Anglo-American legal terms. As an inseparable part of their conceptual apparatus, they carried law in their heads even into the alien territory of Mexican California.[44]

To be sure, most Americans' relationship to law is deeply ambivalent. A strong attachment to law—one observer diagnoses this condition as "hyperlexis"—alternates with a fear of law.[45] (One recalls, for instance, Judge Learned Hand's terror at being dragged to court: "As a litigant, I should dread a lawsuit beyond almost anything short of sickness and death."[46]) Yet whether they view law as the promise of a better society or as vexatious litigation, or both, Americans' identification with law remains extraordinarily strong. Numerous ethnographies describe American communities where the actual behavioral norm is the avoidance of formal law.[47]

But as Carol Greenhouse observes, even in the face of evidence to the contrary, "many Americans are ready to believe in, almost to the point of insistence, their own allegedly litigious national character."[48]

IMAGINING THE CHINESE NONLEGAL NONSUBJECT

If such is the self-understanding of the American legal subject, how do Orientalist discourses perceive the Chinese legal subject? Legal Orientalisms come in many varieties, such as classical European Orientalism and American anti-immigrant Orientalism. Moreover, Orientalist views of China can be both negative and positive. What various Orientalisms share is a tendency to posit the Chinese as nonlegal and lacking in subjectivity—effectively nonlegal nonsubjects.

Although American Orientalism is distinctive, it was not written on a clean slate. It remains indebted to as well as departs from the European prototype. By the founding of the United States, there was already a long history of Sino-European interactions and of European imaginings of China. As Chapter 4 elaborates, over the course of the nineteenth-century wars between Europeans and the Chinese, the United States' initial identification with China's struggles against European imperialism gave way to an increasing identification *with* Europe *against* China. Much of American Orientalism thus pivots around the United States' triangulated relationship with China and Europe. Effectively, after European Orientalist scholarship had created Chinese lawlessness as a globally recognized "fact" (the focus of this chapter and Chapter 3), in the mid-to-late nineteenth century the United States proceeded to fill that lack with American law (as described in Chapters 4 and 5).

It is thus vital to begin by summarizing briefly key terms of classical European Orientalism. I do so by turning to Hegel's *Philosophy of History*. Although I use Hegel as a point of departure, in no way do I mean to imply that he "invented" Orientalism or is somehow singularly responsible for it. Wishing neither to accuse nor to excuse its author, I employ *The Philosophy of History* merely as a textual case study, as it happens to provide a truly classic statement of many Orientalist ideas that continue to structure the perception of Chinese law even today—in Europe, the United States, and indeed even in China.[49]

Hegel asserts that "the History of the world travels from East to West, for Europe is absolutely the end of History, Asia the beginning."[50] In Hegel's dual ontology, Oriental states "belong to mere space," or "unhistorical History," while the West exists in the "Form of time."[51] According to Hegel, "with the Empire of China History has to begin, for it is the oldest, as far as history gives us any information; and its *principle* has such substantiality, that for the empire in question it is at once the oldest and the newest. Early do we see China advancing to the condition in which it is found at this day; for as the contrast between objective existence and subjective freedom of movement in it, is still wanting, every change is excluded, and the fixedness of a character which recurs perpetually, takes the place of what we should call the truly historical."[52] Hegel's statement of China's extraordinary stability is no doubt extreme, yet it has many historical variations. In Marx's scathing metaphor, China "vegetates in the teeth of time," while Max Weber saw in Confucianism a religion that worshipped the status quo and thus radically impeded China's passage into modernity.[53] And in *The Order of Things* Foucault too characterizes Chinese culture—located "at the other extremity of the earth we inhabit"—as one that is "entirely devoted to the ordering of space."[54]

In Hegel's particular teleological view, History's end goal is the accomplishment of freedom, which coincidentally culminates in the political system of Prussia. In contrast, China, standing at the threshold of History, is the paradigmatic example of Oriental despotism. For Hegel, as for Montesquieu before him, despotism is in fact the natural form of Chinese government. As far as Hegel is concerned, the Chinese simply do not exist as individual subjects. In China, "all that we call subjectivity is concentrated in the supreme head of the State," while "individuals remain as mere accidents."[55] This despotic order results in part from a confusion between family and state. "The Chinese regard themselves as belonging to their family, and at the same time as children of the State."[56] By implication, the Chinese also lack a proper distinction between law and morality. Moral dicta are expressed in the form of laws, but, lacking subjectivity, the Chinese obey these laws merely as external forces, like children who fear parental punishment.[57]

Analyzed as an Orientalist discourse, Hegel's account accomplishes several things. First, the purported fact that China is timeless and static implies that the West is not. Second, imputing to the Chinese a lack of individual subjectivity and moral character suggests that Westerners do not lack those progressive qualities. Third, observing that the Chinese are confused about the real nature of "law" establishes the European legal ordering as proper. The Orientalist implications are not difficult to grasp: China is an antimodel and stands for everything that we would not wish to be—or admit to being. This is an entirely negative definition. China is basically just a "glimpse of what it itself is not," namely, we, the Occident.[58]

Montesquieu, Hegel, Marx, and Weber are classical European Orientalists whose work ultimately affirms the superiority of Western civilization and law.[59] However, during its global travels, legal Orientalism has taken on many forms. For example, early American views of China were largely favorable. Thomas Jefferson, for one, held up China's abstemious foreign policy of "non-intercourse" as an ideal for the young United States, while Benjamin Franklin was taken by Confucian ethics and its "wonderful influence on mankind."[60] Indeed, in many respects the Founding Fathers had views on government that were not unlike those of Confucius; the vision of a peaceful, stable agrarian empire governed by a virtuous ruler and a bureaucracy composed of men of letters held great appeal for the young nation.

Moreover, positive views of Chinese politics extended specifically to the Chinese legal tradition as well. One way in which Benjamin Franklin sought to disseminate the political vision of the Chinese sage was by printing a set of essays entitled "The Morals of Confucius" in *The Pennsylvania Gazette,* with approving references to China's restrained judicial administration and discouragement of needless litigation.[61] Even more remarkably, on the eve of the American Revolution Franklin reportedly wished to ask the Emperor of China for permission to use his "code of laws" as a model for the new republic. Although Franklin was quite aware of China's reputation for haughtiness, he is said to have believed that a request coming from a "young people" would be unlikely "to alarm the fears and excite the jealousies of that Cautious Government."[62] Although the Founding Fathers ended up writing their own constitution, rather than copying China's, their positive views of the Middle Kingdom were reflected at least to some extent in the subsequent legal treatment of Chinese persons as well. For example, when Cantonese tea merchants ended up in litigation with their U.S. buyers in Philadelphia courts, their claims were taken seriously and, in general, "received with candor, and treated with impartiality," or so Chancellor

Kent urged American judicial authorities to do in his decision in *Consequa v. Fanning* in 1818.[63]

But although many thinkers of the American Enlightenment admired the political wisdom of Confucianism, such sentiments were ultimately superseded by an anti-immigrant Orientalism, which by the end of the nineteenth century came to exemplify a peculiarly American, and peculiarly virulent, form of legal Orientalism. (Chapter 4 describes this transformation in greater detail, linking it to the rise of racial Anglo-Saxonism over the course of the nineteenth century.) As one historian of Chinese immigration observes, almost every aspect of Chinese life came to be an illustration of backwardness: "wearing white for mourning, purchasing a coffin while still alive, dressing women in pants and men in skirts, shaking hands with oneself in greeting a friend, writing up and down the page, eating sweets first and soup last, etc."[64]

This particular Orientalist discourse found institutional expression in the legal exclusion of Chinese immigrants at the century's end, for which it served as justification. Indeed, the text of a 1878 report by the California State Senate Committee on Chinese Immigration sounds as though it had been excerpted directly from Hegel's *Philosophy of History:* "The Chinese are . . . able to underbid the whites in every kind of labor. They can be hired in masses; they can be managed and controlled like unthinking slaves. But our laborer has an individual life, cannot be controlled as a slave by brutal masters, and this individuality has been required by the genius of our institutions, and upon these elements of character the State depends for defense and growth."[65]

Such sentiments may have a nineteenth-century flavor, but consider also the following analysis of the Chinese immigration exclusion, made by a federal judge in the 1920s: "The yellow or brown racial color is the hallmark of Oriental despotisms, or was at the time the original naturalization law was enacted. It was deemed that the subjects of these despotisms, with their fixed and ingrained pride in the type of their civilization, which works for its welfare by subordinating the individual to the personal authority of the sovereign, as the embodiment of the state, were not fitted and suited to make for the success of a republican form of Government. Hence they were denied citizenship."[66] To the judge it was thus self-evident that Congress's exclusion of the Chinese from immigration was not based on "color" but cultural disqualification for citizenship.[67] That is, the Chinese were so radically unlegal that they were simply not capable of the kind of self-governance that was required by America's "republican form of Government."

Bleak as many characterizations of China and the Chinese are, it is important to reiterate that Orientalist discourses are not consistently negative. The Founding Fathers who held up China as an example of a secular empire run by a rationally organized bureaucracy were in fact also drawing on European precedents.[68] Referring to such idealizations, Jacques Derrida characterizes China as a "sort of European hallucination"—one that represents different things to different observers.[69] In an effortless *volte-face,* Nietzsche, for example, is able to use China as a negative example for Europeans on one page, and then as a model only a few pages later.[70] Instead of being simply a "dull half-conscious brooding of Spirit" in the darkness, as Hegel describes China, for the French *philosophes* China is a source of Enlightenment: *ex Oriente lux,* and even *lex.*[71] An ardent Sinophile, Voltaire, for example, marvels at the religious tolerance of the Chinese bureaucratic state.[72] Similarly, reports by sixteenth-century Jesuit missionaries to China extol Chinese criminal justice "which these Gentiles have great care to performe."[73]

Nevertheless, even such positive portrayals have ultimately far less to do with China than with their authors, who are motivated primarily by their desire to criticize their own domestic conditions—by pointing out that *even* the Chinese had done better. As Derrida concludes, in such cases China still remains a "domestic representation" that is praised "only for the purpose of designating a lack and to define the necessary corrections"[74]—or, in the words of a Portuguese merchant in Macao, to make it "knowen how farre these Gentiles do herein exceed many Christians."[75] Insofar as positive early modern portrayals of China can be attributed to reports provided by Jesuit missionaries, they too had a vested interest in burnishing China's image: in order to gain institutional backing for their mission, it was important to present the Chinese as enlightened proto-Christians on the verge of conversion.[76]

The oscillation in Western evaluations of Chinese law reflects in part shifting evaluations of the rationality of the Chinese language. Rationality, after all, is one of the identifying features of modern law, and law in turn is intimately connected with language and the categories it offers for legal expression. Again, the footprints lead to Hegel, who operationalizes his entire Orientalist arsenal to describe the nature of the Chinese language. That the Chinese language is not phonetic but "represents the ideas themselves by signs" is evidence to Hegel that it has not "matured" and reached the level of Western languages. Indeed, because of the multiplicity of pictorial representations required, the Chinese writing system is a fundamentally inadequate instrument "for representing and imparting thought."[77] The same notion echoes in Weber, who observes that "Chinese thought has remained rather stuck in the pictorial and the descriptive." And, like Hegel, Weber confirms the dire consequences of this unfortunate "fact": "The power of *logos,* of defining and reasoning, has not been accessible to the Chinese," and, indeed, "the very concept of logic remained absolutely alien" to Chinese thought.[78]

As a counterexample, consider Leibniz, a Sinophile *par excellence.* For him, the ideographic, unphonetic Chinese script was a blueprint for the great Enlightenment project of a universal language that communicates ideas directly, like algebraic signs.[79] Leibniz's analysis notably ignores the fact that the Chinese script does include phonetic elements. Yet whether it was considered an anachronism or a kind of potential linguistic algebra, the Chinese language constituted a nearly insuperable barrier to many Westerners. From early on, legal observers of China emphasized the problem of studying a legal system "buried in a language by far the least accessible to a foreign student of any that was ever invented by man," as Sir George Thomas Staunton put it hyperbolically in the introduction to his pioneering 1810 translation of the Qing Code.[80] Given Orientalist assumptions about the close interrelations between language, ahistoricity, and the irrationality of the Chinese, we are hardly surprised to learn that, in the opinion of an officer of the British East India Company, "so arbitrary" are the laws of Chinese as to be "contrary to all reason and justice."[81]

Dated as the debates on the putative irrationality of the Chinese language sound, they have their contemporary variants with contemporary legal implications. With the PRC having assumed sovereignty over Hong Kong, the common law of the former British colony is being translated into Chinese. The debate surrounding this project betrays a persistent Orientalist skepticism regarding the possibility of crossing what Joseph Needham calls "the very great barrier of the ideographic and alphabetic languages," and, by extension, the feasibility of administering justice in Chinese.[82] Indeed, one can only recall the predominantly French origins of the common law and the early Francophones' ardent belief that "really the Law is scarce expressible properly in English."[83]

However, denunciations alone cannot prevent legal influences from traveling. Although Karl Wittfogel updated the vocabulary of Oriental despotism for the Cold War to warn of more modern forms of totalitarianism in the political East, more or less unacknowledged exchanges of legal influences continued to take place.[84] As Mary Dudziak has demonstrated, much of the pressure for the establishment of civil rights in the United States in the 1960s arose from Soviet and Third World critiques of racial inequality in America. In a similar vein, John Quigley analyzes the entire post-1917 "Soviet challenge" to the formal equality of liberal legal orders as a major factor in the enactment of social legislation both in Europe and North America over the course of the twentieth century. (As Roosevelt put it, with the New Deal he hoped to "inoculate" the United States with a moderate dose of socialism so as "to escape the disease.") In the 1960s China in turn became a romanticized placeholder for the revolutionary ideals of Left intellectuals all over the world from France to the United States, drawing on a tradition of positive accounts of Chinese communism dating back to the journalist Edgar Snow's reports from Yan'an in 1936. As William Alford points out, even in 1981 Chief Justice Warren Burger of the U.S. Supreme Court referred to the exemplary efficiency of Chinese courts, relative to that of the United States.[85]

In any event, even as the West lurches from "ethnocentric scorn" to "an hyperbolical admiration" and back—Derrida's characterization of the West's self-referential histories of the Orient—China remains a potent signifier. Continuing this pattern, in an ostensibly dramatic reversal of American Orientalism, Chinese Americans underwent a striking metamorphosis in the late twentieth century. Not only did Orientalist discourses cease to exclude the Chinese formally from immigration, but Chinese Americans were promoted from representatives of the Yellow Peril to members of the so-called Model Minority.[86] Nevertheless, although Chinese Americans are seen as having successfully integrated into the American economy, they are still notably distrusted as legal and political subjects.[87] A few election cycles ago, the media suggested that Chinese Americans use their superior economic power to finance political campaigns rather than express their political will primarily through voting or other regular channels of participatory democracy—or else they simply sell national secrets to China, or to whoever pays the most.[88]

Although the power of Orientalist tropes lies precisely in their irrefut-ability by empirical evidence, it is nevertheless vital to observe that even historically, from the very genesis of the Chinese immigration exclusion, the perception of the Chinese as being either unable or unwilling to resort to law for their rights has been simply inaccurate. A key justification for the Chinese Exclusion Laws was the putative inability of the Chinese even to comprehend the notion of individual rights and thus qualify for America's "Republican form of Government," yet ironically the immediate response of the Chinese to their exclusion was the paradigmatically "American" one: making a federal case out of it (as analyzed in Chapter 4).[89]

Finally, before considering the methodological quandary posed by the history of legal Orientalism, it is useful to issue a set of theoretical as well as historical qualifications. As Chapter 1 emphasized, the point of investigat-ing legal Orientalism as a discourse is neither to prove nor to disprove the existence of Chinese law, nor is it to assess the strengths or weaknesses of China's legal tradition. To state the obvious, the law and judicial administra-tion of the late imperial era undoubtedly left much to be desired by today's standards (say, in its use of corporal punishments and judicial torture). At the same time, many aspects of it do seem also remarkably "modern" and well regulated (including the precision with which both punishments and judicial torture were ordinarily administered). Nevertheless, much of it was no doubt "cruel," to use one of European observers' favorite adjectives.[90]

To avoid anachronistic comparisons, it is important to keep in mind also the state of North Atlantic legal systems in the eighteenth and nineteenth centuries. In the United States chattel slavery—in its extraordinary brutal-ity surely as cruel as any aspect of the Chinese legal system—remained a constitutionally protected form of property until the Civil War, and across the Atlantic petty property crimes were subject to capital punishment in England into the nineteenth century.[91]

To be sure, by the end of the nineteenth century reform movements had transformed the face of continental criminal justice in important ways, and in England too the deprivation of liberty rather than bodily violence be-came the primary form of punishment. At that time and from that particu-lar vantage point, aspects of the Chinese legal system could indeed be regarded as cruel. (Importantly, the practices most deplored by Europeans had been condemned for a long time by many Chinese critics as well.)[92]

However, a contrast between penal practices in Europe and China is hardly the only salient axis of comparison, given that European domestic reforms took place in tandem with the acquisition of colonies elsewhere. Europeans did not simply stop the use of extreme corporal punishments. Rather, such punishments came to be practiced predominantly in the colonies, where they continued to flourish in the cruelest forms.[93]

Lastly, it bears noting that whatever one thinks of the every-day functioning of the late imperial legal order, with the decline of the Qing dynasty over the course of the nineteenth century—precipitated in part by Euro-American imperial actions in China—there were increasing breakdowns of imperial administration. Although some of the perceived lawlessness in China was surely in the eye of the European beholder, there were increasingly numerous instances of "actual" lawlessness as well, caused by internal uprisings such as the so-called Taiping Rebellion (1850–1871)—the most deadly civil war in history.

This book is a primarily discursive analysis of legal Orientalism, however, not a comparative history of Chinese and North Atlantic legal and judicial institutions. Examining legal Orientalism is useful, not necessarily because it can tell us what Chinese law is, or was, "really" like, but because it can tell us why that reality is often irrelevant: China is simply assumed to be lawless and despotic, regardless of evidence. In short, this book is not only an analysis of how, or whether, Chinese law exists *in fact*, but also why it cannot exist even *in theory*.

ACTS OF COMPARISON IN A WORLD OF ORIENTALISM

As the literary scholar Haun Saussy puts it, China is "the reward of the right kind of reading." Analyzing Western readers of Chinese literature, he concludes that "each got the China he deserved and to which his understanding of figural language entitled him."[94] As Saussy's remark suggests, there is no unmediated, uninterpreted China to be had—be that a literary or legal China. There are only different ways of reading China, some surely more rewarding than others, but none "right" to the exclusion of all others.

But before we turn to the task of reading substantive areas of Chinese law—taken up in Chapter 3—it is finally time to ask: How should we go about using law to understand China and its relationship to the United States, and to the modern West in general? It might be rhetorically satisfying simply to denounce legal Orientalism—to issue a categorical imperative that students of Chinese law must cease Orientalizing China and that Chinese law must never constitute a mere means in our own projects of legal self-definition. Alas, a categorically anti-Orientalist morality is simply not possible. Prejudices, in the neutral sense used by Gadamer, can only be managed, not eliminated. As he observes, for better or worse, "the fundamental prejudice of the Enlightenment is the prejudice against prejudice itself, which denies tradition its power."[95]

Belonging to a tradition is the very condition of possibility of interpretation, and traditions inevitably prejudice us in the sense of disposing us to see the world in light of our preconceptions—whether those preconceptions be positive or negative. There is no innocent knowledge to be had. We have little choice but to Orientalize—to always anticipate China and its legal traditions in terms of our own biases. Moreover, not only are we inevitably always engaged in Othering and essentializing China and Chinese law as we seek to understand them, but the Chinese, likewise, essentialize us, the West. Besides, both we and the Chinese essentialize our own traditions as well. The Chinese "self-Orientalize" and Americans "self-Americanize," as it were.

As examples of Chinese self-essentialization, consider again the fact that for centuries it was the official, state-sponsored Confucian view that law played only a minimal role in governance of the Chinese empire that was ideally ruled by morality—yet in fact the state developed a sophisticated legal system to carry out its policies. But insofar as Confucianism privileged morality over law and the state identified Chinese-ness with Confucianism, it was ideologically imperative to insist that China was a government of men (of superior virtue), not of (mere instrumental) laws.[96] Consider again also the notion of a stable, enduring China. This myth is not just a Western fantasy but a Confucian one as well. Confucius himself insisted, rather disingenuously, that his project of reforming the Chinese state and society was simply a return to a past Golden Age—a mere reaffirmation of an ancient tradition rather than a fundamental reorganization of a world that he found corrupt and lacking in morality.[97] In fact, ever since Confucius (and even before him), nearly all Chinese projects of fundamental social transformation have sought to retroject their utopias onto a distant past, so as to honor a cultural prejudice against radical change.

To be sure, upon its establishment in 1949 the PRC rejected the past as a source of legitimacy.[98] However, even that rejection is premised on a self-Orientalization of that past. Although the Sinicized version of Marxism may represent a significant transformation, even the Maoist variety is ultimately driven by a need to see the Chinese past as an irredeemably "feudal" one of imperial despotism, stagnantly waiting for Communism to rescue it from its ahistorical trap.[99] Hence, many Chinese historians have internalized some of Marx's Orientalist understandings of the world as part of their self-understanding. The accomplished legal historian Jing Junjian, for example, paints a rich, even dynamic view of the legal regulation of the economy during the Qing dynasty (1644–1911 c.e.), but almost contradicting his own evidence in the end he nevertheless concludes that "Chinese law was permeated by the same basic principles from beginning to end."[100]

In the past few decades the rising confidence of China and other fast-growing economies in Asia has produced a number of rhetorical and political responses to the hegemony of Western rule-of-law rhetoric. Perhaps the most notable among them has been the assertion of so-called Asian values as an alternative to North Atlantic political ideologies.[101] Although their conscious intent is to challenge some of the chief assumptions of legal Orientalism, in their rhetorical structure they continue to reproduce its logic.

At the risk of caricaturing further an already simplistic position, in the 1990s the proponents of Asian values posited the existence of an indigenous Asian tradition with culturally distinctive notions of rights, duties, and sovereignty, which differ from those of Western liberalism. Somewhat more specifically (although specificity was never among the virtues associated with the proponents of Asian values), they emphasized the priority of collective notions of responsibility over individual rights, the priority of economic rights over political rights, the parity—if not priority—that duties enjoy with regard to rights, and a general cultural preference for the cultivation of social consensus rather than toleration for dissent.

Analyzed as a counterhegemonic discourse, the Asian values position combines an assertion that there *is* such a thing as law in Asia, with an emphatic announcement that Asia's time is *now* and that it need not wait for North America or Europe to emancipate itself into full membership in humanity, at some future point that is forever withheld. In the 1990s this claim was articulated most prominently by Southeast Asian nations (Singapore, Malaysia, and Indonesia) as well as China.[102] That the claim took a specifically cultural form evidently reflects the widespread recasting of the

Cold War's political division between East and West as a clash of civilizations rather than of political ideologies. Rhetorically, Asian values posed at least a moderate challenge to North Atlantic multicultural liberalisms and their deeply held faith in the values of cultural autonomy and local self-determination—which holds only so long as those local values are Western and liberal.

But even if it has the capacity to call attention to the false universalism of a humanitarian will-to-empire, the notion of Asian values as such is no less suspect, at least insofar as it is taken to refer to some stable, prepolitical set of norms that ought to be valued positively simply because of their (putative) cultural particularity and authenticity. The fact that the chief spokespersons for Asian values have been a handful of more or less autocratic leaders of East and Southeast Asian states makes those values even less appealing. As Carl Schmitt notoriously observed, "Whoever invokes humanity wants to cheat."[103] The same goes for Asian values. It is eminently unclear what, or even where, "Asia" is and who has the authority to speak in its name.[104]

Putting aside its value as a political provocation, when analyzed from the perspective of legal Orientalism, the Asian values challenge is in fact less than radical. Whether professed by China or others, in the end many of the so-called Asian values turn out to be little more than transvalued Orientalist clichés: originally negative stereotypes that have been turned into positive ones. Because of their history, at a moment's notice their coding can switch again from positive to negative, and back to positive. For example, an emphasis on family can be coded either as a positive ethic of care or as clannish nepotism; an emphasis on relationships more generally can be construed as a concern for collective welfare or as cronyism; an emphasis on consensus can be valued as either a striving for harmony or as corruption and the stifling of dissent; an emphasis on tradition can be held as a wise regard for precedent or a symptom of rigidity and lack of creativity; an emphasis on morality over law may signify either an admirable lack of litigiousness or a disregard for the values of rule-of-law; and so on. Conceptually, these values are so flat that they are easy to flip—hence their instability and endless oscillation. In short, the Asian values debate is staged largely in terms of binary oppositions grounded in an Orientalist legal epistemology.[105]

At the same time, just as Orientalist assumptions are shared by many people in Asia who essentialize their own traditions as less than legal, I have noted that Americans tend to "self-Americanize" themselves as inherently legal. Intriguingly, although Americans often do "place a high cultural valuation on change," which in turn serves to condemn China's legal tradition as "stagnant," in the domestic context Americans are fully capable of valuing lack of change as well.[106] Just as Confucianism sought political stability in respecting the forms of governance established by the founder of each dynasty, so many Americans too take pride in the fact that the same Constitution has remained in force since its adoption in the wake of the Founding.[107] Yet while a real or perceived lack of change in China's political culture is indeed classified negatively as stagnation, a similar lack of change in the American case represents the positive quality of stability, not slavery to tradition but an admirable fidelity to who We the People "really" are. Indeed, consider the tremendous amounts of scholarly energy that constitutional Originalists devote to explaining why contemporary Americans ought to be ruled by an agreement hammered out by a small group of property-owning white men in Philadelphia in 1787. The expectation that these men should be able to rule us from their graves is surely as much a form of ancestor worship as any advocated by Confucius, yet here it is one that confirms Americans' identity as essentially, solidly American.[108]

If this is indeed the conclusion—we cannot help essentializing others, and even ourselves—what recourse do we have? A simplistic morality of anti-Orientalism—"Thou shalt not Orientalize"—would effectively end all comparative study. In an important sense, comparison is the only way for us to encounter and enter into relationships with others—to enter into a world of similarities as well as differences, which in turn both provide boundaries for our subjectivity and allow us to connect with other subjects in the world.[109] But even if morality has no place in comparative study, ethics must. By morality, I mean normative systems that posit a pregiven moral subject and then elaborate guidelines for proper actions by that subject. By an ethics, in contrast, I refer to a normative system that is concerned not with what a pregiven subject may or may not do but, rather, with the *formation* of that subject. Instead of assuming an ethical subject and then regulating it, ethics in this sense regulates the conditions under which subjects emerge. What comparative study needs, then, is an ethics of Orientalism, rather than an impossible morality of anti-Orientalism.

Even as we continue to compare and necessarily Orientalize as well, we *can* attend to the effects that our comparisons have on others. To the extent that the categories we employ always impose limits on what we can discover in the world, the very act of comparison in part produces the objects that are being compared—for example, the American legal subject and the Chinese nonlegal nonsubject. Therefore we ought to consider the ways in which our comparisons subject others—both in the ordinary sense (limiting their agency as subjects) and in the sense of subjectification (recognizing them as subjects capable of agency).

Whatever the differences among the various Orientalisms sketched thus far, they support a generally idealized self-image of the American legal subject and an overwhelmingly negative view of the Chinese nonlegal nonsubject: Americans are ruled by law, the Chinese by moral proverbs; Americans are individuals, the Chinese lemmings; Americans are democratic, the Chinese despotic; America is dynamic, China changeless; and so on. Together these notions form an analytically indissoluble complex of meanings so that often to invoke one is to invoke all. In the end, the problem is not that these Orientalisms make assumptions about Chinese legal subjectivity—that is unavoidable—but that their assumptions make it exceedingly difficult to negotiate the relationship between the American legal subject and its Chinese would-be counterpart. The assumptions are premised almost exclusively on differences—none contemplate significant similarities, as law's contradictions at home are simply projected elsewhere. Universal, desirable values become identified with America and particular, undesirable ones with China.

To the extent that the American legal subject constitutes the paradigmatic and universal case, its task—its right as well as its duty—is to teach the Chinese, too, how to become (real) legal subjects. It is precisely this duty that animates much of the history analyzed in Chapters 4 and 5, where it takes the form of what I call the white lawyer's burden. And until that lesson has been imparted, there is little that Chinese conceptions of law and justice could possibly offer to American law. This is hardly a promising recipe for cross-cultural understanding. Moreover, insofar as this conception of the legal subject holds the potential for delegitimizing all other legal traditions, legal Orientalism is built into the very definition of law. Law itself, along with the kind of rights-based individual subjectivity it implies, becomes a key North Atlantic contribution to the modern world.

Although legal narcissism may not be fatal and perhaps only gives us the (dim) view of Chinese law that we deserve, the Chinese presumably deserve better. To be sure, it is only because of certain "fundamental, enabling prejudices" that we can communicate with others in the first place.[110] Our preconceptions of others in part enable those others to emerge as subjects. However, the same enabling prejudices inevitably also constrain those others. Subjectivity never implies perfect freedom. What distinguishes one Orientalism from another, then, are its uses and its effects: *How* does it subject the Other, in the two senses of the term?

The ethical distinction is therefore decidedly not a naïve one between Orientalisms with negative rather than positive prejudices (although Orientalist legal myths are in fact predominantly negative). Communitarian idealizations of a Chinese genius for mediation and harmony, for example, tend to rely on similar notions of Chinese nonlegal nonsubjectivity. Often, they represent an uncritical acceptance of the Confucian ideological fiction that the Chinese naturally delight in submitting themselves to the dictates of group morality. And, like their negative counterparts, these positive Orientalisms ordinarily posit law as inherently "Western" and "modern," excluding the Chinese thus from both law and modernity. Admittedly the point of such adoring Orientalisms is typically to criticize the excesses of Western legality, but by using Chinese nonlegality as their counterexample, they reduce the Chinese to the juridical equivalents of the noble savage—primitives happily untainted by legal modernity.

Since it does not insist on a categorical distinction between positive and negative Orientalisms, an ethics of comparison does not require isolating Chinese legal practices from criticism. Enlightenment humanism may well have been implicated in the rise of Western imperialism, but as Dipesh Chakrabarty observes, historically it has provided "a strong foundation on which to erect—both in Europe and outside—critiques of socially unjust practices."[111] Given that the dissemination of European thought is now a global fact and hence affects us all, the task is not, and cannot be, the ultimate elimination of all analytic apparatuses of European thought, such as Western ideas of law. Indeed, we surely have an ethical duty to be concerned about the practices of subjection—the ways in which subjects are both enabled as well as disabled—in China as well as at home. Law provides one important way to address such practices, although certainly not the only one.

At the same time, as Chapter 1 suggested, however we evaluate law's mixed record, it is equally important also to take into account China's own imperial practices in East Asia, both in the past and today. For more than two millennia, it cultivated an official discourse of Sinocentrism, premised on the notion that it enjoyed a unique cosmological status as the Central State. This was not China's only idiom of diplomatic relations (for example, the Qing emperor presented himself as a Buddhist *cakravartin,* or "wheel-turning king," to Tibetans), but it was an ideologically privileged one, and it has sustained a range of institutional and discursive practices that can be fittingly characterized as imperial.[112]

At their founding, both the Republic of China and the People's Republic of China adapted themselves to the modern world by taking on secular, disenchanted forms of sovereignty, yet from the beginning the sovereignty of both was mapped on the giant footprint of the imperial state, at the moment of its widest geographic expansion. To borrow Benedict Anderson's evocative phrase, "the short, tight skin of the nation" was stretched over "the gigantic body of the empire."[113] Tellingly, approximately two-thirds of the territory claimed by the PRC today consists of "minority" areas. (To be sure, given that the sovereignty of the United States is based on Indian dispossession, one might characterize 100 percent of its territory as a minority area.) Beyond the question of Tibet, the Muslim communities of Central Asia, and other so-called minority nationalities (少数民族), there remain old contested imperial borders in Indochina, as well as the question of numerous disputed islands in the South China Sea, to mention only a few prominent problems created by turning the Qing empire into the Chinese nation. As a result, China today confronts more territorial disputes and irredentist claims than any other major or middle-ranking power in the world. Nor are such disputes solely a matter of "questions left over from history" (历史遗留的问题), in the stock phrase by which the Chinese Communist Party refers to its claim to Taiwan and other territorial disputes rooted in the pre-Communist past. Chinese nationalism is visibly on the rise, as Chinese capital is making inroads into Southeast Asia, Africa, and Latin America, and China is cultivating its own, modern forms of economic, political, military, and cultural influence overseas.[114]

Indeed, the temporal logic of Orientalism may be changing. By conventional accounting, China's time is always either already over, with its greatest glories in the past, or else its time is located in a future that is forever receding. Since at least the eighteenth century, one of the most common tropes for characterizing China has been that of a sleeping giant, endlessly and tantalizingly on the brink of a final but elusive breakthrough that will restore its greatness—but that moment is always not-yet.[115] Yet in the early twenty-first century there is a foreboding sense that the moment of truth may finally be at hand. For all the false declarations of China's imminent arrival in the mainstream of history, there is a discernible sense, mixed with fear, that *this time* China's time may actually be arriving—or perhaps already has, while we were not paying attention. It may be that the United States, not China, is finally waking up to the twenty-first century, stirring like Rip Van Winkle from his slumber to discover a post-Revolutionary world.

Nevertheless, because of its particular thematic concerns, this book focuses on the imperial history of Euro-American law rather than the ruling strategies of the Chinese empire, or law's promise to provide a better future. None of this is to suggest that law *cannot* be a legitimate political ideal in today's world. However one defines rule-of-law, whether as an ideal type or as a set of historical institutions, it seems beyond argument—tautological, in fact—that China does not have rule-of-law in the Anglo-American sense of the term. The analytic, and political, mistake is to identify rule-of-law as a universal good-in-itself that requires no justification beyond itself. Michael Dowdle suggests sensibly that we end our fixation with the metaphysical question that currently dominates the field of study of Chinese law: "Is there rule of law in China?" We would be better off asking: "*Should* there be rule of law in China as we currently conceive of that concept?"[116] In answering the latter question, we ought to remain realistic about what law can and cannot accomplish. This is not to prejudge the question. Even if law is something less than universal and associated not only with benefits but costs as well, it may in the end still be worth those costs. Yet it is not to anyone's benefit to call universal what is particular, or costless what is not. Even freedom is not free.

Moreover, as Chapter 6 will consider further, whether we choose to make criticisms of the actions of the Chinese state in terms of rule-of-law, human rights, or some other legal discourse, we must not proceed to condemn China wholesale without a fair hearing. Often, all Chinese legal practices of all eras are judged by irrelevant character evidence, based on timeless assumptions about the despotic and irrational nature of the Chinese. Equally frequently, the Chinese legal system is presumed guilty even before evidence has been offered—or when it is offered, it is Orientalist hearsay with a history of several centuries. And all too often the entire process seems to center around *us,* and the desire to prove the innocence of our norms and practices by challenging those of China. Finally, there is the ultimate structural question of all Orientalist epistemologies: Why is China always cast as the defendant and the West as the judge and the jury—not to mention the law-enforcer?

In the end the interpretation of Chinese law—and the interpretation of just what constitutes law—implicates us inevitably in the process of interpreting ourselves as well. Who are we, as (legal) subjects? Thus, to the extent that "law is truly an interpretive practice and interpretation is ontological, we always risk change through our acts of legal interpretation."[117] In the broadest sense we all engage in legal comparisons routinely in that we necessarily understand ourselves legally against our ideas of others. It is a practice through which we create others as well as ourselves. This power should not cause us to shrink from acts of legal comparison—which we could not do even if we wanted to—but simply to wield that power in ways that enable different kinds of legal subjects to emerge rather than to fix and classify historical subjects on the basis of their relative universality or particularity.

Alas, there is no cross-cultural standard that would help us arrive at a universal definition of law. Although natural law theories have (for the most part) suffered a well-deserved death, in our less self-conscious moments we nevertheless operate as though their discredited notions were still good law, and we forget that even the seemingly most natural legal categories are ultimately cultural artifacts. Yet the only universal law is that in China, as elsewhere, people are born and die—and, in between, they strive to instill the world, and their selves, with meaning. In that project law is one resource of signification. The remaining chapters examine some of the ways in which discourses of legal Orientalism have rendered the world, and its subjects, meaningful. In doing so they seek to universalize neither China nor the United States, and to provincialize both.

CHAPTER THREE

Telling Stories about Corporations and Kinship

> There is a model for the government of the world. It is the family.
>
> —Zhu Xi, *Reflections on Things at Hand*

> The ideal that a great corporation is endowed with the rights and prerogatives of a free individual is as essential to the acceptance of corporate rule in temporal affairs as was the ideal of the divine right of kings in an earlier day.
>
> —Thurman Arnold, *The Folklore of Capitalism*

GIVEN ORIENTALISM AS a general condition of knowledge, how then might a comparative study of Chinese law proceed? This chapter examines the operation of legal Orientalism in a specific field: Chinese corporation law. The subject matter may sound like a rather modern and technical one—neither particularly Chinese nor a very likely candidate for the attention of classical Orientalists. Indeed, as the reader will by now have anticipated, the problem with the study of a Chinese tradition of corporation law is precisely a deeply embedded presumption that no such tradition exists— Chinese corporation law has no history. The task of this chapter is to sketch one possible history of corporate forms of enterprise in China and their legal governance. At the same time, it helps us see in a specific context just how law operates as a technology of personhood—how it makes and unmakes subjects, and how comparative scholars in turn classify those subjects as universal or particular, legal or unlegal, properly modern or improperly Oriental.

To start, then, what is the story of the business corporation in today's China? The conventional wisdom is easy to summarize. As a culmination of its post-1978 reforms in the regulation of enterprises, in 1993 the PRC enacted a Company Law, authorizing for the first time, nationwide, the establishment of corporations owned by shareholders.[1] Except for some experimentation between the twilight of the imperial state and the triumph of Communism in 1949, the business corporation was a radically new transplant in the Chinese legal order, with no indigenous counterpart; historically, most businesses in China have been family businesses.

This story has broad implications. Among other things, it is offered as a key explanation of why capitalism failed to develop indigenously in China. Such an assertion immediately locates China outside of a universal history of capitalism that originates in the West. That the nondevelopment of capitalism constitutes a "failure" implies that its emergence is part of history's natural unfolding. Furthermore, insofar as law is not simply one particular narrative but a privileged language for the articulation of the universal, legal scholars' failure to find corporation law in China both constructs and confirms China's status as essentially particular. At the same time, viewing corporation law from the U.S. perspective, some American legal scholars have already declared an "End of History for Corporate Law" some time ago, anticipating a global convergence of legal development along the lines of U.S. corporation law.[2] In its teleological form, the story combines deftly Hegelian and Weberian elements—a conquest of the world by the spirit of capitalism.

From this perspective, if capitalism is the end of history and the modern business corporation one of its universal embodiments, what is it that has obstructed China's development? It is significant that China's stagnation is attributed specifically to the family—or kinship, to use the "thick" anthropological term that we conventionally use to describe family structures in non-Western societies. In this telling, China is always already a tale about kinship, whereas the history of the West becomes a just-so story about the emergence of the individual. Just as the individual is the paradigmatic political, economic, and legal subject of modernity, kinship is the ultimate regime of particularism and of attachment to tradition.

It is important to emphasize that this story about the predominance of the family is indeed also a story about law's absence in China. Insofar as families are governed by the particularistic norms of kinship, their dominance in the field of production has dire consequences for economic development more generally, impeding the evolution of civil relations on a universal basis, structured by the laws of property and contract—the twin pillars of a market order. Just as damningly, to the extent that there *is* law in China, it is all family law, as family has served as a model for regulating not only domestic relations but political and economic ones as well. This is a major confusion of categories—of the same order as the conflation of laws, manners, mores, and rites that Montesquieu attributes to the Chinese.

This chapter does not so much contest the essential facts on which this Orientalist account is based—the ideological and historical predominance of the family in China—as it reinterprets those facts. To present an alternative story, I argue that in China family law has historically performed many of the functions that modern corporation law performs today. This is evidently a functionalist argument of sorts, although an intentionally perverse one, as it purposely turns the conventional Orientalist story on its head. At the same time, to place the story in an expressly comparative framework, I suggest that there are many aspects of contemporary U.S. corporation law that can be analogized just as easily to the norms of family law as to those of contract law (which is currently a favored paradigm for theorizing corporation law). In short, I offer a way of reading Chinese family law as a kind of corporation law, and of certain aspcts of U.S. corporation law as a kind of family law.

Stated differently, the method of comparison I use here is an antifoundationalist one, a balancing act consisting entirely of moving parts. Rather than taking either the family or the corporation as a given in one tradition and then looking for its analogues in the other, this method examines how the objects of analysis come to be constituted as distinct and oppositional in the first place. In the end, what we call the "family" is not a transhistorical object of analysis. It is not a thing, an object, but a language—an idiom for describing relationships. It is that language that constitutes the so-called family *as* family in the first place. Likewise, the so-called "corporation" is an effect of legal discourse, not its foundation—there is no prelegal or prepolitical reality behind it to which it refers. Stated in the language of Chapter 2, it is the process of comparison that produces the objects that are being compared. The story of Chinese corporation law is thus part of a larger story about the emergence of the modern legal subject, and its Oriental other.

In contrast to Chapter 2, however, which outlined a schematic map of the operation of Orientalist discourses over time, the current chapter proceeds at a more deliberate pace. After presenting the inherited Orientalist narrative, it reads the historical record closely in order to retell the story with a new emphasis. Elaborating the larger argument and developing a model of comparison requires considerable historical detail, but for the benefit of the non-Sinologist reader the analysis that follows assumes no specialized knowledge.[3]

CORPORATE FICTIONS

The conventional story of Chinese corporation law, or lack thereof, is supported by a remarkable scholarly consensus. As Max Weber sums it up, "The legal forms and societal foundations for capitalist 'enterprise' were absent" in traditional China.[4] More recent economic historians concur on the absence of genuine native predecessors for the modern business corporation. Parts of John King Fairbank's restatement of Chinese history could well have been written by Weber: "[The] nondevelopment of Chinese law along lines familiar to the West was plainly related to the nondevelopment of capitalism and an independent business class in old China. There was no idea of the corporation as a legal individual. Big firms were family affairs."[5] Remarkably, whatever their differences with Western students of Chinese legal history, contemporary legal scholars in the PRC agree at a minimum that traditional Chinese law had no concept of legal personality: In the orthodox PRC jurisprudential view, the very notion of "legal person" (法人) is a by-product of the Western commodity economy.[6]

To present an alternative story about traditional Chinese "clan corporations," I draw on developments in two primary areas of Sinology: kinship anthropology and legal history. That Chinese clans often owned property jointly to provide for clan welfare and ancestral sacrifices has been well documented by several generations of anthropologists. Much of the scholarship analyzes families and clans in terms of the ritual significance of their kinship practices. However, Hill Gates has offered an elegant interpretation of late imperial clan organizations as primarily commercial enterprises organized on the sociological foundation of the family.[7]

Starting with Gates's thesis and seeking to give it a specifically legal interpretation, this chapter shows that clan corporations' vehement insistence on kinship as their organizing principle did not mean that they were "just" family affairs. Rather, kinship was often a finely wrought legal fiction that legitimated the existence of private enterprises by profit-seeking individuals in a state in which Confucianism was the official orthodoxy. According to the received view, traditionally, all Chinese law was penal, associated with criminal sanctions. However, as Chapter 1 observed, in the past few decades there have been archival studies of Qing dynasty court records that provide evidence of greater legal regulation of civil aspects of society, including the family and clan, than suggested by previous analyses based largely on the ideological projections and self-representations of the imperial state. Combining the twin perspectives of kinship anthropology and legal history makes it possible to view clan organizations as a species of business corporation with a definite legal status. Together they suggest at least the outlines of corporation law in traditional China, however anachronistic that may sound.

Before proceeding further, it is important to recognize the nature of the conceptual challenge. Because of their different intellectual environments, traditional Chinese and contemporary American corporation law face distinct problems of legitimacy. Americans live in a legal system that thinks in terms of "persons." Consequently, an important task for Anglo-American corporation law has been to justify the existence of collective entities such as corporations in a way that accords with liberal individualism: Every legal actor must be a person, no matter the conceptual violence. This requirement has ultimately given us the fiction of the corporation as a person in its own right—a legal person. Over centuries, this legal fiction has been the object of much jurisprudential controversy. Today, after endless arguments about the nature of corporate personality, U.S. corporation law seems finally to have abandoned further metaphysical speculation. In the relieved words of one scholar, we have worked our way "out of the platonic murk accumulated over . . . two thousand years."[8] Recent American theorists of the corporation take this process to its logical conclusion and thoroughly "individualize" the corporation by conceptualizing it as nothing more, or less, than a "nexus of contracts" among its individual constituents—a set of agreements among shareholders, managers, employees, suppliers, and others.

In contrast, in the Confucian view the collective is morally prior to the individual. Hence, for traditional Chinese law collective legal personality was a given. The main problem for Chinese business enterprises was the antimercantile attitude of orthodox Confucianism and its general ideological hostility to profit seeking.[9] As classical Orientalists recognized all too well, the idealized Confucian view posited a radical isomorphism among the family, on the one hand, and the larger political and social communities, on the other. When functioning properly, they were all governed by a similar kinship logic. Starting from the premise that one is not supposed to take advantage of family members, traditional Chinese corporation law focused on justifying to the state the type of collective that in fact sought profit at the expense of others—and then divided its profits unevenly among various classes of participants. Hence clan corporations' relentless insistence that they were simply extended families. Status as a kinship group entailed legitimacy and recognition by the state. Coincidentally, this also meant that these clan corporations were governed ultimately by family law, which in turn implied fiduciary duties by clan leadership to clan members.

It is also worth noting that while both the kinship and contract metaphors can lend legitimacy to the internal organization of a business corporation, as social epistemologies they have different implications for corporations' duties to society at large. To the extent that the American contractual corporation is viewed simply as a voluntary undertaking by a group of individual citizens, it leaves the political arena and has no inherent social responsibilities. In contrast, the Chinese view of "real" kinship groups and the larger sociopolitical communities as interpenetrating extended families meant that the entire clan corporation owed fiduciary obligations to other groups as well and even to the empire as a whole.

Although it goes beyond the immediate argument of this chapter, it is important to observe that the familial idiom has continued to influence Chinese economic organization even after the official abolition of the traditional legal system. Historically, the several attempts to transplant Western corporation law into China have been remarkable mostly for their irrelevance. In contrast, the family itself has continued to maintain a distinctive legal status—not unlike the one it enjoyed in the late imperial era—and the Chinese have continued to take advantage of that status in organizing their businesses. At the same time, Communists' collective entities have often been conceptualized along the lines of familial analogies, as communities with shared collective interests, rather than contractual arrangements among self-seeking individuals with radically divergent aims.

For clarity, it is important to insist on what this chapter is *not* saying. As Chapter 2 already noted, from the beginning Western legal observers have commented extensively on the prevalence of familial analogies in Chinese social life.[10] In the introduction to his translation of the Qing Code, the trader-Sinologist Sir George Staunton states unequivocally that the "duty of submission to parental authority, whether vested in the parents themselves, or in their representatives," is indeed the very essence of Chinese government.[11] As we have seen, either expressly or implicitly these traditional accounts and their many contemporary variations suggest a contrast with an idealized "West" where the individual is the authentic political and metaphysical subject. The self-serving opposition between a stationary East of oppressed masses and a progressive West of self-sufficient individuals has indeed generated what is perhaps the most stubborn cliché in comparative law, elaborated famously by Sir Henry Maine—namely, that the former are frozen in categories that delimit Status while the latter define their relationships freely through Contract.[12]

Although this chapter takes seriously the rhetoric of family and kinship in Chinese legal and economic organization, it does so precisely in order to destabilize the Orientalist epistemology on which most analyses of that rhetoric rest. For one thing, the fact that the Chinese household owned collective property and engaged in the pursuit of profit hardly differentiates it from its counterparts elsewhere. Indeed, the Greek word οἶκος (oikos), "household," and the Greek study of household management, οἰκονομία (oikonomia), have given us the term "economy." Rather, what is unique about the history of Chinese legal and economic organization is the vehement *ideological* insistence on kinship as the organizing principle—even in the case of large clan corporations in which kinship was the most threadbare fiction and many of the governing relations in fact originated in contract, not kinship. In China, as probably everywhere else, family businesses were among the first types of business organizations. More significantly, even Chinese enterprises that were *not* family businesses often chose to present themselves as such.

Stated more generally, the stories told by Chinese law do not necessarily tell us what the Chinese actually did when they were not telling stories, just as the stories American lawyers tell about corporations do not always correspond to what actually happens in corporations. Although the "nexus of contracts" may be the most individualistic theory of the American corporation to have gained ascendance, it is certainly not the only story that can be told of this legal entity. One need only consider that in their public self-representations—from annual reports to advertising—even the largest Fortune 500 companies prefer to describe themselves as "families."

What, then, is the story of corporation law in late imperial China? I first describe the historical evolution of clan corporations and examine the ways in which they may be viewed as "corporations." Next I explain why the mechanisms by which these corporations were governed and regulated can be usefully regarded as "legal." I also assess how well this corporation law worked in practice and how the ideology of patriarchal kinship provided legitimacy to clan corporations.

MORAL ECONOMY OF THE HOUSEHOLD

To defend the analytic value of interpreting clan organizations as corporations, it is best to start by considering the concept itself. In the blunt verdict of Felix Cohen, seeking to discover the "true" nature of the corporation is "transcendental nonsense": what the corporation "is" depends on the purposes we attribute to corporation law.[13] However, for the purposes of constructing a legal argument, I will adopt the conventional criteria recognized by leading scholars of corporation law: namely, provision for limited investor liability, free transferability of ownership interests, legal personality, and centralized management. In the view of Robert Clark and many others, among all these criteria "the single most important fact about corporate law" is the separation of ownership and management.[14] It is that fact that lies at the heart of the so-called "agency problem," which has defined American corporation law and theory for the better part of the twentieth century.[15] In theory, shareholders are the principals in a corporation, while managers are merely their agents—yet why should investors trust corporate management to guard their capital and use it productively?

Although I insist in this chapter that clan corporations certainly had most—possibly all—of the formal characteristics of the corporation, I rely on the conventional definition only provisionally. For one thing, with the contemporary proliferation of new legal forms (limited liability partnerships, limited liability companies, etc.), the distinctions are increasingly academic, as each form can be tailored into the functional equivalent of almost any other form. Hoping not to get mired in legal semantics, my goal is simply to identify enterprise forms in traditional China that are structurally *analogous* to modern business corporations, not identical—obviously an impossibility. The fecundity of analogy as a conceptual tool is that, by definition, it accommodates both similarities *and* differences. It does not insist on either universalizing itself by demanding self-sameness, or on particularizing the object of analogy by casting it as wholly other. At the same time, it is important to distinguish between two different kinds of analogy. Perhaps the more common approach is to analogize A to B. This is a procedure that holds A constant, as a referent. A more democratic procedure makes analogy *reversible,* not unidirectional. Rather than analogizing A *to* B, it views A and B as analogous *with* each other. It is this procedure that makes it possible to think of Chinese clan organizations as corporations *and* U.S. corporations as families.[16]

In a sense the Orientalist observation that all traditional Chinese law was family law (or, somewhat more precisely, applied family law) is quite accurate. In U.S. legal culture, contract constitutes the dominant paradigm of private ordering, which is then projected onto the public sphere as a hypothetical "social contract." In a parallel fashion, Confucian political and social thought viewed family as the paradigmatic governance model, which in turn implied the notion of a metaphorical "political family" on the level of the state. Even a central pre-Confucian classic proclaimed, "The son of Heaven is the parent of the people, and so becomes the sovereign of the empire."[17] With the eventual emergence of Neo-Confucianism as state orthodoxy in the Song (960–1279 c.e.) and Ming (1368–1644 c.e.) dynasties, the family was given a metaphysical foundation, and filial piety was promoted to cult status.

The familial conceptualization of the polity was reflected even in the terminology used to describe various levels of officialdom. Occupying the role of *parens patriae,* district magistrates were popularly known as "father and mother officials," while higher-up, province-level functionaries were accorded the more reverent designation "distinguished forbears."[18] Just as the ideology of patrilineal kinship extended metaphorically to the state, so the traditional Chinese family provided the prototype of what would evolve into a clan corporation.[19] I begin by analyzing the protocorporate characteristics of the traditional household as well as some key features that prevented it from functioning more fully as a "corporation."

The household was an especially suitable model for the clan corporation in two ways. First, as a kin group celebrating its patrilineal continuity, the household was indeed a "perpetual" corporation in its ritual aspect. Second, because of its hierarchical social structure, it contained an incipient separation of ownership and management. The temporal continuity of the patrilineage was maintained by the performance of ancestral rites. In a form of ritual primogeniture, in each family the eldest male of the most senior line inherited the primary responsibility for ancestral sacrifices. In this respect the Chinese family was a (men's) corporation in just the sense in which Henry Maine used the word in the nineteenth century: "Corporations *never die*, and accordingly primitive law considers the entities with which it deals, i.e., the patriarchal or family groups, as perpetual and inextinguishable."[20] Indeed, the family was a welfare system like no other: in theory at least, it extended from cradle to grave and beyond. In the words of Mencius, the early Confucian second only to the Master himself, "Keeping one's parents when they are alive is not worth being described as of major importance, it is treating them decently when they die that is worth such a description."[21] The *Classic of Filial Piety* maintains that even one's body is not one's own but belongs to one's parents. A father in turn is obligated to provide for his young "not so much because he owes it to the youngsters, but because he is obligated to their common ancestors."[22]

The notion of a personal continuity between fathers and sons was not merely metaphysical. Exemplifying the perpetual corporate nature of the patrilineage, a man's male offspring inherited both his assets and liabilities, even when the latter outweighed the former.[23] At the same time, the Confucian metaphor of kinship as a membership of the dead, alive, and unborn in "one body" (一體) gave rise to an incipient separation of ownership and management—the feature most characteristic of the modern business corporation. In the orthodox Confucian view, kinship relationships are paradigmatically hierarchical, with the senior kin exercising authority over the junior kin. The father-son relationship, for example, was governed by the master principle of filial piety (孝). Early Western comparativists typically read into it the Roman concept of *patria potestas*, or paternal power, which indeed left those under *potestas* at the father's mercy and certainly with little recourse to the law for protection.[24] However, this is an incomplete description, at least in terms of Confucian political theory (as opposed to political practice). The ideal of domestic and political harmony did not result from the observation of hierarchy alone. Parental and political power had to be tempered by concern for those whom one governed. In Tu

Wei-ming's characterization, the ideal Confucian society was a "fiduciary community" in which the corporate effort of the entire membership turned the group into "a society of mutual trust instead of a mere aggregate of individuals."[25]

When this moral hierarchy was projected on the household economy, it had profound material implications. In the strictly Confucian view, membership in the lineage descended in the male line only. Ritually speaking, women were in effect nonpersons, mere begetters of (male) persons.[26] Since all household property was owned by the undivided patrilineage to which women did not belong, they held no rights of their own to lineage property (although they did have the right to be supported by their male kinsfolk). The undivided ownership of lineage property among men reflects in turn the ritual understanding of the patrilineage. As Shuzo Shiga explains the father-son bond, "during the father's lifetime the son's personality is absorbed into the father's, while after the latter's death his personality is extended into that of his son. Father and son are a continuum of the same personality, not two beings in mutual rivalry."[27] Hence, the father lacked testamentary powers, for example. The property of the household was not his personal property.

Given that the father was in effect under a duty to leave the property to his sons, his position has often been likened to that of a trustee for his heirs. An alternative conceptualization is to view him as the manager of a "household corporation," in which capacity he owed a fiduciary duty to the shareholders in the corporation. In effect, so long as sons stayed in the same household and refrained from dividing up their patrimony, the management of family property was indeed functionally separate from its collective ownership. At the same time, the classic agency problem posed by this separation of management and ownership was solved—in good Confucian manner—by the imposition on the family head of a duty not to waste or unlawfully alienate collectively owned property. In a schematic fashion, traditional Chinese family law thus mirrored the structure of modern American corporation law.

But the household as an economic institution also had important limitations. For example, even if the ritual continuation of the patrilineage was potentially perpetual, the ownership of family property was not. The Qing Code expressly mandated equal inheritance among all sons at each generation, which usually ensured the dissolution of even the largest fortunes relatively quickly; the proverbial duration of the Chinese riches-to-rags story was three generations.[28] This result was hardly coincidental, and it was certainly to the liking of the imperial state, which was at least as suspicious of large concentrations of private capital as nineteenth-century America was during the rise of the business corporation.

When it came time to divide up the household property, contract law took priority over the laws of ritual kinship. Household division (分家) was not simply a natural process of property descending in the patrilineage but a distinctly contractual procedure, resulting in a signed document decreeing the division of household assets.[29] Even though partition contracts employed organic metaphors to emphasize collective unity in kinship, their rhetoric cannot hide the unpleasant fact that the contracts were in fact drawn up to settle conflicts over property among individual family members. In practice the fiduciary bonds of kinship usually turned out to be only as strong as the legal unity of property. According to contemporary reports on customary law, once property was divided among brothers, "even though some of them may be unfortunate enough to get poor, the other brothers will not help him."[30]

In short, although the family provided a simple model for the governance of jointly owned property, that property did not partake in the perpetual nature of the patriarchal kinship structure. Ironically, while Confucian officialdom was eager to promote the ritual rather than economic aspects of kinship, its attempts to encourage the maintenance of ancestral worship coincidentally provided the kin group with a means to protect corporate property from dissolution: the institution of ancestral trust.

With familism reaching a fever pitch in the Song period, the emerging Neo-Confucian synthesis called for a renewed commitment to the principles of patriarchal kinship. The leading Neo-Confucians encouraged families to maintain elaborate genealogies out of respect to ancestors and to ensure their continued worship. Taking this advice to heart, many successful imperial officials created charitable trusts for the property they had accumulated over the course of their careers. In these trusts, the property was to remain intact over generations, and the resulting income was to be used for ancestral halls for worship as well as welfare funds providing grants to needy members of the family. To the extent a trust's income allowed, it could also be invested legitimately in cultivating cultural capital in the form of educating promising young males—in the hope that they might one day attain success in the examination system and thus bring glory (and prosperity) to the clan.[31] As the patrilineage multiplied over time, membership in the trust came to constitute an extended kin group identified by the titular ancestor: a clan (总 or 族).

Ancestral trusts were generally safe both from extractions by the state, because of their unquestionable political correctness, and from dissolution at each generation, because of their perpetual nature. However, this very success posed its own problems. As clan membership multiplied and the number of beneficiaries grew over time, a trust's ability to pay for its ritual and welfare functions decreased correspondingly—unless, of course, proceeds from the trust estate were reinvested profitably. In fact, what better way could there be to serve one's ancestors than to work to increase the size of the clan estate? The practice of investing the trust's proceeds in commercial pursuits was a natural, even inevitable, outgrowth of the basic logic of the institution. Reflecting their increasingly mercenary nature, the instructions of many ancestral trusts came to separate completely the managers' qualifications from their genealogical status. In selecting managers, clan members were to focus on criteria such as "honesty, wealth and capability."[32]

The ancestral trust thus had two important corporate characteristics that the household lacked. It provided the family with a means of perpetual ownership of property as well as an institutional structure in which managers were selected by owners rather than genealogically determined. The ancestral trust was thus well equipped to become the template for a kind of business corporation with separate ownership and management functions.

CLAN CORPORATIONS, GENEALOGICAL FICTIONS

Many ancestral trusts were no doubt just what they purported to be— relatively small charitable trusts, the proceeds of which were spent more or less exclusively on the ritual, educational, and welfare expenses of the clan.[33] However, in terms of both their institutional organization and their activities, many ancestral trusts can be usefully interpreted as business corporations rather than merely ritual properties of extended "natural" families. I propose an interpretation of the corporate nature of such trusts in terms of the four formal corporate criteria identified above.

In addition to the conventional criteria, business corporations have two other features that are ordinarily simply assumed yet need to be spelled out when the concept is transposed onto traditional Chinese clan organizations: corporations are voluntary associations, and they are engaged in the pursuit of financial profit (in contrast to some of the other major species of the corporate genus, such as municipal corporations and nonprofit corporations). Therefore, I argue further that ancestral trusts were often voluntary associations rather than natural kin groups, and that their "bottom line" was as much the pursuit of material profit as the satisfaction of the needs of ancestral spirits.

It bears repeating that my checklist of corporate characteristics is only advisory. Ultimately, my goal is to identify entities that can be viewed as meaningfully analogous with the modern business corporation, not exact equivalents—given that the only exact equivalent of a modern business corporation is a modern business corporation. I will begin the analysis by focusing first on the two usually unarticulated features and then the four conventional characteristics: (1) voluntary association, (2) pursuit of material profit, (3) centralized management separate from ownership, (4) legal personality, (5) transferable ownership, and (6) limited liability.

The idea that clan corporations were in fact voluntary associations for private profit seeking sounds especially counterintuitive; surely Chinese clan members did not "choose" their kin any more than any one of us "chooses" our family. Indeed, if the modern American corporation is a nexus of contracts, kinship is the ultimate status regime, and the distance between the two presumably measures the progress from "Status to Contract," as per Henry Maine. However, although many clan corporations presented themselves as trusts set up by a distant ancestor, in fact they were often contractual arrangements formed posthumously by their living members. Indeed, the idiom of the family was frequently only a legal fiction used to recruit members, many of whom were not even related by blood to the clan they joined. To demonstrate that clan corporations were seething with contracts of all sorts, I begin with "charter agreements" that summoned new clan corporations into being and then consider various types of other contracts by which additional members/owners/workers were recruited into existing clan corporations.

In the standard anthropological view, Chinese clans with ancestral estates were divided into segments—房 or branches—by a natural process of fission.

The ancestor who created the trust became the focal point for his descendants, who in turn became his beneficiaries and were entitled to trust proceeds on a *per stirpes* basis. However, recent studies suggest that the segmentary model is largely an idealization of actual kinship practices. Often it was the desire to pool capital that brought a clan into being by transforming the abstract notion of kinship into a self-identified corporate entity: participating kinsfolk would select a long-dead ancestor, in whose name they would set up a posthumous ancestral trust to hold the capital.

As an example, consider the following contract whereby over two hundred kinsmen from four separate branches of a family came together to create an ancestral trust:

> Makers of this contract Kuan Chi-shan [thirteen other names given, all of the Kuan surname] and others, are uncles, brothers and nephews within the [clan] who have lived separately. . . . In the Jen-shen year of the Ch'ung-chen reign [1632], in consideration of their origins, the four [branches of the family] came to an agreement to donate on a per capita . . . basis towards an ancestral trust, to put out capital . . . to seek a profit. . . . Sacrifice was held for several years, and as there was no disagreement, in the Ting-ch'ou year [1637], the silver donated individually and the amounts left after paying for sacrifices, totalling over 80 taels, were used for the purchase of a shop in Sung-kang Market. . . . Subsequently, a plot of land for planting rice seedlings was purchased from Kuan Ch'en-chao, head of the street [on which the market is located], payment for which was made from the same ancestral trust. The land so purchased will be rented out to tenants and the rent collected is to be used for sacrifice. Sums of money left after paying for sacrifice are to be saved in preparation for the building of the ancestral hall and used in connection with winter sacrifice.[34]

The contract goes on to make it absolutely clear that for the purposes of this ancestral trust the relevant kin group is defined monetarily: "The 212 people who have donated have not done so in the name of [their branch of the family] and winter sacrifices are of no concern to those [noncontributing family members] whose names are not listed." Conversely, states the contract, "any person who is to pay .38 tales according to our regulation may have his name listed in the book of the ancestral trust."[35] To be sure, the contract observes the need to provide for ancestral sacrifices. However, if ritual rectitude were truly the sole motivation for the trust, a proper sense of solidarity would seem to argue against the exclusion of noncontributing kinsfolk.

Moreover, one might expect that even if the origins of some ancestral trusts were tainted by the cold contractual logic of commercial enterprise, ultimately familial solidarity and fiduciary obligations to one's kin would in fact result in the "collectivization" of clan capital. Again, evidence supports the opposite conclusion. As a case in point, in 1751 one single-clan Hong Kong village organized a trust in honor of one of its ancestors who had died centuries earlier. At the time, participation in the trust required, as in the above example, both descent from the titular ancestor and monetary contributions to the trust. One group of clan members did not contribute, and, indeed, in 1977—over two hundred years later—the outside group's descendants were still not considered members of the clan corporation, nor were they entitled to the material benefits of its membership.[36] Such a clan is clearly as much a creature of property as of kinship. In fact, in some instances it was property that defined the right to claim kinship. Some clans chose to simply slough off the poorer branches from the clan genealogy, which in turn effectively excluded them from sharing in the proceeds of corporate property. In a real sense, as one historian puts it, "the editing and printing of a genealogy created the organized kinship group, rather than vice versa."[37]

Although the notion that kinship in a clan corporation was as much a property relationship as a genealogical one flies in the face of orthodox Confucianism, at least in the preceding examples kinship was a necessary, though not always sufficient, requirement for membership in a clan corporation. However, in many corporations kinship was simply a fiction. The most extreme instance of this was the merger of two or more unrelated clans. Given that there are fewer than five hundred family names in China, it was not uncommon for unrelated clans in the same locale to have the same name. Relying on the ancient myth that those with the same family name descend ultimately from the same ancestor, unrelated clans with the same name that wanted to combine their capital for business sometimes simply invented a long-dead shared ancestor to whom they began sacrificing.[38]

Of course, even if one was willing to disregard whether those with the same surname were related or not, the random distribution of surnames still often failed to coincide with commercial needs. However, at least in Southeast China, there appeared to be no genealogical obstacle that could not be overcome by creative contracting. The resourceful Li Pang is a case in point. In the early eighteenth century, he combined five unrelated Fujianese families into a single unit with a new surname: the Li, Chen, Su, Zhuang, and Ke families suddenly became a brand-new "kinship group" called Bao. This stunning corporate reorganization quickly spurred a group of rival clans to consolidate in the form of another novel entity, entitled Qi. That the new entities indeed functioned under the guise of kinship is evident in the fact that "contemporary writers quite consciously used the terms, *hsing* [surname], *chia* [family], and *tsu* [clan] interchangeably" in characterizing the mega-clans.[39] In light of such heterodox practices, it is no surprise that concerned eighteenth-century provincial governors were already memorializing the emperor about "ancestral" trusts where the only qualification for participation was a monetary contribution. Actual kinship was simply irrelevant.[40]

The fictive nature of kinship was most obvious when unrelated clans combined, but fictions abounded even in one-clan corporations, which often adjusted kin relations legally in order to recruit more human capital and labor. The adjustments were made by contract—most notably marriage and adoption contracts—but even servants and slaves who could not easily be fitted into the genealogies were treated as quasi-family.

Despite Confucian admonitions to the contrary, adoption was an important and frequently used legal device for rearranging kinship relations contractually. As an extreme example of promiscuous adoption practices, one late sixteenth-century genealogy recorded nearly three hundred adoptions, which certainly suggests that adoption was an important means of redistributing human resources in traditional China.[41] Although in theory Confucianism frowned upon adoption, at the same time for orthodox Confucians there was "no crime . . . more grave than that of filial impiety," and not having offspring was considered the worst form of filial impiety: it meant that one's ancestors would have no one to continue making sacrifices to them, and they would remain unworshipped ghosts.[42] In situations where one otherwise would not have had a male descendant to continue one's line, it was therefore permissible to adopt a son. Yet even in such cases, custom forbade adoption of nonagnates, except when no agnate was willing to provide a son. Indeed, official genealogies invariably professed grave concern regarding unorthodox adoption practices—although not necessarily for Confucian reasons. To the extent that having a son meant an extra person in the household who held a claim to a share in the lineage's common resources, it was understandable that clan rules provided penalties for reporting the birth of a fictitious son or the adoption of one with a different surname.[43] Nevertheless, unorthodox adoptions certainly took place. In the blunt conclusion of one recent study, "the central paradox of adoption in traditional China is that adoption across surname lines was prohibited and that the prohibition was ignored."[44]

Adoption illustrates also the ambiguous relationship between the clan corporation and its male members. On the one hand, males were the "owners" of the clan, or at least of its property (which, in so many ways, included its women); indeed, to maintain accurate "shareholder registers," some clans had a "New Male Book" that listed the births of sons.[45] On the other hand, men were also clan property in the sense that they belonged to the clan. Because poorer clans could not always afford to keep their human capital, it was possible for the more prosperous clans to buy more males in the form of adoptive sons-in-law.

In an orthodox Chinese marriage, the wife left her family and joined that of her husband. Yet in practice it was not uncommon for a husband to join his wife's family in violation of this basic principle. The usual fiction for legitimating these marriages was the adoption of the son-in-law, often as a young boy who was to marry one of his new "sisters" upon maturity. According to a report on customary law near Nanjing in the late Qing, "People who have no male children usually bring in a son-in-law to act as their son. On entering the family the son-in-law changes his name, and a contract is written so there will be proof."[46] The economic aspect of the transaction was evident. To have his son-in-law entered in the genealogy and accorded the rights of a successor, and thus ultimately a part owner of the clan property, the adoptive father was required to pay a fee to the clan. That this represented a material acquisition is fully evident in the adoption contracts whereby the transfers were accomplished. They specified the price of the adoptee, provided for a warranty of title (by representing that the adoptee had not been kidnapped or obtained illegally), and assured the buyer that if something should "happen" to the child later, this was of no concern to the sellers.[47] Girls too were sold, albeit at lower prices and less reluctantly. In areas with high demand for light labor, up to three-quarters of girls were adopted out before age fifteen to be raised as future daughters-in-law.[48] Model adoption contracts were freely available and could be copied from popular handbooks (some of which had rather innocuous titles such as *The Complete Set of Domestic Rites*). Put simply, despite Confucian cautions against the adoption of nonkin, adoption practices were in fact governed "not by the rules of kinship, but by the rules of the marketplace."[49]

Marriage was probably the single most common means of recruiting female labor into clan corporations. Wives and concubines were, in many ways, bought and sold in the market for productive and reproductive labor. Indeed, whatever else traditional Chinese marriage was, it was preeminently a contract, "with its central economic features either written down or clearly recognized."[50] Among the central economic features of any marriage were dowry and bride price, the former an expenditure by the bride's family and the latter the groom's family. As Gates notes, "Without her dowry, a bride ran the risk of being told she came as a beggar, stealing resources for her own upkeep from a husband's family."[51] However, in practice, many marriages entailed a net expenditure by the groom's family rather than the bride's, thus reflecting the net gain in obtaining the value of the bride's labor.

Not only did clan corporations buy women as brides and infant daughters-in-law but sometimes also as maidservants, as the highly ambiguous term 妹仔 is usually translated. Although these girls were "bought and sold like chattels," even they were absorbed into the familial idiom of the clan corporation and, despite their servitude, often were allowed eventually to marry out.[52] The so-called tenant/servants inhabited a similarly ambiguous social location. Especially in areas with a shortage of labor, wealthy clan corporations contracted with poor tenants who agreed not only to cultivate their land but also to take on hereditary labor obligations.[53] Although legally the tenant/servants occupied a low status, within the clan corporation they were considered quasi-kin. Their contractual violations were viewed as "unfilial," they were often mentioned in the clan genealogies, and, indeed, they were even provided with burial places in the clan corporation's ancestral cemetery.[54]

Outright slavery did not figure prominently in the late traditional Chinese political and moral economy—not surprisingly, perhaps, considering the highly developed technologies of servitude made possible by the elaborate kinship system. Yet to the extent that wealthy clan corporations used slave labor (which was considered a luxury, in light of the fact that Chinese slaves typically produced less than they consumed), the slaves' position too was in many ways that of a "contractual" family member. They could be bought with either "white" or "red" contracts, yet at least in the orthodox Confucian view, the slave, too, stood in a quasi-kinship relation to the master, and slaves' disobedience was conceptualized as unfilial behavior.[55]

In short, given the evident plasticity of Chinese kinship practices, much as Chinese kin groups may have wished to present themselves as kin groups, one is well advised to ask whether a particular clan constitutes "a unilineal descent group or a voluntary association posing as a unilineal descent group."[56] The closer one looks, the more the clan corporation begins to look like a nexus of contracts among self-interested, profit-seeking individuals and the less like Confucian familism writ large.

What, then, of the second characteristic in our definition of a corporation, engagement in the pursuit of material profit? Orthodox Confucianism was overtly anticommercial in its rhetoric. While wealth surely mattered in its own right, by far the most socially acceptable road to success was winning a post in the imperial bureaucracy. The state recruited its officials through the prestigious civil service examinations, the content of which had been defined by the Neo-Confucian orthodoxy since the eleventh century. Many successful merchants in fact legitimated their success by buying degrees and thus purporting to become members of the gentry class from which scholar-officials were drawn. In this (ostensibly) unfavorable political climate, the ideological usefulness of the ancestral trust lay in its claim to provide for posthumous worship of a clan's forebears. From the Confucian perspective, an ancestral trust was not morally suspect private property for selfish purposes but a means of perpetuating family solidarity. Nevertheless, clan corporations were analogous to business corporations not only because of their frequent origin as voluntary associations but also because of the profit-seeking activities in which they engaged. Effectively, they contradict the conventional view that extended family organizations were the effect rather than the cause of prosperity—mere "accoutrements of wealth" rather than "techniques of continuing aggrandizement."[57]

Indeed, many ancestral trusts hardly functioned like trusts. Insofar as they purported to be charitable trusts for the purpose of providing ancestral sacrifices in perpetuity, their property was theoretically inalienable. In practice, this was simply not the case. Despite the sacred bonds of kinship and even express trust instructions to the contrary, ancestral trusts could in fact be dissolved by consensus and the properties (including ritual lands held by the trust) could be divided among the beneficiaries.[58] Similarly, ritual land could be used for clan members' private benefit in times of need, even in locales where this may not have been in accordance with "strict custom."[59] To make a sale of trust property valid one only had to recite on the sale deed that the sellers were "in want of means"—usually a "mere fiction," as one observer remarked.[60] At least in Hong Kong, even this fiction may not have been necessary. According to the colonial government's report on Chinese customary law, sales were permitted so long as they were "profitable." There is evidence that ancestral trusts may also have been mortgaged to raise capital.[61]

The need to shroud all mercantile activity in high-minded Confucian rhetoric makes it difficult to judge, in retrospect, in just what activities any particular clan association engaged. However, there is increasing evidence to support the contention that Qing clans ran their estates as "hard-nosed business corporations" rather than Song-style charitable trusts.[62] Absentee landlordism was one of the more lucrative economic activities for many Qing clans. One city-dwelling Taiwanese clan boasted that the rents from its rural landholdings supported four to five hundred clan members.[63] By Qing, commercialized agriculture was already well established, and rice, cotton, mulberry, sugar cane, and tea, among others, were all important cash crops, and, as Philip Huang has shown, the "familization" and commercialization of rural production proceeded in tandem in the Ming and the Qing.[64] While the number of absentee landlords grew steadily in the late imperial period, typically even so-called managerial landlords—landlords who hired and personally supervised outside labor to cultivate their lands—invested part of their proceeds in other capital, such as breweries, oil presses, flour mills, weaving works, and stores of various sorts.[65] Increasing numbers of households also engaged in spinning, weaving, and dyeing cotton for the marketplace, in producing silk, and in building sugar mills, while household handicraft production increased as well.[66]

Indeed, clan activities were hardly limited to land. By some estimates gentry families' income from trading and financial activities in the late nineteenth century was well over half as great as their income from land.[67] The well-documented Lin clan in nineteenth-century Taiwan, for example, held its assets in a complex web of individual accounts, trusts, and partnerships, and its activities ranged from landlordism and urban real estate to money lending, manufacturing, and camphor trading.[68] Around the same time, in certain regions there were family-run silk-weaving enterprises, some of which employed dozens of workers. Evidence of mercantile activity includes clan associations that generated their income by renting land, operating a market or a pawnshop, buying a salt franchise from the state, or producing bricks and tiles in a kiln.[69] The considerable scale of clan business is evident also from the fact that as late as the 1960s, income from clan corporations run by the wealthier rural clans in Hong Kong was sufficient to permit clan members not to work for a living.[70] Anticommercial ideologies aside, there was money to be made. One Qing clan even built a temple and then sold the right to manage it to the highest bidder.[71]

As Susan Mann observes, by the late imperial era the clan organization was not driven simply by wealth drawn from traditional gentry activity and bureaucratic positions; rather, clans "could be sustained by either gentry or merchant activities, and preferably both."[72] Conceptualizing clan associations as business organizations legitimated by their elaborate written genealogies explains also "the otherwise puzzlingly high level of genealogy making at a time when kinship bonds had been thought to be weakening in the face of modernization, especially in coastal China."[73] There is no puzzle: with increasing modernization and commercialization, there were a growing number of clan corporations. That the genealogies themselves made no mention of commercial activities is to be expected. As late as 1948, the anthropologist Francis L. K. Hsu noted that "[genealogical] records emphasize the importance of scholarship and official ranks as achievements, but fail completely to mention trading or commerce," which were nevertheless "the backbone" of everyday life.[74] Or, as Mann trenchantly characterizes the stylized biographies provided by most genealogies, "No one knows how often 'filiality' served as a historical gloss on the lives of entrepreneurs who lacked any other printable distinction."[75]

When it comes to the third element in our definition of a corporation, the separation of management from ownership and the resultant agency problem are generally viewed as *the* key characteristics of the modern business corporation. In the traditional Chinese family, the ritual structure of kinship indeed provided for the ownership of family property by the entire patrilineage and for its management separately by patriarchal authority. Building on this simple model of corporation law, ancestral trusts-*cum*-clan corporations created increasingly complex and bureaucratic governance structures that included full-time professional managers, accountable to "shareholders" in semiannual meetings, and boards of elders whose task it was to monitor the managers in the interim.

The eldest male of the eldest line occupied what was technically the highest position in the clan hierarchy, but his leadership was usually mostly symbolic. Other senior members constituted a council, analogous to a board of directors, which, at least in the case of larger clan associations, left the actual clan management to various corporate officers. Managerial authority was thus distinct from ritual authority.[76] Even the rules of the exemplary Fan clan, generally held to embody Neo-Confucian familism at its best, contain an express rule providing that in the management of clan affairs managers' authority trumps that of their genealogical elders.[77]

As to their social status, managers were usually literati members of the clan; large clans, especially those with highly organized clan associations, were almost invariably economically and socially stratified. In the case of smaller clan corporations, bylaws usually called for the various branches of the clan to rotate the day-to-day management of their affairs annually among the branch heads. In more complex organizations, the clan rules provided for a full-time salaried manager, sometimes with assistants, as well as auditors, registrars, and other functionaries.[78]

Ordinarily, clan corporations held "shareholder meetings" open to the entire membership twice a year, in conjunction with the ancestral sacrifices in spring and autumn. At the meetings, after the sacrificial rituals were completed, the clan's attention turned to financial and administrative matters.[79] The clan membership's role in the selection of corporate officers was often unclear. Short on procedural guidelines, clan rules might advise the clan "to select carefully," "for the members to choose publicly," or "for the members to recommend unanimously."[80] Although real instances of "direct democracy" were possible, the prevailing preference for decision making by consensus made it possible for leading factions of the clan to manipulate the outcomes.[81] (This, of course, hardly makes the clan corporation any less like a modern business corporation, where shareholder meetings are often no less ritualistic window dressing.)

Mindful of the agency problem, clan corporations had various types of specific rules designed to keep the managers and other corporate officers honest, and also to keep other powerful members of the clan from interfering with the officers' work. Among typical requirements for managerial office were integrity and social status, as well as wealth—the last requirement being apparently based on the assumption that the wealthy would be less tempted to steal, or possibly because it would be easier to obtain recovery from them in the case of embezzlement.[82] (In such cases, clan rules were typically satisfied with restitution.) Sometimes the managers were required to give bonds before assuming office. As to account keeping, regulations required managers to make financial reports at clan meetings and to post account documents in the clan hall where meetings took place, and archives of accounting records were kept. As to enforcement, many provisions did not specify penalties, but some did, even severe ones.[83]

As a formal matter, the fourth element of our definition of a corporation, legal personality, is a moot point. In a purely technical sense, Max Weber and his followers are of course correct in denying the existence of the concept of legal person in traditional China.[84] However, in the context of traditional Chinese law, the observation misses the point. It is perfectly clear that family collectives could sue and be sued as well as own and dispose of property in a corporate capacity; in important ways, clan corporations were able to function in the manner of Western legal persons.[85]

That the imperial state never conferred the legal abstraction of "personality" on clan corporations reflects a Confucian social epistemology in which the family was the most fundamental, real, and natural unit. Indeed, in many ways the family was the Confucian "natural person," just as the individual is the "natural person" of modern Western legal systems. As I have emphasized, the personality of corporate entities has been a conundrum for modern Western legal thought because we live in a legal system that happens to think in terms of individual persons.[86] The so-called "endless problem of corporate personality" has plagued Euro-American jurisprudence for distinct historical reasons, not because the notion of collective entities is somehow inherently problematic.[87] Because of different foundational assumptions, the notion of "natural" collective entities was not at variance with the Confucian worldview, and hence traditional Chinese law required no jurisprudential alchemy to accommodate collectives as legitimate and "real." On the contrary, the theory of the indivisible patrilineage on which Chinese kinship is founded makes corporate personality the normative ideal and individual personality the deviation.

Indeed, just as the logic of modern Western law has forced us to personify—or, more precisely, individualize—all legal subjects (every right and duty must be held by a "person," no matter the conceptual violence), so traditional Chinese law constantly sought to analogize everything within its purview to the family, as much the universal subject of Confucian humanism as the individual is that of Anglo-American liberalism. Not infrequently, the imputation of family-hood resulted in the creation of artificial, or what we might call "legal," families, along with the "natural" kind. For example, when thirteen sailors were slain off the coast of Fujian in 1828, the offense was likened to that of killing several members of one family since all the victims had served aboard the same ship.[88] Similarly, in a case appealed to the Board of Punishments, the Board decided that two merchants who traveled together and pooled some of their resources constituted a "family" (家) in a legal sense.[89] In an extreme example of familism at work, even the legal relation between a madam running a brothel and the women working under her was often that of a mother and her adoptive daughters, and to conform to the ideology of the family, even successful eunuchs took pro forma wives and adopted sons for the purposes of succession.[90]

In sum, by virtue of its status as a kinship group—real or fictional—the clan corporation acquired some of the ideologically unimpeachable and legally cognizable personality of the family. Even if the social universe was ultimately a unified whole, the family provided a legitimate means of partaking in that universal source of personality.

Transferability of ownership—the penultimate element of our definition of a corporation—is the characteristic most difficult to identify in the structure of the clan corporation. Nevertheless, in limited ways printed copies of the clan genealogy functioned in the manner of stock certificates. In many clans, member households were given a numbered copy of the genealogy, and at least in larger clan corporations, distributions of clan proceeds required the presentation of a registered copy of the genealogy. The existence of clan regulations providing penalties for those who sold their genealogies suggests that there was at least a small market for the sale of shares in large clan corporations, and there are reports of instances where shares were sold even to nonkin.[91] Nevertheless, there is little evidence of wide transferability of ownership in clan corporations, which obviously provided limits to their ability to raise capital—no matter how creative and ingenious they were in their ability to turn potential, biologically unrelated contributors into legally and socially cognizable kinfolk.

With regard to the final element of the corporation, as defined here, just as the market for clan shares was limited, it is not quite clear to what extent

clan corporations enjoyed limited liability.[92] Part of the difficulty in defining limited liability in the clan corporation is conceptual. It is not clear just
what it would mean for clan members to have unlimited individual liability
for corporate acts. At least under the preferred Confucian theory of the
family, there was no individual property: whatever property a person acquired, it belonged to the family as a whole.[93] Recent scholarship suggests, however, that individual property could coexist with jointly owned
household property. Custom apparently distinguished between property a
household head acquired solely through his own efforts, on the one hand,
and property acquired through inheritance or with the assistance of his
sons, on the other. As far as individually acquired property was concerned,
the household head was permitted to disinherit his heirs or to devise his
property to nonrelatives by gift, for example. Insofar as any of his sons contributed to the acquisition of new household property, they had the right to
demand division of that property at any time. Arthur Wolf and Chieh-shan
Huang indeed maintain that, in practice, the division of property would
often "respect individual effort and not flow directly from genealogical status."[94] To the extent that there existed individually held property of this
sort, distinct from family property, there was at least the conceptual possibility of limited liability in the family and the clan. At a minimum, the
British colonial administration in Hong Kong interpreted Chinese customary law as providing for limited liability. When the Partnership Ordinance of Hong Kong was amended in 1911 to provide that an ancestral
trust may register as a legal person with limited liability, the government's
stated purpose was to bring the Ordinance in line with actual Chinese
custom.[95]

To summarize, then, the Orientalist story of Chinese law is one where kinship overwhelms the entire system, seemingly crowding out even the conceptual possibility of the corporation as a legal form. Nevertheless, we *can* read
traditional Chinese family law as a species of corporation law. Many clan
corporations met evidently most, if not all, of the conventional corporate
criteria of Anglo-American law. They were voluntary associations; their
primary goal was the pursuit of material profit; their ownership was sepa-
rated from management; they functioned as legal persons; their ownership
was transferable to some extent; and, finally, even their liability may have
been limited, at least up to a point.

CORPORATION LAW IN ACTION

Even if it is useful to view ancestral trusts, at least in their more complex forms, as corporations, it is worth pausing to consider further the extent to which they were regulated by *law*. After all, the received notion that China traditionally had no concept of business corporations is associated with the claim that all Chinese law was penal by nature, with civil and commercial affairs being of little concern to the state. The claim for law thus seems particularly difficult to make in the familial context of the clan.

Indeed, according to the orthodox Confucian view, the family was ideally the sphere of moral, rather than legal, control—it was a locus in which the Chinese genius for mediation and informal dispute resolution reached its highest development. A large proportion of Western scholarship has accepted this assertion more or less at face value.[96] At the same time, a considerable minority have portrayed the Chinese family as the exact opposite: a beginner's course in Oriental despotism, and a place where fathers tyrannized their sons into filial submission, juniors surrendered to the whims of their seniors, and wives served their husbands with abject humility.[97] Diametrically opposed and caricatured as these portrayals are, they converge on their unwillingness to consider seriously the possibility of meaningful legal controls within the family sphere.

That the Chinese term for civil suits was "minor matters" (细事) surely tells us something important about the official Chinese attitude toward civil law.[98] In a Confucian utopia, law is just as redundant as it is in a Marxist one, and largely for the same reason: when people put aside the selfish pursuit of power, prestige, and profit, they will realize the unity of their interests, and there will no longer be a cause for litigation. In one of his two references to law in the *Analects,* Confucius notes: " 'In hearing litigations, I am like any other body. What is necessary, however, is to cause the people to have no litigations.' "[99] Yet the profusion of popular antilaw proverbs and attitudes need not mean that there was not plenty of law, penal and civil, and that people did not resort to it on a regular basis—any more than one should conclude from the proliferation of lawyer jokes in the United States that Americans must be peculiarly averse to litigation. Philip Huang insists that the state's actions often spoke louder than the official Confucian rhetoric: "the Qing legal system . . . embodied the practical reality of civil law and property rights without their representational realities."[100] This accords with Madeleine Zelin's conclusion, based on her study of land-related litigation in mid-Qing Sichuan: "Tenants were not inhibited in filing suits against landlords who violated what they perceived to be their rights, and in many cases tenants were able to gain redress."[101]

In keeping with Huang's and Zelin's observations, I outline below more fully the legal dimensions in the governance of the clan corporations. I do so by focusing on corporation bylaws, customary law, administrative regulation, and statutory law. The internal governance rules of clan corporations were often written down and included in the clan's genealogical record, which also contained title deeds and other important clan documents. These written rules, adopted by the clan, are best analogized to corporation bylaws—essentially the private law of the corporation. The rules were frequently registered with the local magistrate whose commitment to enforcing them gave the rules the express force of law.[102]

As the perceptive nineteenth-century observer Ernest Alabaster (who in Chapter 1 bemoaned the general lack of awareness of Chinese law) put it: "The family or clan is . . . much in the position of an English corporation: with powers, within certain limits, to frame bye-laws: subject to have its local regulations construed by ordinary tribunals: and liable to the ordinary law for exceeding its powers. As the innermost of two concentric circles is of necessity bounded on all sides by the outer, so is the family or clan encircled by the law."[103] Alabaster, to be sure, only meant that the clan was governed *like* a corporation, not that it "really" was a business association. Although clan rules have received considerable scholarly attention, they have been tapped mostly by social historians and anthropologists interested in their ideological and sociological significance for understanding Chinese kinship and family organization. However, given the economic aspects of the clan corporation, there is no doubt that clan rules were an important legal technology of economic organization.

In terms of their content, clan rules were filled with moral maxims calling for the protection of the young, weak, and powerless members of the clan. Overall, they tended to lie in the intermediate territory "beneath the idealistic value scheme of Confucian theory and above the *ad hoc* expediency of everyday family, clan, and social life."[104] Although many genealogical regulations are on the order of such Confucian platitudes as denunciations of "bullying the weak by relying on one's strength," many are remarkably sophisticated and quite reminiscent of modern corporation bylaws in their structure.[105]

As a taxonomic matter, to characterize clan rules as corporation bylaws rather than as customary law carries some important implications. "Customary law" is a notoriously unstable legal category: Is it descriptive or prescriptive, "custom" or "law"? Moreover, to characterize an aspect of the Chinese legal tradition as "customary" carries overtly colonial overtones. The positivist jurisprude John Austin, for example, describes rules based on "brute custom" as "monstrous or crude productions of childish and imbecile intellect."[106] Henry Maine states equally emphatically, "What an Oriental is really attached to is his local custom."[107]

In any event, customary law was one part of traditional Chinese corporation law. For example, in the case of smaller clans without written bylaws, rights and duties among clan members were based on customary norms. Indeed, even clans with written bylaws did not typically make their rules up from scratch. Many clans copied entire sections verbatim from authoritative historical models, such as the rules of the Fan clan. Over time, the pool of models grew increasingly uniform, coming to constitute a kind of "common law" of corporations. At least in the absence of written bylaws stipulating otherwise, they provided a set of default rules for clan governance.[108]

Part of this common law was, for example, the structural division between a ritual and managerial hierarchy, with the clan elders constituting a kind of board of directors overseeing the managers.[109] Furthermore, gentry status and wealth were widely seen as qualifications for managerial office. The practice of rotating managerial positions among the various branches of a clan was another standard feature, especially in the case of smaller clans which did not necessarily have full-time managers.[110] By the Qing, there had evolved a common vocabulary, used throughout China, for describing clan management, and "the elaboration and revision of clan rules reached a saturation point around 1880."[111]

Apart from lending its support to the enforcement of corporation bylaws and customary law, the imperial state also sought to regulate clan corporations with its own and society's interests in mind. It did so, among other things, by issuing measures that constituted a form of administrative regulation. The state frequently saw clans as a potential source of disputes and public disturbances, and in 1736 an imperial memorial even promised to reward clan associations that stayed out of court for three consecutive years—a gesture that also serves as an indication that clan associations did engage in litigation.[112] In 1757, the Qianlong emperor imposed a disclosure obligation of sorts on larger clan associations. Each was to appoint a member responsible for making periodic reports to the government regarding "the good and bad elements of the clans."[113] A few years later, it was recommended that the government establish a bureau to control the proliferation of spurious genealogies that were used as fronts for selfish activities wholly unrelated to kinship.[114] The state also regulated the content of genealogical records on which the legitimacy of the entire institution of clan association rested. For example, the records of families whose genealogies made fabricated claims to imperial kinship were to be destroyed by the emperor's order.[115] In a 1768 edict, the emperor addressed the state's concern that powerful members of clan associations used their power to control the clan and to oppress its less powerful members.[116] Finally, in perhaps the most extreme form of state regulation, the Qing Code contained a type of "antitrust law"-*cum*-public security ordinance. Overly powerful clan associations that used their ancestral income for arming themselves and subsequently got involved in violent disputes were to be dissolved and their property was to be distributed to clan members.[117]

These various regulatory measures flatly contradict the traditional view of Chinese clans as *imperia in imperio*—entirely private havens within the state.[118] To view them as such is, first, to buy into the fiction that they were "merely" family groupings and, second, to assume that their purportedly familial nature would naturally exempt them from state regulation. The latter assumption is likely a projection of Roman law categories onto Chinese intellectual topography, as the recurring use of the expression *imperium in imperio* evidently suggests. On a more fundamental level, the Confucian tendency to conceptualize the entire state as a single fiduciary community united in "one body" makes a public/private distinction ultimately meaningless. Where Roman law viewed the family head and the state as distinct sources of authority, Chinese political theory posited a continuum of shared interests throughout the polity and, indeed, the cosmos. To the extent that clan corporations legitimated their existence by purporting to enforce fiduciary relations among their members, the same fiduciary logic was equally applicable to the corporations' relationship to the outside world. For example, the Yongzheng emperor issued an edict in 1731 proclaiming that "the ideal way for a wealthy household to perpetuate itself" included the need "to be constantly vigilant, even in peacetime, in dispensing relief and aid to the poor."[119] In fact, wealthy merchants typically responded positively to local officials' appeals for financial contributions to relief aid in the wake of natural disasters, public projects of various sorts, and other social welfare assistance. In essence, clan managers owed fiduciary duties not only to corporation members but also to the ultimate parent corporation: the Middle Kingdom.[120]

A more recent alternative to the *imperium in imperio* thesis indeed views the power wielded by clan organizations as a controlled delegation by the state—a brilliant way of co-opting the family into the state hierarchy.[121] In this view, clan elders were unofficial administrative arms of the state; in a vast empire where there was only one district magistrate per 250,000 people, administration of justice through the clan was an inexpensive means of enforcing the Confucian norms on which the state had staked its legitimacy.[122] Indeed, when clans registered their rules with magistrates, the state clearly had an opportunity to pass judgment on the content of the rules. This recognition of particular clans was thus, in a sense, analogous to the Anglo-American concession theory of the corporation in the era of specific incorporation.[123]

However, to say that the clan corporation received its authority in a straightforward delegation from the state gives too much credit to the state and too little to clans. The private lawmaking power of clans was surely in many ways an "involuntary" delegation. Insofar as the state, with its limited resources, could not exert much actual power on the local level, it may have made a virtue out of necessity. When it could not control clan organizations, the second-best option was to claim that it did, and to persuade the clans to pay lip service to the notion. Even clans that had not been expressly sanctioned by the state often recognized its theoretical authority. Many genealogies in the Pearl River Delta in South China included foundation legends invoking mythical state documents that conferred on these clans the right to their lands.[124] Thus, at least in theory, though perhaps not always in practice, a clan corporation registered with the government was subject to state regulation and owed duties to the community as well. Or, as the Kangxi emperor put it, "the profit of all" is "the real profit."[125]

Beyond ad hoc administrative regulation, clans' corporate property was the subject of permanent statutory enactments as well. The Qing Code contained a statute prohibiting "fraudulent" sales of land, and one of the substatutes under the general prohibition made it clear that the prohibition applied to fraudulent sales of ritual properties as well.[126] Given the official status of clan property as a sacrificial trust—whether actually established by an ancestor or pooled by contemporaries in an ancestor's name—it came under the protection of the substatute.[127] Thus the substatute functioned as a safeguard for the clan corporation against managers who tried to sell off capital assets without clan members' approval.

LEGITIMATING INEQUALITY

It is evident that several aspects of the governance and regulation of clan corporations provide a basis for describing them as "legal" entities. To be sure, it is one thing to identify a set of legal norms and another to consider how such norms are enforced. How well, then, were the fiduciary duties implied by the Confucian family metaphor observed in everyday life? It is impossible to provide meaningful statistical estimates. However, there is no question that despite the conventional view that most clan disputes were resolved through intraclan mediation, many clan members did in fact invoke the law to protect their rights against clan leaders and at least sometimes magistrates were willing to enforce those rights.

According to a turn-of-the-century account from Northern Shandong, "The causes of litigation . . . are endless, but a large proportion of the cases are the results of more or less trivial family quarrels."[128] Property disputes ranked among the most frequently mentioned disputes in clan regulations. As Jonathan Ocko observes, "property—especially its management and its division—was a major source of family disharmony," and "suits about the failure to discharge fiduciary responsibilities were . . . a regular, but unwelcome, feature of magistrates' dockets."[129] This may sound surprising in light of the fact that the Qing Code provided penalties for bringing complaints against one's status superiors, which presumably made it easy for powerful clan members to loot common property at will.[130] However, this feature, like many others in the Qing legal system, had more to do with official idealization of hierarchy and harmony than with legal reality. The provision did not apply to accusations regarding a breach of fiduciary duty.[131] In Northern Taiwan, for example, challenges to the illegal sale of common property could be initiated by male clan members who had been minors at the time of the sale. With remarkable frequency, even widowed women plaintiffs asserted rights to clan property as representatives of their minor sons.[132]

Given the official Confucian preference for "alternative dispute resolution," one might wonder whether the local magistrates truly adjudicated the conflicting claims in accordance with the clan regulations. Rather than basing their decisions on the law, perhaps they engaged in something more akin to arbitration, or even mediation. If so, there would presumably have been more pressure on the poor, female, and/or junior members to settle their charges of mismanagement by clan leaders.

However, Ernest Alabaster's 1899 transcription of two decisions given in clan disputes suggests that, at least sometimes, legal rights did triumph over Confucian social hierarchy. The first case, decided by a magistrate Fang, concerned "land dedicated to the maintenance of ancestral worship." The land had been set aside by the ancestors of the Chen family, with provisions for rotating the management of the land among the various branches and a prohibition against the diversion of the land to "other uses." Taking advantage of his status and seniority, "an old but reprobate graduate [of the civil service examination system,] Chên Chi-yi, disregarding the pious intentions of his ancestors, greedily and avariciously trie[d] to appropriate twenty *mu* to his own ends." Apparently the reprobate clan elder had rented out some of the clan land in his own name. Magistrate Fang annulled the lease and ordered that "the trusteeship [of the common land] go on as before . . . and that the tenants pay no heed to the terms of the underhand lease." By annulling the unlawful transaction, Fang clearly acted as an adjudicator upholding the letter of the law rather than as a mediator concerned primarily with the preservation of family harmony.[133]

In the second case a prefect was confronted with a dispute between two branches of a lineage over the distribution of income from their collectively managed ancestral trust. One branch had just produced a successful candidate in the imperial examinations and claimed that the settlor-ancestor had intended the proceeds to belong to "any of his descendants who might devote himself to study." The representatives of the other branch contended that the land was intended for ancestral sacrifices and cultivation. The prefect observed that "neither party have any proof, for the original deed merely says [the land is] 'to be zealously cultivated' and does not say anything about diligently studying." The prefect assumed that the settlor-ancestor knew "how much more necessary property would be to common cultivators, than to those possessing the resources of their pen." He therefore flatly rejected the claims of the more powerful branch to more than its proportionate share of the clan income.[134]

All of this may not prove much. Yet it does show that, conventional wisdom notwithstanding, the fiduciary duties in management of common property in Chinese clans constituted a distinctly legal obligation: They were at least potentially enforceable at law. Indeed, both of the above cases were included in an official case compilation, which suggests that clan rules were intended to be taken seriously. Although the compilation did not have precedential value in a formal sense, the cases included in it had been selected and edited with care and were hence studied closely by officials.[135]

That fiduciary obligations were the aspirational norm is clear. As one sixteenth-century observer put it, clan members "should treat each other 'as parts of a single body, like bone and sinew, hand and foot,'" and clan resources should be shared accordingly, with "'no wealthy and no poor families.'"[136] Yet it is equally clear, in most commentators' view, that this ideal remained largely unrealized: "The constant inroads made upon the common property by powerful [male] clan members" were among clan corporations' most egregious failures.[137] Although many clan regulations expressly provided that no one, regardless of genealogical rank, was above corporation managers' authority, in practice managers were often susceptible to pressure from powerful clan members. In the absence of detailed procedural rules for the election of leaders, corporations were frequently controlled by the literati and other powerful clan members.

Legal fictions often helped cover the flouting of kinship obligations. In places where customary law prohibited sales of property to a relative—a transaction with an evidently high risk of favoritism—transfer documents would not use the words "purchase" and "sale" (買, 賣); instead, they purported to give the transferor a right of redemption, even though in practice no such redemption was possible. As one notable scholar of Chinese customary law explains: "The custom prescribing this formality here gives the impression that an absolute sale has not taken place. It presumes what it likes or desires to be rather than what is and therefore creates this legal fiction in order not to violate the virtue of filial piety and thus harm good understanding among members of the same family."[138] In a similar fashion, instead of selling his property outright, a landowner in Sichuan would "rent" his land to a tenant, but the rental agreement would provide for a large one-time deposit and no periodic rental payments. "In this manner [the seller] was able to receive most of the benefits of sale without having to bear the shame and economic consequences of having alienated his patrimony."[139]

Moreover, vague rules often made it easy to label poorer members of the clan as "immoral" and to use this as an excuse to expel them from economic membership, resulting in what Rubie Watson calls "inequality among brothers."[140] Some genealogies frankly admit their failure to live up to clan rules. One simply noted that because membership had grown so large and corporate income had become so limited, the clan was forced to discriminate between the two branches of the family in distributing proceeds.[141] Another genealogy spelled out with equal candor the priority of wealth in ordering relations among clan members: "If the wealth is about equal, they call each other brothers."[142] Yet other clans went even further, permitting wealth not only to level genealogical hierarchies but to reverse them: with utter disregard for proper Confucian generational order, in some clans a genealogical senior sometimes addressed his junior as "uncle," in recognition of the junior member's greater wealth and social power.[143]

Overall (and less than surprisingly), the conclusion is clear. Even in Chinese clan corporations the "haves" tended to come out ahead of the "have-nots."[144] This too would seem to confirm, rather than to disqualify, the characterization of Confucian family as a corporation law. However, it is worth considering the deeper causes of such inequality, embedded in Confucian notions of subjectivity. Even if Confucian corporation law failed to redeem its promise in full, that failure was not—at least not necessarily—merely the result of the abuse of power by those in the higher echelons of the social hierarchy. Paradoxically, part of the problem lay in the radical, organic unity upon which the legal subjectivity of the family was premised. Understood in terms of the Confucian metaphor of the family as "one body," the family head is virtually infallible.[145]

In a body, the head may well rank over the limbs and make decisions on their behalf, yet it is difficult to conceive that the head would purposely try to take advantage of the limbs. By definition, what is beneficial to the head is beneficial to the rest of the body as well. Although this may sound like a barely concealed ideological justification for Oriental despotism in the sphere of the family, it is the same logic that lay behind Blackstone's dictum that in English law "husband and wife are one person"—what is good for one spouse is by definition good for the other as well. Of course, as Justice Black later noted in his famous paraphrase, in the construction of this marital "one" person, ultimately "the one is the husband."[146] Similarly, even if members of the Chinese clan were "one body," more often than not the "ones" were really the literate, well-placed members of the family.

For a Confucian who takes seriously the family metaphor and the notion of collective unity it suggests, the concept of self is best conceived as interpersonal.[147] By definition, this self is an altruistic one: "As a member of society the person must subordinate his selfish desires (ssu-yü 私慾) to the good of the community or public good (kung 公). His true personhood is thus achieved by disciplining his desires so that they serve rather than conflict with the public good."[148] A "selfless" concern for other members of the larger body is the very fulfillment of authentic personhood. Indeed, true filiality is realized "only if one's filiality is expressed not as an obligation toward an outside authority but as an integral part of one's self-realization."[149]

The radical unity of the family, as expressed by orthodox Neo-Confucian ideologues, made it effectively an oxymoron to "steal" from one's family. Looting an ancestral trust was tantamount to trying to steal from oneself. Consider the following words of reproach from a magistrate about a clan elder who had attempted to divert clan property to his own uses: "This was foolish, for his grey hairs were many; he was like a burnt-out censer at night when day is about to appear; little earthly enjoyment was before him, and dead he would not have lost the property, for if he died without children, would he not in the next world have fared with the rest of his ancestors— sharing alike with them the common provision for their spirits?"[150] By stealing from the ancestral trust, the foolish old man was simply stealing from his future spirit. From this perspective the imperative that clan corporations be managed for the benefit of the living and the dead was eminently sensible, and in fact it provided a perfect incentive for long-term planning; while it is undoubtedly true that in the long run we are all dead (in John Maynard Keynes's immortal observation), a clan manager will be able to reap the fruits of "selfless" management even generations later.[151]

That the meaning of both selflessness and selfishness depends entirely on how one defines the legal and moral self was painfully evident when a

British colonial court in Singapore held, in 1869, that ancestral trusts by the Chinese were "void, 'as a perpetuity, not being a charity.' "[152] By viewing the "ancestral trust" as a trust, rather than as a corporate entity, the court made it subject to the Rule Against Perpetuities—a decision that misconstrued the Chinese legal definition of the family, the very essence of which was perpetuity. In the court's view, the only thing that might have saved the trust was a charitable purpose. Alas, as an Orientalist legal epistemology collided headlong with Chinese law as a lived social practice, no such purpose could be found. In the conception of the family as one body, a selfishness/selflessness distinction among family members makes little sense. On the one hand, an ancestral trust is in the settlor's "own" interest, as it will benefit him after death; on the other hand, it is also an act of great filiality that benefits all family members past, present, and future and, indeed, as an act of civic morality contributes to the flourishing of the entire community.

Reading Chinese law through the lens of the common law, the colonial court deemed that an ancestral trust's object was "solely for the benefit of the testator himself." Although English law applied to the native inhabitants of the Crown Colony "subject to such modifications as are necessary to prevent it from operating unjustly and oppressively on them," the common law's Rule Against Perpetuities was held to require no such modifications in this context:

> Certainly it would require very strong evidence to establish that it was regarded as a duty, in any religion, to disregard the claims of natural affection, and, as in this case, to dispose of the bulk of one's property in providing for the supposed benefit and comfort of his own soul, while he left his sons and daughters almost wholly unprovided for. As there is no such evidence, I am unable to see any reason for holding that the rule against perpetuities is less applicable to property in the hands of a Chinese and Buddhist than to property in the hands of an Englishman and a Christian.[153]

It simply eluded the court that eventually the trust would provide for the worship of the younger generation's ghosts as well; it was in fact a selfless attempt to care for them for aeons to come.

Yet even when properly understood, the concept of intersubjective family unity made the administration of justice exceedingly difficult. That the family, for social and legal purposes, was likened to one body meant that intrafamily exchanges were often impenetrably ambiguous. Although the Confucian fiduciary community was based on an assumption of reciprocity even among unequals—care and concern for those below in return for their submission—its key values of loyalty and filial piety "enjoined inferiors to keep giving to superiors even when no reciprocation was possible," in Hill Gates's crisp formulation.[154]

This ambiguity in turn illuminates the divergent interpretations of property rights in the traditional Chinese family. On the one hand, it is true that the father's right to manage family property did not imply absolute ownership. It was his fiduciary obligation to preserve it for his descendants, who were in fact co-owners of the land. Hence technically he could not dispose of it without junior members' consent. On the other hand, it is also well recognized that there was "practically no limit to the extent to which a man may dispose of or squander his property during his lifetime."[155] The practical implication of the theory was that, by virtue of the interpersonal unity between a man and his sons, expressions of assent to a father's judgment were redundant. As a fiduciary, he had—in modern legal idiom—constructive consent to his actions. In the end the Chinese father did not simply guess what might benefit his sons the most. He knew. As Duncan Kennedy describes the phenomenology of true paternalism, "The actor is not in the position of 'supposing' or 'hypothesizing' that the other feels in a particular way—it's much more immediate than that. It feels like unity."[156] That is, even if clan members' interests should not have been truly in harmony, the metaphor simply postulated a hypothetical harmony in its place. This is precisely what happened in litigation over clan property, as described by Melissa Macauley: "Appeals to common descent [were] made in the very process of dispossession, as if the loser was unable to perceive his or her own economic interest."[157] Besides, even if a father were to have asked one of his sons for consent, say, to a land sale, how could the son have said "no"? As legal historian Paul Ch'en observes, a disloyal person "who violated the basic [Confucian] bonds, was no longer regarded as a human" but was "an animal or brute creature" instead.[158] Presumably a son would not oppose his father lightly if it entailed risking his very humanity.

What should we make of this analysis then? It seems that much of traditional Chinese corporation law was irrelevant and ignored, and, perhaps more disturbingly, even when it *was* properly observed its chief achievement appears to have been to perpetuate an ideology of inequality and

dispossession, by manufacturing the conditions in which dispossession became normatively desirable. At worst, clan corporations were ruled by outright despots, and at best their despotism was cloaked as kindness and
concern. There is much to this analysis. However, it is not necessarily an
indictment of Chinese corporation law *as* corporation law. In an important
sense, it makes traditional Chinese corporation law *more* like its contemporary American counterpart. Consider, again, the notion of interpersonal
continuity in the father-son relationship. Its hierarchical implications are
captured perfectly in the general Confucian belief that parents are always
right.[159] Such filial norms are in fact the functional equivalent of the so-
called business judgment rule of American corporation law—a critically
important doctrine developed by courts that leaves virtually all business
decisions to managerial discretion. Gerald Frug's assessment of the business
judgment rule describes the clan corporation perfectly. In Frug's words, the
rule effectively allows "corporate managers [to] set the limits of their own
activity by describing it as consistent with a concept—shareholder
interest—that they themselves define."[160]

In short, traditional Chinese corporation law told a highly idealized story.
The logic of kinship and family made it not only tolerable but natural that
some stood above others in the family and the clan—and, by implication
of its homologous constitution, in the state. Within the internal structure
of the corporation, Confucian kinship ideology thus legitimated intracor-
poration inequality by making hierarchy an ostensibly *natural* function of
familial relationships, much as the nexus of contracts metaphor of recent U.S.
corporate jurisprudence renders it *voluntary* among individual participants in
a joint enterprise. Different conceptions of the normative legal subject—
family and the individual—thus generate distinctive ideologies of corporate
hierarchy.

PROVINCIALIZING U.S. CORPORATION LAW

It is important to reinterpret Confucian family law as a species of corporation law. However, to pause here would be mostly an intervention in the
politics of recognition, a demonstration that "China, too, has corporation
law." Effectively, it is a move that merely rescues China from its particularity and absorbs it into the universal, defined in Euro-American terms. Is it

possible to use the analysis above to destabilize, rather than consolidate, U.S. corporation law as the universal standard? If legal Orientalism operates as a kind of epistemological imperialism seeking to colonize China, can we use China to provincialize legal theory? The analysis below reverses the analogical operation and reconsiders the nature of U.S. corporation law in light of a broader notion of what constitutes a family, using Chinese law to generate insights about U.S. law. Seeing familial elements in the constitution of U.S. corporation law makes it seem, paradoxically, unfamiliar. When the two analogical moves are considered part of a single analytic procedure, they might be able to unsettle the universal-particular opposition that haunts so much of legal analysis.

If we consider family not as a thing in itself but as language for describing and creating social relationships, we can indeed interpret key aspects of American corporation law as a kind of family law. Admittedly, at least upon first impression, what one finds is quite the opposite of the Chinese ideal of the corporation as a natural collective unit. As Blackstone summed it up, "A corporation . . . has no soul."[161] To critics of late capitalism, the notion that corporations are soulless has no ring of scandal, yet this achievement reflects in part the vast expenditure of legal energy, over centuries, to make sure that the corporation really was "dead"—a mere *persona ficta* rather than a real, organic entity in its own right. The metaphysical debates about corporate personality in the formative era of the business corporation reflect in part the difficulty with which the doctrine was swallowed and the contested place it occupies in an individualist legal system. In the bipolar political ontology of Anglo-American liberalism, between the state and the individual there is precious little room for metaphysically "real" intermediate entities. Either such entities are creatures of the state ("public"), or else they are merely associations composed of individuals ("private"). In Hobbes's stark words, the existence of "corporations" within the state is like having "wormes in the entrayles of a naturall man."[162]

The so-called concession theory of the English common law in effect reduced corporate personality to a discretionary grant—a concession—by the sovereign; hence Blackstone's declaration that corporations were "artificial persons."[163] There was a notable intellectual rebellion against this view in the wake of the U.S. Supreme Court's 1886 declaration that corporations were not just legal but indeed constitutional persons.[164] By the turn of the century, a number of American corporate academics argued boldly that corporations were not fictions at all—a cause with a rich continental tradition that spread from Germany, via England, to America.[165]

In the end, these defenders of corporate autonomy lost, and what used to be known as "the endless problem of corporate personality" seems finally to have ended its career as a problem.[166] Today we accept limited corporate liability, and the vast concentrations of capital it helps make possible, as premised on necessary legal fictions. But if corporate personality is little more than a metaphor, a legal fiction, just what is the corporation then? There are legal doctrines such as "piercing the corporate veil" and of using the corporation as an "alter ego," which suggest that *something* lies behind the veil and *some* egos are involved in the creation of the fiction. As I have already suggested, the latest understanding to take hold of the American legal imagination cuts the Gordian knot by defining the corporation as a nexus of contracts: the set of agreements among the constituent parties whereby the parties organize their relations.[167] In this seemingly straightforward and democratic view, the corporation is neither a metaphysical entity of its own nor a privilege bestowed by the sovereign, but simply a private undertaking by a group of citizens.

This view of the corporation as basically an artificial aggregate of individual constituents stands in sharp contrast to the traditional Chinese corporation, which claimed to be a natural collective entity in its own right. Yet as this chapter has shown, even the Chinese clan corporation was seething with contracts and individual self-seeking of all sorts that hardly accorded with the pursuit of the collective good. Similarly, the contractarian theory of the corporation is also just a story—a convincing (if not always appealing) story in some ways and one approaching the implausibility of science fiction in other regards. For if the nexus of contracts were the *whole* story, there would be literally no need for corporation law: all corporate relations would be governed simply by the common law of contracts. The most committed contractarians indeed view the tendency of corporate statutes to impose fewer and fewer mandatory terms in corporate relations as evidence of a legislative and judicial recognition of the contractarian nature of law. In the absence of mandatory provisions, the corporate parties are free to devise their own terms. To the extent that the parties fail to negotiate complete contracts providing for every contingency, corporation law merely provides default terms to fill in the blanks. Thus the existence of corporation law as a separate field of law does not vitiate the contractarian paradigm: in the absence of express contract terms to the contrary, corporation law constitutes "a standard-form contract."[168]

Yet as Harold Laski puts it, "the contractual theory of voluntary associations can result in fictions compared to which the fiction of corporate personality has less than the ingenuity of childish invention."[169] Just as the Chinese clan corporation was not simply a familial entity characterized by altruism, as the official ideology would have had it, but also a hotbed of contracts and economic self-seeking, so the contractarian theory of the corporation is at odds with many explicitly *paternalist* assumptions that inform the regulation of American business corporations. Most notably, contractarians have difficulty accounting for the concept of fiduciary duties, which stands at the very center of corporation law. As the shareholders' agents, managers owe a fiduciary obligation to manage the corporation in the shareholders' interest rather than their own. In the words of a leading critic of contractarianism, "At the heart of fiduciary analysis is an assumption that individuals can act in a selfless manner and a desire that, for the good of society, they do so."[170] Although classical Neo-Confucian ideologues could hardly agree more, the neoclassical economics which informs the contractarian paradigm rests on very different assumptions: it first postulates "maximizing behavior on the part of all individuals" and then uses the notion of contract to explain "how the conflicting objectives of the individual participants are brought into equilibrium."[171] Yet according to the strongest formulation of contractarianism, fiduciary duties are "the same sort of obligations, derived and enforced the same way, as other contractual undertakings."[172] Just like the rest of corporation law, we are told, they "fill in the blanks and oversights with the terms that people would have bargained for had they anticipated the problems and been able to transact costlessly in advance."[173] Courts' task in enforcing fiduciary duties is therefore not to write their own law over the corporate contract but to divine how the parties *would* have addressed the particular problems that arise *if* they had thought of them beforehand.

This solution is simple and elegant. Like sophisticated social contract theory, by postulating a hypothetical contract it is able to draw on the immense legitimating power of the contract metaphor. However, it is also open to the same criticisms as its philosophical counterpart. As Ronald Dworkin pointedly observes, "A hypothetical contract is not simply a pale form of an actual contract; it is no contract at all."[174] The contractarian definition of

fiduciary duties as "presumptive rules that maximize the parties' joint welfare" is ultimately a utilitarian, not contract, argument.[175] As long as the
parties are defined as welfare maximizers and fiduciary duties as welfare
maximizing, to say that the corporate parties would hypothetically "agree"
to the imposition of fiduciary duties is tautological. The hypothetical contract does not justify fiduciary duties; their utility does. What is more, this
definition of fiduciary duties necessarily implies that those who define them
have some special "insight into the characteristics of people's utility functions."[176] Thus, in the end, fiduciary duties are inescapably paternalistic. The
contractarians—or courts—will decide just what type of fiduciary constraints will maximize corporate contractors' utility.

Yet, for the most part, history may seem to be on the contractarians'
side. Corporation law has moved from specific incorporation as a privilege
granted by the sovereign or legislature to general incorporation statutes,
which in turn have come to contain fewer and fewer mandatory provisions
for structuring corporate affairs. However, while the statutory law of corporate *organization* has surrendered much of its earlier ambition, regulatory
impulses have resurfaced in the creation of a Byzantine web of federal regulations to govern the issuance and *sales* of corporate securities. Mandatory
disclosure of corporate affairs is one of its centerpieces. At least in theory, it
will result in more stable securities markets by making more information
available and thus protecting the public from making unreasonably risky
investments. Corporate contractarians recognize that mandatory disclosure
is theoretically problematic for them. In effect, it takes the sale of securities
out of the unregulated corporate contract envisioned by general incorporation statutes. If people are willing to buy securities even without adequate
disclosure, why should this be the law's concern? Robert Clark, for one,
argues that mandatory disclosure provisions in securities regulation are "an
example of fundamentally paternalistic legislation masquerading as a response to market imperfections"; in the end, mandatory disclosure requirements imply that "a person's actual preferences for risk-taking should not be
dispositive as a normative matter."[177]

The point, of course, is not whether the contractarian story is "true" or
not. What this chapter has sought to do is to listen to both Confucian and
contractarian stories carefully to learn what they tell and what they omit
and what kinds of legal subjects they summon into being. At a minimum,
the contractarian story is *one* way of conceptualizing corporations. Yet there

are clearly many other stories that can be told about corporate entities, such as the paternalistic one above, along with recent communitarian stories of various kinds.[178] The latter stories draw on notions of altruism, paternalism, and fiduciary duty that are more commonly associated with the particularistic regime of family obligations than with economic relations organized on the universal basis of the market.

Moreover, it is important to recognize that the role played by the family in U.S. corporation law is not only a metaphoric one. Much of U.S. corporation law too is literally a matter of family law. That is, most of the case law involving corporations in the United States concerns so-called close corporations rather than large public ones—small corporate entities that are predominantly family enterprises. Hence much of what is designated as Corporation Law in the law school curriculum is effectively family law, involving the adjudication of disputes among family members and adjustment of domestic relations in the context of family business.

Going a step further, just as much of U.S. corporation law can be reinterpreted as family law, both literally or metaphorically, U.S. family law too can be reinterpreted in terms of economic organization. Anticipating just that, the Nobel Prize–winning economist Gary Becker has analyzed the nuclear family as an economic enterprise, suggesting at least the outlines of reading of *U.S.* family law as a kind of corporation law.[179] In short, although the family and the corporation seem oppositional to each other—and as idealized subjects, they are—as sociological and historical entities they are better thought of as complementary. Neither the family corporation nor the corporate family is an oxymoron.

EITHER/OR VERSUS BOTH/AND

Strikingly, then, viewed as stories, the Chinese clan corporation of a "truly" collective nature and the American contractual one offer two diametrically opposed justifications for what is, in important ways, a functionally similar separation of ownership and management. The legal ideologies that undergird them could hardly be further apart. From the perspective of Confucian humanism, the family is the universal subject, while individualism represents a deviation and the risk of selfish particularism. Conversely, from the point of view of Anglo-American liberalism, the individual is the unencumbered universal subject and kinship a regime of parochialism, at least if not confined to its proper sphere. Analyzed in terms of legal Orientalism, what are we to make of a notable functional convergence of two legal orders supported by such divergent ideologies?

One way of reading the story of traditional Chinese corporation law is to view it as a cautionary tale of ideology's relative unimportance in the harsh world of material incentives. Even the traditional Chinese, despite the ideological obstacles posed by Confucian moral utopianism, were driven to employ what is the most efficient form of economic organization, the corporation—a triumph of the laws of economic rationality, if not Hegelian laws of history. From the opposite end of the political spectrum, the moral of the story might be a crude Marxian one. The stories that the masses tell, or are told, about their economic and material activity are just that—stories, opium for the people—while what truly matters are the "real" relations of production.

Both of the above conclusions are too easy, as the analysis of legal Orientalism in Chapter 2 has already suggested. Law's stories are not mere fairy tales. They stir into being certain kinds of subjects while disabling others. Phenomenologically, the rhetorics of contract and kinship are simply not interchangeable. However commercialized and commodified many of the relationships in clan corporations may have been and however thin they may have stretched the fictions of kinship, it matters that kinship ideology was still generally accepted as an accurate reflection of social practices. Even clan corporations that made a perfectly conscious, mercenary distinction between shared descent and capital contribution to clan—by stipulating that descent alone was not a sufficient condition for clan membership— nevertheless still *viewed themselves* as unilineal descent groups, rather than mere voluntary associations of kinsmen.

Indeed, legal distinctions often have very practical implications. Even if the metaphors in which we conceptualize corporations—whether as a familial, organic community or a network of contracts among discrete individuals—are not *all* that matters, they surely *do* (sometimes) predispose us to act in certain ways. William Alford, for example, suggests that, in traditional China, the Confucian family ideology had a "sharp restraining impact" on power holders in kinship groups.[180] This makes it exceedingly difficult to make generalized normative assessments of the rhetorics of contract and kinship. For even if the Chinese did experience their clan corporations *as* kin groups rather than as just legal fictions designed to evade Confucian moralism, this fact alone does not necessarily make the notion of corporations as real, organic entities either more or less desirable than the individualistic view of a nexus of contracts. It may seem evident that being treated as an adopted (even if "bought") son or daughter rather than a fungible employee makes the experience of labor less alienating. Yet that rhetoric may just as easily permit subordination to persist under the guise of familial affection. As a scholar of Chinese adoption practices observes astutely, "An adopted son is more reliable than an ordinary employee, yet more expendable than a biological son."[181]

Furthermore, in seeking to make sense of the various stories about corporate organization, it is not clear just whose story one should be listening to. The Confucian elder may offer us a story of bona fide benevolent paternalism, while his kin juniors might tell a very different tale of indignity and oppression. One need only consider how the ranchero class in Mexican California considered Indian servants their "children," assuring outsiders, "Those people we considered as members of our families. We loved them and they loved us; our intercourse was always pleasant."[182] Or, even more starkly, slaveholders in the antebellum South were similarly fond of absorbing their human property into the idiom of "family members."[183]

The stories that law tells about us and the stories we tell about law both form part of our identities. Legal Orientalism is one such story—a tale we tell about who does and does not have law. This chapter has demonstrated that what counts as law is, in the end, law's interpretation of itself. In the tautological world of legal Orientalism, law is a narrative that defines itself as legal. As we have seen, the discursive nonexistence of corporation law has served to mark China as essentially particular, waiting for the universal history of capitalism to introduce it to modern legal forms. It is in response to that tale that this chapter has re-narrated the story of family law in China while also suggesting the outlines of a possible retelling of Anglo-American corporation law.

Admittedly, it may seem anachronistic at best and perverse at worst to interpret family law in terms of corporation law, nor is the analogy any less jarring when it is reversed. When I first began exploring Chinese clan corporations and presented my interpretation to academic audiences, I was always ultimately asked a version of the same frustrated question: "At the end of the day, were they *really* corporations or were they *really* families?"

The formulation misses the very point of the comparative exercise, for the answer is ultimately undecidable. They were *both* families *and* corporations, and no less of one for being also the other. The capacity of human beings to imagine various ways of organizing factors of production is vast, if not limitless, and our facility in telling different stories that justify those arrangements is even greater. Like all stories, they are local and historical—fully intelligible only in the world they create for the people who tell them. They are always also plural. No one story ever exhausts the meaning of the social and moral universe, no matter how great its claims to universality.[184]

Certainly the world of Chinese clan corporations is not the world in which we live today—at least not the dominant, ideologically privileged world, although there are indications that at least some aspects of that world remain, as Chapter 6 suggests. For the time being, we live in a world of unevenly distributed legal modernity where narratives of legal Orientalism enjoy global currency. This fact is an effect of legal Orientalism's world-making power and makes it more than mere academic speculation. If the historic erasure of Chinese clan corporations constitutes an instance of epistemological imperialism, Chapters 4 and 5 examine how such acts of scholarly conjecture justified increasing material interventions in Oriental legal systems over the course of the nineteenth century. Stories told by European and American comparative lawyers were eventually translated into international legal institutions that marked China's declining standing in the global order.

Although the analysis will shift from the academic field of comparative corporation law to the politics of international law, the story will take a familiar form—that of a failed legal subject. Just as Confucian kinship norms make individual Chinese persons less than individual and thus locate them outside of modern law, in the nineteenth century China in its entirety fails as a sovereign subject of international law. In anticipation of that story, it is important to note that the fundamental Euro-American postulate that all rights and duties must be held by a "person" encompassed not only corporations but *states* as well. In the jargon of international law, states were (and still are) "international legal persons," and the legal relations among them were (and continue to be) analogized to those among private individuals—what legal scholars refer to as "the private law analogy." As it turns out, what was missing in the Orient, among other kinds of law, was the most universal legal order of all: international law. China, as we would expect, modeled even its interstate relations on the ideal of Confucian kinship: the central and outer states form one family (中外一家). Indeed, the emperor customarily referred to the rulers of Korea and Vietnam, for example, as his "younger brothers" or "younger cousins." We might call this "the family law analogy" of East Asian interstate law.[185]

Yet the notion of Confucian kinship norms as a type of international law did not impress nineteenth-century international lawyers, as they began to limit China's authority to subject Europeans and Americans to Chinese law. We now turn from stories about corporations and kinship to tales of jurisdiction—central narratives in the development of legal Orientalism.

CHAPTER FOUR

Canton Is Not Boston

> We have a separate and different Law of Nations for the regulation of our intercourse with the Indian tribes of our own Continent; another Law of Nations between us, and the woolly headed natives of Africa; another with the Barbary Powers and the Sultan of the Ottoman Empire; a Law of Nations with the Inhabitants of the Isles of the Sea . . . and lastly a Law of Nations with the flowery Land, the celestial Empire, the Mantchoo-Tartar Dynasty of Despotism.
>
> —John Quincy Adams, "Lecture on the War with China"

> How different is the condition of things out of the limits of Christendom! From the greater part of Asia and Africa, individual Christians are utterly excluded, either by the sanguinary barbarism of the inhabitants, or by their phrensied bigotry, or by the narrow-minded policy of their governments. To their courts, the ministers of Christian governments have no means of access except by force, and at the head of fleets and armies. As between them and us, there is no community of ideas, no common law of nations . . .
>
> —Caleb Cushing, Opinion of the Attorney General

WHEN THE ABOUT-TO-BE-BORN United States of America rose in rebellion against Great Britain in 1776, the very first sentence of its Declaration of Independence appeared to envision a world of states that are "separate and equal," calling for Great Britain simply to acknowledge that the United States, too, rightfully occupied that equal status—nothing more, nothing less. While the language of the Declaration of Independence was stirring in its magnificent simplicity and its righteous invocation of "the Laws of Nature" and of "a decent respect for the opinions of mankind," eventually a very different juridical conception of the world came to structure the nation's relations with various non-European states, including China—a conception that was ultimately far closer to John Quincy Adams's unapologetic formulation, quoted above, than to that of the Declaration of Independence.

How and why did that happen? This is a vast and complex historical question that does not admit of a single answer, yet legal Orientalism is certainly part of any comprehensive explanation. Thus far we have focused on Euro-American scholarly representations of Chinese law as essentially particular, in contrast to the universal qualities of "real" law. In the remainder of the book we see how such legal epistemologies came to justify the establishment of legal institutions that sought to overwrite the Orient in the name of civilizing and modernizing it. With comparative lawyers having characterized Chinese law as particular, that view became the ground for a series of exclusions from the universal order of legal modernity. Paradoxically, however, the legal institutions that evolved to exclude China came to embody the very contradiction between the universal and the particular that they sought to resolve; rather than safeguarding the imagined border between "law" and "Orient," they *became* that contradiction.

To summarize, the first half of this book has examined legal Orientalism as an ideology of personhood, with a focus on the study of comparative law as an important element in the production of an idealized modern legal subject—namely, the individual, who becomes the model for the subjectivity of both persons and corporations. The second half of the book expands the scale and turns from self-making to world-making, analyzing how the Orientalist premises of comparative legal scholarship were absorbed into international law, the primary discursive resource in the recognition, and the derecognition, of states. Structurally, Chapters 2 and 3 began with a general account of the making of legal and unlegal subjects, followed by a detailed historical examination of Orientalist analyses in one specific field of comparative study, Chinese corporation law. In a similar manner, the second half of the book begins by first outlining in broad strokes a larger story about shifting global positions among China, the United States, and European states. In Chapter 5, the focus then turns to a detailed examination of key institutions in this changing global equilibrium: the operation of the United States Court for China and one of its sister tribunals, the International Mixed Court.

In a sense, we have thus far focused on a set of mostly academic North Atlantic narratives about Chinese law, whereas we now turn to examining how those narratives configured, and reconfigured, global maps of the reach of Euro-American law—how they became, in effect, "tales of jurisdiction," to use Robert Cover's phrase.[1] Although the idea of jurisdiction may sound arcane, in the end every claim to jurisdiction demands a narrative to justify it. This chapter recounts an Orientalist narrative of international law that came to justify expansive U.S. claims to extraterritorial jurisdiction in China, and elsewhere in Asia.

Stated differently, Chapters 4 and 5 illustrate how legal scholars' conjectures became internationally recognized legal "facts" with dramatic political and legal consequences. The primary vehicle for translating the knowledge produced by the academic discipline of comparative law into political institutions was the emerging profession of modern international law. As the preceding chapter noted, European states did not recognize the diplomatic institutions of East Asia as an authentic international legal order. At the end of the Opium War (1839–1842), China became formally absorbed into the regime of Euro-American international law, finding itself bound by a series of so-called Unequal Treaties that effectively constituted it as a second-class sovereign in a world that was increasingly defined by a European race for colonies. Remarkably, most observers in the United States initially sided with the Chinese in the Opium War as they sought to resist British imperial overreach. Yet by the century's end the United States itself had become a practitioner of formal empire, inheriting Spain's colonial possessions in 1898. This chapter identifies the Treaty of Wanghia, entered into in 1844, as a constitutive moment in the United States' relations with China, and with Asia more generally, that paved the way for this imperial turn more than half a century earlier.

To anticipate the story, the extraordinary treaty that laid the foundation for American extraterritoriality in the Orient was negotiated by Caleb Cushing—the first American minister to China as well as a former Congressman, a future justice of the Massachusetts Supreme Judicial Court, a future attorney general of the United States, and a future (abortive) nominee to the United States Supreme Court. In the wake of the British victory in the Opium War, Cushing was charged by President John Tyler with the pretextual mission of going to Peking to inquire after the emperor's health and to deliver the president's wishes for his longevity. Backed by his own little armada as well as the presence of the U.S. naval forces in the Pacific, Cushing persuaded the Qing Empire to enter into a Treaty of Peace,

Caleb Cushing, on the eve of
his mission to China, 1843.
*Courtesy of the Historical Society of Old
Newbury.*

Amity, and Commerce with the United States. That innocuously entitled
treaty was signed on July 3, 1844, in the village of Wangxia (望廈, translit-
erated as "Wanghia" by Cushing) in Macao. Under its terms China was
obligated to allow Americans to trade freely in Canton as well as in four
other ports that had been closed to Euro-American traders. Moreover, U.S.
citizens obtained the privilege of extraterritorial jurisdiction in China.[2] As
a result, for nearly a century—from 1844 until 1943—Americans in China
were formally subject only to the laws of the United States. Put differently,
when Americans entered China, American law traveled with them, effectively attaching to their very bodies. Significantly, in addition to providing
for the extraterritorial application of U.S. law in China, it also created a
framework for the United States' political relations with the states of Asia
generally. That framework indeed constituted a specifically *legal* version of
an American Orient, where Americans were to remain free of the oppression of Oriental law, subject only to their own.

The material effects of globally circulating Orientalist projections of lack
of law were not limited to international law and to relations among sovereigns. Just as China as a state was excluded politically from the Family of
Nations, with the establishment of anti-Chinese immigration laws around
the world Chinese individuals too were excluded physically from the territorial space of a growing number of states. The political exclusion of China
as a state and the physical exclusion of Chinese as persons were both

grounded in the epistemology of legal Orientalism. As a subject of international law, China failed to live up to the normative ideal of a fully sovereign nation-state, just as the Chinese masses fell short of the normative ideal of personal subjectivity, that of the sovereign individual.

Yet the consequences of legal Orientalism were greater still, as we will see in the last part of this chapter. In the United States, the enactment of Chinese Exclusion Laws had a direct and deeply damaging impact on the development of U.S. constitutional law in the late nineteenth century. When the U.S. Supreme Court upheld the laws, it did so on a remarkable basis, holding that with regard to immigration the U.S. government possessed a plenary power that was unchecked by the Constitution.

From a global perspective, this chapter sets out the little-known story of America's extraterritorial empire in the Asia-Pacific. There is a robust literature examining various forms of semicolonialism in nineteenth- and early-twentieth-century China. However, as Chapter 1 noted, most students of colonialism in China have focused on the actions of the British rather than those of the United States. In American studies, U.S. imperialism is studied mostly in terms of the United States' territorial expansion in North America, the Caribbean, and the Pacific (notably Hawaii and the Philippines). What is still missing in both Chinese and American studies is a recognition of the extent and nature of the United States' *extraterritorial* empire in the Orient—a key form of American legal imperialism.

Two caveats are in order. First, the core of this chapter focuses on changing conceptions of sovereignty in the nineteenth century. To examine those conceptions in context, I provide thumbnail sketches of long stretches of American, Chinese, and British political and economic history. Necessarily selective, these interpretive summaries are intended only to illuminate relevant parts of the core thesis. Second, while the focus of the previous chapter was predominantly on China, the story of the legal encounter between China and the United States is narrated here primarily from the perspective of the United States. Consequently, in this chapter China often appears as an all but inert object of Euro-American legal and diplomatic actions. Needless to say, that is an effect of the discursive structure of legal Orientalism, not a fact about China.

EXTRATERRITORIAL EMPIRE

China, according to received wisdom, was never colonized, except for the minor British and Portuguese outposts of Hong Kong and Macao, respectively, and the United States never established even its own little Hong Kong in the Chinese empire. To be sure, in 1856–1857 the American commissioner in China tried to sell the idea of a U.S. occupation of Taiwan, arguing that under international law it "ought not to be allowed to exist in the hands of such a people" who could not even control the island's "cannibals."[3] The commissioner went so far as to bring to the State Department's attention Americans who would be willing to assist in Taiwan's "colonization,"[4] but the State Department nevertheless rejected the plan. President McKinley was equally unsuccessful half a century later in trying to talk his secretary of state into acquiring a "slice" of China, as if the Middle Kingdom were a pizza.[5] Although the United States ultimately rejected the idea of territorial imperialism in China, it of course came to approve of it elsewhere, after its victory in the Spanish-American War left it with the remains of the Spanish empire in the New World and in Asia.

It is remarkable, however, that as late as 1901 the government had not given up wholly the idea of territorial acquisitions in China. It specifically asked the Supreme Court to keep in mind, when adjudicating the constitutional status of the territorial spoils of the Spanish-American War, that "the question might be as to the powers of this government in the acquisition of Egypt and the Soudan, or a section of Central Africa, or a spot in the Antarctic Circle, or a section of the Chinese empire."[6] Significantly, though, the road to territorial colonialism opened up by the war occasioned a constitutional crisis, as the U.S. Supreme Court was called upon to determine whether, and on what terms, the nation could annex the Philippines, Puerto Rico, and Guam. The answer came in a complex and contradictory series of decisions known as the *Insular Cases,* in reference to the islands whose legal fate they determined. In contrast, as we will see, the establishment of an extensive extraterritorial empire in the Orient did not cause even a constitutional ripple.

Exclusive territorial jurisdiction is one of the defining features of the sovereignty of the modern nation-state. Ordinarily we take it for granted that it is where a person is that determines what law applies to him or her. The assertion of extraterritorial jurisdiction—a state's claim to apply its laws beyond the borders of its territory—contradicts this basic principle. It is critical to recognize that exclusive territoriality would be neither desirable nor workable as an absolute jurisdictional principle. Taken to its logical conclusion, it would render states into hermetically sealed boxes, unable to communicate or interact with each other. Ambassadorial immunity is perhaps the most explicit recognition of that fact, permitting diplomatic envoys to remain subject to their own sovereigns' laws even while in foreign territory, but there are numerous more mundane exceptions as well to strict territoriality. As Chapter 5 elaborates, what is distinctive about the kind of extraterritoriality that the United States, among other nations, came to assert in China was the sheer audacious breadth of it, as well as its ideological justification based on civilizational superiority.

Some *fin-de-siècle* international lawyers described even such extreme assertions of extraterritoriality as simply a kind of sentimental "habit" of Western peoples who wished to "carry with them, as far as their rights of law and protection go, a little bit of their home country" into exotic lands.[7] Yet stated more bluntly and more accurately, by virtue of its treaty with China the United States suddenly obtained "the attributes of sovereignty in China."[8] How did the relatively recently emancipated world's leading anticolonial power reconcile its extraterritorial jurisdiction in China with the ringing statement made by Chief Justice Marshall in 1812, "The jurisdiction of a nation within its own territory is necessarily exclusive and absolute . . . being alike the attribute of every sovereign, and being incapable of conferring extraterritorial power"?[9]

As I have already suggested, the nearly forgotten century of American extraterritorial jurisdiction in China is a story not only about China and the United States but also of international law—or, as John Quincy Adams might say, of several international laws, each for a different region of the world. The history of the United States' extraterritorial jurisdiction in China both served to constitute it as a state in a global order of international law, while at the same denying it full admission into the international society of states into which it was apparently being inducted.

The origins of American extraterritorial jurisdiction in China must be considered together with the free trade rationale that it was deemed to serve. In their classic article on "free trade imperialism," John Gallagher and Ronald Robinson caution against a rigid qualitative distinction between formal and informal empire in the analysis of British expansion in the nineteenth century. As they put it, studying imperialism in terms of formal empire alone is "rather like judging the size and character of icebergs solely from the parts above the water-line."[10] Specifically, they observe that in the mid-Victorian era "perhaps the most common political technique of British expansion was the treaty of free trade and friendship made with or imposed upon a weaker state."[11] This chapter argues that in the Treaty of Wanghia the United States laid the foundation for this imperial practice in Asia, where it utilized and refined the practice even beyond the British precedent. For it was the updated American version that in turn became a model for the British themselves and other European states with imperial aspirations in Asia. Although it is true that we are liable to "recognize the existence of U.S. imperialism only when qualified as 'informal,' 'accidental,' 'involuntary,' or otherwise differentiated from the European kind," below I analyze the story of the Treaty of Wanghia as evidence of a fundamental continuity between the imperial practices of Britain and the United States.[12]

The notion of an informal American empire is of course not new, whatever its relationship to British imperialism may be.[13] However, as noted in Chapter 1, the vocabulary for analyzing U.S. power overseas is largely military and economic, as exemplified by the widespread use of terms such as "gunboat diplomacy" and "dollar diplomacy." A discursive analysis of legal Orientalism allows us to consider law as an important currency in its own right in American overseas imperialism. The exercise of American power has been rarely based merely on the assertion of sheer economic and military might. From the beginning, and in keeping with the peculiarly legal mythology of the nation's birth, that power has been mediated through the language of law, as a matter of *right*. Although the United States' independence was seemingly premised on the view that not only all men but also all states were born to be equal, in the mid-nineteenth century earlier professions of the liberal norm of sovereign equality gave way to an open embrace of imperial American sovereignty in the Pacific. In China, Caleb Cushing essentially renarrated the nation's early diplomatic history and substituted in its place an invented tradition of U.S. extraterritoriality in Oriental states. This extraterritorial empire in turn protected American commercial interests in Asia, while real or alleged violations of extraterritorial privileges justified the occasional use of military power to protect America's newly acquired rights under the law of nations.

To appreciate the unstable ideological underpinnings of early American diplomacy, evolving from a widely (though not universally) shared assumption of equality among states to an increasingly aggressive expectation of extraterritorial privileges for American citizens among "uncivilized" peoples, we must first consider broadly America's historic place in the global expansion of (Western) international law before analyzing how the United States reconfigured its legal relationship to Europe and the rest of the world in the post-Revolutionary War era.

It bears noting that I am certainly not suggesting that extraterritoriality has been historically the chief form of American imperialism, informal or otherwise. It is an axiom of U.S. constitutional law, announced by Chief Justice Marshall in the landmark decision *Johnson v. McIntosh*, that the title of the United States to the land on which it was established derives ultimately from the European "discovery" of the Americas—an expressly colonial notion that denies legal subjectivity to the indigenous inhabitants of the continent.[14] The original union of the thirteen newly independent colonies was decidedly not the end of imperialism in America but simply a new chapter in its evolution. The union's further expansion from the Atlantic to the Pacific was a landgrab of world historic proportions, claiming half a continent as the new homeland of overseas settlers. Nevertheless, this was not regarded as imperialism at all but only as the young nation's manifest, preordained destiny. From this perspective, it was only in 1898 with the Spanish-American War that the United States took on full-fledged territorial colonialism.

What this chapter emphasizes is that even this turn to the European-style territorial model was not an abrupt reversal—as understood by many—but was preceded by more than half a century of extraterritorial imperialism, providing a continuity between informal and formal practices of empire as they continued to unfold in tandem thereafter. Moreover, while formal empire suffered major ideological damage in the twentieth century, the United States' contemporary claims of extraterritorial jurisdiction and programs of overseas law reform form part of this longer history dating back to the nineteenth century. Without minimizing the brutality of U.S. territorial colonialism in the Philippines, for example, it is crucial to recognize the deeper roots and continuing vitality of a longer tradition of legal imperialism with which it is imbricated. At the same time, by no means does this chapter's focus on U.S. extraterritorial empire in Asia suggest that the United States was the *sole* practitioner of legal imperialism in Asia (although it was a leading one). Extraterritorial jurisdiction in the Orient is a well-recognized part of the history of British imperialism, for example.[15] America's extraterritorial empire in the Asia-Pacific, in contrast, has not received the attention it warrants.

THE UNITED STATES AND CHINA: A BRIEF LEGAL HISTORY

Standard accounts of the origin of modern international law trace its birth to the Treaty of Westphalia in 1648 and the end of the post-Reformation religious civil wars in Europe. With the establishment of the principle of *cuius regio, eius religio* ("whose region, his religion"), each sovereign was to determine the religion of his state, and all states were to enjoy formal equality under the law of nations.[16] Collectively, these accounts provide a history of the emergence of the liberal norm of sovereign equality among nation-states. Analyzed in terms of the key concepts that structure the discourse of legal Orientalism, this history is paradoxically at once particular and universal: a historically specific European law of nations is presented as proto-universal at its inception, unfolding in space and time toward a final completion.

Yet the global picture changes significantly when it is reframed geographically, beyond Europe, and temporally, to an earlier date. Consider Carl Schmitt's invitation to view the Discovery of the New World in 1492 as the origin of modern international law.[17] From this perspective the narrative is no longer one of increasing inclusion and equality *within* Europe. Rather, it becomes a story of the violent exclusion of others *outside* of Europe, first on the basis of religious, then cultural, difference. Law, in turn, becomes a medium not for the global recognition of universality but for the differential allocation of universality across the globe. Viewing the history of international law from this earlier date, then, how did the New World fit into what was still by and large the public law of the "Christian republic" of Europe? It is important to recall that Columbus ended up in America while looking for a route to India. America hence began its European career as Asia. Columbus believed until his dying day that the New World he had found was in fact Asia. Thus America originated as the "West Indies" in European historical consciousness, in contrast to the East Indies in the "real" Asia.

Originally both the East and West Indies were regarded as lying beyond the pale of civilization, or, as John Locke put it epigrammatically, "In the beginning, all the World was *America*."[18] Yet with the American Revolution the United States indeed rose to assume, in its own words, "among the powers of the Earth, the separate and equal station to which the Laws of Nature and Nature's God" entitled it. Although the new nation emerged from what had once been the West Indies, the United States now claimed to exceed, and supersede, that categorization. It asserted its political parity with Europe, and ultimately even its superiority. With the Revolution, Americans came to believe that theirs was the *real* West: the New World embodied the universal values of Europe even better than Europe did. Its values did not, in short, simply happen to coincide with universal principles: they embodied them with *particular* effectiveness. With the rise of the New World, the Old World in turn became precisely what the designation suggests—old and anachronistic. Whatever may have remained of the Indies in the New World was expelled geographically outside of North America proper, where it still languishes, mostly in the islands of the Caribbean. And insofar as some actual "Indians" still remained physically within the borders of the United States, they were not considered citizens of the new polity but became ultimately "domestic dependent nations," in the memorable words of Chief Justice Marshall.[19]

As far as Europe was concerned, in 1776 the law of nations was still limited in its application to the Family of Nations, or European international society consisting of "civilized" states. Nevertheless, despite some early hesitation, the admission of the United States into this European political family was fairly uncontroversial. Given the colonists' genealogical connection to the Old World, the young nation was soon recognized as civilized and hence fully sovereign.[20]

But although the American Revolution reconstituted America's legal relationship to Europe on the novel basis of sovereign equality, it remained an open question how the young nation would organize its political relations with the rest of the world. Even after the American Revolution, Europeans deemed themselves fully authorized by the law of nations to continue their project of colonizing the extra-European world. With a high degree of self-consciousness, the young United States rejected that European understanding of sovereignty and the "will to empire" that it implied.[21] It was self-evident to patriotic early Americans that they ought not to establish territorial colonies on the European overseas model (but, again, on their own continental one, which constituted the march of freedom, not imperialism).[22]

Nineteenth-century international law, however, did not divide the world solely into civilized states that were fully sovereign and savages whose lands were either mere *terra nullius* that was only there waiting to be "discovered" or else could be won through colonial conquest. A binary civilized-versus-savage opposition was simply not adequate in the face of the enormous diversity that European states encountered in their global expansion. Such a distinction was useful so long as the colonizers were dealing with peoples that they could characterize at least to their own satisfaction as barbarians or savages. This had been generally the case with American "Indians" and Australian Aboriginals, for instance. However, as the imperial project expanded further, the law of nations accorded differing degrees and kinds of legal personality upon societies that could not be fitted neatly into the civilized-savage dichotomy. Consequently, in certain circumstances, less-than-civilized peoples might indeed possess a degree of sovereignty, yet they could not impose their laws on "civilized" men even when they entered their territory. This exemption from local law became established as the right of extraterritorial jurisdiction.[23]

Over time, it became a common practice in Asia, which indeed defied European legal and cultural taxonomies. China, for example, was organized functionally in the form of a centralized bureaucratic state and could thus hardly be dismissed as a grouping of tribal savages. Yet rhetorically its sovereignty was structured in the moral terms of Confucianism. To European international lawyers, this signaled a paradigmatically Oriental confusion of the logics of politics and kinship. Over time, China came to occupy a queer intermediate position in the European legal imagination, located uneasily somewhere between civilized and savage, fully sovereign and colonizable. Extraterritorial jurisdiction in turn became the chief institutional expression of that status.[24]

The secular international law of the nineteenth century justified the practice of extraterritorial jurisdiction in Asia and elsewhere on explicitly civilizational grounds. However, it is important to recognize its religious origins in the much earlier system of the so-called Capitulations, which once mediated Europe's relations with the Ottoman Empire. In the pre-Westphalian era when religion provided the predominant framework for European interstate relations, the privileges of the law of the European *Respublica Christiana* could not be extended to infidels and, concomitantly, Christians sojourning in the Ottoman Empire could not be subjected to Muslim law but adjudicated their disputes under their own law. The arrangement began as a favor granted by Turks to Europeans. Yet as the Ottoman Empire became increasingly weak relative to Europe, the Capitulations ultimately solidified into a resented imperial imposition. By the nineteenth century, they were a well-established, nonterritorial form of imperialism.

As the newborn United States began looking outside its borders and turned its gaze across the South Seas, how was it to constitute its relationship to Asia? Having (ostensibly) rejected outright territorial colonialism, would it decline to follow the European practice of extraterritorial jurisdiction in Asia as well? The matter was far less urgent than the relations with Europe, for example (the clarification of which required a revolution), or the relations with Africa (which were troubled because of slavery). Unsurprisingly, it was also decided much less self-consciously. China figured only minimally in the early American diplomatic consciousness, and from the beginning, U.S.-China relations were inextricably intertwined with questions of trade. Moreover, Asia was hardly the relevant contemporary category anyway: America's China trade was viewed as part of a larger "East Indies trade."

Officially, the history of Sino-American commercial relations begins only with the United States' independence. Before 1776, Americans were not legally permitted to trade with China directly—a fact of such economic and political significance that it ultimately became the immediate cause of the American Revolution. During the colonial period, the East India Company enjoyed a Crown monopoly on Britain's China trade, and Americans were permitted to function only as middlemen. In the case of Chinese tea, for example, the Honorable Company first shipped the tea to England, and Americans then transported it to the colonies, subject to much resented import duties. This basic framework was altered by the notorious Tea Act of 1773. It gave the Company the right to sell tea directly to the colonies, thus displacing the American middlemen from the trade. Outraged American patriots responded by raiding the Company's boats in Boston and dumping the tea into the harbor. (To compound the irony, as they attacked the property of the East India Company, the Americans were dressed as Indians, the original inhabitants of Columbus's "West Indies.")

It was thus one of the consequences of American independence from Britain that the Chinese market now opened legally to the United States for the first time. In 1784, with the ink on the peace treaty with Britain barely dried, China trade was inaugurated with the celebrated voyage of the *Empress of China* from New York to Canton. (Notably, in his journal the captain described the ship's destination as "Canton In India."[25]) The following year, excited by the prospect of entering China's mythically vast markets, the Continental Congress appointed one of the supercargoes of the *Empress of China* as a consul in Canton.[26] Yet the gesture was purely unilateral, and the Chinese government in no way recognized the consular post.[27] As a contemporary observer put it ambivalently, upon hearing of the reception of the *Empress of China* in Canton: "It seems our countrymen were treated with as much respect as the subjects of any nation, i.e., the whole are looked upon by the Chinese as Barbarians, and they have too much Asiatic hauteur to descend to any discrimination."[28]

Although American trade grew considerably in volume over time and sizable personal fortunes were made from it, overall it did not live up to the unrealistically wild expectations that had inspired it. Even the consular post remained unstaffed for most of the time during the first several decades of its existence. Nevertheless, the trade generated a fair number of legal skirmishes. The main Western presence in Canton continued to be the British East India Company, and British sailors in particular appear to have gotten into violent, drunken brawls with the local Cantonese with some frequency. In an oft-repeated pattern, if and when British subjects were tried under Chinese law, the British government voiced its protest.[29]

In the one major controversy involving the United States, in 1821 sailor Francis Terranova, who served onboard an American ship, was accused of killing a Chinese woman who had come to the ship to sell food. The Chinese government demanded the surrender of Terranova and ultimately ended up sentencing him to death by strangling. In response, some American merchants—most notably the fur merchant John Jacob Astor—voted with their feet and withdrew from China trade altogether.[30] Others wrote in protest to the Chinese authorities ("We consider the case prejudiced"), but even they recognized the legal weakness of their complaint: "We are bound to submit to your laws while we are in your waters, be they ever so unjust. We will not resist them."[31] The State Department evidently also believed that Americans in China violated the empire's laws at their own risk, for it made no protest in the matter. The British, meanwhile, took notice of American "weakness" in submitting to Chinese jurisdiction.[32]

Indeed, when the British searched a U.S. vessel in Canton in 1804 for deserters from the East India Company's ships—claiming a right to seize all sailors who could not give indisputable proof of American citizenship—the American consul in Canton issued an objection in which he called on China for protection from such attacks, thus expressly acknowledging China's jurisdiction over foreigners in the city. Not only did he emphasize that "the citizens of the United States have for many years visited the city of Canton in the pursuit of honest commerce, [and] that their conduct during the whole period of intercourse has been regulated by a strict regard and respect for the laws and usages of this Empire, as well as the general law of nations,"[33] but he also described China expressly as "a sovereign and independent" empire, presumably thereby implying that it enjoyed the rights and privileges of the law of nations.[34]

As late as 1839, the American consul strongly disapproved of Britain's exercise of jurisdiction over a Briton accused of murdering a Chinese man. He stated that the trial aboard a British ship was "considered illegal, and of course the man is subject to a new trial."[35] Even the Americans who most resented Chinese jurisdiction observed reluctantly that "as a question of the law of nations and casuistry, it would bear an argument whether the United States could rightfully go to war against the Chinese for administering their own laws on persons voluntarily coming within their jurisdiction."[36]

These perceptions by Americans about their legal status in China were consistent with the explicit terms of the only existing political relationship into which the United States entered with an Asian state prior to its extraterritoriality treaty with China. In addition to providing commercial access, the 1833 Treaty of Amity and Commerce with Siam stated expressly that Americans in Siam would be subject to Siamese law.[37] Consistent with this spirit, as early as 1808 Thomas Jefferson had agreed to make an exception to the Embargo Act for a Chinese mandarin, justifying the exception as a matter of "national comity." A less than precise international legal doctrine, comity referred to the discretionary courtesies that civilized states owed one another, thus suggesting that Jefferson indeed regarded China as a sovereign.[38] As a general matter, until the outbreak of the Sino-British Opium War in 1839, it thus appeared that the United States was in fact ideologically and politically inclined to respect the sovereign equality of Oriental states such as China—unlike European imperialists such as the British, who had an imperial tradition of extraterritoriality in dealing with barbaric and semicivilized peoples.

CHINA AND BRITAIN: FREEDOM TO SELL OPIUM

Yet despite the ostensibly promising outlook in U.S.-Chinese relations, in 1844 the United States insisted on formalizing its right to extraterritorial jurisdiction in the nation's first trade treaty with a major Asian state. To appreciate more fully the genesis of the treaty, it is useful to consider briefly the conventional account of Sino-British relations, and especially the role of the British in opening China for Western trade.

Mainstream historiography in the West as well as in the People's Republic of China offers an essentially Orientalist narrative, regarding the Opium War as the beginning of modern Chinese history. The war is seen as an unfortunate but unavoidable stimulus for the modernization of China. It launched a transition from a "traditional" and unchanging China to a "modern" and dynamic one by beginning the process of displacing a naïve Sinocentric worldview and inducting China into the global economic and legal order. The official Chinese worldview—as described in stereotypical terms by historians of modernization—regarded China as a universal empire, surrounded by uncivilized barbarians. Yet its borders did not constitute a point of absolute exteriority: barbarians who paid economic and symbolic tribute could become Sinified and included in the purportedly universal Chinese civilization.[39]

The most common illustration of China's smug isolationism is the fate of the notorious Macartney embassy in 1793. There is a vast literature on the subject, yet the standard interpretation of the embassy is easy to summarize. Since 1744, Western trade in China was restricted to Canton, where foreigners were permitted to trade as a matter of imperial grace. Lord Macartney was the first British ambassador to China, dispatched by George III to negotiate an agreement that would open up the Celestial Empire as a whole for British trade. The Qianlong emperor treated Lord Macartney perfectly courteously but not any more so than he treated tributary envoys coming from Vietnam, Korea, and elsewhere. In keeping with imperial protocol, the emperor expected the British ambassador to perform the requisite kowtow—a series of prostrations and "knockings" of the forehead on the ground.

From the perspective of the British ambassador, however, to perform the kowtow would have constituted nothing less than a scandal of sovereign equality. He insisted that he could not show greater deference to an Oriental monarch than he did to his own sovereign, before whom he would only kneel, not prostrate himself in slavish abjection. A series of complicated diplomatic negotiations ensued. To gain access to the emperor without surrendering his insistence on equality, Lord Macartney at one point even offered to kowtow to the emperor on the condition that an imperial official of equivalent rank perform the same series of prostrations before a portrait of George III (which Macartney had conveniently brought with him). This offer was declined and followed by further negotiations. The end result was a tense imperial audience—with Macartney agreeing only to kneel—no trade agreement, and the beginning of a British obsession with Chinese "arrogance."[40]

Taking this iconic diplomatic fiasco as its point of reference, much of post-War area studies scholarship views the Sino-Western encounter in the nineteenth century as a tragic cultural misunderstanding, demonstrating that the Chinese simply did not understand modernity and the West in general. As a corollary, they were also unable to appreciate the fundamental concepts of political and economic universality: sovereign equality and the concomitant idea of free trade among independent states. The key piece of evidence cited to support this proposition is the notorious message the Qianlong emperor asked Lord Macartney to deliver to George III. After thanking the British monarch for sending an ambassador to pay tribute to the Middle Kingdom, the Emperor declared, "We have never valued ingenious articles, nor do we have the slightest need of your Country's manufactures."[41]

Whatever one wishes to make of the emperor's tone, his underlying point was indisputable. The Chinese economy was self-sufficient, and stubbornly remained so, despite heroic British hopes of convincing the Chinese of the superiority of knives and forks over chopsticks, for example.[42] At the same time, the British appetite for Chinese tea and silk was only growing. In Marshall Sahlins's words, "for nearly three centuries, China was the tomb of European silver—from which none ever returned."[43] The East India Company ultimately devised a brilliant solution to its ever-increasing trade deficit. It started shipping opium grown in India to pay for Chinese tea and other goods, which it then shipped to England. Finally, here was a commodity that created its own demand, once introduced to the Chinese market.

The only problem with this solution was that it constituted an open violation of Chinese law, which prohibited the importation of opium. Despite repeated official Chinese protests and even an appeal to Queen Victoria's moral conscience and the rules of the law of nations, the British refused to stop the trade.[44] When the Chinese in 1839 finally confiscated some of the smuggled opium and destroyed it, Britain condemned this violation of its subjects' private property. Determined to "open" China for free trade once and for all, the British declared war—freedom of trade evidently not including the right not to buy opium. At the end of the ensuing Opium War in 1842, China signed the Treaty of Nanjing as well as the supplemental Treaty of the Bogue the following year. Although the war was blamed on China's arrogant refusal to submit to diplomatic and legal parity, the treaty settlement made it clear that Britain's true goal was not simply to denounce Sinocentrism in the name of equality but to establish *British* superiority, with Eurocentrism as the true standard of universal civilization. Collectively, the British treaties required China not only to open four additional ports for British trade but also to cede the island of Hong Kong to Britain as a colonial possession in perpetuity. Moreover, invoking an increasingly authoritative discourse of legal Orientalism, the British insisted that they could not submit to the arbitrary and cruel practices of Chinese justice. As a result, Additional Regulations of Trade that accompanied the treaties provided for the privilege of extraterritorial jurisdiction—seemingly as an afterthought, but with remarkable consequences.

CHINA AND THE UNITED STATES: "SPECIAL FRIEND"

In short, the conventional history of the Opium War is a story of China's introduction to the universal categories of political and economic modernity: a world of formally equal sovereign nation-states trading freely under the rules of international law—notions the Chinese originally "misunderstood" but subsequently learned to appreciate (at gunpoint, admittedly regrettably). This story is largely a Sino-British one.[45] There is also a prominent narrative of the same events that is told from the perspective of American studies, primarily by American diplomatic historians. Theirs is a story about America's "special relationship" with China, self-consciously contrasted to the violent Sino-British one.[46] Unlike the British in Hong Kong and Portuguese in Macao, Americans never set up colonies in China on the European imperial model. Equally important, they also declined the British invitation to join the Opium War and subsequent European military campaigns in China (with the important but again largely forgotten exception of American participation in the punitive multinational expedition sent to North China in the wake of the Boxer Rebellion). Indeed, American diplomatic historians emphasize that throughout a century of increasing European encroachments in China, Americans typically actively *opposed* such encroachments.

Admittedly, after Britain did euphemistically "open" China in the Opium War, Americans were perfectly happy and indeed very eager to participate in the "free trade" the war had made possible. No sooner had the British won in Canton than President Tyler turned to Congress for an authorization to send the first American minister to China. The New England lawyer and Congressman Caleb Cushing was charged with the task of matching the trade concessions the British had obtained.

Aware of the Qianlong emperor's demand half a century earlier that Lord Macartney kowtow before him, Tyler and his Secretary of State Daniel Webster were both at least somewhat concerned about China's putative arrogance. On the matter of the kowtow, Webster's instructions to Cushing emphasized that, should he receive an imperial audience, Cushing should "do nothing which may seem, even to the Chinese themselves, to imply any inferiority on the part of your government, or anything less than perfect independence of all nations." However, it was left ultimately to Cushing's discretion to determine just what a kowtow would signify and whether its performance would compromise U.S. sovereignty. He was also specifically instructed that in his dealings with the Chinese he should "avoid[ ], as far as possible, the giving of offence either to their pride or their prejudices."[47]

This concern about Chinese pretensions was reflected also in President Tyler's letters to the Son of Heaven, which Cushing was charged with delivering. To start with, the letters opened with the rather familiar salutation "Great and Good Friend"—a form of address that crowned heads of Europe used typically in diplomatic correspondence among themselves.[48] Cushing himself also wished to impress the emperor, and he had a special uniform made for his mission: "a Major-General's blue frock-coat with gilt buttons and 'some slight additions in the way of embroideries', gold-striped trousers, spurs, and a hat with a white plume."[49] The uniform was lost, alas, when one of Cushing's four ships was destroyed in Gibraltar.[50] However, upon his arrival Cushing nevertheless sought to cut an aristocratic figure, and apparently successfully so. An American eyewitness in Canton referred to him as having "spurs on his heels, and mustachios and imperial, very flourishing!"[51]

In the end, Cushing never made it to the Chinese capital and thus never had to confront the audience question, with or without his uniform. However, he did succeed in negotiating a commercial treaty. In accordance with his instructions, Cushing obtained free commercial access to the same ports as the British had. In addition, the treaty provided for extraterritorial privileges for Americans in China. Finally, it also contained a Most Favored Nation clause, which was to guarantee that the United States would not find itself in a position inferior to anyone else in China: it would share equally in all the privileges that any European imperial power might obtain from China in the future.

Over the ensuing decades, as more gunboats appeared at its doorstep and further wars were fought by the British and the French, China in fact surrendered further privileges. The process culminated in the so-called Scramble for Concessions at the turn of the century, which for the first time presented the real possibility that China might actually be divided up among various European powers as well as Japan (which had just succeeded in overthrowing its regime of Western extraterritoriality). It was this race for territorial possessions that provided the immediate impetus for President McKinley's behind-the-scenes plea for a "slice" of China, his appetite having been whetted by the territorial gains of the Spanish-American War. In the end, Secretary of State John Hay talked McKinley out of his China fever and into condemning the actions of the Europeans and Japan in

China. Moreover, in an articulation of what had been implicit in the terms of the Treaty of Wanghia, in 1899 and 1900 Hay issued his famous Open Door notes: all foreign powers were to have commercial access to China on equal terms, while at the same time they were to respect China's territorial integrity.[52]

Admittedly, the policy was not designed with the primary goal of advancing China's interests. As a very recent owner of the Philippines and other newly obtained "Insular Possessions," the United States was a latecomer to European-style colonialism in the Pacific and would have been left behind in a race for the acquisition of territory. However, it was evident to both critics and supporters of the Open Door policy that in an economic competition with the European powers the United States would come out ahead. As *The Nation* put it succinctly in 1901, "We do not need to seek an unfair advantage. An open door and no favor infallibly means for the United States . . . the greater share and gain in the commercial exploitation of China."[53]

At the same time, however, until the Chinese reformed their imperial legal system, Westerners would remain exempt from Chinese jurisdiction. It was quite evident that the United States did not intend to surrender its extraterritorial privileges anytime soon. But although American extraterritoriality in China ostensibly violated the principle of exclusive national territorial jurisdiction, its very point—the Chinese were told—was to prepare for its own demise and help China take full legal control of its territory, thereby permitting it to become a full member in the universal community of states.

For all the differences between the British and American attitudes to China, in retrospect it seems natural and self-evident that Americans sided in principle with the British on the question of free trade. Although Americans refused to take up arms to gain commercial access, the disagreement between the two countries was over the means, not the end—how best to incorporate China fully into the capitalist world system. Ultimately, Britain and the United States represented modernity and freedom, while China stood on the side of constraint of tradition.

Despite the intuitive appeal of this conventional narrative, it is an anachronistic projection of attitudes that were not yet preponderant. In fact, most of the public opinion in America sided with the *Chinese* in the events leading up to the Opium War. When John Quincy Adams argued in a lecture in 1841 that "the cause of the war is the Ko-tow!" and "the arrogant and insupportable pretension of China," he was employing a British idiom, and his position was considered so extreme and controversial that the *North American Review,* which had already agreed to publish the piece, ultimately declined to do so.[54] Importantly, even most merchants recognized that China had "a perfect right to regulate the character of her imports," and many considered the Opium War "one of the most unjust ever waged by one against another."[55] The fact that the immediate *casus belli* was opium hardly made the war any more respectable.

Indeed, with confiscated British opium being flushed into the Canton harbor, it was difficult *not* to view the event as a kind of Canton Opium Party, analogous to the Boston Tea Party—two heroic acts of struggle against British imperial regulation of trade, in China and America, respectively. Admittedly, John Quincy Adams, most notably, rejected this analogy strenuously: "It is a general, but I believe altogether mistaken opinion that the quarrel is merely for certain chests of *opium* imported by British Merchants into China, and seized by the Chinese Government for having been imported contrary to Law. This is a mere incident to the dispute; but no more the cause of the War, than the throwing overboard of the Tea in Boston Harbour was the cause of the North American Revolution."[56] The point, however, is that this *was* the analogy to be rejected, and that many Americans did in fact find it persuasive.

For a contrasting view, consider the 1841 lecture delivered by the New York lawyer John W. Edmonds, who did believe that the Opium War was in fact fought over opium. He condemned England squarely for acting "for a purpose revolting every principle of justice and humanity" and providing "the first instance in the annals of civilization" in which "indemnity for smugglers has been demanded at the cannon's mouth." As far as China was concerned, Edmonds was effusive in his praise, stating that the Middle Kingdom "may truly be ranked high in the scale of nations" and "regarded as one of the greatest of the family of nations." Indeed, he concluded his lecture by urging, "Let us not forget, that, in most of the arts of civilization, the Chinese are our equals, and in its virtues of mildness, forbearance, and love of peace, they are our superiors."[57]

However, while it was still plausible at the time of the Opium War for many Americans to see China's struggle against British imperialism in the light of their own not so distant past, by the end of the century America itself had become an imperial power in Asia and its fate aligned with that of Britain *against* China. Although the United States continued to reject the British model of territorial imperialism (at least in China, except for some erratic interest in Taiwan), it adopted, with a vengeance, the key form of British nonterritorial imperialism: the cultivation and elaboration of the privilege of extraterritoriality in connection with various Treaties of Peace, Amity, and Trade (or some combination of the trinity). Indeed, the Treaty of Wanghia of 1844 can be viewed as a turning point in American political relations with Asia more generally. Not only did it "plac[e] our relations with China on a new footing, eminently favorable to the commerce and other interests of the United States," as President Tyler buoyantly informed Congress, but once ratified it became the model for subsequent American extraterritoriality treaties elsewhere as well.[58]

In short, prior to America's adoption of the European practice of extraterritoriality in Asia, it was still possible at least in principle to view China as a sovereign state that enjoyed a political status equal to that of the United States and to condemn England as a nation that cloaked itself in an illegitimate imperial sovereignty that purportedly made it politically superior to both China and the United States. However, by taking on the practice of extraterritoriality, America took on a form of imperial sovereignty that rendered it *Britain's* equal in extraterritorial imperialism in China. From this perspective, U.S. imperialism in Asia evidently did not begin with the arrival of the U.S. forces in Manila in 1898, or even with the arrival of Admiral Perry's black ships in Tokyo Bay in 1854, but with the signing of the Treaty of Wanghia in 1844.

CANTON IS NOT BOSTON: INVENTING AMERICAN IMPERIAL SOVEREIGNTY

If the privilege of extraterritoriality itself is extraordinary, it is equally extraordinary how the United States came to obtain that privilege in China and how the main author of the Treaty of Wanghia renarrated the history of the law of nations to justify its extraterritoriality clause—and even played an important role subsequently, as U.S. attorney general, in interpreting extraterritoriality's scope and meaning.[59]

Caleb Cushing's primary charge in 1844 was simply to match the British trade concessions. Yet in the Treaty of Wanghia he far exceeded his mandate. While the instructions he received were ambiguous at places (for example, with respect to the kowtow), they certainly did not call for him to acquire the right of extraterritoriality for American citizens. Indeed, President Tyler's letter to the emperor, which Cushing was charged with delivering, expressly pledged the president's respect for the emperor's jurisdiction over Americans. It assured the emperor solemnly, "We shall not uphold them that break your laws." The letter ended on an ominous note, asking the emperor to agree to a "just" commercial treaty in order that "nothing may happen to disturb the peace between China and America," yet the letter provided no suggestion whatsoever that "just" trade relations demanded that Americans be exempted from the normal operation of Chinese law.[60]

Cushing's actions seem all the more surprising considering that in 1840, before his appointment as an envoy to China, he had proudly declared in the House of Representatives that "the Americans in Canton, and they almost or quite alone, have manifested a proper respect for the laws and public rights of the Chinese Empire, in honorable contrast with the outrageous misconduct of the English there."[61] To be sure, Cushing was a political opportunist extraordinaire and flip-flopped on any number of issues that would seemingly have demanded a categorical position (most importantly, slavery), and his public pronouncements can hardly be taken at face value. Instead, the above statement is probably best interpreted not as an expression of Cushing's heartfelt respect for China but as a denunciation of British imperial ambitions there. Yet putting Cushing's private views aside, evidently the politically expedient position was to take China's side against the British, and it was indeed perfectly intelligible to suggest that China did enjoy full "public rights" under the law of nations.

Regardless of what motivated his earlier statements, during his stay in China Cushing apparently became convinced that China's disinterest in trade and diplomatic relations was not motivated by a mere harmless desire to be left alone. Rather, he came to see it as evidence of a civilizational superiority complex—what the British had been calling Chinese "arrogance" at least since the Macartney embassy. When subsequently confronted by his earlier inconsistent remarks, Cushing did not deny the contradiction but simply unhesitatingly disavowed his prior views, declaring, "I do not admit as my equals either the red man of America, or the yellow man of Asia, or the black man of Africa."[62] From such a perspective of racial superiority, it was only a short step to conclude that China's isolationist foreign policy was nothing less than an *insult* to the honor and dignity of the United States as a sovereign nation.

Indeed, Cushing's correspondence from China is filled with accounts of various indignities he suffered. When he was told, for example, that it would not be appropriate for him to proceed to Peking for an imperial audience, as there was no precedent for American ambassadors being received in the capital, he responded with the rather astonishing statement that a refusal to receive an envoy constituted among Western nations "an act of national insult, and a just cause of war."[63] Disingenuously, he huffed that the "sole object" of his diplomatic efforts was "to signify my high personal respect, and that of my Government, for the August Sovereign, by seizing the earliest moment, after my arrival in China, to make inquiry for his health."[64]

And when one of Cushing's ships was requested not to fire twenty-one guns in salute—because, he was told (quite accurately), "China has no such salute as firing twenty-one guns," and gunfire from a foreign vessel would therefore likely have caused terror among the population—Cushing declared in response that it was his "*duty*, in the outset, not to omit any of the tokens of *respect* customary among Western nations."[65] And in case the threat was not clear enough, he added that "China will find it very difficult to remain in peace with any of the Great States of the West" if it was unwilling "either to give or to receive manifestations of that peace, in the exchange of the ordinary courtesies of national intercourse."[66]

With such shows of "respect" by the United States, it is little wonder that Cushing was able to negotiate the Treaty of Wanghia, complete with an extensive extraterritoriality clause. Cushing himself was fully aware that obtaining extraterritorial jurisdiction had *not* been part of his instructions and that the provision for it was in fact quite exceptional. His ship had barely departed the South China Seas when he started composing a long and remarkable memorandum to the State Department. He began by refuting classic publicists' characterizations of international law as universal, asserting that they had all completely missed "the all-important fact, that what they denominate the law of nations, as if it were the law of *all* nations, is, in truth, only the international law of *Christendom*."[67] Significantly, rather than insisting that international law was universal and the

Negotiating the Treaty of Wanghia, 1843,
with Cushing seated at the table on the right.
Courtesy of the Historical Society of Old Newbury.

Chinese legal tradition particular, and therefore excluded from it, he insisted on the particularity of international law itself. He was not quite as willing to proliferate multiple international legal orders as was John Quincy Adams in his 1841 anti-Chinese polemic (quoted in one of the epigraphs of this chapter), but Cushing insisted that there were at least *two* international legal orders: a Christian and a non-Christian one, or, stated in geopolitical terms, one order for the West and another for an ill-defined Orient.

He next reviewed the origins of the concept of extraterritoriality in the religious exemption of Christians from the jurisdiction of the Ottoman Empire. He stated that, "as far as I remember," Great Britain, for example, had never permitted its subjects to submit to the jurisdiction of non-Christian states in Asia, Africa, or America. Therefore, scholars' general pronouncements about exclusive territorial jurisdiction in fact only "apply to the international intercourse of no states but those of Christendom."[68] Cushing acknowledged that the United States had treaties with France, Sweden, and Russia that provided for consular jurisdiction, but he stressed that

European consuls enjoyed only limited civil jurisdiction among their own countrymen. In "states not Christian," in contrast, Christians enjoyed a much wider general exemption from local civil *and* criminal jurisdiction.[69]

Not content to rest his case on general principles alone, Cushing observed that the United States too in fact had *already* entered into a series of extraterritoriality treaties with non-European states. "If any reasonable question could exist on the subject, so far as regards the Mohammedan states, our treaties with the principal among them, (to wit, the Barbary states, the Porte, and the Imam of Muscat,) have put an end to such questions."[70] Having thus settled the issue of the "Mohammedan states" of North Africa and the Middle East—the predominant Orient of the European imagination—Cushing concluded that the right of extraterritoriality certainly applied with equal force in the "pagan" states of East Asia, which came to define the core of America's Orient.

Yet if the law of nations as well as American diplomatic practice were so clear on the matter, why had the United States not apprehended their relevance in its political relations with China before the Opium War? Why indeed had it not insisted on exemption from Chinese jurisdiction in the Terranova incident of 1821, when a sailor on an American ship was executed for murder under Chinese law, without official protest by the United States? Cushing admitted, "Questions of jurisdiction have arisen frequently in China; and these questions have not been without difficulty, arising from the peculiar character of that empire, and the want of clear and fixed ideas on the subject among Europeans as well as Americans."[71] In Cushing's view, the problem was that "Europeans and Americans had a vague idea that they ought not to be subject to the local jurisdiction of barbarian governments, and that the question of jurisdiction depended on the question whether the country were a civilized one or not."[72] This generally accepted nineteenth-century notion, however, was an "erroneous idea" that "confused all their reasonings in opposition to the claims of the Chinese; for it is impossible to deny to China a high degree of civilization, though that civilization is, in many respects, different from ours."[73]

The real cause of the confusion was, in Cushing's view, the secularized nature of nineteenth-century international law. Its main justification for imperialism was the *mission civilisatrice* rather than the older Christian mission of religious conversion (accompanied, when necessary, with the conduct of a just war against infidels). Insofar as the law of nations provided for the exemption of subjects of civilized states from the laws of barbaric and semibarbaric peoples, China provoked a catachresis in this classification. Cushing recognized the inadequacy of civilizational discourse with regard to Oriental states that undeniably had the conventional markers of a high civilization, even as defined by Europeans. The key, therefore, was to recover the originally *religious* justification of the doctrine of extraterritoriality and to reinstitute Christianity as the standard of admission into international society governed by the law of nations. After all—Cushing emphasized— even in the nineteenth century the states of Christendom continued to possess "many of the qualities of one confederated republic."[74] In effect, while he recognized that Euro-Americans were not in possession of the sole, universal civilization, he more than made up for this concession by grounding full sovereignty in a religious universalism.

Cushing's extensive historical account of why American extraterritoriality in China was not only desirable but necessitated by the law of nations was a considerable rhetorical feat. Much of his historical account was exaggerated, distorted, or simply untrue. Among other things, the young republic's treaties with "Mohammedan states" which Cushing invoked hardly supported his extensive claims. Insofar as extraterritoriality did figure in those treaties, it was simply incidental, outranked by other, far more urgent concerns—such as the suppression of raids on American ships, in the case of the Barbary States. Indeed, they were peace treaties, not commercial ones, and the provisions relating to extraterritoriality were apparently simply copied from earlier European models, given the young nation's inexperience in diplomacy.[75] As such, they hardly amounted to a considered practice of extraterritoriality.

More significantly, the actual extraterritoriality provisions in treaties with the Barbary States, for example, were quite limited in scope—more akin to the kind of consular jurisdiction that European states accorded even to each other than to the extraordinary grant of jurisdiction wrested from China in the Treaty of Wanghia, for which they were supposed to serve as precedent. For instance, the first Barbary treaties provided for a *reciprocal* right of primarily *civil* extraterritorial jurisdiction that was limited to disputes involving *only* U.S. citizens. It was only in later treaties that extraterritorial jurisdiction came to extend to criminal matters as well, and even then only to crimes committed by Americans against other Americans. Importantly, and ironically, one of the justifications for the eventual extension of extraterritorial privileges in the Barbary States in the second half of the nineteenth century was precisely the existence of even greater privileges in Asia—even though the radical nature of *those* privileges had originally been justified by Cushing's spurious claim that they simply mirrored the Barbary treaties. The circular logic of legal Orientalism was self-fulfilling. As a specifically legal discourse, its Orientalist narratives always had the potential of hardening into legal *facts* simply on the basis of their own authority.[76]

In short, the Treaty of Wanghia exceeded in key regards the extraterritoriality provisions of the Barbary treaties, even as they were claimed as its precedent. Importantly, the extraterritoriality provisions of the Treaty of Wanghia were not reciprocal and contained no privileges for the Chinese in the United States; they applied not only among U.S. citizens but also in disputes involving Chinese defendants; and they exempted U.S. citizens from both civil and criminal jurisdiction in China.[77] Furthermore, as he drew on the discourse of one historically and politically specific Orient to craft policy in another—that is, using the Capitulations of the Orient of North Africa and the Middle East as an inspiration in dealing with the Orient of East Asia—Cushing did more than simply exaggerate the radical nature of the extraterritoriality the United States had obtained in its treaties with the Barbary States. In several cases, even the Barbary treaties themselves expressly disclaimed the notion that the United States made distinctions among states on the basis of religious difference—the very idea that Cushing was trying so hard to prove. Contradicting Cushing's claim that American extraterritoriality in "Mohammedan states" was based on religious grounds, several of the Barbary treaties asserted expressly that "the government of the United States of America is not in any sense founded on the Christian religion," and that the United States "has in itself no character of enmity against the laws, religion or tranquility of Musselmen."[78]

Cushing's invented history of neatly compartmentalized legal regimes for interactions with Christian states, on the one hand, and non-Christian ones, on the other, was contradicted not only by treaties he mischaracterized but also by treaties he omitted from consideration altogether. Remarkably, he did not even mention the 1833 Treaty of Amity and Commerce with Siam, which was the sole prior treaty with a "pagan" state in Asia and the closest thing to a directly applicable precedent. Moreover, the treaty with Siam was specifically a trade treaty, like the Treaty of Wanghia, in contrast to the peace treaties with the Barbary States. As already noted, it provided *expressly* that Americans in China were obligated to submit to Siamese jurisdiction, flatly refuting Cushing's revisionist account of American diplomatic history—a simplistic narrative that collapsed all distinctions among Oriental states, whether in the Middle East, East Asia, or Southeast Asia, all of which Cushing subsumed under the single attribute of "non-Christian."

Other relevant but ignored precedents of prior relations with "non-Mohammedan states" in the Pacific would have included U.S. treaties with the Sandwich Islands (i.e., Hawaii, 1826), Tahiti (1826), Samoa (1839), and Sulu (1842); none of them provided for American extraterritoriality.[79] Like the Siamese treaty, the treaty with Hawaii specifically obligated Americans in Hawaii to "behave themselves peacefully, and not infringe the established laws of the land," thus expressly disavowing the European practice of extraterritoriality.[80]

But all of this was conveniently left out of Cushing's narrative explaining why extraterritoriality in China was "essential" to the "honor" of the United States, as he put it.[81] "In China, I found that Great Britain had stipulated for the absolute exemption of her subjects from the jurisdiction of the empire; while the Portuguese attained the same object through their own local jurisdiction at Macao," he explained.[82] Given these circumstances, he argued it would have been "ignominious" for Americans to remain subject to Chinese jurisdiction. The reference to the British and Portuguese imperial practices is telling. While Cushing had indeed earlier dismissed Britain's imperious acts that led to the Opium War, once the war was over and the United States too was about to enter into legal relations with China, surely the nation should not accept a position inferior to that of the British—or, worse still, the Portuguese. Once Chinese law had been characterized authoritatively as despotic and arbitrary by the Europeans, the United States would *in fact* have humiliated itself in European eyes by submitting to Chinese jurisdiction. This was a crucial illocutionary effect of legal Orientalism as a globally circulating discourse. Cushing's preoccupation with the honor of the United States is evident in the Treaty of Wanghia itself. Apart from the extraterritoriality clause, the most extraordinary provision it contains is its call for the Chinese government to defend Americans in China "from all insult or injury of any sort on the part of the Chinese."[83]

Remarkably, the United States made its signal contribution to a seemingly modern form of nonterritorial imperialism in Asia by justifying its precedent-setting extraterritoriality claims by invoking a medieval religious discourse of a *Respublica Christiana*.[84] However, apart from Cushing's personal religiosity (he held twice-daily religious services in the U.S. legation during his sojourn in China), it is hardly surprising that a religiously inspired discourse of legal Orientalism did emerge at this time in China, precisely by drawing on Europe's relations with *its* primary Orient—the Muslim Orient of North Africa and the Middle East—which had indeed been cast in religious terms. From the very beginning, American diplomacy in China relied on missionaries. In addition to a segment of U.S. merchants in Canton, missionaries were the main lobby for the treaty. Peter Parker, an American medical missionary in Canton, urged Secretary of State Daniel Webster during his 1841 visit in Washington, D.C., to send a minister to China at once. Subsequently, because of his putative command of Cantonese (likely quite questionable), Parker became one of two "Chinese Secretaries" for Cushing's mission and played a role second only to Cushing in the negotiations leading to the Treaty of Wanghia. Indeed, Parker apparently regarded the diplomatic mission as "an opportunity of doing more in a few months than in all the rest of his life."[85] In fact, many of the substantive provisions of the Treaty of Wanghia were informed directly by articles published in the *Chinese Repository,* a missionary periodical edited by Parker and his joint Chinese Secretary, Reverend Elijah Coleman Bridgman.[86] In effect, from the 1830s through the 1860s, a handful of missionaries were in charge of most official U.S. government contacts in China.

In the end, whatever hesitation the United States might have had about fashioning its relationship to the Orient on the inherited European model of extraterritoriality, by the time Cushing had finished his mission those doubts had vanished. With the establishment of treaty relations with China in 1844, the United States took on unambiguously the European discourse of imperial, aristocratic sovereignty, which made sovereignty available only to the states with the right genealogy: namely, members of the Euro-American Family of Nations. Only these states were born to be equal and possessed their sovereignty as a matter of birthright. All others would have to *earn* their sovereignty and prove that they deserved it.

Cushing was remarkably successful in convincing the State Department that the extraterritoriality provisions of the Treaty of Wanghia, far from providing a novel basis for American political relations with Asia, was simply a continuation of what had been implicit, and even explicit, prior policies. Over the next several decades, this invented tradition of extraterritorial empire in the Orient turned into a settled expectation in U.S. relations with states in Asia and the Pacific. The 1850 Treaty of Peace, Friendship, Commerce and Navigation with Borneo provided for full extraterritoriality, civil and criminal.[87] In 1854 Commodore Perry arrived in Japan with the task of opening it for the West, as Britain had done in China. Carrying the Treaty of Wanghia with him as a model, Perry acknowledged encountering "great difficulties" in winning immunities for Americans at first, but in 1857 the United States obtained an express right of extraterritoriality in Japan.[88]

Despite a minor delay in getting Japan to fit into the emerging structure of American extraterritoriality in the Pacific, in 1856 the United States went back and revised its earlier treaty with Siam, insisting now on extraterritoriality there as well.[89] In the last quarter of the nineteenth century, the United States obtained similar privileges in Samoa (1878), Korea (1882), and Tonga (1886).[90] By the time it entered into the treaty with Tonga, extraterritoriality for Americans in the Asia-Pacific was well on its way to becoming a virtually irrebuttable presumption: according to Article 12 of the Tonga treaty, Americans were to enjoy extraterritorial jurisdiction in Tonga, not only on the basis of the treaty itself but also "in conformity with the statutes of the United States and the law of nations"—a statement evidently seeking to turn America's extraterritorial jurisdiction in Tonga into an entitlement based not only on treaties but customary international law as well.[91]

As the quoted language suggests, the United States had indeed passed domestic legislation for the creation and regulation of consular posts to exercise extraterritorial jurisdiction in Asia and elsewhere.[92] Yet the most remarkable enactment of all was the congressional provision, passed in 1860, that boldly extended the right of extraterritorial jurisdiction to all "consuls and commercial agents of the United States at islands or in countries not inhabited by any civilized people, or recognized by any treaty with the United States."[93] Under this law, U.S. citizens who found themselves in "uncivilized" countries could be exempted from local jurisdiction even without the formality of a treaty, solely by virtue of being American. The law made no reference whatsoever as to the source of Congress's authority; evidently it derived from the law of nations itself. Effectively, American law now reigned everywhere in the Orient where lawlessness prevailed.[94]

Not only did the United States adopt European imperial institutions in its political intercourse with Asia, but it perfected them so well that it came to serve as an imperial model in its own right. Although the British had been the first to obtain extraterritoriality in China, the American statement of extraterritorial rights in the treaty language itself was regarded as "superior" in terms of precision and coverage, and it came to be hailed as "one of the distinct contributions of the treaty to the diplomacy of the Far East."[95] In the envious admission of a high-ranking contemporary Briton, "The United States government in their treaty with China, and in vigilant protection of their subjects at Canton, have evinced far better diplomacy, and more attention to substantial interests than we have done."[96] In the end, it was the American, rather than the British, extraterritoriality provision that became the model for the other European nations that entered into their own treaties with China in the following years. In sum, the United States played a crucial role in designing the legal architecture of the semicolonial century of Unequal Treaties that structured China's entry into modernity.

Similarly, the 1858 revision of Perry's original treaty with Japan provided the first clear statement of extraterritoriality in Japan, and it too came to serve as the model for subsequent European treaties.[97] And in a repetition of the same pattern, the American treaty with Korea in 1882 was also that country's first treaty with a Western state, and again it set the precedent for later treaties by other powers.[98] Within decades, Cushing's invented tradition, woven out of Orientalist clichés, had become an institutionalized norm in U.S. diplomatic practice, which in turn was eagerly emulated by European states.

As Chapter 5 details, over time extraterritoriality in Asia developed into a unique form of colonialism without colonies. In many ways the regime seems almost postmodern. In fact, the increasing extraterritorial application of national laws is today often viewed as a by-product of twenty-first-century globalization, associated with the rise of cyberspace and the decline of the territorially based Westphalian order of the modern era. (It is notable that, apart from historical literature, the sole reference in contemporary legal scholarship to the U.S. Court for China is by a cyberlaw scholar who proposes it as a model for a "United States Court for the District of Cyberspace"![99]) Since Euro-American accounts of international law generally do not take note of the longer extra-European history of extraterritorial juris-

diction, that history is invariably characterized as "exceptional."[100] Jurispru-
dentially, the express or implicit point of reference for such claims is nineteenth-
century positivism—the notion that all law emanates from nation-states,
each sovereign within its territory. Yet characterizing extraterritorial jurisdiction as a historic exception within the overall international legal architecture
amounts effectively to bracketing much of the planet from consideration.

From a global perspective, in the nineteenth century extraterritorial jurisdiction came to be the *rule* rather than the exception for much of the
so-called Orient. To exaggerate only slightly, Euro-American international
law declared the Orient to be in a permanent state of exception—a state of
emergency where "normal" rules did not apply.[101] Legal Orientalism, in short,
was built into the very institution of international law, or, stated differently,
international law itself became a discourse of legal Orientalism.

CONSTITUTIONALIZING ORIENTAL DESPOTISM

The discursive operation of legal Orientalism is evident in the extension of
U.S. law into China. At the same time, ideas of Chinese lawlessness had
important consequences also for the development of *domestic* U.S. law in
several areas, including the intersecting fields of constitutional law, immigration law, and administrative law. To start with, although Americans in
China were exempt from the operation of Chinese law starting in 1844, the
Chinese in America were absolutely subject to American law. American law
in turn absolutely discriminated against them—sometimes with considerable
effort and ingenuity. For example, in *People v. Hall* the California Supreme
Court held in 1854 that the prohibition of "Indians" witnessing against white
persons applied to Chinese witnesses as well. One of the court's justifications
was the fact that Columbus *thought* he was in Asia when he called the natives
of North America "Indians."[102]

And although the United States was pleased to refer to its China policy
as Open Door—thus distinguishing itself from the Europeans hungry not
only for Chinese markets but for territory as well—it hardly escaped the
Chinese that the door swung one way only. Starting in 1882, in response to
rising anti-Chinese sentiment and a general economic downturn, a series
of Chinese Exclusion Laws enacted by Congress barred the Chinese from

entering the United States and from naturalization.[103] In 1888 Congress went so far as to retroactively terminate the right of some twenty thousand Chinese residents to reenter the United States after visiting China, without permitting the excluded even to recover or sell any of their personal property left in the United States.[104] These racially motivated laws were harsh in consequence as well as in direct violation of the nation's obligations to China under the 1868 Burlingame Treaty and its subsequent amendments. This treaty was one of several revisions and extensions of Cushing's Treaty of Wanghia, and in it the United States had solemnly pledged to permit Chinese immigration, at a time when Chinese labor was still needed in the West for railroad construction and mining.

To appreciate the full historic significance of *Chae Chan Ping v. United States* (1889), known as the *Chinese Exclusion Case* for its affirmation of the constitutionality of anti-Chinese immigration laws, it is important to realize that earlier in the nation's history control over immigration was not seen as an incident of *national* sovereignty. It was precisely in the context of Chinese Exclusion Laws that immigration came to constitute a key index of what it means to be a sovereign power in a world of nation-states. It was the misfortune of Chinese immigrants—and of the U.S. Constitution—that the Chinese were America's constitutive Other in not only a figurative but *legal* sense: a group outside the nation against which the United States defined itself in terms of its constitutional law at a historical juncture when control over the flows of people across borders became a matter of national concern.

From the nation's founding, immigration had been a matter of local and state regulation. As there were few privileges associated with federal citizenship, the federal government had little reason to concern itself with immigration. For example, under nineteenth-century poor laws the support of indigent immigrants fell to state governments. Towns were obligated to take care of their "own" poor, while state governments were responsible for the welfare of foreigners. Perversely, this provided an incentive for towns to characterize even their African American residents as "immigrants" and thus not entitled to local poor relief—whether or not they had been born in the United States and whether or not there was any conceivable moral or legal sense in which the Middle Passage could have been characterized as immigration.[105]

However, as noted above, in the Burlingame Treaty the U.S. government had insisted on free emigration from China, and the treaty came to facilitate large-scale emigration to the United States, mostly to California and Western nonstate territories—areas that were only recently settled by pioneers and sorely needed railroad and mining labor for their economic development. With mass migration and the eventual emergence of a strong anti-Chinese labor movement in the West, control over Chinese immigration became of increasing concern to the federal government. After the completion of the transcontinental railroad, California began to restrict Chinese immigration, thus dishonoring the obligations of the federal government under the Burlingame Treaty—a matter of international embarrassment.

The ensuing struggle between state and federal governments gave Chinese immigrants their first, ultimately misleading, judicial victories. Ironically, as Chapter 2 noted, a large part of the rhetorical justification for Chinese Exclusion Laws in the United States was the premise that the Chinese, as born slaves of Oriental despots, were incapable of understanding the notion of individual rights and could therefore never assimilate into America's republican system of values. Yet the Chinese responded to their exclusion by immediately challenging it under the Constitution. The U.S. Supreme Court consistently invalidated anti-Chinese immigration restrictions promulgated by states, reserving the regulation of immigration to the federal government.[106]

Indeed, what was at issue in the *Chinese Exclusion Case* was the authority of the U.S. Congress to exclude aliens from the nation. In sweeping terms, the U.S. Supreme Court held that the right to do so was an inherent power of sovereignty—a core attribute of what it means to be an independent nation. It did not derive from the Constitution, but from the law of nations and the very notion of sovereignty itself. Therefore, however that power was exercised, there was no appeal from it, for it was simply not constrained by the Constitution. Quoting the authoritative words of Chief Justice Marshall from 1812, the Court declared, "All exceptions, therefore, to the full and complete power of a nation within its own territories, must be traced up to the consent of the nation itself. They can flow from no other legitimate source."[107]

Yet even if only the U.S. government itself could limit its sovereign right to exclude the Chinese from within its borders, seemingly it had already done precisely so in the Burlingame Treaty, which in turn *was* a binding obligation under international law. After all, if it was not, then all American privileges in China, including the right of extraterritoriality, would also appear to be in doubt. With breathless indifference to this implication, the

Court "conceded" that the 1888 legislation was "in contravention of express stipulations of the treaty of 1868, and of the supplemental treaty of
1880," but that it was not, because of any such technicality, "invalid, or to
be restricted in its enforcement."[108]

The Court held that since the power to exclude foreigners was in its view
"an incident of sovereignty," a core attribute of nationhood itself, it "cannot
be granted away or restrained on behalf of any one." That is, despite its apparent willingness to restrict its sovereign right to exclude immigrants from
China, the United States had in fact not succeeded in doing so. It *could not*
impair its sovereignty in such a radical way as to surrender its right to exclude Chinese immigration. Hence, any promises it had made to China on
the subject could be retracted unilaterally by subsequent legislative action.
Sovereign states, like individuals, were simply not free to negotiate away their
inalienable rights by treaty. Or as the Court put it, the right to exclude the
Chinese could not be "the subject of barter or contract."[109] To add insult to
injury, the Court noted that if the Chinese government was displeased with
the result, it was free to pursue diplomacy or "resort to any other measure
which, in its judgment, its interests or dignity may demand."[110] Of course,
it was evident to all informed observers that the exclusion of the Chinese
from the United States could not possibly injure China's "dignity" in the
same way that American dignity was offended at not being allowed to exercise its "right" to trade freely with China.

Yet in discussing the American policy of Chinese exclusion, the Court
made no mention of how the United States had responded to the *Chinese*
policy of seeking to exclude Americans and Europeans. While the American
right to exclude the Chinese was an inalienable right of sovereignty that inhered in the United States' nationhood, the efforts of the Chinese government to exclude Americans from China outside of Canton were seen as anti-
social behavior that could not be tolerated in international society. And
whereas the United States could not—even if it wanted to—give away its
ontological freedom to keep foreigners outside, the extraterritoriality treaties
by which China had signed away far bigger chunks of its sovereignty were
regarded as perfectly valid exercises of whatever "sovereignty" China had.

As Sarah Cleveland characterizes the Supreme Court's nineteenth-
century jurisprudence on the government's foreign affairs power, which included the right to regulate immigration, "the Court repeatedly utilized
international law as a source of authority for U.S. governmental action but

did not recognize it as a source of constraint."[111] Remarkably, the law of nations was thus seen to give Americans *both* the right to exclude the Chinese from the United States *and* the right to "open" China for the entry of Americans, thereby permitting the United States to export its (universal) values to China and to keep China's (particular) values out. Indeed, with the establishment of Euro-American extraterritorial jurisdiction in Asia and the subsequent rise of Chinese Exclusion Laws in settlement colonies across the world, from Canada to South Africa to Australia, legal Orientalism took on increasingly institutionalized forms everywhere.

Even as the new laws contradicted squarely the liberal norms professed by the excluding states, the discourse of legal Orientalism enjoyed planetary circulation, with the high courts of various countries citing each other as precedent in a global chain of judicial tautology. For example, the Privy Council relied on the reasoning of the U.S. Supreme Court in upholding Australian exclusion laws, while the U.S. Supreme Court subsequently cited the Australian precedent as further justification for its decisions.[112] When Congressman Geary in 1892 defended the extension of the 1882 Exclusion Act—known as the Geary Act by virtue of his sponsorship—he stated that he had modeled the new act expressly on Australian anti-Chinese legislation, which he regarded as exemplary.[113] Aristide Zolberg characterizes the global rise of such measures aptly as the "Great Wall Against China," observing that U.S. immigration laws in turn were invoked in Western Europe to justify restrictions aimed at Asians as well as Jews and East Europeans.[114]

But the institutional expressions of legal Orientalism were not limited to the erosion of Chinese sovereignty (through extraterritoriality) and the further consolidation of the sovereignty of Euro-American states (with the erection of walls against Chinese immigration). Legal Orientalism played a significant role in how the United States exercised its sovereignty not only externally but also internally within its domestic constitutional structure. Although one of the stated goals of the Chinese Exclusion Laws was to protect the American shores from Oriental despotism, ironically the bodies of constitutional and administrative law that grew out of the *Chinese Exclusion Case* and its progeny came to reflect the very values that the exclusion laws sought to keep outside the nation's borders in the first place.

Indeed, when the Supreme Court expanded on its ruling in the *Chinese Exclusion Case* and held, in *Fong Yue Ting v. United States* (1893), that the United States had a plenary power not only to exclude Chinese entrants but also to deport long-term Chinese residents after their lawful admission, the dissenting justices understood perfectly well what was at stake, announcing that it gave rise to an "unlimited and despotic power" over aliens. Questioning the expansive notion of plenary powers, the dissenters asked rhetorically, "Is it within legislative capacity to declare the limits? If so, then the mere assertion of an inherent power creates it, and despotism exists."[115]

Chapter 6 considers in greater detail the Chinese immigration cases' continuing legacy in the field of administrative law. It is important to recognize that these cases are part of a larger set of judicial decisions arising in multiple contexts beyond immigration. Precisely as the dissenters in *Fong Yue Ting* feared, collectively those decisions came to stand for the proposition that in certain areas the U.S. government possesses "plenary" or "inherent" powers that are part of its authority simply by virtue of its being a sovereign state in a world of other sovereign states, and hence not subject to constitutional restrictions. Indeed, the notion has all the appeal of an Occidental version of unqualified despotism.

In the constitutional crisis provoked by the Spanish-American War, the *Insular Cases* held, among other things, that although the text of the U.S. Constitution did not envision the annexation of permanently disenfranchised colonies, such a power was "inherent" in the very notion of sovereignty—much like the federal government's right to exclude aliens. This in turn was an extension of earlier cases holding that the Constitution operated fully only in properly admitted states. Even within the continental United States, only some constitutional rights had been made available to the inhabitants of nonstate territories prior to their eventual admission to the Union as states.

Creating an even more disenfranchised category, the *Insular Cases* instituted a further distinction between so-called incorporated and unincorporated territories. The former (such as the Territory of Alaska) were destined for eventual full membership as part of the United States, while the latter (such as the Philippines and Puerto Rico) could be kept in abeyance forever—or else let go of altogether, in the case of the Philippines. Unless and until they were admitted into full statehood, the populations of both kinds of territories remained subject to the plenary authority of the U.S. government, without a right to democratic self-government. These populations were all Orientalized in the sense that they were seen as more or less lawless by nature. To be sure, frontiersmen in the continental U.S. territories were not bona fide ethnic Orientals like, say, Filipinos, but both groups were regarded as semicivilized.[116] (Fililpinos, in particular, were seen as afflicted with "Tagalog despotism," in the U.S. government's view.)[117]

In addition to immigration and territorial administration, the plenary powers doctrine grew out of federal Indian law as well. Under the logic of the U.S. Constitution, Indians were de jure foreigners in their own land: the constitutional provision for birthright citizenship to "persons born . . . in the United States" was limited to individuals "subject to the jurisdiction thereof," and it was held not to apply to members of Indian tribes.[118] In the view of the U.S. Supreme Court, the federal government was therefore at liberty to regulate Indian tribes at its pleasure, again with plenary authority unchecked by the Constitution.

In short, it is hardly a historical accident that the plenary powers doctrine grew out of cases involving immigrants, territorial populations, and Indians. The three groups, ranging from Chinese sojourners to Filipinos to settlers on the American frontier to native Americans, spanned the gamut from Orientals "out there" to America's "internal Orientals," as it were—populations excluded from membership in a nation that was conceptualized in expressly Anglo-Saxon terms in the late nineteenth and early twentieth centuries. Although Chinese immigrants, Indians, and territorial populations were distinctive in numerous ways, the favored rhetorical justification for their constitutional exclusion was such groups' asserted lack of "civilization."[119]

Although the inhabitants of continental U.S. territories are the least obviously "Oriental" of the groups subjected to plenary government authority, apart from the generic lawlessness attributed to them, they too could be Orientalized as needed. For example, the Territory of Utah with its predominantly Mormon—albeit white—population evoked many Oriental fears, inspired by institutions such as polygamy, theocracy, and collectively held property. As Christine Talbot states, "By showing that Mormons were 'really' Orientals in American clothing, Orientalism could make sense of the oxymoron of polygamous Americans."[120]

Indeed, when the U.S. Supreme Court held that Mormon plural marriage in the Territory of Utah did not come under the Second Amendment's protection of freedom of religion, it had a ready-made Oriental analogy at hand: "No doubt, the Thugs of India imagined that their belief in the right of assassination was a religious belief; but their thinking so did not make it so." And likewise, the Court noted, although "the practice of suttee by the Hindu widows may have sprung from a supposed religious conviction," such practices were "open offenses against the enlightened sentiment of man-kind."[121] Indeed, it was evident to the Court that Mormons' notions of fam-ily had potentially grave political consequences for the nation. In an earlier case, Chief Justice Waite had already stated—on the authority of the legal scholar and political theorist Francis Lieber—that polygamy was a crucial element of "the patriarchal principle," which in turn was a one-way road to "stationary despotism."[122]

The Orient was evidently a locus of the legal imagination that existed both inside and outside the nation's borders. In the plenary powers doctrine it found a place inside the Constitution as well.

AMERICAN EMPIRE AND THE RISE OF RACIAL ANGLO-SAXONISM

By the end of the nineteenth century, the global expansion of Western in-ternational law was well on its way to turning the entire planet into a juridi-cal formation consisting of nation-states. At the same time it was eminently clear that even in a world structured on the notional basis of formal sover-eign equality, some sovereigns were more equal than others. It was not only a geographical but also a social, historical, and political fact that Canton was not Boston and that access from the "Mantchoo-Tartar Dynasty of Despo-tism" (in John Quincy Adams's lyrical phrase) to the shores of New England was far more limited than the other way around. Treaties of "free trade" with imperial conditions became one of the pillars of the informal empire on which the emerging global structure rested.

Although the United States still prefers to view itself historically as China's "special friend," the story of the Treaty of Wanghia casts it in the role of a precedent-setting imperial power in its own right, in China as well as elsewhere in the Pacific region—a global leader in the practice of extra-territorial empire. It is noteworthy that in their analysis of British free trade imperialism, Robinson and Gallagher cite as one of their main examples Britain's 1858 treaty with Japan, while that treaty was in fact modeled on the prior American precedent, as noted above. A conventional distinction between a British policy of "imperialism" in Asia and an American one of

free trade thus masks a fundamental continuity in the two nations' practices. An analysis of legal Orientalism—of the construction of America's
legal Orient—makes such a continuity visible.

Nevertheless, American exceptionalism retains much persuasive force in
the telling of the history of America in China. Although few would state
the point quite as starkly today, Tyler Dennett's statement of the United
States' universalist values is exemplary: "England was approaching China
through the old world, through India and other Oriental countries, where
every precedent was in favor of the policy she was laying down; the United
States was approaching China as one independent nation to another, and the
negotiations were in the hands of Yankees who recognized no color line and
prided themselves that they yielded to no race prejudice."[123] Caleb Cushing
was certainly a Yankee, but he wore his racial prejudice on his sleeve, with
great Anglo-Saxon pride. (Nor were his prejudices limited to the Chinese. He
took part in the Mexican-American War as a brigadier general, and the *Dred
Scott* decision cited approvingly his opinions as attorney general in which he
asserted with great conviction that "free persons of color are not citizens,
within the meaning of the Constitution and laws.")[124]

Indeed, it is noteworthy, and hardly coincidental, that the rise of American legal Orientalism in Asia coincides with the development of what Reginald Horsman calls American racial Anglo-Saxonism.[125] He observes that
while the beginning of the nineteenth century is dominated in the United
States by a pervasive sense of the country's Manifest Destiny, the notion
did not yet connote the "rampant racialism" that was evident by the midcentury.[126] With respect to China, Jonathan Goldstein's study of the first
American merchants in Canton likewise argues that while there were tensions between Americans and the Chinese government prior to the Opium
War, those tensions did not have the kind of "racial overtones" that emerged
later: the attitudes of the vast majority of early Philadelphians involved in
the China trade were "entrepreneurial, cordial, and tolerant."[127] In Horsman's view, however, by midcentury the country's "sense of idealistic mission had been corrupted" and replaced with the view that "the peoples of
large parts of the world were incapable of creating efficient, democratic and
prosperous governments; and that American and world economic growth,
the triumph of Western Christian civilization, and a stable world order
could be achieved by American commercial penetration of supposedly
backward areas."[128] The United States' territorial conquest ended on this

side of the Pacific Coast, culminating in a Congressman's exuberant declaration that with title to Oregon, "we shall be neighbours of the Chinese."
But even if America ended at the water's edge, its mission did not. From
Oregon, "civilization was to be carried into Asia along the paths of commerce."[129] Yet, as this chapter suggests, commerce did not replace an earlier discourse of civilization, nor even a prior one of religion. All three
discourses survived, each available for invocation when the other two failed
in their imperial purpose.

In sum, during the first decades of the nineteenth century, while relatively positive views of Asia still prevailed—or, at a minimum, the picture
remained radically ambivalent—the United States paid little diplomatic
attention to Asia and articulated no express policy.[130] When the nation finally focused on Asia around the midcentury (only to be distracted again
by the Civil War, and to remain so until the Spanish-American War), the
policies that developed reflected increasingly negative views of Orientals in
general and the Chinese in particular. With growing contact, what had
once been "fabulous had become mundane," and the notion of "race" took
the place of an earlier concept of merely strange, alien peoples.[131] The Chinese
discovered that they were "yellow," along with all the other attributes that
this implied—and, by definition, they did not include what Cushing called
"the marvellous qualities of Anglo-Saxon blood."[132] Accordingly, the United
States took upon itself the imperial sovereignty to which its heritage entitled it, and the civilizing mission that it implied.

While many important recent studies of American imperialism have focused on law's role in America's territorial possessions, it is crucial not to
ignore law's role in nonterritorial forms of American imperialism as well,
more than half a century earlier. Concomitantly, the story of America's extraterritorial empire in the Asia-Pacific region puts in question our epistemological commitment to such discrete, territorially determinate categories
as "China" and the "United States." Although we may be increasingly aware
of how culturally, socially, and ethnically heterogeneous nations are, legally
at least we are inclined to think of them as defined by their territorial borders.[133] Thus, we tend to view American law as if it emanates from the very
ground of the United States—as if it bears a necessary, even natural, relationship to it. Yet this is merely the relatively recent modern mental habit
of associating law (real, authentic, proper law) with the territorially defined
sovereign nation-state.

As the following chapter describes in greater detail, in China, among other places, American law did not attach to American territory but to the *bodies* of American citizens, each one of them representing a floating island of American sovereignty.[134] In effect, the story of American law in China helps us see law as an almost ontological character of American *being*—the glory of the law-loving Anglo-Saxon race, a kind of white lawyer's burden.

CHAPTER FIVE

The District of China Is Not the District of Columbia

> It seems that American citizens residing for the purpose of trade in the ports of China are not regarded as subjects of that government, but that, for purposes of government and protection, they constitute a kind of colony, subject to the laws and authority of the United States.
>
> —*Forbes v. Scannell*, 13 Cal. 242 (1859)

> China, in so far as the administration of estates of American decedent therein is concerned, is a separate, distinct and complete jurisdiction, similar to that of one of the unorganized territories of the the United States.
>
> —*Cunningham v. Rodgers*, 1 Extraterritorial Cases 109 (1907)

THIS CHAPTER CONTINUES to trace the transformation of legal Orientalism as a regime of comparative knowledge about China into a regime of legal institutions, as well as the ultimate collapse of that distinction. Chapter 4 told a story of how legal Orientalism shaped the international legal basis for extraterritorial jurisdiction in China as well as the development of the domestic legal order of the United States. This chapter examines in greater detail just how American lawyers took up their civilizational burden in the Orient and how U.S. legal institutions functioned in the paradoxical conditions created by extraterritoriality. It is an exploration not only of law's history in China but also of the largely uncharted diasporic history of U.S. law.

The bulk of the chapter consists of an investigation of the jurisprudence of the U.S. Court for China—a woefully little-known chapter in the history of U.S. law, which is, by definition, associated with the territory of the

United States. Even for its contemporaries, the court remained obscure. Faced with a will probated in the U.S. Court for China, the surrogate of Westchester County, New York, confessed his puzzlement to the Department of Justice (understandably but erroneously assuming that the court operated under its supervision): "I have examined the law as far as I have been able to find it to see what is the jurisdiction of this Court and in what it is organized or constituted but can find nothing about."[1] For the first time, then, this book sets out a detailed jurisprudential analysis of the operation of America's extraterritorial legal empire. Unfortunately, the records of the U.S. Court for China have not survived. The analysis that follows draws on the court's published cases, State Department records in the National Archives, and contemporaneous journalistic as well as scholarly accounts of its operation.

As we have seen, the empire of U.S. law in the Orient extended from China to Japan, from Korea to Siam, from Borneo to Tonga, and beyond. In addition to Asia, it included the Ottoman Empire and its dependencies in the Middle East and North Africa, the first Orient of the early modern European imagination. To be sure, as we saw in Chapter 4, although the system of Capitulations that developed in the Levant served as a model for America's legal Orient in the Asia-Pacific, the Capitulations were not as draconian in substance as the legal order that evolved in China and East Asia more generally. Equally significantly, there were no permanent extraterritorial communities of U.S. citizens in the Middle East that came anywhere near the size of the American community in, say, Shanghai, with its armies of merchants, missionaries, beachcombers, and others. Consequently, America's extraterritorial empire reached its greatest elaboration in China, in the jurisprudence of the U.S. Court for China.

To make sense of the extraterritorial jurisprudence of the court, it must be analyzed as part of the histories of both U.S. and Chinese law, and indeed of the history of law's globalization. The story of law's empire in China is one of a progressive breakdown of the constitutive distinctions of legal Orientalism. Rather than part of a universal history of law's progress in China, it is a story in which the posited elemental difference between law, on the one hand, and the Orient, on the other, finally contracts to the vanishing point. As the previous chapters have sought to demonstrate, legal Orientalism as a system of knowledge entails the projection of law's contradictions elsewhere. All of law's universal virtues become associated with an idealized Euro-American rule-of-law, while all its particular shortcomings are conceptualized as a despotic rule-of-man attributed to others. However, once the imagined Orient becomes a field of direct Euro-American legal action, mediated through the institutions of international law and extraterritorial jurisdiction, those contradictions reemerge with a vengeance, in forms so exaggerated that law becomes its own caricature. As the contradictions become more difficult to manage, they can often only be denied or repressed—or simply blamed on the Orient, in whose name despotism now becomes law's ground, rather than its Other.

Within the legal universe of extraterritorial China, law operated in Byzantine ways. In the end, a total of nineteen powers came to enjoy the privilege of extraterritoriality, thereby superimposing nineteen foreign legal systems on top of China's own.[2] The result was a true Babel of legal tongues—a cacophony of particular legal systems without a universal foundation. From 1905 until 1940, there were twenty-eight courts of first instance in Shanghai, only two of which were part of the same constitutional order.[3] In addition to foreign extraterritorial legal systems, there were three competing city governments in Shanghai: those of the so-called International Settlement, the French Concession, and the Chinese City. Eventually, there was also the so-called Green Gang, a criminal confederation that arose in large part in response to this administrative chaos. Unencumbered by law or jurisdictional boundaries, it constituted an extralegal institution providing order across Shanghai.[4]

Norwood Allman, a leading American lawyer in Shanghai, describes the city's legal world as follows:

> [A lawyer in Shanghai] might be in the Chinese court one day, the British the next, the French or American court another. . . . A fluency in French, plus a good working knowledge of the Code Napoléon and of Chinese and English law, was highly desirable. . . . It was taken for granted that the American lawyer in Shanghai knew something about international law, maritime law, the laws of the District of Columbia, the decisions of the federal courts, equity, and the laws of most of the forty-eight of these United States. Cases in the American court frequently turned about the law of any one of the states, not to mention the laws of the Philippine Islands.[5]

This complicated regime of extraterritoriality paved the way for increasing territorial encroachments of Chinese sovereignty as well, although most

of them fell formally short of colonialism proper (with the important exceptions of Hong Kong and Macao). Leases and associated railroad concessions became the major technologies of territorial penetration in China,
whose sovereignty came to be little more than a shell perforated from all
sides. Indeed, as noted in Chapter 4, in the post-1895 Scramble for Concessions there was genuine fear that China might be divided into actual colonial enclaves among the so-called Treaty Powers, or Euro-American states
with Unequal Treaties with China. Befitting China's ambiguous international legal status, the scramble was precipitated by a novel legal form, the
so-called public international law lease. It had no clear historical precedent,
and it defied international lawyers' attempts at precise definition. Although
it fell short of a formal cession of territory, the public international law lease
was a form of *direct* territorial control, on the model of outright colonialism.[6]
Germany, for example, referred to its lease in Jiaozhou formally as a *Schutzge-
biet,* a protectorate, and it treated Jiaozhou the same way as its recently established protectorates in Africa—the preeminent form of colonial control
on that continent. Indeed, it was hardly an accident that the race for concessions in China came to be known by the same term as the Scramble for
Africa.[7]

   In addition to direct territorial control within the leasehold, public international law leases in China typically entailed concessions for building
railroads, both inside *and* outside the leased territories. The Jiaozhou lease,
for example, provided for a right to construct a railroad outside the German
leasehold, along with a right to establish mines within a fifteen-kilometer-
wide zone on each side of the railway line. In addition, the treaty secured a
fifty-five-mile buffer zone outside the leasehold that was to be patrolled by
German troops.[8] In other words, the territorial leasehold represented only a
beachhead, a point of departure for extending the lessor's power beyond the
formal territorial boundaries established by the lease. Over time, the prolif-
erating foreign railroad concessions both inside and outside of leaseholds
came to constitute another mutant form of nonterritorial imperialism, a
reticular quasisovereignty superimposed on formally sovereign Chinese territory. This emerging "railroad sovereignty"—a term current in China at
the time—was epitomized by the South Manchuria Railway Company,
chartered by Japan in 1906 to operate its railroad concessions in Manchuria. Officially a commercial operation, the company became an extension
of the Japanese state itself, establishing militarized company towns as well

as agricultural settlements along its extensive railroad zone in nominally sovereign Chinese territory.[9]

In addition to railroad concessions and other semicolonial privileges, China granted (under duress) a number of residential concessions to foreign sojourners in major cities. As already noted, the city of Shanghai, for example, had a multinational International Settlement as well as a French Concession. Technically, these concessions remained under Chinese sovereignty, yet the International Settlement in Shanghai, most notably, came to enjoy an independence equivalent to that of a nation-state, imposing and collecting its own taxes and operating even its own defense force.[10] Overwhelmed by the need to observe Chinese law, the regulations of several competing municipal governments, and a growing number of extraterritorial foreign legal systems, U.S. consul general David Bailey complained as early as in 1879 that Shanghai constituted "the most cumbersome system of judicature known to exist in any considerable commercial center in the world."[11]

Within this system—if it can be called that—U.S. law performed multiple, and often contradictory, roles. This chapter will draw attention only to some of them, as they emerged in the jurisprudence of the U.S. Court for China. First, the greatest contradiction exemplified by the U.S. Court for China was the simple but profound fact that one of the main justifications for it was to provide a model of rule-of-law for China, yet its own operation was far from exemplary. Perhaps most notably, the court came to rely on the codes of the Territory of Alaska and of the District of Columbia, thus externalizing the law that obtained in two internal colonies of the United States. As we will see, U.S. law has its own spatial and temporal structure—a constitutive set of territorial and historical associations—that did not allow for one-to-one translation to the circumstances of China. In the end, the U.S. Court for China constructed an extraordinarily idiosyncratic version of American law—a *particularly particular* law, as it were, which had neither a coherent territorial referent nor a constitutional one. It was a placeless law that was justified, ultimately, by the Orientalist axiom that China itself was a fundamentally lawless place.

Second, and perhaps more surprisingly, the U.S. Court for China sought to colonize *Americans* in China as well. While the United States as a nation sought to represent the idea of law in China, numerous Americans in Shanghai were associated with crime—the very opposite of law. The court did not hesitate to employ its full arsenal of judicial despotism to transform criminal U.S. citizen-subjects into proper subjects of rule-of-law. In order to do so, it developed a hybrid definition of U.S. citizenship, reflecting the diasporic population of America's territorial and extraterritorial empires in the Orient, in China and beyond. In the end, much as the Chinese immigration cases created a lawless zone for the treatment of Chinese wishing to enter the United States, Americans in China found themselves in a similar constitutional black hole.

Finally, this chapter will consider the so-called International Mixed Court that operated in the International Settlement of Shanghai from 1864 until 1926. The International Mixed Court was originally a Chinese court, charged with applying Chinese law in disputes involving Chinese defendants. However, over time the foreign consular body took over the court's administration, thereby finding themselves able to simply invent the law the court applied and calling it "Chinese law." At that point, legal Orientalism ceased to be a discourse of *representations* about Chinese law to a global audience. It became Chinese law itself.

"THE LARGEST DISTRICT OF OUR FEDERAL COURT SYSTEM"

For more than sixty years, the United States followed the model of the European powers and exercised its right of extraterritorial jurisdiction in so-called consular courts. That is, it vested its consular representatives in China with the power to adjudicate legal disputes. Institutionally, this was simply an extension of the way in which European powers exercised the reciprocal and limited extraterritorial jurisdiction that they recognized even amongst the members of the Family of Nations. Most consuls in Europe had no legal training—often they were merchants—but since their chief judicial function was attending to civil disputes among merchants of their own nationality, they were usually perfectly well suited for the limited judicial tasks they performed.[12]

However, as we saw in Chapter 4, the consular jurisdiction exercised by European powers in the Orient was radically more extensive than among other European states. Hence, the generally low judicial quality of the consuls in the Orient became eventually a matter of concern. For example, untrained U.S. consular judges in China exercised not only civil but also criminal jurisdiction. In fact, at least one person was hanged in the U.S.

consulate in Canton, in 1864.[13] Nevertheless, one particularly notorious American consul prided himself on being "short on law" but "hell on equity."[14]

To be sure, even the establishment of U.S. consular courts in China was an improvement over what preceded them—which was nothing. After Caleb Cushing succeeded in obtaining the Treaty of Wanghia in 1844, he requested that the State Department immediately urge Congress to pass legislation to establish consular courts, as Americans in China were now no longer subject to Chinese laws. Remarkably, Congress did not establish consular courts in China until 1848.[15] That is, from 1844 until 1848, Americans in China existed in a legal vacuum in which they literally got away with murder: they were no longer subject to Chinese jurisdiction, but the U.S. government had not yet authorized anyone to exercise U.S. jurisdiction over them either.

But even after Congress set up rudimentary consular courts, some U.S. critics entertained severe doubts about their quality, and even their constitutionality. In fact, whether the Constitution applied to them at all was an open question for some time. Caleb Cushing himself believed firmly that it did, under the extraterritorial regime he had helped create. When he subsequently became U.S. attorney general, he indicated so in an opinion he gave in 1855.[16] In 1881, the matter became unexpectedly a subject of debate in the Senate. As part of the system of consular courts, which by now was well established, the Senate was called on to consider a request for funds for the maintenance of an American jail in Shanghai. Most senators were not even aware of the existence of U.S. consular courts in China, and Senator Dale Carpenter queried, with dismay, "I would like to know, just for the peace of my own conscience as a Senator, what authority we have to vote money to keep [Americans] in jail [in China] until somebody can hang them by judicial murder." And he answered his own question, "I assert here that they are in prison there in violation of the Constitution of the United States."[17]

This concern was shared by Secretary Blaine in the State Department who suggested twice, in 1881 and 1884, that the United States replace the makeshift consular courts in China with a proper judicial tribunal, complete with a jury and the full panoply of constitutional guarantees. He drew special attention to "the strange and incompatible blending of executive, judicial, and legislative functions" concentrated in a single officer. As Blaine put it, a consular judge in China enjoyed powers "greater than ever the Roman law conferred on the pro-consuls of the empire," which made him an "officer who, under the terms of the commitment of this astounding trust, is practically irresponsible."[18] Evidently, if the courts' purpose was to save Americans from Oriental despotism, they were part of the problem rather than its solution.

Blaine concluded that "a reform, on the part of the United States, is naturally to be sought in the erection of tribunals; purely judicial in character, and conforming in principle and practice to the standards of jurisprudence in the United States." That is, the United States should import American law to China in its full-fledged, completely institutionalized form. In Blaine's view, "despotic" American extraterritorial justice in China was clearly not compatible with the Constitution. To frame the issue squarely, he quoted Senator Carpenter's formulation: "The question is whether this government can derive any power denied to it by the Constitution from a treaty with a foreign nation?" As Blaine saw it, even if the Qing government was willing to permit American kangaroo courts in China, the U.S. Constitution did not.[19]

Yet such concerns were brushed aside definitively by the Supreme Court when it announced, in 1891 in *In re Ross*—an appeal from Japan—that the Constitution did not apply outside the territory of the United States; it was therefore permissible for a consular court in Kanagawa to convict a defendant for murder without a jury. Hence, extraterritoriality treaties could empower the government to administer justice in China in ways that would have been impermissible in the United States. The constitutional basis for America's extraterritorial empire was now fully in place. Indeed, the unanimous Supreme Court opinion in *In re Ross,* authored by Justice Field, adopted Caleb Cushing's dubious historical account of the development of extraterritorial jurisdiction almost verbatim, citing his 1844 memorandum to the State Department, analyzed in Chapter 4. While acknowledging that a criminal defendant might have to forego some constitutional niceties in consular courts established in "non-Christian countries," Justice Field thought this was quite acceptable as the defendant was still a "gainer," being spared from "barbarous and cruel punishments" inflicted by "arbitrary and despotic" local officials. Cushing's Orientalist narrative had now been written into the constitutional law of the United States.[20]

Of course, as we have seen, the dubious character of consular justice was not the only legal complaint the Chinese had about the United States.

Dismayed at the Chinese Exclusion Laws as well as outbreaks of violence against Chinese laborers in California and elsewhere in the West, increasingly assertive Chinese merchant classes responded by organizing a large anti-American boycott in 1905, which swiftly caught the attention of the policy establishment in Washington, D.C.[21] Apparently still invigorated by U.S. victories in the Spanish-American War, President Roosevelt at the time even entertained the option of seizing Canton with the support of approximately 15,000 troops.[22]

The bad news from China was compounded in 1905 by a *Report on the United States Consulates in the Orient*, commissioned by the State Department. It confirmed what everyone already knew about U.S. extraterritorial justice: American consular courts were plagued by incompetence, inefficiency, and corruption, which in turn resulted in increasingly lawless behavior by Americans in China.[23] And although the extraterritorial jurisdiction of consular courts was limited by treaty as well as by statute to disputes involving American defendants, there were numerous reports of consuls seeking to adjudicate even among Chinese parties, which was an egregious violation of Chinese sovereignty. Many U.S. missionaries supported the practice, insisting that converted Chinese should not remain subject to Chinese legal superstitions—as if Christian baptism amounted to naturalization. In short, the state of American law in China was becoming intolerable, and the stage was set for a new phase in the exercise of America's extraterritorial empire in the Orient.

When in 1906 Congress passed an act for the establishment of the U.S. Court for China, the idea was unprecedented in American diplomatic and legal history.[24] Although the court has been called "the strangest federal tribunal ever constituted by Congress," it remains largely unknown.[25] It was only in China that the United States decided to establish a "real" court to exercise its extraterritorial jurisdiction; everywhere else, it relied on consular courts. The court was modeled, in many respects, on His Britannic Majesty's Supreme Court for China, created in 1865 (at the time named for Her Britannic Majesty) and also located in Shanghai. Indeed, the American and British courts in China—or "for China," in the more generous formulation entailed in the two courts' official names—were the only two full-fledged national courts operated by foreign states in China. All other Treaty Powers relied on consular courts. (There were two other important courts that were controlled wholly or in part by foreigners—the International Mixed Court of the International Settlement and the French *Cour mixte* in the French Concession—but neither court was a foreign court in a formal sense. In principle, both were Chinese tribunals operated with foreign "assistance," although France did not disavow its desire to operate the French Concession on the legal model of a territorial colony. For now, the operation of the *Cour mixte* remains an understudied subject.)[26]

The advocates of the U.S. Court for China invested the tribunal with high hopes. As the high tide of U.S. imperialism overseas coincided with Progressivism at home, the motivations of the court's advocates are perhaps best characterized as Progressive imperialism. The imperial aspect was evident in that one of the court's main tasks was to provide a model of rule-of-law for the Chinese—a classic *mission civilisatrice.* But what gave it a (perhaps) Progressive slant was the fact that it also had a second civilizing mission: in addition to civilizing the natives, it was charged with civilizing Americans in China, by bringing law and order to the increasingly ill-behaved U.S. community.[27]

As far as the first mission was concerned, Congressman Edwin Denby, a missionary's son and the author of the court's organic act, envisioned the judge of the U.S. Court as "an ancillary, unofficial ambassador of the United States," charged with the promotion of rule-of-law in China.[28] While the right of extraterritoriality might have struck most observers as an extraordinary privilege, the court's supporters described it soberly in a rhetoric of America's "obligations" to China, viewing the U.S. Court for China "as the place where the Chinese may come in and receive justice."[29] The Far Eastern American Bar Association likewise emphasized Americans' "special duty to China."[30] In the extraterritorial regime of the International Settlement, it was said, even the Chinese could receive "many of the benefits of constitutional government at a time when those benefits cannot be made generally available to the Chinese population in the country at large."[31] Overall, institutions such as the U.S. Court for China were believed to "impress upon the Asiatic mind" that Americans are "governed by law and not by an imperial or presidential edict."[32] "The common law of England" was viewed as the great responsibility of English and American lawyers and nothing less than "the great heritage of their race."[33] In short, members of the American bar in China stopped just short of describing their mission as a white lawyer's burden, in language of which both Caleb Cushing and Rudyard Kipling would have approved.

In the end, the necessity for (Western-style) legal reform in China was implicit in the very system of extraterritoriality, given that it was justified by a despotism that allegedly inhered in the very nature of Chinese law. Self-evidently, the price for its elimination was to become schooled in the civilized ways of the West. As Antony Anghie puts it in his characterization of nineteenth-century international law, "a non-European state was deemed to be civilized if it could provide an individual, a European foreigner, with the same treatment that the individual would expect to receive in Europe."[34] Hence, extraterritoriality would be lifted as soon as it became redundant and China became a replica of Europe and America. To help China reach that state, the U.S. Court for China would serve as a model for Chinese legal reform.[35]

THE LEGAL CONSTRUCTION OF "AMERICA" IN THE DISTRICT OF CHINA

Whatever else rule-of-law might mean, the minimal requirements for any system of rule-of-law include the existence of a reasonably determinate body of laws and an institutional structure for applying those laws in a reasonably consistent manner. The U.S. Court for China provided the institutional basis for the exercise of U.S. jurisdiction in China. But insofar as the term jurisdiction refers, literally, to the power to "say" (Latin, *dicere*) what "the law" (*ius*) is, just what law was the U.S. Court for China supposed to use as the basis of its holdings? This deceptively simple question turned out to be extraordinarily difficult to answer, and the answers the court produced are indeed so ad hoc as to be lawless.

To begin, the oath to be taken upon admission to the bar of the U.S. Court for China required members to swear, among other things, that they would not bring suits that were "unjust" except insofar as the justice of such suits was "honestly debatable under the law of the land."[36] But what was the law of the land? Or, rather, the law of *which* land was the bar to uphold? At first glance, the answer seemed quite easy. According to

Sino-American treaties as well as the court's organic act, the court's task was to apply the "laws of the United States."[37] In the peculiar conditions of American extraterritoriality in China, however, even the innocent phrase "laws of the United States" led to serious interpretive difficulties. For example, did it cover only federal legislation passed by the U.S. Congress, or did it include the common law as well? If so, the common law of which state—or states?

At the heart of some of the most difficult questions was the court's irregular place in the institutional structure of American law, articulated in terms of territorially defined state legal systems, on the one hand, and a further distinction between state and federal courts, on the other. At the most basic level, was it a federal or state court? Obviously—or perhaps not?—China was not a "state" of the United States. In the end, the only thing truly obvious was that the court was *sui generis*. Some did in fact seek to analogize China (along with the U.S.-occupied Philippines) to a state, at least as far as the organization of the bar was concerned. Chauncey Holcomb, district attorney for the District of China, explained to the House Committee on Foreign Affairs, "We have a bar association which is a branch of the American Bar Association, just the same as the States of Delaware or New Jersey."[38] The local branch, the Far Eastern American Bar Association, indeed convinced the American Bar Association to amend its definition of "state" so as to include the District of China within it.[39]

The court itself, however, much preferred to associate itself with the prestige of the federal system. In the preface to the first volume of the court's case reports, *Extraterritorial Cases*, Judge Lobingier—the court's second and longest-serving judge—described his jurisdiction confidently as "territorially the largest district of our Federal Court system."[40] Elsewhere, he referred to his tribunal slightly more equivocally as "a part of the Federal Judicial system, corresponding in grade mainly to the District Courts."[41] In the opinion of Lobingier's former district attorney, the judge of the U.S. Court for China was just a "regular district judge"[42] (although he did recognize the rather anomalous fact that the judge's district was "as large as our whole home land"[43]). The State Department, too, happily referred to the U.S. Court for China as "a regular district court of the United States."[44]

Nevertheless, all these claims about the court's utter ordinariness were belied by Judge Lobingier's efforts on behalf of legislation that would "expressly" confer on him "the powers of a judge of the district court of the United States."[45] In an appeal from China, the Ninth Judicial Circuit in San Francisco indeed deliberately declined to address the status of the court. The China Trade Act, one of the few pieces of congressional legislation passed specifically for application in China, provided that, for its purposes, the term "federal district court" included the U.S. Court for China.[46] Confronted with a dispute under the act, in dicta, the Ninth Circuit merely "assum[ed], without deciding, that the United States Court for China is a court of the United States."[47]

Of course, the court *was* like a federal court in that even the most minimal definition of the law it was charged with applying—"the laws of the United States"—undoubtedly included general legislation enacted by Congress. However, this body of law was largely irrelevant to the lives that Americans lived in China. They married, divorced, entered into contracts and breached them, embezzled, raped, murdered, wrote wills, and died. Within the federal system of the United States, these were ordinarily matters of state, rather than federal, law. Judge Lobingier himself acknowledged that although his court "derive[d] its entire authority from the Federal Government," it nevertheless exercised "much of the jurisdiction commonly possessed by a state court."[48] Hence, the court's main problem from the very beginning was that the only body of law which it had an unquestionable authority to apply—general acts of Congress—was simply irrelevant to the disputes that were typically brought before it.[49]

Fortunately, Congress had seemingly anticipated the potential inadequacy of federal legislation in the extraterritorial conditions of China. In setting up the court, it had provided that where "the laws of the United States . . . are deficient in the provisions necessary to give jurisdiction or to furnish suitable remedies, the common law and the law as established by the decisions of the courts of the United States shall be applied."[50] The good news was that this enactment did provide Americans in China with basic rights based in common law—those of "property, succession, the contract, which constitute the staple matter of ordinary life."[51] The bad news was that this turned out to be an archaic common law frozen in a much earlier time.

That is to say, in addition to its spatial logic of territorially delineated jurisdictions, American law has a temporal structure as well, rooted in a historically based English common law. In light of the revolutionary break in its reception by the United States, it was not possible to transport the common law tradition across the Pacific as if it were a single monolithic entity. As the common law had been modified in distinctive ways by the various states as well as federal courts since the separation from England, the U.S. Court for China concluded that "*the* common law" as a singular body of law had to refer to the common law of England as it existed in American colonies "at the date of the transfer of sovereignty."[52]

That view may have been logically defensible, but in practical terms it meant that the court was called on to "ascertain the common or unwritten law in force in the colonies prior to the Declaration of Independence" and then to "attempt to apply it to modern conditions in China," as one eminent Shanghai lawyer put it, adding that this was certainly an occasion for some "amazement."[53] Significantly, though, the only thing that seemed to amaze him was the temporal disjunction—not the fact of applying American law in China, so long as it was state-of-the-art American law.

Functionally, then, the U.S. Court for China was left with the hybrid task of serving as a federal court *and* a state court, yet as far as the latter role was concerned, its misfortune was to be a state court without a state and a corresponding slice of American history. The court's very first judge, Lebbeus Wilfley, and the Ninth Circuit that upheld him, resolved the dilemma with the simple act of borrowing the municipal code of the District of Columbia and the code of the Territory of Alaska.[54] As congressional statutes, these codes were certainly laws enacted *by* the United States, even though this still left room to argue about whether the two codes were laws *of* the United States, in terms of their limited territorial applicability.[55] Equally importantly, since neither the District of Columbia nor the Territory of Alaska enjoyed the full rights of self-government (Alaska would not become a state until 1959), the subject matter coverage of the congressional codes included what would ordinarily have been state-law matters. As we saw in Chapter 4, by the end of the nineteenth century the federal government came to enjoy extraconstitutional discretionary authority not only over Asian immigrants wishing to enter the United States but over the nation's internal Orientals as well: Indians and territorial populations, including those of Alaska and the District of Columbia. Ironically, the undemocratic form of law whereby the nation's internal colonies were governed, justified by a constitutional doctrine that grew in part out of a policy of excluding Chinese immigration, was now exported back to China.

Judge Wilfley's solution was strikingly effective, although it ignored altogether what Congress could possibly have intended in passing the D.C. and Alaska codes.[56] The court nevertheless insisted that "Congress may enact a law for a limited area under its exclusive jurisdiction, such as Alaska or the District of Columbia," and that the law may "by its terms . . . have no force whatever outside of such area."[57] Yet the court concluded that so long as such a law was both necessary and suitable for the purposes of its extraterritorial jurisdiction in China, it was the law in China.[58] Quite simply, in the court's view "any pertinent act of Congress" was in force in the District of China "regardless of the limits within which it was originally intended to apply."[59]

This reasoning had startling implications for the court's double bind. In the words of the prominent Shanghai lawyer Stirling Fessenden, in one bold stroke it got the court out of "the wilderness of colonial common law."[60] After a dearth of applicable law, the U.S. Court for China was suddenly awash in a *surplus* of law. As a dismayed member of the House Committee on Foreign Relations summed up the situation, "Any law enacted from the foundation of the Government of United States up to the present time that the court may think applicable is applicable"—regardless of whether such an act had been originally passed for the United States as a whole, or for Washington, D.C., Alaska, the Philippines, or any other federal territory.[61] In short, the court's holding resulted in an explosion—or perhaps more properly an *implosion*—of American law into China. *All* federal law applicable *anywhere* in the United States and its territories was now potentially the law in China.

In Judge Wilfley's opinion, it had originally been one of the court's "worst embarrassments" that it lacked "an adequate body of laws to be applied."[62] Instead, the court was now faced with the novel problem of choosing among an exhilarating excess of law. When the House Foreign Relations Committee protested the broad judicial discretion such a choice entailed, a decade later Judge Lobingier disingenuously denied the need to resort to any discretion at all: "The policy of the court has been to apply every act that could be applied, and it has not seemed desirable to exclude anything that seems to have any bearing on the conditions [in China] at all."[63] Admittedly, just as Lobingier seemingly never confronted a case over which he did not want to take jurisdiction, so he never appeared to come across a law that he did not want to apply in China.[64] Yet this hardly eliminated the need for choosing among several potentially applicable bodies of law, since territoriality— the key criterion in traditional choice-of-law analysis—was by definition of little use in the *extra*territorial application of U.S. law. For example, which law should the court apply when legislation for the various territories was in conflict? Or, if a special act, say, for Alaska, conflicted with a general congressional statute, which should govern?

To address the problem the court applied two basic rules. First, when two special acts (that is, federal laws of limited territorial application) conflicted, the later enactment was to control over the earlier one. Second, in a conflict between a special act and a general one, the general act was to take precedence.[65] When these rules were applied to the choice between the codes for the District of Columbia and for the territory of Alaska, presumably the slightly newer D.C. code should have controlled over the Alaska code, as both codes were special acts of limited territorial application. Yet in the opinion of Judge Lobingier, "Much of the District of Columbia legislation is inherited from colonial Maryland and is therefore antiquated," which was the very infirmity the court was trying to avoid. Moreover, Lobingier noted, D.C. legislation was enacted for an urban community whose life was "complex" and "highly advanced." Therefore, it was "ill adapted to conditions in a country like China"—those conditions being, by implication, simple and primitive. In contrast, "the Compiled Laws of Alaska afford a fairly modern and up to date piece of legislation," and, besides, they were designed for "a primitive, frontier community," and thus seemed "far more suitable and workable" for China. Apparently, then, D.C. legislation was both too old *and* designed for such a highly developed community as to be inappropriate for China; the laws of Alaska were preferable because they were more modern *and* suitable for primitive conditions.[66]

By whatever leap of logic Judge Lobingier arrived at his preference for the laws of Alaska, those laws did not necessarily always take precedence over legislation for the District of Columbia either—except when they did. In the opaque legal universe of the District of China, observers could not agree on what was, even in theory, the jurisdiction's primary source of law; some claimed it was the D.C. code, while others believed it was the territorial code for Alaska.[67] This was no wonder, considering the patchwork of law the court created. Not only were its choices often inconsistent, in that it preferred D.C. legislation in one area of law and Alaska law in another, but the court felt free to mix and match even within a single area of law. For example, although D.C. law applied to divorce generally, the court never-theless applied the law of Alaska to determine the parties' residence for purposes of divorce.[68]

The laws of Alaska experienced some especially dramatic twists. For ex-ample, once the court had declared that the federally enacted corporation law of Alaska was available for the creation of American corporations in China, the court then insisted that Alaskan corporation law would remain valid in China even after it was repealed in Alaska.[69] In effect, the corpora-tion law of Alaska continued to live on as a ghostly presence in China, long after its demise in Alaska. Alarmed at this extraordinary situation, Con-gress passed the 1922 China Trade Act, a special law applicable only in China, for the creation of American corporations for the purpose of doing business in China.[70] When the court still refused to let the Alaskan corpo-ration law die, in 1925 Congress amended the 1922 act to make it perfectly clear that from then on the China Trade Act was to be the only law under which American businesses were to incorporate in China.[71]

It is also noteworthy that even after the court had selected a law and found it both "necessary" and "suitable" in the requisite sense of these terms, it then declared itself free to ignore the penalties prescribed by the otherwise applicable law. The court admitted frankly that "the case must be exceptional where one part of a statute is applicable and the other part not." However, the court adverted to "obvious difficulties" that would arise given that "the penalties fixed for similar offenses in the [codes of Alaska and District of Columbia] differ from each other." The court never explained what these "obvious difficulties" were; seemingly, either one or the other code would have been applicable in a given case, and the penalty would likewise have been governed by the same code. The court simply asserted that the applicable section of the code of Alaska "leaves the fixing of penal-ties for criminal offenses committed within this extraterritorial jurisdiction to the discretion of trial officers. For that reason it is not believed that the Court is bound by the penalties prescribed in [the codes of Alaska and Dis-trict of Columbia]." Almost as an afterthought, the court noted that "while the penalties fixed in those codes are not binding on this Court they may be well utilized as guides and treated with great respect." At least the court was permitted to follow the law, even if it was not required to do so.[72]

Evidently much of the court's work could not have withstood constitu-tional scrutiny. However, the U.S. Court for China was perfectly aware of the Supreme Court's 1891 decision in *In re Ross*, which had upheld trials without jury in consular courts in Japan, as we have seen. As the court put it emphatically, there was not even a "hint" that the Constitution was in force in the District of China.[73] Remarkably, even though every other federal law in force in the United States and its territories—and even some that had been repealed—was exportable to China, the supreme law of the land was not.[74] Seemingly, whenever the Constitution came into contact with either China or the Chinese, it ceased to apply—whether with respect to Chinese immigrants wishing to enter the United States or Americans in China.

The court's declaration that it was free to mete out whatever penalties it preferred was hardly the sole practice in which it engaged that might have run afoul of the Constitution, had it been applicable. Chauncey Holcomb, after having left his post as a district attorney for the District of China, explained to the House Committee on Foreign Affairs, "If a man is arrested and locked up when the Judge happens to be away, sometimes we have to keep that man locked up for six months waiting for trial."[75] The judge might have been away for several reasons. For one thing, he was required by statute to hold sessions at least once a year in Hangzhou, Tianjin, and Canton. This was indeed roughly equivalent to a New York judge being required to take his court periodically to Boston, Chicago, and San Francisco, and the demands of such travel could result in lengthy absences from the court.[76] Moreover, when the U.S. constituencies in Shanghai were unhappy with the justice they received in the U.S. Court for China, they often exploited diplomatic and political avenues and took their grievances to Washington, D.C. During hearings on a petition for Judge Wilfley's removal, for example, the court did not sit for nearly a year, and, likewise, when Judge Lobingier went to Washington, D.C., to address charges made against him, the court's work came to a halt.[77] Tellingly, though, such situations were perceived as commercial crises for Americans in China, not constitutional ones.[78]

Even when it was in session, the court itself expressed little concern about the absence of the Constitution. Judge Lobingier, for example, felt confident that he could do very well without the assistance of juries, as he had done in his previous post as a judge in the U.S.-occupied Philippines. The U.S. Supreme Court had already expressly upheld the absence of juries in the Philippines in *Dorr v. United States*, among the first *Insular Cases*.

Although the Constitution applied in the Philippines *after* it was acquired by the United States—at that point it was indisputably under U.S. sovereignty—it did not apply in full force but required the observation of "fundamental rights" only. In the Supreme Court's view, jury trials did not happen to be such a right. Hence, if juries were not required even in the Philippines, which was sovereign U.S. territory, perforce they could be dispensed with in the extraterritorial District of China. Proleptically, the decision in *Dorr* relied in part on *In re Ross*, which had approved of jury-less trials in U.S. consular courts, including those in China.[79]

But although China was not a territorial U.S. colony, like the Philippines or Puerto Rico, it was evidently part of a wider circulation not only of legal ideas throughout the American empire but also of officials. It was hardly coincidental that not only Judge Lobingier but also his predecessor on the U.S. Court for China had both served previously in America's preeminent colony in the Pacific: Lebbeus Wilfley was a former attorney general of the Philippines—and coincidentally also a great admirer of the British colonial empire. When the constitutional controversy over the status of the Philippines and Puerto Rico was raging, Wilfley published an article in the *Yale Law Journal* praising Britain's "wonderful record" of colonial administration, predicated on a racial distinction between Anglo settler colonies and crown colonies inhabited primarily by "Negroes, Asiatics, and Polynesians." As Wilfley explained approvingly, while the former could be trusted with the institutions of self-government, the latter were best governed "despotically."[80]

Apparently sharing Wilfley's sentiments about the dispensability of rule-of-law in the Orient and in order to boost his claim that allowing juries in China "would not be wise," Judge Lobingier assured Congress that "there is no popular demand for anything of the sort."[81] The latter claim at least was patently untrue. Those wary of the powers of the judge of the U.S. Court for China constantly complained of the lack of juries as a check on his power. They noted poignantly that even His Britannic Majesty's Supreme Court for China had jury trials, while in contrast the American judge was entrusted precisely with a kind of autocratic power "consistent with the practice under the barbarous system obtaining in China, against which we were attempting to guard when we demanded our extra-territorial jurisdiction."[82] One member of the American bar in Shanghai described the procedure of the court as a "star-chamber proceeding." Even the less-than-radical

Associated American Chambers of Commerce insisted that, at a minimum, the court should adopt a system in which the judge sits with lay assessors in cases that would ordinarily be entitled to a jury trial.[83] It hardly escaped Americans in China that they were subject to a despotism of their own.

Despite the absence of constitutional due-process guarantees, the court did not function wholly without procedural guidelines. Although general federal rules of civil procedure were not promulgated until 1938, at which point the U.S. Court for China did deem them applicable in China as well, in the interim there was a set of regulations governing the procedure of American consular courts in China.[84] These regulations had been originally enacted in 1864 by the U.S. minister to China, and the China Court Act made them applicable to the U.S. Court for China, although it authorized the judge "to modify and supplement" them.[85] Judge Lobingier, however, wanted to go further and draft an entirely new code of procedure, not only for his own court but for the consular courts as well. Speaking before Congress in favor of a bill that would have authorized him to do so, he promised, "As soon as this measure passes, which confirms the authority to make rules, it is my intention to promulgate them, and they will cover the subject of procedure pretty generally."[86]

The bill never passed, but Judge Lobingier wrote his own rules anyway, and then proceeded to apply them under the title of the Extraterritorial Remedial Code.[87] Their legal status remained ambiguous (and despite the name of the compilation it included many new substantive rules of law as well). In an appeal from the U.S. Court for China, the federal appeals court for the Ninth Judicial Circuit in California speculated about what it thought "the practice prevailing in the China court" likely was, but ultimately it conceded its ignorance: "We do not have access to the rules."[88] The State Department was no more knowledgeable, although it was charged with administrative supervision of the court.[89] (Tellingly, until 1933 the court operated under the supervision of the State Department, not the Department of Justice.[90]) When the chair of the Senate Committee on Rules asked for information regarding the procedure of the court,[91] he was told politely that "the Department is not informed as to the rules under which the Court is now proceeding."[92]

In addition to applying its own curious mix of American law, the court believed that there was authority even for applying the municipal regulations of the International Settlement.[93] What was, legally, most peculiar

about this willingness to apply those regulations was not simply that they
were not American law, but the fact that they existed, even in the State
Department's view, "outside of any general system of law."[94] As the last section of this chapter elaborates, technically the International Settlement was
on sovereign Chinese territory in Shanghai, yet in the second half of the
nineteenth century it essentially seceded from China and set up its own
municipal government that was constitutionally accountable only to its
multinational electorate.[95] Consequently, the regulations of the government
of the International Settlement were not promulgated under the authority—
direct or delegated—of *any* national government. To be sure, the court had
overwhelming practical reasons for cooperating with authorities of the International Settlement. America's extraterritorial empire was a distinctively
judicial one, extending the reach of U.S. law overseas. Yet law does not enforce itself, and in its day-to-day functioning the U.S. Court for China had
no choice but to rely on the cooperation of the authorities of the International Settlement for enforcement. Had it refused to apply the municipal
regulations of the Settlement, it could hardly have expected the Settlement
authorities' cooperation in return.

Finally, the court recognized even Chinese law among its sources of law.
It enforced what it called "compradore" or "Chinese custom," and it adopted Chinese law with regard to real property insofar as it followed the
British Supreme Court for China, which had ruled that land in Shanghai
would be governed by *lex loci rei sitae*.[96] In 1933, Judge Lobingier went so
far as to propose—unsuccessfully—that the U.S. Court for China should
adopt newly enacted modern Chinese codes as the law of the court. That
way, finally, a "uniformity of law" would obtain in China, as he put it, and
it would resolve the contradictions inherent in applying American law in
China.[97] Presumably, it would also have cleansed the exercise of American
extraterritorial jurisdiction in China from the charge of imperialism. With
a modernized Chinese law modeled on Western law and then adopted as a
form of U.S. law in China it would have been increasingly impossible to
distinguish between U.S. law and Chinese law.

This, then, is a description of key aspects of the jurisprudence of the U.S.
Court for China, born of the jurisdictional crisis precipitated by extraterritoriality. On the one hand, Alaska and the District of Columbia were
among the court's predominant sources of law. On the other hand, the law

it produced was a remarkable synthesis that was not reducible either to the law of Alaska or the law of the District of Columbia. Indeed, it was not the law of any identifiable territorial jurisdiction anywhere, other than the jurisprudential wonderland of the District of China. The final product constituted a unique body of law of its own—a kind of American common law of China—which the court constructed for its own purposes.[98]

This should not surprise us. The court was caught in the impossible act of seeking to resolve several irresolvable contradictions. The most fundamental one was the simple fact that the court was authorized to apply only U.S. law and that for jurisdictional purposes China was to be treated as if it were literally part of the United States—a mere District of China. Formally, China as such simply disappeared behind the judicial horizon. Yet like colonial courts everywhere, in practice the U.S. Court for China simply could not ignore Chinese law completely. Hence, without either statutory or treaty-based authority, the court applied Chinese law at least occasionally, as well as local "compradore" or "Chinese custom."

Conflicting imperatives for the application of U.S. law and Chinese law were not the only contradiction the court had to manage. Equally importantly, it faced numerous contradictions among different bodies of U.S. law. Ordinarily, making selections among them would have been just the kind of technical questions—far removed from the politically charged matter of dealing with Chinese law—that any moderately competent U.S. court could handle. To ensure the proper functioning of a complex federal system, there existed a settled body of rules for managing conflicts of law. Yet significantly the U.S. Court for China had tremendous difficulties precisely with these mundane conflicts.

Ultimately the problem lay in the very notion of extraterritoriality on which the court's jurisdiction rested. In the United States, the main criterion for choice of law was territoriality—determining the location of the relevant acts and actors. To be sure, in numerous instances a single act or actor might be associated with several locations, but once a court did decide on a relevant location (say, Massachusetts), there *was* a more or less determinate body of law it could apply (that is, Massachusetts law). In China, the criterion of territoriality was simply not adequate. Given that the District of China was not a state of the United States, it was eminently unclear which of the several state common laws should apply to legal acts and actors in

China. And although the court resorted to the codes of Alaska and the District of Columbia precisely as a way of avoiding the problem, it found itself equally unable to choose consistently between the two codes; evidently, the District of China was not the District of Columbia, or the Territory of Alaska either.

In the final analysis, jurisdictional events that took place in China had no evident territorial or jurisprudential referents in the United States. It should therefore come as no surprise that the body of law the court created seems so arbitrary and so unmoored from "real" (that is, territorial) U.S. law. Legal fictions aside, China was not the United States, and no judge could overcome that profound fact. The impossibility of simply projecting the spatial and temporal logic of American law into China in turn gave the court extraordinary discretion in fashioning an extraterritorial law of its own.

Indeed, the pages of *Extraterritorial Cases* read at times not unlike entries from Borges's "Chinese encyclopaedia" (discussed in Chapter 2), juxtaposing disparate sources of law in weirdly disjunctive ways. The above analysis of the jurisprudence of the U.S. Court for China could well be summarized as follows, in the language of magical realism:

> In China, American law is divided into: (a) compradore custom belonging to the Emperor, (b) Unequal Treaties written at gunpoint, (c) anything but the Constitution, (d) the Code of the Territory of Alaska, except when not, (e) parts of the Code of the District of Columbia (perhaps) but not its penalties (unless we like them), (f) innumerable, (g) the common law, but only if really old, yet not too old, (h) fabulous, (i) again, not the Constitution, (j) prisons in the Philippines, (k) not included in the present classification, (l) et cetera, (m) having just been repealed in Alaska, (n) that from a long way off looks like law.

The United States Court for China was, in short, an imperial court that was left to fashion its own peculiarly placeless law, justified by the conviction that China itself was a lawless place. In America's extraterritorial empire in the Orient, U.S. law became its Oriental Other. Considered as part of a global story of American law, it took a *particularly particular* form, divested even of its seemingly most universal feature, the constitutional rights of U.S. citizens.

LAW'S EMPIRE: HOW TO CIVILIZE AMERICANS IN CHINA

China was, in fact, in many ways a lawless place. From the point of view of the U.S. State Department, the problem was that its lawlessness was hardly limited solely to the Chinese. The American community in Shanghai, for example, was increasingly associated with crime—the exact opposite of the image of law the United States wished to project. It therefore became an urgent task for U.S. law in China to stop Americans from going native, by turning its imperial gaze not only on the Chinese but on U.S. citizens as well. As Eileen Scully has shown, in its mature form extraterritoriality was as much about the U.S. government seeking control over Americans overseas as it was about releasing them from Chinese jurisdiction. That is, *freedom from* Chinese law implied *submission to* U.S. law—and as we have seen, in the view of many Americans in China, the exchange of Oriental despotism for a despotism of law.[99] The U.S. Court for China, however, saw no contradiction in cultivating civilized subjects of law by despotic means.

It is important to recognize that as Americans set about constructing their own extraterritorial America in China, the enterprise was not solely the white lawyer's burden. It entailed ultimately the cooperation of all kinds of Americans in China—lawyers as well as missionaries, businessmen, and others.[100] Among the American institutions created were Chambers of Commerce, Boy Scouts, Girl Scouts, the Salvation Army, an American University Club in Shanghai, a YMCA, a Short Story Club, and a Far Eastern American Bar Association.[101] The immediate milieu in which the U.S. Court for China existed in Shanghai was not China but, in the phrase of Norwood Allman, "America in China"—the final fruition of the illogic of extraterritoriality.[102]

Alas, as the American community in China grew, it attracted not only law-abiding citizens such as lawyers, missionaries, and Boy Scouts but also lawbreakers of various kinds—or, worse still, not even all the lawyers, missionaries, and Boy Scouts who came to China turned out to be law-abiding. Together with beachcombers and other American undesirables that turned up in Shanghai, they were giving the United States a bad name and, significantly, provided increasing ammunition for Chinese critics of American extraterritorial jurisdiction. Given the damage they wrought on U.S. diplomatic prestige in China and the danger they posed to extraterritoriality as an institution, a central mission of the U.S. Court for China was to discipline the unruly elements of the American population in China.

Jurisdiction for prosecuting American citizens in the court was based on the extraterritoriality provisions of the 1844 Treaty of Wanghia and its several revisions over time. Together they set up a system where jurisdiction depended on the defendant's nationality. "Citizens of the United States" who committed "any crime in China" were triable "only by the consul or any other public functionary of the United States, thereto authorized according to the laws of the United States." Similarly, "subjects of China" who were "guilty of any criminal act towards citizens of the United States" were to be punished "by the Chinese authorities according to the laws of China." In civil suits as well, a Chinese plaintiff could sue an American citizen only in an American court, while an American citizen would have to sue a Chinese subject in a Chinese court.[103] This arrangement was subsequently codified by Congress in legislation that formally set up the system of American consular courts in China, as noted above. When the U.S. Court for China was created in 1906, it inherited the principles of consular jurisdiction.[104]

In theory, the system was simple enough and even had a certain formal symmetry to it: the Chinese could be sued only in Chinese courts under Chinese law, and Americans in American courts under American law. This symmetry, of course, was limited and entirely misleading. As Chapter 4 emphasized, the Chinese *in America* had no equivalent extraterritorial privileges. On the contrary, they were barred even from entering the country after the enactment of the Exclusion Laws. Indeed, in tandem with the expansion of America's extraterritorial empire in the Orient, in 1917 the immigration exclusion came to entail an entire "Asiatic Barred Zone"—a startlingly candid term reflecting the expanding borders of America's legal Orient.[105]

Americans, in contrast, could enter China without legal difficulty, yet their activities while there were frequently illegal. The foreign enclaves of China were notorious for the gamblers, adventurers, prostitutes, and other Treaty Port flotsam that landed on their shores—or at least this was how less than prosperous Euro-Americans were typically portrayed. Shanghai in particular was famed as the Far East's capital of sin and vice, or even more pruriently, as "the Whore of the Orient." Accordingly, the U.S. Court for China started its career by prosecuting Americans in China with a vengeance. Among its first targets were lawyers, prostitutes, and vagrants.

According to State Department officials, Chinese Treaty Ports were "favorite resorts for adventurous and irresponsible lawyers" who "by reason of their lack of knowledge of the law and lack of character were not fitted to perform the duties of the office of attorney at law." Indeed, by one account, such lawyers were said to be "the greatest hindrance to the promotion of decency and virtue that the American missionaries, both men and women, encountered in the Empire."[106] If America was to be identified with law and distinguished from Oriental lawlessness, lawyers of ill repute were evidently a major concern. Dissatisfied with the state of the bar, Lebbeus Wilfley, as the first judge of the court, took it upon himself to institute a bar examination for admission to the court. The reaction was one of dismay and disbelief. Although the exam was elementary in content, of the nine lawyers who took it on its first administration, only two passed—and one of the disqualified ones was so enraged by the action that he petitioned for the judge's removal.[107]

Prostitutes were another main object in Judge Wilfley's cleanup campaign.[108] "America" had in fact become synonymous with prostitution in Shanghai; brothels were generally called "American houses," prostitutes were referred to as "American girls," and going to the red light district was described as "going to America."[109] In short, a more express association of "America" with lawlessness and immorality was hard to fathom. Judge Wilfley thought it vital to restore the respect for law among American women in particular. However, when he tried to crack down on "keepers of American bawdy houses" in Shanghai, many of his targets quickly married foreign men.[110] Under the patriarchal logic of derivative spousal citizenship, these women instantly lost their American citizenship and acquired the husband's foreign one, which in turn protected them from prosecution in the U.S. Court for China. As contemporary observers noted, several brothel keepers "jumped [Judge Wilfley's] jurisdiction by hurried marriages with men of other nationalities, mostly sailors who conveniently sailed away after the ceremony, the 'bride' having paid over a marriage fee which ranged anywhere from one hundred to one thousand Chinese dollars."[111] Put simply, citizenship could be bought and sold in Shanghai, which made it exceedingly difficult for the court to bring American prostitutes before the law.

"Vagrants" constituted another early target of the court. Like European colonizers elsewhere, American sojourners in China were invested in maintaining "the illusion of a homogenous white race, affluent, powerful, impeccable, aloof."[112] In the racial economy of Shanghai, in particular, there was little room for a Euro-American working class, or, as the journalist Edgar Snow noted, "in Shanghai every occidental is supposed to be a gentleman."[113] A 1898 Shanghai editorial put it even more starkly: "just as a Senator from the Southern American States once declared that most of the pleasure of his trip to Europe was spoiled by the sight of white men doing menial labour, so we wince at the sight of a destitute foreigner."[114] The court was not at all shy about admitting that the elimination of lower-class Americans from China was in fact one of its main aims in seeking to enforce the law against vagrancy. The district attorney for the U.S. Court for China complained to the State Department of "a certain class of unemployed Americans" whom it had convicted on vagrancy charges.[115] Indeed, the court was careful to point out that while vagrancy was defined as "the idle or dissolute wandering about," the idle rich "who are under no obligation to work" would not be encompassed in that definition.[116]

Yet there still remained the problem of what to do with the vagrants after their conviction. Observing that "the presence of American vagrants in China injures our country's prestige," the court decided to send them to the Bilibid Prison in Manila. Sending them out of China was viewed as necessary for the reason that vagrants "rather liked a short term of imprisonment in our American jails where they were well fed, etc."[117] In the Bilibid Prison, in contrast, they would be subject to "mild tho exacting discipline," all in accordance with the methods of "modern penology."[118] In short, there they would be turned into proper, law-abiding citizen-subjects of the United States.

Once this practice was approved, in yet another twist of legal Orientalism the Philippines became effectively an American penal colony in which to house lawless Americans whose presence in China was deemed to injure America's diplomatic interests.[119] Extraterritoriality could thus mean not only the right not to be subject to Chinese law but also *expulsion* from China. Because America's extraterritorial empire in China lacked a comprehensive enforcement apparatus and sufficient prison facilities, it made sense to ship those who failed to observe extraterritorial U.S. law to a U.S. colony in the proper sense of the term—a place where American laws could be applied with minimal process and maximal force. Indeed, this was yet another way in which U.S. extraterritorial imperialism was articulated with its territorial counterpart.

At the same time as it was seeking to impose stricter standards on what it meant for Americans to behave lawfully in China, the U.S. Court for China also loosened its definition of *who* counted as an American in China, for the purposes of the court's jurisdiction. In ambiguous cases, the court preferred to take jurisdiction. Such was the case with American "subjects" from the Philippines and Guam, and Chinese Americans, for example. As we have seen, both the treaties and congressional acts in which the court's jurisdiction originated limited it expressly to cases in which defendants were "citizens of the United States," yet the court not only sent U.S. citizens to the Philippines but also took jurisdiction over Filipinos and Guamanians who came to China, without pausing to consider the legal niceties of citizenship in the increasingly complex imperial legal order of the United States.

Under the convoluted reasoning of the *Insular Cases*, the legal status of the former Spanish colonies was ambiguous indeed. In the words of one commentator, the U.S. Supreme Court managed to find, in a single day in 1901, that Puerto Rico, for example, was "in and/or out of the United States in three different ways."[120] Most memorably, the Court characterized the island's territorial status as "foreign to the United States in a domestic sense"[121]—a phrase fittingly parallel to Chief Justice Marshall's designation of Indians as "dependent domestic nations," both in and outside of the United States as expedience demanded. Much as the precise status of the newly acquired insular territories was unclear, so was the status of the residents of those territories. The U.S.-Spanish peace treaty was written so as to avoid conferring citizenship on them, and as Christina Burnett observes, "they were neither aliens nor, apparently, citizens, but something in between."[122] Such a denial of full citizenship was evidently permissible under the doctrine of extraconstitutional plenary powers. At the same time, while Filipinos in the Philippines were deemed sufficiently un-American *not* to enjoy the full range of rights afforded by U.S. law, Filipinos in China *were* considered American enough to bring them under America's extraterritorial empire in the Orient, even if they were not deserving of U.S. citizenship.

Just as former, current, and would-be Americans in China were frequently opportunistic about their social and legal identities, so the United States too hedged its bets, not always willing to claim all of its own as American citizens. The status of American citizens of Chinese origin was especially fraught. The State Department worried about their trying to reap the benefits of being Chinese vis-à-vis the Chinese government and the benefits of being American vis-à-vis the U.S. government. The concept of dual nationality was itself viewed as a perversion of true citizenship, the civic equivalent of polygamy.[123] In the words of the Solicitor's Office of the State Department, American-born Chinese who might also be claimed as Chinese citizens "as a rule do nothing for the United States" and therefore the U.S. government "would gain nothing but the resentment and ill will of China if we should insist that, although residing in China, they must be subject to the jurisdiction of our courts."[124]

Robert Lee was a case in point. He was born in 1868 in St. Louis, Missouri, as the son of a "Chinaman" and an "American woman." He moved to China at the age of twelve with his parents, and he lived in Shanghai and Hangzhou until his death in 1917. To avoid the risk of expatriation while in China, he had duly maintained a registration with the American consulate. After the periodic registration again expired in 1915 and "thru an oversight was not renewed," the consulate refused Lee's new application for registration. Lee was told that while the ordinary presumption of voluntary expatriation could be overcome by "sound reasons for remaining abroad," such as "advanc[ing] American interests" through missionary activity and business, his business as a "dealer in vermillion and yellow lead" did not overcome that presumption: there was "considerable doubt" as to whether his motivation was "purely for the advancement of American interests" or for selfish pecuniary gain.[125]

Putting aside the highly questionable notion that most—or any—U.S. businessmen were in China for the primary purpose of advancing American interests rather than making money, Robert Lee had other disqualifications as well. Notably, he was married to "a Chinese woman" who "wears Chinese clothing," "has not been in the United States and does not associate with the American people." To be sure, the children were "taught the English language" and wore "European clothing."[126] This, however, was hardly enough to indicate a desire "to return to resume the obligations of citizenship" in the United States.[127] Ultimately, the State Department justified the denial of Lee's registration on its right to refuse protection "to one who has left the United States for permanent residence abroad."[128] In Lee's case, the State Department was perfectly willing—indeed, eager—to let go of him as an American citizen. Nevertheless, the U.S. Court for China decided to uphold Lee's registration, insisting on the legal fiction of extraterritoriality in China: "An American citizen in China, whether residing temporarily or permanently, remains as much under the jurisdiction of his government, its laws and its institutions as if he were residing at home."[129]

The ambiguous and shifting definitions of what counted as U.S. citizenship in China for jurisdictional purposes made it possible even for many local Chinese to benefit from some of the privileges of extraterritoriality. One common way of doing so in Shanghai was for a Chinese owner to have his land held in trust by an American citizen. In keeping with treaty restrictions, foreigners residing in Shanghai's International Settlement did not technically own their lands in fee simple but, rather, held them under "perpetual" leases.[130] The foreigner lessees ordinarily recorded their leases in their own consulates, which gave rise to a system of so-called consular title deeds. These perpetual leases were not only as good as full ownership as a practical matter, but, more importantly, the consular title deeds to which they gave rise could be challenged only in foreign extraterritorial courts; this in turn rendered them "practically indefeasible."[131]

One Western observer proudly claimed, "The Chinese have not been slow to learn that the property of a foreigner in China is in a far more secure position than that of a Chinese." To obtain the benefit of such a "practically indefeasible" title, a Chinese landowner in Shanghai could enact a "fictitious transfer" of his lands to a foreigner, who would then register the land with his consulate, thus "possessed of that land nominally and to the world as beneficial owner, when he in fact is a bare trustee for the Chinaman." The system was one where a "Chinaman . . . avail[s] himself of the services of his foreign friends in order to employ their names for his property and enterprises."[132] Indeed, a senior American lawyer admitted candidly, "In addition to the ones I own personally, numerous consular title deeds are registered in my name and in the name of my [law] firm."[133] Clearly this "service" was not a purely humanitarian gesture; it came at the price of a lawyer's fee. The result of this commodification of citizenship was, effectively, a "market in foreign privilege"—a legal Orientalism available for Orientals as well, at a price.[134]

Yet whether one was defined constitutionally as an American citizen, subject, or national, one might have thought she was nevertheless beyond the jurisdiction of the U.S. Court for China as long as she stayed *out* of China. For instance, when a woman living in Gettysburg, Pennsylvania, was sued for divorce in the U.S. Court in Shanghai, her attorney immediately questioned the court's jurisdiction, querying the State Department about the court's authority to hear a divorce action "against [a] wife in America who has never been in China."[135] In response, the State Department simply referred the attorney to the court's previous holding that "jurisdiction of the respondent's person was not essential" in a divorce action that did not seek other relief.[136] Indeed, the court went even further, as it determined that in divorce actions there was neither a residency nor even a *nationality* requirement for defendants, as long as the action was solely for a decree of divorce, without property claims; in such cases, only the *plaintiff* had to be an American.[137] The court held that it had analogous jurisdiction in actions for the annulment of marriage: such suits could also proceed "regardless of defendant's nationality."[138] These cases struck the editors of the *Harvard Law Review*, among others, as creating exceptions "in plain disregard" of the terms of the Sino-American treaty, which predicated jurisdiction precisely on defendant's nationality.[139] Nevertheless, the court's reasoning was not challenged either on appeal or by the State Department.

Considering the court's civilizing mission among U.S. citizens in China, it is filled with several paradoxes. Insofar as the court's mission was to bring law and order to the American community in China, it fell far short of its goals. Rather than decriminalizing Americans, frequently the main effect of the court's actions was to de-Americanize criminals: in response to the threat of prosecution by the U.S. Court for China, American criminals simply assumed other identities and nationalities.[140] In the description of the State Department, the jurisdictional competition—or lack thereof—among the several Treaty Powers led to a kind of criminal race to the bottom: "The vice which seems to thrive in the atmosphere of the Orient has long tended to seek shelter under the flag of the country whose administration is the most lax and ineffective."[141] Even the loudly proclaimed success of the American antiprostitution campaign was largely rhetorical. At the very moment of his triumph Judge Wilfley was reduced to celebrating the mere fact that "at present not a single lewd woman within the jurisdiction of this court *admits* she is an American."[142]

Moreover, not only did the court de-Americanize criminals (admittedly inadvertently, as American citizens sought refuge in other nationalities), but it also effectively Americanized some *non*-Americans, such as foreign spouses of American citizens. On the one hand, the jurisdictional net cast by the court missed many Americans in China, while on the other it also caught many non-Americans. The result was a classic hybrid colonial identity—not the citizenship of the United States in its ordinary sense but, rather, the citizenship of "America in China" or "the American community in Shanghai," that is, the court's own, self-defined idea of who needed civilizing. Indeed, just as the court arrived at a syncretic definition of the "laws of the United States," it arrived at an equally hybridized definition of "citizens of the United States."

At the same time, it is vital to recognize that although the extraterritorial rendition of U.S. law and its subjects in China may have been about as "American" as Borges's encyclopaedia is "Chinese," the territorial grounding of "real" American law in the United States is no less self-evident. In its original conception, the common law was limited in its operation to the King's courts in England. Over the course of the settlement of North America, it remained an open, and contested, question to what extent English law traveled with the colonists across the seas.[143] The official reception of English common law by the newly established United States of America in 1776 thus already represented the extraterritorialization of a European legal system. It is an irreducible fact of the intertwined constitutional histories of the British empire and the United States that U.S. common law *in America*—like the American common law of China—already operates on somebody else's land: land that once belonged to Native Americans.

Significantly, in the collision of European and indigenous political and legal worlds from which North America emerged, Indian nations were transformed into tribal "sovereigns" in the European sense, and over time their lands were taken from them in accordance with international treaties to which the tribes formally consented—in a process not unlike the one in which China consented to American extraterritorial privileges under the Unequal Treaties.[144] Yet even with Indians' diminished existence as "domestic dependent nations," a multitude of tribal legal orders remain in operation in the United States to this day. Remarking on the U.S. Supreme Court's continuing, and growing, willingness to divest Indian tribes judicially of the quantum of sovereignty that they do retain, Philip Frickey observes pointedly that colonialism in the United States "did not end at some point in the distant past": Congress and courts are engaged in an "ongoing colonial process." He describes the Supreme Court's ad hoc decisions in federal Indian law, or what he calls an "American common law of colonialism," as nothing less than a "jurisprudential land of ultimate incoherence"—a striking characterization equally fitting for the American common law of China.[145]

Without implying a false equivalence between the legal construction of "America" in China and the legal construction of "America" in America—to do so would be willfully obtuse—one must recognize that legally the United States, too, is an edifice of extraordinary complexity, a Babel of jurisdictions not unlike extraterritorial Shanghai. Not only does the United States consist of a federal government superimposed on fifty state governments superimposed on hundreds of tribal jurisdictions, the relations among which are the subject of endless legal and political contestation, but there are also numerous non-state territories, including such "unincorporated" territories as the Commonwealth of Puerto Rico, the Commonwealth of the Northern Mariana Islands, Guam, the U.S. Virgin Islands, and American Samoa—each territory occupying a distinctive legal status. And while the District of China may be history, the District of Columbia endures—subject to taxation without representation to this day, the American Revolution notwithstanding.[146]

Despite the numerous regards in which U.S. extraterritorial jurisdiction in China is distinctive from the territorial jurisdiction of the United States, the fact remains that the ways in which the claims of American law attach to, and detach from, Earth's surface and the bodies of human beings is always an imperial achievement (even if it is not *only* that). A distinction between territorial and extraterritorial jurisdiction is not meaningless, but it may not be as consequential as we might think, given our reflexive commitment to the idea of territoriality. In the end, *all* claims to jurisdiction—territorial and otherwise—rest on a common foundation. That foundation, as Oliver Wendell Holmes put it simply, is "physical power."[147]

From a larger perspective, it is evident that the establishment of the U.S. Court for China was not part of a universal history of law's unfolding in China. It is better understood as a chapter both in a global history of U.S. law and a global history of legal Orientalism—interlinked and inextricable.

INTERNATIONAL MIXED COURT: A FLOATING WORLD OF CHINESE LAW

While the body of American law produced by the U.S. Court for China was *sui generis*, the so-called Chinese law generated by the International Mixed Court of Shanghai was even more so. Indeed, it remains one of the most extraordinary jurisprudential artifacts of legal Orientalism. In theory, the Mixed Court was a Chinese court applying Chinese law only, in disputes involving Chinese defendants and typically Chinese plaintiffs as well. However, because of the putatively lawless nature of Chinese law, the foreign consuls in Shanghai ultimately took over the operation of the court. Formally, the law applied by the court always remained Chinese law, yet it became a Chinese law that was fabricated by foreign assessors who shared the bench with Chinese magistrates. In the end, the extraterritorial population of Shanghai colonized not only the territorial space of the International Settlement in which they lived but even the very category of Chinese law.[148]

This foreign colonization of the power to apply Chinese law, and concomitantly to determine just what Chinese law *was*, was no small matter. By the early twentieth century, the International Mixed Court was described as "the most powerful court in the world."[149] It enjoyed unlimited subject matter jurisdiction in one of the leading commercial centers of the world.[150] By 1925, its reach extended over all 810,000 Chinese residents of the International Settlement as well as any foreigners there who were not protected by extraterritoriality treaties and hence remained subject to Chinese law.[151] (However, most foreign residents of the International Settlement enjoyed extraterritorial privileges and therefore could be tried only by courts of their nationality.) Over its lifetime, from 1864 until 1926, the Mixed Court handled over a million cases.[152] The sanctions it meted out included capital punishment. The death penalty was in fact administered quite liberally. In 1924 alone, ninety-six persons were executed at the behest of the Mixed Court.[153]

Even though Chinese law remained formally the sole body of law the Mixed Court was authorized to apply, the foreign-controlled court paid no heed to the Qing Code, which was the chief statutory compilation of China until 1911, and even thereafter the court applied the statutory law of the Republic of China only selectively.[154] Frequently, the court applied simply its own sense of justice, without citing any authority whatsoever for its decisions.[155] Remarkably, after 1911 even the court's records were kept only in English, notwithstanding the fact that the court's "official" language was Chinese.[156] (That foreign court officials and law enforcers could not speak Chinese often had serious consequences for defendants. The Municipal Police of the International Settlement who prosecuted in the court ended up periodically charging and imprisoning the wrong Chinese defendant.[157]) The Supreme Court of the Republic of China inevitably refused to recognize the legitimacy of the Mixed Court's judgments, but this was ultimately irrelevant, as there was no appeal from the Mixed Court's decisions.[158] It was its own legal universe, a floating world of Chinese law, wholly unmoored from China.

How did a small Chinese police court in the British-American concession of Shanghai evolve into a nearly all-powerful and all-but-lawless foreign institution? As noted above, the International Settlement evolved over time into a de facto colonial enclave, seeking to provide a system of municipal government for foreign residents of Shanghai. However, as the foreign population came to depend on the labor and services of a growing number of Chinese who resided within the Settlement, it was no longer enough that the foreigners themselves were not subject to Chinese law by virtue of their extraterritorial privileges. They soon wished to obtain legal control over the Chinese population as well. They did so by taking over the Mixed Court, which was originally merely a subunit of the Shanghai magistracy, charged with providing justice to the Chinese population in the Settlement. By doing so, the foreign population was able to apply foreign laws to itself and a Chinese law of its own assemblage to the Chinese.

The court and its history are worth a closer look, analyzed from the perspective of legal Orientalism. For what became one of the most influential courts in the world, the beginnings of the International Mixed Court were modest indeed. As we have seen, the first Unequal Treaties, including the British Treaty of Nanjing in 1842 and the U.S. Treaty of Wanghia in 1844,

provided access to several ports as well as the right of extraterritorial jurisdiction. As part of such access, foreign sojourners in Shanghai were assigned separate residential areas. To that end they drew up a set of Land
Regulations in 1845, with the assistance of local Chinese officials. Significantly, there was nothing in the treaties to suggest that China in any way
conceded its territorial sovereignty in the newly opened Treaty Ports. Foreigners' residential areas were meant to be just that—areas for foreigners to
reside, not to set up a government of their own.[159]

However, when the British and American concessions decided to merge
to form a new entity, what had begun as a Committee of Roads and Jetties
in the British settlement in 1845 became the foundation of what would ultimately constitute, effectively, a city-state of its own. Over time, the original Land Regulations were revised, setting forth a rudimentary charter of
self-governance with a Municipal Council. Once created, the Municipal
Council assumed a number of political functions in the International Settlement that would have been simply unimaginable when the imperial
government authorized the foreign presence in the first place. Most notably,
the Council promulgated municipal regulations to be enforced by a Municipal Police. As we have seen, those regulations were enforced even by the
U.S. Court, although they were most certainly not U.S. law under any definition. During the Taiping Rebellion, the Municipal Council also set up a
militia and a defensive force, ultimately barring Chinese troops from even
entering the Settlement, which became a city literally apart from China.
The Municipal Council built not only roads, jetties, and public buildings,
but it also assumed unilaterally the power of taxation over both the foreign
and Chinese population of the Settlement.[160]

The International Settlement is remarkable in numerous respects. It was
evidently not subject to Chinese rule, but it did not operate under the authority of any one Western national sovereign either. In effect, as noted
above, it had withdrawn not only from Chinese sovereignty but also from
the direct control of British, American, or *any* state authority. By using
Euro-American extraterritorial empire as their springboard, the residents of
the International Settlement were able to turn their enclave into a de facto
territorial colony, even if it had no international legal status de jure. The International Settlement was, in the words of an early twentieth-century jurist,
"a unique example of an International Consortium exercising executive

authority within a district over which it has no territorial rights."[161] Even as precise an observer as the American lawyer and codifier David Dudley Field referred, inaccurately, to having stayed in the "colony" of Shanghai.[162] Tellingly, he conflated the legal status of a colony in the territorial sense, such as Hong Kong, and that of an extraterritorial jurisdiction, such as Shanghai—a distinction that became increasingly academic. Regarding themselves as "Shanghailanders"—a hybridized local identity—at least some foreign residents of Shanghai in fact considered declaring themselves officially an independent city-state, even though such a proposal was never adopted formally.

That the International Settlement was a self-governing Western territory in the middle of Shanghai that had essentially unilaterally seceded from Chinese sovereignty is not the only striking fact about it. In the scholarly literature on Shanghai, this is invariably regarded as a form of semicolonialism, or some other type of *modified* colonial form. Yet there is very little about its actual functioning that warrants such a qualification. A territorially limited and militarily defended jurisdiction, governed by Western residents for Western residents, while exercising plenary authority over the local Chinese population, sounds far more like direct control than any kind of informal imperialism. In important ways the International Settlement is less akin to state-led nineteenth-century imperialism than, say, earlier forms of settlement colonialism by which the first Europeans occupied the New World: they too left behind their own states and set up their own governments, among more or less hostile native populations. Similarly, Shanghailanders at times defied both the sovereignty of China *and* that of their home governments by establishing a system of self-governance that did not depend on outside state authorities—the Shanghai Bund as Plymouth Rock, as it were.

Beyond its ambiguous—or, more accurately, nonexistent—international legal status, two additional legal problems ensued from the fact that the International Settlement did not exist under the sovereignty of any Western government. First, as we have seen, although extraterritoriality allowed Westerners in China to escape Chinese jurisdiction as *individuals*—thus obviating the need to declare a colony in a formal sense—it also meant that the foreign population of Shanghai as a whole was governed by an unsystematic conglomeration of several national legal systems. Whatever types of rights and duties these foreign legal orders provided through their extraterritorial operation in China, one thing, by definition, that they could not provide was a constitutional basis for operating the municipal affairs of the multinational settlement as a whole. In response, the Municipal Council simply arrogated to itself the power to do so. Even though the extraterritorial national courts in Shanghai, including the U.S. Court for China, struggled with how to deal with the Council formally—given its lack of a formal legal status—they nevertheless enforced the regulations it promulgated and came to rely on it institutionally for the enforcement of their own sentences.

As already suggested, the second, related problem pertained to the legal status of the Chinese population in the International Settlement. Formally, they remained Chinese subjects, living in China, subject to Chinese law. Over time, as the number of Chinese residents in the International Settlement increased, and ultimately vastly exceeded the size of the foreign population, this came to be regarded as a problem, and the International Mixed Court in turn was the answer to that problem. Its beginnings were as deceptively modest as those of the Municipal Council. As we have already seen, under extraterritoriality treaties foreign plaintiffs who wanted to sue a Chinese person had to do so in Chinese courts. (As defendants, foreigners could only be sued under their own law, in courts of their own nationality.) To facilitate foreign suits against the Chinese, in 1864 Settlement authorities asked the Shanghai Daotai to appoint a submagistrate to hear such disputes within the Settlement. At the same time, the British consul-general Sir Harry Parkes also requested that a foreign "assessor" be permitted to observe the proceedings in order to ensure that foreign interests were properly protected.[163]

This arrangement formed the foundation of the Mixed Court, its "mixed" character referring to the dual composition of the bench. In 1869 the Shanghai Daotai and the British consul agreed to rudimentary Mixed Court rules (intended as temporary, for one year only), which gave the Mixed Court jurisdiction in all cases involving foreign defendants as well as in civil and commercial disputes among Chinese residents in the Settlement—essentially, all the cases that were required by treaty to be decided under Chinese law, except for criminal cases involving anything more than a minor punishment (which were still to be decided by the Shanghai district magistrate). Ultimately the foreign assessors came to insist not only on a right to be present in suits involving foreign defendants—which was consistent with treaties—

but also whenever foreign *interests* were involved, even if all the parties to a suit were Chinese. In practice, as Tahirih Lee explains, from then on "virtually any excuse justified an Assessor's assignment to the bench."[164] From 1911 an assessor was assigned automatically to *all* cases, even those involving only Chinese parties.[165]

Although at this point the court employed a hybrid Sino-Western procedure and included Western observers, it was still an identifiably Chinese court applying Chinese law. Yet over time the assessors took on a role equal to, and even greater than, the Chinese magistrate. The court's original jurisdictional limitations were overcome as the initial Mixed Court rules were simply rewritten by the consular body in Shanghai. After 1905 assessors decided that their views would trump those of the Chinese magistrate in case of disagreement.[166] From 1910 the assessors, on occasion, even announced the court's judgments formally, despite their putative status as mere observers. When the imperial government fell in 1911, the Municipal Council and Municipal Police took over all of the court's functions: they began to appoint the Chinese magistrate, prosecuted all the cases, paid all court salaries, and operated all the jails in the Settlement. Although the Chinese government protested this takeover bitterly, the system continued until 1927. At that time the Shanghai city government declared that it would no longer enforce the court's judgments. Thereafter, to escape its judgment, Chinese defendants would only have to cross from the International Settlement to the Chinese city, and the court finally lost all its effective power.

Nevertheless, during its entire history the Mixed Court purported to be a *Chinese* court authorized to apply *Chinese* law only. This was precisely its utility. While extraterritoriality exempted the foreigners in the International Settlement from Chinese law, they had no plausible justification to apply Western law to the Chinese. The perfect formal solution was to colonize the body of law that did apply to the Chinese residents of the Settlement—Chinese law. As we might expect, what the Mixed Court produced was probably even closer to a Borgesian hallucination of "Chinese law" than the U.S. Court's jurisprudence was of "U.S. law." However, in the case of the U.S. Court for China, the incoherence of its jurisprudence posed an ever-present threat to its legitimacy. With the Mixed Court, an opposite logic prevailed. Since the body of law it applied was at least notionally "Chinese," the *more* despotic it made that law appear, the *greater* its original justification: the administration of Chinese law in the Settlement could not be trusted to a purely Chinese court *because* Chinese law was arbitrary and despotic—a spectacular instance of legal Orientalism's capacity to produce the conditions that validate it in the first place.

Indeed, the application of Chinese law in the Mixed Court was little more than an act of legal ventriloquism. Since it was the assessor's opinion that was enforceable, not the magistrate's, the foreign assessors ultimately determined what Chinese law was. And as to how they made that determination, one British assessor admitted openly that he had "not been guided by any legal principles or any rule of law" other than his own sense of justice. This was evidently a Chinese law that was fashioned by foreigners. The court criminalized a number of uncodified offenses, and even when the court did refer to written authority, those authorities were only incidentally Chinese.[167] The court eventually recognized the Provisional Criminal Code of the Republic of China, but it enforced it only selectively, determining the applicability of each provision separately and at its own discretion— and even when it found a provision to be applicable, it did not deem itself bound by the prescribed punishment. (We already saw the same questionable strategy of statutory interpretation practiced by the U.S. Court for China, which would follow parts of the codes of Alaska and the District of Columbia only in order to ignore the penalties they provided.[168]) The other main source of criminal law in the court were the Police Regulations of the International Settlement—again, as we have already observed, a body of law that was evidently *not* Chinese law of any description, as it was promulgated despite China's bitter protests to the contrary.[169] As to civil law, especially commercial law, the court regarded itself even freer to construct its own jurisprudence, operating as it did from the Orientalist assumption that Chinese law was exclusively penal and that there was consequently no such thing as Chinese commercial law.[170] All of this is perhaps explained in part by the fact that most assessors were laypersons without *any* legal training, in either Western or Chinese law—something that was problematic enough even in less formally constituted consular courts, but far more so in a tribunal with a vast jurisdiction, complex cases, and a huge volume.[171]

Considered in terms of legal Orientalism, whatever the court's failings, they were always seen as reflections of the inferior nature of Chinese law—

rather than, say, shortcomings caused by the court's mixed composition and dubious administration. With reference to the Mixed Court, a member of Parliament in London regarded both its procedural and substantive law simply as evidence of "Chinese barbarism, unmixed with the faintest trace of European sense of humanity."[172] The concern with barbarism was not unjustified, but it is eminently unclear whether such barbarism should be attributed to "Chinese law" or its Western inventors and administrators. The one penalty whose execution was in fact delegated to the Shanghai magistracy itself, outside the International Settlement, was capital punishment. Until the very end, the Chinese magistrates in the Mixed Court insisted on referring death penalty cases to their superiors, in keeping with a historic tradition whereby all death sentences had to be affirmed by the emperor himself.[173] Nevertheless, the Municipal Police of the International Settlement did not trust the Shanghai authorities to execute Chinese defendants whom the Mixed Court had sentenced to death, and they insisted on attending the executions in person, ready to assist as needed— for example, by making convicts drink cement before being hanged, to ensure a successful result. Not-so-humane pre- and post-execution practices of the Municipal Police included parading the convicts around the streets of the International Settlement beforehand, and hanging their heads on telegraph poles after the execution.[174] It is easy to concede that such procedures were barbaric, but their inhumanity was surely no less European than it was Chinese.

In the end, there was a remarkable Western consensus that, in the final analysis, the Mixed Court "really" was a Chinese court. That was the verdict of the British Supreme Court of China as well the U.S. Court for China, both of which recognized the Mixed Court's decisions *as* Chinese law.[175] Anatol Kotenev, the official historian of the court, has likewise insisted on the court's irreducible Chineseness. While he could not but admit that the court was in fact run by Settlement authorities, he insisted that this did not in any way reflect a Western disregard for the Chinese administration of law. Rather, it was "nothing more than the natural result of an unavoidable historical process," due to "an immutable law of logic which has forced the Chinese nation to give up a part of its sovereign right."[176]

Kotenev was a White Russian refugee in Shanghai, and it may not surprise us that he was an apologist for the court. What *is* genuinely surprising is how enduring the appeal of his Orientalist narrative has proven. To consider its appeal, it is useful to analyze Thomas Stephens's 1992 history of the court, *Order and Discipline in China: The Shanghai Mixed Court, 1911–27.* (Regrettably, except for Kotenev's partial and dated account of the court's work, published in 1925, this is the only published monograph on the subject.)[177] Stephens urges that we approach the tribunal's jurisprudence precisely in terms that this book identifies as the discourse of legal Orientalism. For Stephens, the contrast between Western and Chinese law could not be starker. He describes Western legal systems as embodiments of "transcendent, rigid, universal imperatives of conduct," while he regards Chinese law as an instance of a "disciplinary"—as opposed to properly "legal"—system, based on hierarchical subordination to particularistic norms.[178] Ultimately the notion of "Chinese law" is an oxymoron for Stephens, a monstrous confusion of two different normative orders, for it is as impossible to combine the two systems as to mix "oil and water."[179] For Stephens, as for Kotenev, the tension between them is ultimately unsustainable and has its own built-in historical logic. Just as the particular must yield to the universal, so Westerners in Shanghai had little choice but to take over the Mixed Court. Therefore, their actions were not an instance of legal imperialism but of legal assistance: they provided a crucial object lesson for the Chinese in the universal values of rule-of-law.

The basic structure of Stephens's argument is simple enough. In general terms, it is the same argument the U.S. Court for China used to justify its mission, as we have seen. Yet there was one major difference between the U.S. Court for China and the Mixed Court. The Mixed Court and Stephens are placed in the dilemma of having to use *Chinese law* as a model of rule-of-law for the Chinese—a position that would seem to be an impossible one. The way in which Stephens manages this contradiction is worth analyzing in some detail.

When Stephens enters through the looking glass into the world of the Mixed Court, anything that corresponds to the definition of law becomes identified as Western, while everything that is not law is identified as Chinese. He makes it clear that in his estimation the Mixed Court had no claim whatsoever to legality by the standards of Western jurisprudence. Its authority was grounded in nothing more than the brute force of power—the fact that it could enforce its judgments, since it was ultimately backed by the military might of the Treaty Powers. However, rather than reflecting poorly on the Powers, their reliance on sheer domination becomes a sign of *Chinese* lawlessness. That is, the Mixed Court's lack of legality did not bother the Chinese under its jurisdiction because they *expected* to be ruled not by law but by "discipline"—a term that in Stephens's usage has only a slightly less pejorative ring than "Oriental despotism." Since the court's procedures had been "formally promulgated by an acknowledged superior authority," Stephens explains, their application as compulsory "was accepted by all subordinate Chinese without a murmur."[180]

Yet Stephens's argument goes further, as he insists that the Mixed Court is not only evidence of Chinese lawlessness, but, paradoxically, the court also constituted a positive example from which the Chinese *should* have learned Western law, and that their failure to do so in turn signifies China's inability "to be drawn into the mainstream of Western jurisprudence."[181] The court's jurisprudence thus counts simultaneously as both Chinese nonlaw and Western law. The ways in which it fell short of law and acted in a disciplinary mode count against the possibility of Chinese law and prove its nonexistence, whereas the ways in which it did approximate the adjudicative mode count as Western law from which the Chinese should have learned—and their alleged failure to learn provides even greater proof of the unlegality of the Chinese. Stephens's analytic framework makes his "findings" ultimately inevitable: nonlaw is Chinese while law is Western.

Simply as a matter of logic, it may thus be a non sequitur for Stephens to use the Mixed Court first as an instance of law's absence in China and then as an example of law's promise and potential from which the Chinese should have learned. His analysis evidently participates in the continuing circulation of discourses of legal Orientalism. In the Mixed Court—as well as in the U.S. Court for China—the contradictions of rule-of-law are so apparent that they can be seen with a naked eye. It is instructive that Stephens insists that any perception of "law" in the operations of the Mixed Court is only a kind of optical illusion, "an instance of the projection of the images of Western jurisprudence upon the realities of the Chinese disciplinary system."[182] When we look at China as legal outsiders, much of the time law seems to recede to the periphery and all we can see is the residue that is discipline.[183] And conversely, when we look at our own courts, what we tend to see is law, while discipline remains an invisible aura around it.

Yet what makes the International Mixed Court perhaps most amenable for an analysis in terms of legal Orientalism is the fact that in all but form, the International Settlement was a perfect replica of territorial colonialism proper. As a de facto foreign settlement colony inside China, the International Settlement in Shanghai had a classic system of legal dualism for its governance: foreign law for the foreign settlers and native law for the natives. The foreign law was delivered through extraterritorial Western courts and Chinese law through a territorial, nominally Chinese Mixed Court. The fate of Chinese law in Shanghai was the same as that of native law in other colonial settings. When administered by foreign judges in accordance with foreign procedures, it became essentially a foreign fabrication. The main functional difference was that the International Settlement embodied a system of legal pluralism that went far beyond legal dualism. There was not *one* system of Western law in Shanghai but more than a dozen extraterritorial ones.

Moreover, given that the role of the foreign-controlled Mixed Court in this structure was indeed to apply Chinese law, any distinction between legal Orientalism as *a system of representation* of Chinese law and Chinese law as the *object* of such representations simply collapsed. Euro-American representations of Chinese law *became* Chinese law. In short, the International Mixed Court took over the signal function of modern sovereignty—the power to define and apply the law that applies within a territorially defined jurisdiction. In the International Settlement, the foreign residents were not only exempt from Chinese law but defined what *was* Chinese law, and then applied it to Chinese subjects living on sovereign Chinese territory.

Stated differently, while the application of U.S. law in China was justified by the legal fiction of extraterritoriality, the application of Chinese law in China required no such fictions: it was the law of the territorial sovereign. Instead, Chinese law itself became a fiction, in order to suit the imperial purposes of its foreign administrators. In a legal landscape where the line between fact and fiction blurred into indistinction, the difference between territorial and extraterritorial application of law likewise hardly mattered— while American law was *extra*territorialized, Chinese law was, in a sense, *de*territorialized in the multinational International Settlement.

There were, of course, true believers, such as Caleb Cushing who complained of certain "speculative publicists" of international law who dismissed extraterritoriality "*as if* it were a mere fiction of law." For Cushing, extraterritoriality was real. While he may have taken his categories rather literally, in one key regard he was right. Whatever else one might say about legal fictions, they are *true in law*. In the end, law provides its own foundation.[184]

Consider, for example, the ease with which U.S. district courts took jurisdiction over actions brought by Cantonese tea merchants in the nineteenth century, seeking to collect on U.S. buyers some of whom owed staggering sums. In their pleadings, the Chinese merchants' U.S. lawyers employed a jurisdictional fiction of the utmost transparency. When suing Pennsylvania merchants, for example, they simply asserted that Canton *was* Philadelphia. Their complaints baldly recited agreements made "at Canton, to wit, at Philadelphia." In his study of such suits, Frederic Grant, Jr. concludes, "This fiction was used, without recorded challenge, in every American action brought by or against a [Chinese] hong merchant."[185] In the asymmetrical world of legal Orientalism, Canton was perhaps not Boston, but in certain circumstances it *could* be Philadelphia.

What we have witnessed in this chaper is thus a series of collapsing distinctions: distinction between legal Orientalism as a system of representation of Chinese law versus Chinese law itself as a historical and institutional practice; opposition between law versus Orient; territorial versus nonterritorial forms of law and colonialism; and, finally, an imperial inability to maintain a distinction between self and other—as evidenced by Judge Lobingier, who wanted to promulgate the law of the Republic of China as the formal law of the U.S. Court for China, and the International Mixed Court, which simply called its law "Chinese." And confusing the other for oneself of course also allowed one to characterize one's legal enterprise in the Orient as legal aid, not legal imperialism.

Together with Chapter 4, this chapter has sought to demonstrate that there is an important, albeit remarkably unknown, history of American extraterritorial empire in the Orient in the nineteenth and twentieth centuries. That empire was conjoined with a larger multinational enterprise of subjugating China, represented by the municipal government of the International Settlement (upon whose police powers the United States relied) and the pseudo-Chinese International Mixed Court (which permitted Americans in China to sue Chinese defendants under a Chinese law literally dictated by foreigners). And as we have seen, this extraterritorial empire in Asia was also closely articulated with territorial forms of American imperialism, both in internal U.S. colonies and overseas ones, even as it remained distinct from them—in the form of prisoners being trafficked from China to the Philippines, judges from the Philippines to China, and bodies of law from the District of Columbia and Alaska to China.

The history of this empire is in turn part of an uneven global history of legal Orientalism. At the same time, seen from the opposite perspective, it is part of an unrecognized global history of American law. That the multiple histories and trajectories of Chinese law and U.S. law are so inextricable reflects precisely the global nature of both. American extraterritorial jurisdiction in China is a critical moment in the rise of the United States and of U.S. law over the course of the nineteenth and twentieth centuries, rooted ultimately in a long-standing tradition of European prejudices about the despotic constitution of the Orient. From the vantage point of the twenty-first century, the forcible introduction of North Atlantic legal institutions in China in the nineteenth century can be viewed as the fraught point of origin of Chinese legal modernization, a crucial juncture in the globalization of modern law. As we enter the Asian century with China at its center, law's appeal remains ambivalent, its timeless promises of freedom troubled by a long history of legal imperialism.

CHAPTER SIX

Epilogue: Colonialism without Colonizers

> The rule of law signifies that a political civilization has developed to a certain historic stage. As the crystallization of human wisdom, it is desired and pursued by people of all countries.
>
> —PRC White Paper on Rule of Law

IF SUCH IS the historical itinerary of legal Orientalism, or at least a partial account of its global travels, what is its contemporary status, especially in light of the extraordinary law reforms that have taken place in China since 1978? Given that U.S. extraterritorial jurisdiction in China was abolished formally in 1943—it had already ended de facto with the Japanese occupation—what is the standing of U.S. law in China today? And what is the status of China in the American legal imagination? Even as China's economic and political status has risen globally, its legal standing seems to be in permanent decline since Tiananmen and the concomitant post–Cold War rise of the twinned discourses of rule-of-law and human rights.

This final chapter is an epilogue that begins by briefly reviewing China's postimperial legal history and then considers the afterlife of America's extraterritorial empire and its replacement by a range of multilateral institutions after World War II. Today, these new organizations—especially the World Trade Organization—have transformed not only China but the entire world in profound ways. As a result of the globalization of liberal and neoliberal institutions discourses of legal Orientalism are today as commonplace in China as they are in the United States. If extraterritorial empire was a kind of colonialism without colonies, one might view many aspects of China's modern law reforms as a colonialism without even colonizers. As the language of rights, and especially those of property and contract, come to play increasing roles in the PRC, the Chinese lifeworld itself is changing.

This epilogue is not an indictment of change—anything that is alive is always changing—but an attempt to understand the nature and political as well as cultural significance of contemporary Chinese law reform. At the same time, while it can be instructive to examine certain aspects of modern Chinese legal development as a form of self-colonization—the colonization of Chinese subjectivity—law's triumph in the Orient remains far from complete, as an analysis of corporation law in China today will demonstrate. Perhaps unexpectedly, the changing world of business enterprise contains resources for imagining new—and re-imagining some very old— legal, economic, and political subjects.

Apart from the living law of business enterprise, Chinese legal thinkers have challenged conventional legal categories in theoretical work as well. Indeed, legal theory constitutes an important arena in which state power is negotiated in the PRC. Chinese liberals and communists alike share a tendency to decry what they regard as a historical inheritance of despotic imperial rule. But however persuasive Orientalist discourses may be and however great their cross-ideological appeal, the contemporary Chinese legal imagination necessarily exceeds their boundaries. New ideas continue to emerge, as do novel configurations of old and new ideas.

At the same time, legal Orientalism's history continues to reverberate in the United States. Congress has repealed the Chinese Exclusion Laws and the U.S. Supreme Court has overruled *In re Ross* and the extraconstitutional application of American law overseas that it authorized.[1] However, the U.S. Supreme Court has never overruled the *Chinese Exclusion Case* that upheld the enactment of exclusionary immigration laws in the first place. Although the ugly legacy of that case and its progeny is largely hidden today, it remains available to be invoked against new groups of Orientals—such as Muslim terrorists, most recently. In the end, law's Orient designates a discursive position, not a static group of persons associated with a determinate geographic region. Today, as before, law needs its Others.[2]

After a summary of China's twentieth-century legal history and a consideration of America's extraterritorial empire today, the bulk of this chapter focuses on Chinese legal reforms after 1978, examining first some of the ways in which law has indeed colonized the Chinese lifeworld. It analyzes this phenomenon as a kind of self-Orientalization resulting from the internalization of the norms of legal subjectivity. It then turns to two sites where different types of non-normative subjects—old and new, legal and nonlegal—continue to live: the "real" world of Chinese business organization and the imaginative world of legal theory. Finally, the chapter returns to the contemporary status of legal Orientalism in the United States, and it concludes by speculating on the future of both China and the United States in the world that legal Orientalism has made.

THE DISENCHANTMENT OF CHINA'S POST-IMPERIAL SOVEREIGNTY

It is not the aim of this book to provide a comprehensive account of Chinese law reforms up to the present. Yet before turning to a closer analysis of China's post–1978 legal developments, it is useful to summarize by way of background some key aspects of its prior legal history in the twentieth century. With the collapse of the imperial state in 1911 and the subsequent establishment of the Republic of China (ROC), China self-consciously sought to establish itself as a modern nation-state, in accordance with the norms of (Euro-American) international law. This entailed the reconceptualization of Chinese sovereignty as a constitutionally defined legal order in a world of other similarly organized sovereign states—a process that Mayfair Yang has aptly called the "disenchantment" of Chinese sovereignty.[3] No longer insisting on its singularity as a Middle Kingdom, China is today a member of the United Nations, one nation among others, and in the process it has historicized its imperial past on the basis of equivalence with other national histories. The Qing empire of the nineteenth century has become simply another "international legal person" (in the jargon of international lawyers), with the proper name "China."[4]

During the interwar years, the United States and France proved to be particularly eager to provide assistance to the ROC in this project. American attention to Chinese legal development was part of a larger missionary mentality. As President Woodrow Wilson phrased it messianically, it was "the obligation of the United States to promote the modern trinity—

democracy, the rule of law, and Christianity."[5] Among the first legal missionaries from the United States to China was Frank Goodnow—a scholar of administrative law, professor at Columbia University, and the first president of the American Political Science Association. His dubious chief contribution to China's legal development was to recommend the establishment of a constitutional monarchy, a form of government he found fitting for a populace that suffered from a "total lack of any idea of law."[6] Yuan Shikai, the second president of the ROC, was only too happy to exploit Goodnow's intellectual prestige to justify a short-lived coup in which he declared himself emperor. After World War II, Goodnow was followed by Roscoe Pound, the former dean of Harvard Law School, who became an adviser to the ROC until 1949.[7]

Although the Nationalist government was never able to exercise effective jurisdiction over the entire country—at various times the Chinese mainland was in the throes of competing warlords, a Communist-Nationalist civil war, and eventually under attack by Japan as well—its law reforms were ambitious, and driven by the express goal of throwing off the yoke of extraterritoriality. At least on paper, and to a limited geographic extent even institutionally, it set up a "scientific" legal system on the model of the European civil law tradition, precisely to defeat long-lived Orientalist prejudices and to show that China was in fact fully capable of establishing a system of rule-of-law.[8]

However, with the Nationalist regime's 1949 retreat to Taiwan, the law reform efforts of the first half of the twentieth century came to naught in the Chinese mainland. Among the first acts taken up by the PRC was the abolition of the ROC legal system.[9] During the Maoist period law was in radical decline, ideologically and institutionally. One important exception to a general indifference to policy making by legislation was the passage in 1950 of the Land Reform Law and the Marriage Law, designed to achieve a redistribution of land and patriarchal privilege, respectively. Predictably, the former was carried out with far greater zeal than the latter.[10]

As a matter of socialist legal theory, such inattention to law was perfectly defensible. In the orthodox Marxian view, articulated most forcefully by the Soviet legal theorist Evgeny Pashukanis in the 1920s, there is no such thing as "socialist law," as law is simply code for the protection of bourgeois class interests, a mere ideological reflection of the material relations of production on which capitalism rests.[11] Nevertheless, as a political matter

Stalin refused to give up law as an instrument of rule, insisting that Soviet law differed fundamentally from its bourgeois counterpart because it reflected the interests of the working class—a position that was articulated by the jurist Andrei Vyshinsky who came to stand for Soviet jurisprudential orthodoxy.[12] In the 1950s China at first sought to follow the revisionist Soviet model of "socialist legality." However, early experiments with law soon gave way to mass campaigns and, ultimately, the Cultural Revolution during which law sank to its ideological nadir, exemplified perhaps best by the title of a 1967 editorial in the *People's Daily*, "In the Praise of Lawlessness." Effectively, Mao Zedong became a living *nomos*, a law unto himself, and what mattered in politics was not the juridical distinction between legal and illegal but the political one between friend and enemy.[13]

Whatever one thinks of China's legal past, it is a singular historical fact that no state has ever produced as much organizational, procedural, and substantive law as quickly as China has since 1978.[14] To cite just one statistic, the country's enormous judicial system today consists of more than 3,000 basic courts and nearly 200,000 judges.[15] Significantly, the principle of rule-of-law itself is today an official part of the governing ideology of the nation. In 1999 the Constitution was amended to declare China a "socialist rule-of-law state" (社会主义法治国家), and in 2008 the State Council issued a white paper entitled "China's Efforts and Achievements in Promoting the Rule-of-Law." Writing the principle of rule-of-law into a Constitution that references also the laws of dialectical and historical materialism poses a major epistemological challenge, which the white paper seeks to overcome by insisting that the Chinese idea of rule-of-law is simultaneously universal (it "signifies that a political civilization has developed to a certain historic stage") *and* particular ("in line with the basic tasks of socialism, and has distinctive Chinese characteristics"). To set the historical record straight, it also declares that the Chinese legal system has a five-thousand-year history and has contributed significantly to "the legal civilization of mankind."[16]

Although the United States plays an oversized role in the Chinese legal imagination and legal politics today—in human rights as well as in the legal structures of capitalism—it is important to recognize the diverse genealogical origins of modern Chinese law. While the PRC initially turned to the Soviet Union as a model, the Communist Party studied the earlier reforms of the ROC as well, which in turn were influenced primarily by the German legal system, mostly as it was interpreted in Japan. As we have seen, the common law model offered by the U.S. Court for China hardly impressed the Chinese in the first half of the twentieth century, while the international prestige of the German civil code—the revered *Bürgerliches Gesetzbuch*—was at the time at its zenith, representing the state of the art in legal science.[17]

Although the PRC legal system is still based formally on a more or less Sinified version of the civil law model, with socialist adaptations, the United States is today the chief source of transplanted substantive law, especially in the area of economic law. At the same time, U.S. law is shaping Chinese legal practices more generally as well, through daily encounters with common lawyers and, especially after China's entry into the WTO, with the general "Americanization" of transnational legal practice.[18] The hegemonic status of U.S. law is in turn part of a larger economy of knowledge and expertise. For much of the generation that came of age after the Cultural Revolution "the only worthwhile knowledge comes from the West, particularly from the United States."[19]

EXTRATERRITORIAL EMPIRE OF AMERICAN LAW TODAY

Having sketched the broad outlines of Chinese law's twentieth-century trajectory, let us turn to that of U.S. law, especially in terms of Sino-U.S. relations. Given the unfortunate history of U.S. extraterritorial jurisdiction in China, how did American legal thought become an object of such admiration and emulation?

World War II was followed not only by the decolonization of formal empires but also by the final disappearance of consular jurisdiction of the Oriental kind. The United States surrendered its extraterritorial jurisdiction in China in 1943. (It held onto the last vestiges of its Barbary Treaties until 1956, when it finally gave up extraterritorial privileges in Tangier, Morocco.)[20] However, emerging from World War II as a global superpower, the United States could easily afford to see old forms of imperial power vanish. In their place it built a new kind of international order that recognized American hegemony without the considerable administrative and ideological costs associated with formal territorial imperialism.

As Kal Raustiala sums up the nature of America's leadership in the post-War world, "It was predicated not on *territorial* control but on *extraterritorial* power and presence."[21] From this perspective, the century of U.S. extraterritorial jurisdiction in China, together with the Open Door policy of which it was an integral part, is better understood not simply as an institutional relic of early modern European–Ottoman relations that somehow found its way into the Far East and survived there into the twentieth century. Rather, it becomes visible as a precursor of modern—even postmodern—forms of neocolonial power, predicated on legally protected freedom of trade without formal territorial control.

It was precisely the desire to extract economic profit from other lands without assuming administrative responsibility for them that underlay the British notion of "free trade imperialism" in the mid-Victorian era, which in turn sought to realize the vision announced by Thomas Babington Macauley in British India: "To trade with civilised men is infinitely more profitable than to govern savages."[22] For in no way does trade's freedom imply substantive equality among those trading. As Bertrand Russell observed in 1922, at the conclusion of his Chinese lecture tour, "It is quite possible to dominate China without infringing the principle of the Open Door. This principle merely ensures that the domination everywhere shall be American, because America is the strongest Power financially and commercially."[23]

In his analysis of America's post-War role, Raustiala identifies three contemporary forms of extraterritorial power: the establishment of a global network of military bases in other countries, the selective application of U.S. laws extraterritorially, and the creation of a system of multilateral institutions that extend American influence globally. It is illuminating to consider each in turn. In order to protect members of the military stationed at U.S. bases overseas as well as military contractors and accompanying civilians, so-called Status of Force Agreements (SOFAs) provide them with extraterritorial immunity.[24] Collectively these agreements represent a major extension of American law abroad, covering U.S. bases all around the globe; in 2007, the U.S. military operated 823 facilities in thirty-nine countries.[25] The SOFAs constitute the closest modern analogue to the Unequal Treaties of old, as they provide a blanket exemption from local law—civil and criminal—to those under their protection.

At the same time the United States has extended the extraterritorial reach of its domestic legislation unilaterally, without even formal consent provided by treaties. Claiming jurisdiction based on the extraterritorial *effects* of a person's actions (rather than merely the territorial location of the person acting), the United States has begun to regulate increasingly aggressively activities that take place outside the nation's borders. The extraterritorial enforcement of American law has been especially notable in securities regulation, antitrust law, environmental law, anti-corruption legislation, and criminal law—foreign protests notwithstanding.

Yet by far the most important means of extending the reach of American power has been the establishment of a set of multinational institutions whose charters collectively make up the constitution of the world as we know it today: the World Bank, the International Monetary Fund, the General Agreement on Tariffs and Trade, the North Atlantic Treaty Organization, and the United Nations. Under American leadership, these institutions, together with the World Trade Organization (WTO)—the successor to the General Agreement on Tariffs and Trade—have sought to reconstruct the world essentially in the image of the United States: a global community of liberal-democratic states committed to free trade. (Importantly, the promotion of democracy globally does not mean the promotion of *global democracy*: the United States continues to insist on its exceptional status as an international leader.) These post-War institutions have been so effective in harmonizing legal regimes across the world that in many areas, especially ones pertaining to the economy, it would be largely redundant for the United States to assert its laws extraterritorially.

Indeed, the earlier regime of U.S. extraterritoriality in China, together with the U.S.-brokered Open Door policy, was in important ways functionally similar to the WTO— with the critical difference that China's participation in the WTO is consensual.[26] (China was neither consulted about nor did it consent to the Open Door, which was an understanding by others *regarding* China, not a policy by China.) Both regimes are premised on respect for China's territorial integrity, with open and equal access to Chinese markets. As we have seen, as part of the Open Door the United States and other Treaty Powers insisted on extraterritorial jurisdiction until China modernized its legal system. "Modernization," in turn, was shorthand for adopting a legal system based on the Euro-American model that would in turn make Western rights of extraterritoriality superfluous. In this regard, the WTO regime is even bolder, insisting on obtaining directly what the Open Door sought only indirectly. As part of the price of admission into the WTO in the first place, China had to agree to alter its legal institutions to conform to North Atlantic standards.

As the ideology of rule-of-law has become a key component in the globalization of norms of free trade and liberal democracy, the World Bank
and the WTO count among its most dedicated adherents today. Yet the
rule-of-law discourse today remains one of contradictions, as before. When
China entered the WTO in 2001, its accession protocol was of record
length and filled with unprecedented ad hoc directives for the reorganization of China's economic and legal systems. Collectively, these directives
exceeded both quantitatively and qualitatively what had been demanded of
any other member of the WTO, including other so-called transition economies. Ironically, in order to ensure that China comply with the requirements of rule-of-law, the WTO ignored its *own* constitutional rules—much
as the United States suspended the operation of the U.S. Constitution in
excluding Chinese immigration in the nineteenth century. While WTO
rules are based on market economy assumptions, they do not legally require
that member states structure their political economies in a particular way.
China's accession protocol, however, makes it an international legal obligation for the PRC to convert to a market economy—an extraordinary surrender of China's freedom to structure its political economy. As Julia Ya
Qin points out, the singling out of China creates different classes among
the member-states of the organization and thus violates the WTO's fundamental principle of nondiscrimination, while also contravening the organization's overall commitment to a rule-based trading system.[27]

No doubt the sheer size of China's economy was one major cause of Western anxiety about its WTO membership, but equally importantly, now as
before, China continues to be defined by not-having-law, and as before, this
means that China must be *made* lawful. As a goal, lawfulness is surely defensible, but its defense still needs to be articulated. It is not simply self-
evident, and it must take into account the historical and logical contradictions that it necessarily entails. What does it mean for the WTO and others
to *demand*, possibly even impose, a regime of rule-of-law, even as they suspend their own rules in dealing with China? As an ideal, rule-of-law is far
more attractive than forcing China to open its markets for opium, yet that
fact alone does not relieve its advocates from the burden of a history where
demands for law were often window dressings for other agendas.[28]

Indeed, China continues to occupy an unstable position in teleological
schemas of U.S.-led legal development. The Chinese economic and legal
systems are today said to be in transition, much in the same way as the post-

Socialist states of Eastern Europe have been described by the ever-growing academic subfield of "transitologists."[29] As Chapter 1 suggested, the unstated implication of the seemingly innocuous notion of transition is that whatever distinctive forms China may have adopted for now, those forms are ultimately not authentic. Until it has fully "modernized," China will remain in transit. Moreover, to the extent that "we" are *not* in transition, by implication "we have arrived" at the ultimate destination: a (highly idealized) U.S.-style market economy.[30]

Even if the naïve evangelism of the Law and Development movement of the 1970s has receded, at least in its overt form, it has been replaced with the ostensibly more generous assumption that China and the rest of the world will, one day, simply "catch up" with the West (趕上).[31] Benign as this sounds, this developmental model is only one recent example of neo-Hegelian evolutionary schemes in which "China always furnishes a beginning to be improved on," in Haun Saussy's phrase.[32] It should be evident that the relationship between the Chinese legal tradition and modernity cannot be simply a one-sided affair, with the West providing the blueprint for a modern legal order and China merely executing it.

JURIDIFICATION OF THE CHINESE LIFEWORLD

From this perspective, how should we understand the stunning legal changes, and changes in attitudes to law, that have taken place in China since 1978? In many ways, they would seem to represent the triumph of the logic of legal Orientalism, with China slowly clearing away the obstacles posed by its (particular) political traditions to make way for law's (universal) development—exemplified in turn by a U.S.-championed rule-of-law model as the new "standard of civilization," the ultimate measure of constitutional fitness for inclusion in international society.

Insofar as we have analyzed the history of America's extraterritorial empire in China as a colonialism without colonies, much of China's modern law reform can be interpreted as a colonialism without even colonizers. No matter how the Chinese government chooses to characterize its political and legal values—"socialist," "Asian," or informed by "Chinese characteristics"—it remains a fact of fundamental importance that the PRC today has in fact "juridified" itself in terms of how it exercises its sovereignty both externally vis-à-vis other states and internally over its citizens. As far as the source of its external sovereignty is concerned, it has been inducted into the system of nation-states organized under the aegis of (Euro-American) international law, and today it is a member not only of the United Nations but also the WTO.

These developments stand in stark contrast to China's erstwhile disinterest in accommodating itself to North Atlantic modernity. If indeed the tragic irony of the Opium War was its use of force in the name of free trade, it is an equally great irony that some one hundred and fifty years later China waged a major political battle to gain admission into the trade regime of the WTO. While it is possible to analyze China's membership in the WTO as "extraterritoriality by other means"—territorializing Euro-American law *in* China *as* Chinese law—there is an even more profound sense in which the colonial project of modern law has been successful. That is its ability to colonize the legal subject, and even the notion of the political itself. Today law *is* universal, not only in a geographic sense—having literally colonized the planet—but also in the phenomenological sense of having colonized the lifeworld. Evidently the modern legal project has succeeded in creating Chinese subjects who desire law and conceive of politics in juridified terms.

From this perspective, the juridification of Chinese sovereignty is indeed one of the crowning achievements of international law in the twentieth century. At the same time, China's national subjects too have been clothed in the legal garb of modern citizenship. It goes without saying that Chinese citizenship remains a distinctive one. As Elizabeth Perry notes, the Chinese term for citizen (公民) means, in its literal translation, a "public person"— connoting "collective membership in the polity, rather than a claim to individual or inalienable rights vis-à-vis the state."[33] Nevertheless, even in the PRC citizenship is a *legal* status, conferred on a modern political subject. And whatever the official Chinese conception of politics may be today, there is no question that Chinese citizens are conscious of their rights as citizens: they are increasingly suing their employers, landlords, each other, and even the state. The putatively nonlegal nonsubject of the Orientalist imagination seems to be well on its way to becoming a legal subject.[34]

Consider, also, the simple but remarkable fact that the PRC has yielded even on the ideologically fraught question of (bourgeois) human rights, a foundational element of the United States' post–Cold War ideological mission. Conceding that being opposed to the idea of human rights is no longer a tenable position in global politics, the PRC enshrined human rights in its Constitution in 2004 and now publishes even its own white papers on human rights.[35] Rather than remain simply an object of withering human rights critiques by others, the PRC now monitors the rest of the world's compliance with human rights—notably, that of the United States. If Confucian humanism once defined personhood in terms of *rites,* while orthodox Marxism does not even acknowledge legality as a principle, there could hardly be better proof that the modern Chinese subject is today a bearer of *rights.*

To recognize the relatively recent provenance of a rights-based notion of political subjectivity in China is not to dismiss it as nothing more than a foreign imposition, nor to yearn nostalgically for vanishing indigenous notions of politics. For one thing, while rights consciousness is a real phenomenon in China, its triumph remains far from complete and its spread uneven, geographically as well as demographically. More significantly, the Chinese surely have as much of a "right" to think in terms of rights as anyone else. Just as notions of political subjectivity have changed dramatically over time in the North Atlantic world, it would be unreasonable to expect that Chinese conceptions would remain frozen in time.

It is worth pausing here to consider the peculiarly spare ontology of the modern state, at least in its dominant liberal version. In the final analysis it recognizes only two kinds of authentic subjects—the state itself and the individual. Between the two, there is no room for other metaphysically "real" subjects. Any would-be independent entities mediating between them are ultimately reduced either to creatures of the state ("public") or to associations composed of individuals ("private"). As we saw in Chapter 3, it is precisely this bipolar nature of Anglo-American liberalism that has made the corporation such a tortured object of jurisprudential speculation. Theorists have worked hard to stabilize it as a legal subject—as a person in its own right, amenable to a logic insisting that all rights and duties must be held by a person modeled on the individual. On the one hand, we might regard the state-individual dichotomy as a practical, and even elegant, way to conceptualize politics. On the other hand, we might also see it as a reflection of a woefully impoverished modern legal imagination—impoverished if we compare it, say, to the overabundance of subjects in medieval political cosmologies, consisting of numerous overlapping jurisdictions and multiple sources of law and sovereignty. (This is not to idealize or romanticize the medieval political world, only to note its more complex theories of political and legal subjectivity.)[36]

Yet today the centralized modern state has successfully colonized the entire juridico-political field, carefully evacuating the intermediate space between itself and the singular individual of all other autonomous sources of authority. It is precisely this reductive political logic that rendered the events in Tiananmen Square on June 4, 1989, instantly intelligible to a global audience. In Michael Dutton's acute observation, there is only one street scene in China that is "worth remembering in Western eyes": the iconic image of the Tank Man on Tiananmen Square.[37] There could be no starker depiction of the solitary encounter between the two main protagonists of the liberal political universe than the image of a lone but heroic individual facing off the power of the state. Significantly, as Gloria Davies points out, the Tank Man image does not enjoy anywhere near the same currency in China, where its appeal has been superseded by an image of three students kneeling to petition the government on the steps of the Great Hall of the People, weeks before the massacre—an image invoking a Confucian-inflected conception of politics, based not on rights but on reciprocal duties of loyalty and protection.[38]

However, while rights possess no magical powers, they may in fact be necessary in a modern centralized state, which is precisely the form that both the PRC and ROC have taken.[39] Again, this should not surprise us, given that it is the only political form that international society today recognizes *as* a state. In the face of the overwhelming centralization of political authority and the state's monopoly on the exercise of legitimate violence on Earth, political life without rights may be literally unlivable today. It remains an undeniable fact of political life that social contracts can be breached and constitutions disregarded. While all states justify themselves by purporting to protect their citizens, when the modern state with its unprecedented concentration of power fails, it fails spectacularly. That, indeed, seems to be the grim lesson of the twentieth century.

At the same time, the nature of abstract individual rights is in fact never abstract once they are deployed in the world. There is no doubt that there is more political mileage left in them in contemporary China than in the United States, for example. In a Chinese legal order that at least officially still prioritizes "the people" over the "individual," the language of individual rights can still perform a counterhegemonic role—although much more so in the political rather than economic arena, given the rapid marketization and contractualization of Chinese society.[40] In any event, even if radical individualism has yet to become the *lingua franca* of Chinese politics, something like the notion of individual rights has clearly captured the imagination of many—though not all—Chinese. These increasing signs of rights consciousness are nothing to be belittled, so long as there remains a strong authoritarian state. As described in countless journalistic accounts, there are numerous brave, indeed heroic, "rights protection lawyers" (维权律师) working at great personal risk in China today.[41]

Even in the economic realm, individual rights can be a mode of resistance to both state-led and private development in China. Although the Tank Man may not enjoy the same popular recognition as he does in the West, there is at least one symbol of possessive individualism—to use C. B. Macpherson's term—that *is* recognizable to all Chinese today: the so-called Nail House (钉子户) in the city Chongqing, in Sichuan province. The most famous instance of a widespread phenomenon, the owner of the Chongqing house refused offers made by commercial developers who wished to build a huge shopping mall on the site occupied by the house. Even as all the land around the house was excavated for the foundation of the mall, the single house remained teetering for over three years in the middle of an enormous ten-meter-deep hole dug up by the developers—sticking out literally like a single nail that could be neither hammered down nor pulled up out of the way of progress.[42]

Nevertheless, it remains crucial to acknowledge the limits as well as the power of the discourse of individual rights even in China, both as it imagines atomistic property owners in a zero-sum contest against each other (as exemplified by the standoff between the Nail House occupants and the developers) and as it positions a lone individual against the state (like a man facing a tank in an empty square—with no context, history, or a community of others). As Anne Orford puts it with reference to human rights more broadly, "By adopting the liberal programmatic vision of human rights, the shape of the politics of our time seems predetermined—all over the world, the individual confronts the all-powerful apparatus of the state." Even if at the current historical moment we find ourselves in a discursive and political double bind in which there is no other vocabulary available, it remains

"Nail House," in Chongqing, Sichuan.
Courtesy of Derek R. Kolb.

critical to recognize the nature of the subject position into which it inter-
pellates those who invoke it—a position that Orford describes as "the tragic
subject of human rights."[43]

In any event, however we assess Chinese rights discourse, it is an integral
part of the language in which state power is negotiated and by which an
ever-growing number of social relations continue to be contractualized and
commodified. Although there is a real sense in which this discourse is a
foreign import, no colonizing discourse, including law, is able to replicate
itself unchanged across space and time. In Homi Bhabha's oft-quoted formulation, even the most obliging colonial subject is necessarily one of difference as well as similarity—*"almost the same but not quite."*[44] The modern
Chinese legal subject is not just a (poor) reproduction of its Euro-American
counterpart.

Furthermore, to characterize modern Chinese legal discourse as a colonial one in its origins is not to imply that there exists a wholly uncolonized
Euro-American legal subject of unqualified freedom. As Chapter 2 insisted,
law is a discourse of state power and hence a discourse of subjection as well
as subjectification. In an important sense it makes "Orientals" out of all of
us. As this book has insisted throughout, law's Orient is ultimately not
locatable in place or time but in the discursive and political structure of
law itself.

LOOKING FOR NEW SUBJECTS

It would thus be a grave theoretical and factual error to assume that all legal
discourses in China today are nothing more than self-Orientalizing bun-
kum. They are multiple, frequently contradictory, and they continue to
produce subtle, enduring effects. Failing to recognize this would be to leave
us with a bleak conclusion indeed—a cramped political and legal vision offering only a false and foregone ideological "choice" between idealized liberal individualism, on the one hand, and a socialist adaptation of Oriental
despotism, on the other.

Given the changing nature of the Chinese legal world, where then might
we look for other possible legal and political subjects? Let us reconsider a
specific area of Chinese law we already examined in detail in Chapter 3—
corporation law. As the preceding chapters have illustrated, law plays a key

role in articulating not only larger social and geopolitical relations but also foundational notions of modern subjectivity. In this regard corporation law forms part of a larger structure of the jurisprudential imagination. Admittedly, the law of business organization may strike one as an unlikely place to look for alternative visions of social and political life. However, we have already observed its uncomfortable fit in the political ontology of Anglo-American liberalism, consisting ultimately of the state and individuals. Structured in the form of administrative bureaucracies, corporations constitute state-like islands of vertically organized hierarchy in an ocean of otherwise horizontal market relations among individual actors.[45] It is precisely because it straddles the public-private distinction so awkwardly that the business corporation is a useful place to explore elements of already-existing socioeconomic life that do not map neatly on the elemental logic of political liberalism.

To be sure, in the United States today corporate jurisprudence is not necessarily the most dynamic area of theoretical speculation. Methodologically, it has been taken over almost entirely by economic analyses. It is obviously not inappropriate to analyze corporation law in economic terms. Corporations *are* economic institutions. However, they are also political, social, and cultural entities, and an exclusively economic approach simply cannot capture their complexity. Although corporation law seeks to affirm a foundational commitment to a distinction between public and private domains, it necessarily also unsettles that very boundary. Historically, a corporate charter was once a special privilege conferred on enterprises that promoted a public good of some kind, and as we saw in Chapter 3, the legal and metaphysical status of the corporation has been the subject of keen and shifting debates. Do corporations exist solely by a concession of the sovereign, or are they "real" entities in their own right?

Today we accept the personhood of the corporation as nothing more than a legal fiction—it is a creature of law, existing by virtue of the state's recognition only. At the same time, however, the nature of corporations remains politically contested, especially as the U.S. Supreme Court has recently recognized corporations' right to "free speech," empowering them to spend money on political candidates.[46] (We have thus been asked to entertain not only the fiction that corporations are "persons" but also the auxiliary fantasies that corporations can "speak" and that money *is* "speech.") While corporations may be owned privately, incontestably they play a fundamental role in the political economy and must hence be regulated pub-licly. In effect, corporation law is the "constitutional law" of much of private governance and deserves a similarly close political analysis.[47] Yet as we saw in Chapter 3, many U.S. legal theorists committed to an economic paradigm insist on understanding the corporation as essentially private, defining it as nothing more—or less—than a "nexus of contracts." In this economic *Welt-anschauung*, a corporation is merely a set of agreements among the constitu-ent parties whereby those parties organize their relations.

Against this background, the story of Chinese corporation law takes on considerable significance. Until the beginning of the economic reforms, the major form of industrial enterprise in the PRC was the state-owned enter-prise (SOE)—a form of public ownership that was conceptually as well as organizationally indistinct from other forms of state administration. After the enactment of a Western-style corporation law in 1993 (amended in 2005), the ambivalent nature of the corporation—an unstable mixture of public and private governance—has become a matter of utmost urgency. Twenty years after the enactment of the PRC Company Law, the following question still awaits a definitive answer: What *is* a corporation? Is it best understood as analogous to a contract among enterprising individuals (as U.S. Law and Economics scholars would have it), or as a quasi-kinship group (in Confucian terms), or as a form of government (in the vision of state so-cialism)? There is no *right* answer to this question, but there are clearly many *possible* answers. If we give up the teleological vision of a China "in transi-tion," perhaps we will be able to discern some entirely new kinds of corpo-rate subjects that exceed the possibilities we have considered thus far.

At a minimum there is evidence that both Confucianism and Commu-nism inform the operation of economic enterprise in China. For example, familial norms continue to structure certain aspects of contemporary Chi-nese business organization. We have already observed that imperial Chinese law tended to analogize everything to Confucian family structures, while in the Marxist-Leninist-Maoist view the politically correct collective entity is (still) "the people." Yet even the relationship between SOEs and the state bureaucracy has often been colored by familial conceptualizations reminis-cent of the rhetoric that defined clan corporations' role within the imperial state. In principle, each state entity in China is supervised by an adminis-trative agency, colloquially known as a "mother company" (母公司).[48] In addition, each state entity typically owes a subsidiary duty of loyalty to a number of other administrative units as well. When these other units interfere with enterprise management, the problem is referred to as having "too many mothers-in-law" (婆婆多).[49]

Beyond their external relations, even in their internal governance SOEs have functioned—or at least purported to function—like families. SOEs form part of a household registration system in which each citizen is assigned to a "unit" (单位). For its members, historically the SOE as a unit has been much more than a workplace. It has been also "a place to live, raise children, socialize, grow old, and die."[50] As one observer states, "The Chinese manager typically describes the danwei production unit under his auspices as a 'family'—a Big Family."[51] Although the work unit and the household registration system no longer play the all-encompassing role that they once did, SOEs are among the most important last bastions where the work unit remains socially and economically significant. In thousands of enterprises, work units continue to operate hospitals, schools, and community centers for their employees and retirees.[52]

Today, SOEs in China are being converted into corporations under the Company Law. It is crucial to recognize that from the beginning the Law's main aim has not been privatization (私有化) but what is called "corporatization" (公司化): converting SOEs into legally independent economic units to ensure that the state will no longer be ultimately responsible for their losses. Although the corporatization of SOEs ordinarily entails the raising of private capital, the state remains the chief owner and controlling shareholder, at least in the case of the major SOEs that continue to play a key role in the Chinese economy. In a policy of "grasping the large and letting the small go" (抓大放小), since the late 1990s outright privatization has been typically reserved only for smaller, publicly owned enterprises.[53]

It is difficult to discern with precision to what extent the older "customary law" of enterprise governance and the notions of kinship-based subjectivity that inform it continue to influence the practices of corporatized SOEs. However, there is a large literature on so-called township and village enterprises (TVEs, 乡镇企业). That body of scholarship is highly illuminating, as TVEs are a form of semiprivate industry that played a key role in China's economic growth until the 1990s. Nominally most TVEs have been created locally as collective rather than as private undertakings, but in fact "they are typically set up, financed, and operated by a small partnership of local officials who benefit as private owners of the enterprise."[54] A leading political scientist argues that with the establishment of TVEs "local governments have taken on many characteristics of a business corporation, with officials acting as the equivalent of a board of directors."[55] Others have tellingly described the relationship between local governments and TVEs as a "father-son" relation.[56] Yet what is probably most striking about this development is that even when the TVE boom was at its height it did not—or did not invariably—result in the opportunistic privatization of public wealth: "Unlike the case in a true capitalist corporation, profits are not always the driving force. The former emphasis on strict egalitarianism has been rejected, but leveling of incomes still seems to figure in the decision-making process."[57] In a form of "redistributive corporatism," local governments have sought to make sure that at least one member of each family is employed in industry.[58]

For better or for worse, the TVE explosion of the 1990s is over. Today some of the biggest profits are generated by real estate development rather than manufacturing. It turns out that similar kinds of collectivist norms play an important role in this new context. Because of the historically segregated structure of the PRC land ownership regime, real estate speculation has been a specifically urban phenomenon. Under China's Land Administration Law—and under the PRC Constitution as well—rural lands controlled by rural governments remain collectively owned and designated for predominantly agricultural use. Nevertheless, when economic development reaches the city limits, lands belonging to rural villages and townships next to cities become increasingly desirable sites for urban investors. However, legally they can be diverted from agricultural use only if they are first converted formally into urban land.[59] The takeover of collectively owned rural land for economic development has been aptly described as a new "enclosure movement," leaving behind peasants without lands, jobs, or social security. By 2004, the process had already produced over forty million dispossessed villagers.[60]

To be able to take advantage of urban growth while also protecting themselves economically, more recently numerous village collectives have established new landholding companies on the foundation of old lineage organizations—that is, the kinds of clan corporations analyzed in Chapter 3. You-tien Hsing describes this phenomenon as "village corporatism." When villagers agree to place their land under the jurisdiction of a neighboring urban government—making the land thus eligible for development—in return they are permitted to retain a portion of the converted, formerly rural land. Legally the villagers continue to hold that land collectively, organized now as a shareholding cooperative (股份合作制企业).

With feverish real estate speculation, lands belonging to shareholding cooperatives have generated significant profits for the villages that have developed them. In a familiar pattern, these profits have been used to look after the villagers as a group. Consider Shuping Village in the Pearl River delta. Reorganized as Sanwan Group Shareholding Company, it became the primary provider of welfare programs of numerous kinds, in the form of medical care, day care centers, primary and secondary schools, nursing homes, financial aid to college students, and even living expenses and funerals. Yet, as before, the limits of such generosity are defined by the operation of the logic of (real or fictive) kinship: it does not extend to labor migrants from other villages, for example.[61]

Political economists as well as sociologists have had considerable difficulty analyzing such phenomena. It is telling that the question of whether TVEs are more properly characterized as public or private entities has been an especially vexing one. Scholastic debates on the question have yielded no single unambiguous answer, for the simple but profound reason that there probably is none, as exemplified by so-called red hat (红帽) enterprises—a phenomenon in which private entrepreneurs choose to put on a "red hat" and register with local authorities as ideologically unimpeachable collective enterprises.[62] For their favors, local officials earn a management fee.[63] In post-Maoist China legal personality has evidently become an attribute that can be borrowed, bought, or rented—part of a larger phenomenon that David Wank identified as the "commodification of communism" in the early reform era.[64] What emerges from the study of contemporary Chinese legal practice is an appreciation of "the diversity of the entities that obviously have some sort of legal capacity."[65] Like traditional clan corporations, even (more or less) private PRC entities with "customary personality" seek the imprimatur of the state by affiliating themselves with collective entities identified with "the people." Moreover, even if an enterprise incorporates under the Company Law, its stated purposes include the protection of the social and economic order generally and the promotion of China's "socialist market economy" (社会主义市场经济) specifically.[66]

Needless to say, to observe conceptual and operational continuities between traditional and contemporary notions of kinship and corporate organization is not to suggest that the Chinese somehow remain so trapped in an archaic Confucian ideology that they cannot see vital differences between a state-owned enterprise, a clan, and a household. One need not be a sociologist to agree that a multimillion-dollar manufacturing company is not just "a peasant clan writ large," nor need one believe that Chinese corporation law reflects a higher "natural" law of kinship, which is itself somehow hardwired into the genetic code of people of Chinese descent.[67]

The point, in short, is not that there is an essential, enduring structure of Chinese subjectivity but, rather, that kinship metaphors have not lost their currency as a language for articulating relationships. Today, as before, they continue to call forth certain kinds of legal and economic subjects. Sometimes those metaphors are reproduced almost unchanged; at other times they have mutated into socialist rhetoric; and sometimes they combine with profit-driven economic activities of seemingly capitalist variety. And, just as before, sometimes the familial rhetoric is just that: little more than ideological window dressing (as is the case in many SOEs). At other times it produces subjects that have internalized the logic of kinship in various degrees, sharing their material resources with others, as has been the case with at least some TVEs and village landholding enterprises.[68]

In short, there exist subject formations in post-Maoist China that combine aspects of normative Confucian, socialist, and liberal selfhood, thus transcending a simplistic public-private dichotomy with the state on one side and the lone individual on the other. They may or may not augur the arrival of a progressive future, but there is little doubt that they *are* distinctive.

THE CHINA PROBLEM: THEORIZING UNLEGALITY

While the sheer volume of law in China today is awe-inspiring, it is equally critical to appreciate how much China has been able to do *without* law. Even if legal institutions have colonized much of China, they have not colonized all of it. It is an axiom of contemporary Law and Development discourse, and of institutional economics more generally, that economic growth demands well-defined property rights enforceable at law: only they can provide the security and predictability that make long-term investment possible and worthwhile.[69] Remarkably, the PRC did not promulgate its first Property Law until 2007—almost thirty years into the era of economic and legal reforms, during which time China experienced economic growth unrivaled by any other economy on the planet. While the *homo economicus* of the U.S. variety is always also a *homo juridicus*—operating within the logics of property and contract—it is evidently entirely possible to be a modern *nonlegal* Chinese economic subject without thereby becoming simply a lawless subject of Oriental despotism. Just as formal law—and, more specifically, a U.S.-style system of rule-of-law—is not the only way of articulating social and political subjectivity, it is not the sole effective means of channeling material resources either.[70]

For all of law's strides, significant aspects of Chinese life remain outside of law altogether. Obviously there are many kinds of social activity in the United States as well that are arenas of private activity, beyond direct state regulation. In China, however, some aspects of life take place outside law in a more radical sense, seemingly existing beyond the binary code of legal versus illegal altogether. It is a key index of the modern state's ultimately boundless will-to-power that it insists on characterizing everything within its jurisdiction as either legal or illegal. Any conceivable activity must fall into one category or the other, as law simply does not recognize anything beyond its reach. In China, in contrast, there appears to be a third category outside this binary—considerable areas of activity that seem best characterized as *unlegal*, or perhaps nonlegal or extralegal, rather than either legal or illegal.

There is no question that much of Chinese economic life, for example, does fit under the category legal—it takes place in legally recognized markets. Similarly, there are numerous economic activities that are unequivocally illegal—they occur in legally proscribed black markets. However, there are also various kinds of gray markets and many other activities that apparently have not (yet) been the object of legal contemplation at all. Until, and unless, the state passes legislation that addresses them, such activities seem destined to remain *un*legal—neither illegal nor simply tolerated by law (which would make them in fact legal) but outside law's scope altogether.

Consider, for example, the so-called "individual households" (个体户). This was a legal category designed specifically to legitimate the operation of family businesses early in the reform period.[71] Since other forms of private enterprise had not yet been recognized, evidently family businesses were meant to be limited to what the legal term designated—households. A household might presumably include non-kin as well, in light of the elastic kinship practices we have considered, but in a socialist understanding it would certainly seem to exclude the employment of wage labor. However, family businesses soon began hiring outside help. Although such practices were widespread and not authorized by law, it would not be useful to characterize them as simply illegal. Rather, they are better seen as taking place in a social and economic space that was unlegal—outside the law unless and until the law took note of them. Indeed, ultimately a set of interim regulations were promulgated, stating that an "individual household" was permitted to hire up to five "apprentices" and two "assistants."[72] It was only at that point that the (limited) use of wage labor in family businesses became a matter of legal determination, one way or another.[73]

A (Western) legal theorist might view the notion of the unlegal as a misunderstanding of law at best and a pathology at worst, given that it is in the DNA of the modern state to pronounce on the legality of all human activity under its purview.[74] Nevertheless, the simple fact that the Chinese economy has experienced extraordinary growth for decades without the blessing of a Property Law suggests that legal theorists may have something of significance to learn from China. Effectively, the U.S. Law and Development orthodoxy's response to this has been a shrug—a variation on the academic witticism, "It may work in practice, but it'll never work in theory." That otherwise sophisticated scholars' first impulse is to blame China for not complying with their conjectures is striking. If a theory of law fails to account for China—a larger phenomenon that Donald Clarke has dubbed "the China problem"—that would seem to leave an irreparably large hole in such a theory, downgrading it to the status of a North Atlantic prejudice.[75]

Yet in order to truly provincialize legal theory it is not sufficient to "test" it in China—to make sure that we can fit Chinese facts into Western theory. On a more fundamental level, we must consider: Why is it that even within the academic field of comparative law the study of Chinese law ultimately provides only *comparative*, rather than absolute, legal knowledge? Why couldn't the study of China generate *primary* knowledge—theory itself—rather than merely secondary data to confirm or disprove theories developed elsewhere?

It may sound utopian to ask for U.S. scholars to treat China not only as an empirical datum but also as a source of theory. American legal thought may seem insular today, but there is nothing in the U.S. politico-legal tradition that makes it inevitably so. As we have already seen, several of the founding fathers admired Chinese political institutions, including its legal system. In Jedidiah Kroncke's observation, they were in effect willing to see China as *part* of the universal—not opposed to it—and thus potentially capable of imparting lessons to the United States.[76] Moreover, throughout its career the common law has been influenced to a far greater extent by continental civil law than nationalist historians of English law would care to admit, and in the post-Revolutionary era, too, the civil law tradition continued to influence the development of American law.[77] Despite the provincial turn of U.S. legal theory in the twentieth century, the common law and cosmopolitanism are not inevitably incompatible.[78]

USING LEGAL THEORY AS A WEAPON

The PRC is in fact producing legal theory of its own, even if few U.S. theorists are interested in it.[79] As we might expect, much of it invokes the standards of U.S. constitutionalism as the measure of rule-of-law—but much of it does not. Just as Chinese law of business organization has not yielded to a Euro-American institutional logic, neither is Chinese legal theory merely a reinscription of ideas developed elsewhere.

To be sure, when China's post-Mao "legal construction" began in earnest in the 1980s, to crack open a Chinese law review was to enter an incongruous world of liberal thinkers of various eras and multiple ideological stripes, ranging from Max Weber to Friedrich Hayek to Henry Maine. (At a certain point, citations to Maine alone exceeded those to Karl Marx.)[80] They were invoked in the name of rule-of-law and in order to realize a radical break with the Maoist past. Such invocations were perhaps naïve, or so they appear from the perspective of a post-Tiananmen China, but they were offered with sincerity and consideration. Insofar as they constructed an essentially despotic past—or a "feudal" (封建) one, in the terminology of Chinese communism—from which China will be liberated through modern law, they were certainly a form of self-Orientalism.

Again, to characterize a phenomenon as self-Orientalism is not to deride it. Simply because something is identified as Western and liberal assuredly does not mean that it cannot work in China (although one can be fairly confident that it will operate *differently*, no matter what). Nevertheless, this particular invocation of liberal legality did *not* produce desired results in the 1980s, as disappointed Chinese liberals soon came to realize themselves, conceding that they had placed far too much faith in the emancipatory potential of freedom of contract, for example.

It was from that pervading sense of disappointment that the so-called New Left (新左派) thinkers emerged in the 1990s. Apart from the political standpoint signaled by the moniker New Left—originally applied by detractors as an epithet—these intellectuals were united methodologically by their affinity for critical theory. This was also the moment when the status of Orientalism as an *academic* discourse became a matter of impassioned debate among Chinese theorists. In 1993, Zhang Kuan—at the time a graduate student in comparative literature at Stanford University—encountered Said's *Orientalism* and published a polemical essay on it in *Dushu* (读书), the leading Chinese theoretical journal. The essay ignited a heated conversation about the nature of representations of China in the West.[81]

Although Orientalism (东方主义) and postcolonialism (后殖民主义) have remained on the intellectual agenda since then, it is notable that subsequent analyses have focused largely on the elucidation of the work of U.S. theorists. As the leading New Left critic Wang Hui observes, critiques of Eurocentrism have tended to lead back to a Chinese nationalism rather than a critical examination of the nature of Chinese modernity within a longer global history of colonialism.[82] Although there are numerous contemporary U.S. scholars who are cited with great frequency by Chinese legal thinkers—ranging from John Rawls to Richard Posner to Harold Berman—both postcolonial theory and Critical Legal Studies remain marginal in Chinese legal thought.[83]

Nevertheless, China's judicial elites regard legal theory with utmost seriousness, whether produced in China or outside. Wang Shengjun, the ideologically conservative President of the Supreme People's Court, has gone so far as to issue a warning to those who "deploy Western legal theory as a weapon" (利用西方法律理论作武器), using pieties about rule-of-law to question the leadership of the Communist Party. Admittedly, concerns about the weaponization of legal thought may strike an outsider as overblown. In the United States, legal theory is a marginalized occupation of academics, and few U.S. scholars would see themselves as capable of producing weapons-grade legal theory. But the ideological stakes in theorizing rule-of-law in China are high, and they are recognized as such.[84]

In his mapping of the diversity and contradictions of those debates, Samuli Seppänen characterizes the official Chinese account of rule-of-law aptly with the label of conservative socialism—an idiosyncratic and ostensibly oxymoronic ideological location that generates a series of paradoxes regarding the nature and operation of law.[85] An outstanding example is the doctrine of the Three Supremes (三个至上), championed vigorously by Wang Shengjun since his appointment as head of the Supreme People's Court in 2008. In brief, Wang believes that adjudication must remain subject to the supremacy of the party, the supremacy of the popular interest, and the supremacy of the Constitution and law.[86] The idea of three "equally supreme" supremes may seem incoherent, absent guidance on how to proceed when the three frameworks point in different directions. However, as Seppänen explains, the notion is not necessarily unintelligible on its own terms, even if it is subtended by a degree of cynicism. From the perspective of Chinese-style developmental socialism, certain elements of rule-of-law are at the same time intrinsically valuable *and* potentially harmful to the Party-state's goals.

This is more than a simple acknowledgment that contradictions are inherent in the very notion of law. To be sure, as this book has insisted, it is in fact one of the key tasks of the ideology of rule-of-law to manage and repress such contradictions—by projecting them in an Orient of the legal imagination, for example. Rather, what is distinctive about the conservative socialist position exemplified by Wang is that instead of seeking to harmonize, regulate, or simply repress the coexistence of incommensurate yet equally authoritative normative orders, it consciously *embraces* the undecidability among them. The effect of this highly "useful paradox" identified by Seppänen is that it permits the decision-maker to choose among competing sources of authority as needed in order to maintain the status quo.[87]

As an account of rule-of-law, this may not be an especially appealing one, but it is a self-conscious theorization of law's rule—not a misunderstanding of liberal rule-of-law but its intentional rejection. Equally importantly, it is only one Chinese position among many, albeit an ideologically priveledged one. For example, a cadre of elite human rights and criminal rights lawyers in the PRC espouse the liberal version of rule-of-law as self-consciously as conservative socialists reject it. In search of determinacy, the liberal scholar-activist He Weifang has pointedly asked Wang to identify just which of the "three supremes" is *the* supreme one.[88] His own answer, of course, would be, "the Constitution and law," although that is precisely what Wang's ambiguous formulations and double meanings refuse to specify.

But conservative socialism and liberalism do not exhaust the universe of PRC legal thought, although they are the easiest to characterize in terms of legal Orientalism—one an embrace of liberal rule-of-law, the other its disavowal. In fact, they are not even the dominant positions in the Chinese legal profession at large. Significantly, many of the more recent analyses seek to give a theoretical account precisely of the kinds of emergent, hybrid subjectivities identified earlier in this chapter in the context of contemporary business enterprises—combinations of socialist, liberal, and Confucian aspects.

The prominent New Left critic Wang Xiaoming has expressly bemoaned the progressive decline in the variety of types of political and ethical subjects in China, wrought by the modernizing revolutions of the twentieth century—analogous to the radical post-Enlightenment simplification of the Western juridico-political field.[89] What is perhaps most distinctive about Chinese legal thinkers is their willingness to extend their consideration beyond the state-individual dichotomy that structures so much of Anglo-American legal thought. For advocates of socialist rule-of-law (社会主义法治), the relationship between the state and the individual is evidently mediated by a vitally important third party—namely, the Party itself. The Party's existence in turn is both legal and extra-legal, befittingly paradoxical. In Schmittian terms, it is the Party that ultimately decides on "the state of exception" and thus constitutes the true source of sovereignty.[90]

It is nevertheless important to recognize that Chinese socialist rule-of-law today is in fact distinct from a crude Marxian one that would simply regard the Party as above the law. Undesirable individuals can no longer be labeled "enemies of the people" to be dealt with politically; the state must employ other legally cognizable categories of social regulation and criminal prohibition. Flora Sapio, for one, believes that a friend-enemy distinction still endures, underneath a veneer of legality. In her view, Chinese legal reforms have served to consolidate rather than dismantle "zones of lawlessness," especially in the field of criminal law where critical exceptions to ordinary procedural norms are defined in increasingly technical legal terms. In effect, areas of lawlessness have simply become *legal*—an analysis that agrees with the conservative socialist position, although the latter would welcome the paradox, not bemoan it.[91]

Without trying to assess the ultimate merits of "rule-of-law with Chinese characteristics"—and recognizing that there are competing interpretations of just what the term means—it is vital to be aware that the legacy of China's revolutionary history is not limited to the continuing dominance of the legal system by the Party-state. As Benjamin Liebman explains, that history has provided support for many reforms that are widely regarded as successes, both inside and outside of China. With a growing perception that law reform has favored the interests of economic and political elites, over the past decade Chinese courts have become increasingly responsive to popular pressures. The Supreme People's Court today emphasizes the importance of "justice for the people" (司法为民)—a concept whose history dates back to the Jiangxi Soviet of the 1930s. Speaking as President of the Supreme People's Court, Wang Shengjun has gone so far as to declare that "upholding the massline" is just as important as the continuing professionalization of the judiciary. It is of course true that all courts must implicitly balance flexibility and predictability, substantive and procedural justice, but as Liebman emphasizes, when Chinese judges do so, they "are not acting contrary to an idealized conception of their roles": they are acting precisely as they *should*, given China's revolutionary legal tradition. Indeed, that tradition helps explain China's embrace of innovations that many have regarded as straightforward transplants from Western liberal democracies, such as legal aid.[92]

At the same time, with an increasing emphasis on the need to avoid mindless imitation of foreign models and a desire to remain faithful to China's own historical tradition, even recognizably Confucian elements have become part of official rule-of-law discourse. This is perhaps most notable in the emergence of "socialist harmonious society" (社会主义和谐社会) as a political and legal ideal promoted by President Hu Jintao. Rhetorically, it is an unobjectionable call for both stability and social justice, echoing Confucian clichés to the same effect. Politically, it is a response to increasing unrest resulting from growing social and economic inequality. In practice, it has become a justification for silencing dissent and maintaining the status quo at any cost—not unlike the 1990s Asian values version of autocratic Confucianism.[93]

Although nearly everyone in China pays at least lip service to the universality of some version of rule-of-law as an ideal—while they might be unable to agree on what it means—Zhu Suli, the prolific Marxian sociolegal scholar and former dean of Beijing University Law School, does not. Paradoxically, he is the most famous PRC advocate of the notion that law is not inherently Other to China, tirelessly urging Chinese law reformers to draw on the country's "indigenous resources" (本土资源).[94] In an important article entitled "Taking the Rule of Man Seriously," Zhu identifies traditions of both rule-of-law and rule-of-men in Chinese history. Yet while recovering an indigenous concept of rule-of-law, he insists that the rule-of-men is *also* a perfectly rational and desirable form of rule, at least in certain historical and social conditions.[95] Resisting the allure of self-Orientalism, Zhu neither idealizes nor demonizes Confucianism: he hedges his bets on *both* the rule-of-law *and* the rule-of-men. Even if unstated by Zhu, the implication of his analysis is that rule-of-law is not the only possible way to live and to be human.

In addition to Zhu's controversial jurisprudence—grounded in an unlikely postmodern/pragmatist epistemology that draws in roughly equal parts from Friedrich Nietzsche, Karl Marx, and Richard Posner—there are a handful of scholars offering genuine alternatives beyond the opposition between a jurisprudence of developmental socialism and U.S.-style liberal rule-of-law. They include self-identified advocates of New Confucianism (新儒学) such as Xia Yong. He seeks to harmonize the notion of a "people-centered" virtue ethic—based on the classical concept of virtue (德)—with the modern idea of civil rights. In an effort to do so, he argues that China's so-called legal modernization is not at all a departure from Chinese tradition but instead a *return* to classical discourse, "only now couched in the Western language of rights."[96]

Xia Yong's Confucianism is relatively conventional, essentially a Confucian-inflected liberalism. The legal theorist Jiang Qing, in contrast, wishes to render Confucian values *foundational*—politically, morally, and epistemologically. Audaciously, he proposes that China establish a tricameral legislature to be populated by representatives selected on the basis of merit, (more or less) popular elections, and historico-cultural status. Drawing on the correlative cosmology of Dong Zhongshu (178–104 B.C.E.), the philosopher who first formulated Confucianism as a state ideology in the Han dynasty, Jiang identifies distinctive kinds of political legitimacy deriving from Heaven, Man, and Earth, each associated with one of the three houses of his Confucian legislature. In sum, what Jiang proposes is nothing less than a new legal cosmology for the sovereignty of the Chinese state.[97]

In effect, Jiang offers Confucianism as a competing universalism, in contrast to more modest New Confucianisms that ultimately regard Confucianism and liberalism as distinctive but complementary (like Xia Yong, who wants to avoid having to choose between the two). Jiang in fact regards himself as a critic of self-identified New Confucians; he dismisses their appeals to Confucianism as merely *moral*, in contrast to his own *political* theorization of it. Nevertheless, even Jiang's political Confucianism has remarkable structural consistencies with contemporary PRC legal thought, albeit decidedly not with its liberal version. As Daniel Bell points out, Jiang's proposal entails no mechanism for resolving potential conflicts among the three different legislative chambers with distinctive sources of sovereignty. In this regard Jiang's constitutional vision is not unlike that of Wang Shengjun's: all three houses of his constitutional schema are "equally supreme," as it were. Such a vision is of course liable to the same kind of totalitarian subversion as Wang's.[98]

Although the theories canvassed above are genuinely varied—ranging from conservative socialism to Confucian socialism to liberal Confucianism to conservative Confucian constitutionalism—it is noteworthy, as Seppänen points out, that many of the scholars most invested in articulating a distinctively Chinese theory of law are also among those most keenly engaged with Western legal theory. Seppänen cites Zhu Suli and Xia Yong as key examples.[99] Indeed, Zhu Suli, the preeminent advocate of China's "indigenous resources," holds a PhD from Arizona State University as well as an LLM from the University of the Pacific in Sacramento.[100]

The genesis of Xia Yong's Confucian legal theory, too, is traceable to the United States, to two years spent at Harvard Law School in the mid-1990s. That encounter with U.S. law caused Xia to ask, in his own words, three "axial questions": "How do others see us; how do we see ourselves; and how do we see others?"[101] In a cliché of cross-cultural comparison, when recalling his time in Cambridge, Massachusetts, Xia likens himself to Alexis de Tocqueville, as he discovers a sense of community and family in New England—not merely "lone rights-bearers" of the legal imagination, as he had expected.

More surprisingly, as Xia describes his participation in a Ford Foundation survey of rights consciousness in the *Chinese* countryside, he again likens himself to the French observer—eager "to encounter the 'spirits of village and township' described by Alexis de Tocqueville" on his travels in

America in the 1830s.[102] That is, in order to arrive at a "Chinese" theory of Confucian civil rights, Xia performs a complex act of self-alienation and self-discovery in which he anthropologizes the Chinese peasant, temporalizes the countryside as a living past, and positions himself as a modern Chinese observer interpreting the nation's past, refracted through the lens of a French traveler reading the American legal landscape. The theoretical imagination of Confucian legal thought is clearly a transnational one— routed in this case not only through rural China but also Cambridge, Massachusetts, as well as post-Revolutionary France. However one assesses its political appeal, to call it simply self-Orientalization would be to fail to appreciate the multiple circuits of identification whereby it is constituted.

AMERICAN LEGAL ORIENTALISMS TODAY

Having investigated the status of legal Orientalism in the PRC today, as well as hybrid legal and nonlegal formations that challenge it, it is important to consider, by way of conclusion, Orientalism's ongoing legacy in the legal order of the United States. As we have seen, at the heart of the history of American legal Orientalism are late nineteenth-century anti-Chinese immigration laws, upheld in the *Chinese Exclusion Case,* which remains good law even though the exclusion acts themselves have been repealed.[103]

However, it is not only the constitutional law of immigration that is frozen in an earlier era of Orientalism, but also constitutional doctrines regarding the authority of the United States over its "internal Orientals" considered in Chapter 5—Indian tribes and populations of nonstate territories. Examining the cases that over a century ago established the United States' plenary power over them, Alexander Aleinikoff states, "Despite tectonic shifts in our constitutional law, these cases remain largely untouched and continue to dominate their areas of law."[104] As a concession to contemporary sensibilities, the more recent cases on immigration, Indians, and nonstate territories cite policy considerations to justify their holdings. Yet they continue to rely on outmoded precedents, sanitizing their reasoning by selective quotations and paraphrasing overtly Orientalist concerns with "civilization" into questions of "culture" instead.[105]

Similarly, as far as the U.S. government's powers of external sovereignty are concerned, Congress still enjoys the indisputable constitutional right to breach foreign treaties—another direct legacy of the *Chinese Exclusion Case*. It is hard to resist the temptation to speculate how American constitutional law might have developed if the treaty disregarded by Congress in the *Chinese Exclusion Case* had not been a Sino-American one and if the group of immigrants at issue had not been Chinese—an international obligation owed to a declining Oriental power and a group of deeply unpopular Oriental immigrants. Indeed, the Supreme Court "appears to have envisioned Asian immigration as a form of war that justified extreme government intervention"—a suggestion with disturbing contemporary implications for the extension of state power in the age of an endless War against Terrorism. As Leti Volpp notes, today it is the terrorist who is the primary Other of the U.S. citizen.[106]

That Orientalist discourses both reflect and shape changing political situations with such expedience should not surprise us. Consider the Cold War, for example. Although the federal government's plenary authority to exclude aliens was first recognized in the context of the "obnoxious" Chinese race in the late nineteenth century, in the 1950s it was extended to authorize the exclusion of Communists as well as homosexuals—a legal and discursive move enabled by overdetermined racial, political, and sexual associations among yellowness, redness, and queerness. As the U.S. Supreme Court characterized in 1950 the legitimate expectations of such populations upon presenting themselves at the nation's borders, "Whatever the procedure authorized by Congress is, it is due process as far as an alien denied entry is concerned."[107]

The unedifying story of the Chinese Exclusion Laws as part of U.S. immigration law is well-known among historians as well as legal scholars, if not among the general public. However, the constitutional jurisprudence generated by litigation over the Exclusion Laws has another, largely obscured legacy that extends to the way in which the United States exercises power over its *citizens* as well. Ironically, that legacy hides in a field of U.S. law that is viewed universally as progressive—in contrast to immigration law, which is routinely denounced as a nineteenth-century relic by the standards of more recent constitutional jurisprudence. This ostensibly progressive field is administrative law, a distinctly modern branch of law that has made possible the rise of the regulatory state in the twentieth century and everything that is associated with it—welfare, health care, environmental regulation, and the administrative management of innumerable aspects of modern society that are simply beyond the capacity and expertise of the U.S. Congress to regulate directly.[108]

As Gabriel Chin recounts the progressive and dark sides of administrative law's history, the progressive one begins with the establishment of the Interstate Commerce Commission (ICC) in 1887. It had become woefully evident that Congress had neither the time nor the capacity to regulate the railroad industry effectively, along with other burgeoning industries of national scope. Hence Congress created the ICC and empowered it to promulgate appropriate regulations, to enforce them, and to perform adjudicative functions as well. Under a categorical view of the separation of powers, such a delegation of legislative, executive, and judicial functions to a single agency would have been an impermissible combination—indeed, a form of administrative despotism. However, since the New Deal the Supreme Court has blessed the creation of innumerable administrative agencies of a similar kind, in the name of efficiency and expert governance.

This familiar progressive account is not so much inaccurate as it is incomplete. As Chin insists, there is an earlier genealogy that becomes visible if we view the Chinese immigration cases as part of a longer history of administrative law. The account of administrative law beginning with the establishment of the ICC in 1887 is essentially a story about enlightened government regulation of business corporations, based on Progressive Era notions of scientific rationality and expert governance. Chin calls attention to an alternative story of administrative law, seeking to regulate *individuals* in order to enforce a restrictive federal immigration policy reflecting another type of scientific rationality—that of scientific racism. Over a decade before the establishment of the ICC, in 1875 Congress passed the first Immigration Act—the beginning of anti-Chinese immigration legislation—for the same reason that it subsequently chose to regulate railroads: states had become unable to regulate both arenas effectively. As a national immigration bureaucracy was built to exclude the Chinese, it exercised its responsibility in overtly racist ways and in express denial of Chinese immigrants' individual rights, as we have seen. Crucially, the Supreme Court cases that upheld the Chinese Exclusion Laws and the procedures by which they were administered are also among the earliest and most important sources of constitutional administrative law more generally. As Chin summarizes, "Almost all contemporary due process cases, in all fields, rely in part on the Asian Exclusion cases or their progeny."[109]

As a result, while the Chinese Exclusion Laws themselves are indeed long gone, the minimal—all but absent—standards for administrative procedure set by the judicial decisions upholding and interpreting those laws remain to a remarkable extent the constitutional baseline to this day. Moreover, with the twentieth-century explosion of the administrative state, it is not only immigrants who are subject to administrative regulation by the federal government. We have all become, or are at risk of becoming, "internal Orientals" of the United States. This may not have happened yet (at least not to some of us) because Congress has in fact recognized the risks posed by unchecked administrative power. It has enacted protections such as the Administrative Procedure Act (APA): a "high-end administrative model" that, among other things, provides for judicial review of administrative actions that are "arbitrary or capricious." The standard of review could hardly be more evocative: the adjectives "arbitrary" and "capricious" are among the most clichéd characterizations of Oriental despotism.[110] (Strikingly, one of Roscoe Pound's objections to administrative law was that it subjected citizens to "a season of oriental justice."[111])

However, although the APA applies to a wide range of areas of administrative regulation, it is not universally applicable.[112] Equally significantly, the protections provided by the APA and other statutes are legislative grants only, not constitutional entitlements. It is up to Congress to determine just who deserves the protections of the APA and who are the internal—and external—Orientals who can be properly subjected to administrative despotism. Chin observes that heightened statutory protections are in fact far more prevalent in the regulation of corporations than they are in the regulation of individuals. Moreover, even in the regulation of individuals it is persons belonging to socially disfavored categories that enjoy the fewest protections against state power.

LEGAL ORIENTALISM OR ORIENTAL LEGALISM

The legal imagination of modernity is a global one. In the circulation of legal Orientalism from Asia to America and back, it is impossible to pin it down for more than one moment in more than one place. However, while law is an extraordinarily potent discourse with an imperial history, "China" as a sign as well as a political and cultural formation has an equally impressive imperial record of its own.

Hence the future of law's world is, above all, a political—indeed, a geopolitical—question. Although the possibilities of politics are always limited in some ways, by our constrained imaginations as much as by history, the future is never foreclosed. As the global distribution of universality and particularity is being recalibrated—and there is no question that it is—it would be futile to predict what the new equilibrium might be. Perhaps China will in fact one day submit to rule-of-law in its modern Euro-American form, thereby confirming its universality. Or maybe it will recast law's rule in the form of an evolving Chinese universalism—an Oriental legalism, as it were. If law can resignify China, we must be prepared to accept that China can also Sinify law.

Yet one thing seems clear. As the relationship between U.S. law and Chinese law continues to be negotiated, the high-flying notion of rule-of-law hinders that negotiation more than it aids it. Perhaps most fundamentally, as an idea it is simply too broad and all-encompassing. Inevitably, it obscures more than it illuminates. To achieve greater precision and to enable more effective communication across legal traditions, we would do well to stay away from a quasitheological contrast between rule-of-law and rule-of-men and replace both with more modest and more definable concepts instead. As David Kairys believes, "Criticism or praise in terms of a grand, amorphous notion of the rule of law, which we cannot define without controversy among ourselves, is not constructively focused, useful, or fair."[113]

Admittedly, whether we invoke it directly or not, it is unlikely that we can give up the rule-of-law versus rule-of-men dichotomy altogether, simply through a heroic act of will. This is possibly even desirable. Certainly the analysis of legal Orientalism in this book suggests that it is the very suppression of law's contradictions that makes it "work." It may be that the very idea of rule-of-law *demands* that we regard it in an overwhelming, and overwhelmingly negative, contrast with rule-of-men. It is entirely possible that honest views of law may result in psychological changes in how we view it, including a certain loss of faith in law's purity.[114] A perfectly accurate view of law might in the end undermine its very basis, insofar as law depends on our faith in its transparence, even transcendence.

Nevertheless, if we wish to take Chinese politics seriously—indeed, if we wish to take *ourselves* seriously—that is the risk we have to accept: the possibility of discovering that law is as much a religion as a political institution. While that is a genuine risk, it seems hardly fatal, for it is unlikely that any political system can function unless supported by the faith of those it governs. As Antonio Gramsci insists, no political system that relies on sheer domination can last. To survive, it must be able to produce and reproduce the consent that sustains it, through the hegemonic institutions of civil society.[115] Law is evidently a critically important institution in producing the subject of consent, as Chapter 2 emphasized.

In a historical sense, the story told by this book is a genealogy of the universal: a partial account of how one particular idea of law has become a global standard for constituting free individual subjects as well as free and democratic states. To point out the historically contingent nature of this particular political soteriology is to say nothing about its emancipatory potential. It is, however, to point out that the freedom of rights is just *one* kind of freedom, not freedom as such—whatever that might mean—and thus to remind us not to give up on other kinds of freedom as well.[116] Although the discourses of legal Orientalism rely on an opposition between the universal and the particular, it does not seem especially useful to insist that any place or any time is more or less universal than any other. Rather than identifying law with the universal—or the particular, for that matter—it is best seen as a critical transnational discourse that gives rise to the oppositions it seeks to manage. It is both the universal and the particular, and the very moment of their making.

In the end this book invites the reader to step back from the present, so overwhelmingly saturated with abstract talk of rule-of-law, and to consider the longer history of legal Orientalism, both as a general discourse of Chinese lawlessness and as a specifically American ideology of law's rule. That history cannot tell us what law's global future will be, or what to think of either Chinese law or U.S. law as they exist today. It will, however, help us see both more clearly and aid us in recognizing the stakes in legal comparison. It is only through a critical awareness of this past and its continuing legacies that we can understand the world that legal Orientalism has made. This does not mean that we cannot continue to engage in an impassioned dialogue about the demands of justice globally and locally. It does mean giving up law's universalism as the foundation for such a dialogue—without either uncritically assuming or fully rejecting the more particular terms in which ideas of justice are ultimately understood, and lived.

Although in late modernity the direction of cross-cultural legal exchange has been disproportionately from West to East, one heavy symbolic cost of the United States' largely extralegal War on Terror has been that the nation's claim to being the chief custodian of the principle of rule-of-law is less persuasive today than it was at the end of the Cold War. To be sure, the United States continues to insist that it represents an ideal legal order. However, its claim to universality is no longer *particularly* strong, or at least *as* particularly strong as it once was.

If that is so, where in law's world is China today? Understanding China's past is difficult enough, even without trying to predict its future. But while China is certainly still regarded in many ways as *sui generis*, it also seems that its values are no longer seen as invariably and necessarily unique—that is, they appear to be not quite as *universally* particular as they were only some time ago. Yet even today, while China's claims to economic universality, and even political dominance, are growing stronger, the idea of "Chinese law" continues to strike many as an oxymoron, haunted as it is by a long history of legal Orientalism.

Notes

1. Edward W. Said, *Orientalism* (New York: Pantheon Books, 1978), 3. See also Said, "Orientalism Reconsidered," in *Literature, Politics, and Theory: Papers from the Essex Conference, 1976–84*, ed. Francis Barker et al. (London: Methuen, 1986), 210–229; Said, "Orientalism: An Afterword," *Raritan* 14, no. 3 (Winter 1995): 32–59. In describing Orientalism as a "discourse," Said employs it in an explicitly Foucaultian sense. Yet just as Foucault has been faulted for lacking a concept of agency that would allow for more than merely local resistance to disciplinary discourses, Said's concept of Orientalism as a discourse has also been criticized as too hegemonic for not allowing "the Orient" a role in its construction. See, for example, Dennis Porter, "Orientalism and Its Problems," in *The Politics of Theory: Proceedings of the Essex Conference on the Sociology of Literature, July 1982*, ed. Francis Barker et al. (Colchester, UK: University of Essex, 1983), 179–193. In later work Said provides a broader study of imperialism that encompasses "a general world-wide pattern of imperial culture" and incorporates also "a historical experience of resistance against empire." See Said, *Culture and Imperialism* (New York: Knopf, 1993), xii. Indeed, much of the subsequent development of postcolonial theory—most notably the work of Gayatri Spivak and Homi Bhabha—can be

viewed as an effort to resist totalizing readings of Orientalism, with increasing emphasis on the cultural hybridity, psychological ambivalence, and geographic diaspora of (post)colonial subjects. In this volume I draw on the field of postcolonial theory as a whole, as it has developed since *Orientalism*'s first publication.

2. The most important exception is Piyel Haldar, *Law, Orientalism and Postcolonialism: The Jurisdiction of the Lotus Eaters* (London: Routledge-Cavendish, 2007). Haldar focuses on the "colonization of legal subjectivity" specifically in the context of the British colonization of India, while this volume's "Orient" is of course China, and East Asia more generally. Notable essays on legal Orientalism include Veronica Taylor, "Beyond Legal Orientalism," in *Asian Law through Australian Eyes*, ed. Veronica Taylor (Sydney: LBC Information Services, 1997), 47–62; Hilary McGeachy, "The Invention of Burmese Buddhist Law: A Case Study in Legal Orientalism," *Australian Journal of Asian Law* 4, no. 1 (July 2002): 30–52; Jean Allain, "Orientalism and International Law: The Middle East as the Underclass of the International Legal Order," *Leiden Journal of International Law* 17, no. 2 (June 2004): 391–404. There is also a forthcoming volume of the *Journal of Comparative Law* based on a symposium on "Law and Orientalism." See Teemu Ruskola, "Foreword: The World According to Orientalism," *Journal of Comparative Law* (forthcoming 2013).

3. Act of June 30, 1906, Pub. L. No. 59–403, 34 Stat. 814.

4. Lewis Carroll, *Alice's Adventures in Wonderland & Through the Looking-Glass* (New York: Signet Classic, 2000), 102–118.

5. While the story of Manifest Destiny is well known, the Confucian civilizing mission is probably less so. See Stevan Harrell, "Introduction: Civilizing Projects and the Reaction to Them," in *Cultural Encounters on China's Ethnic Frontiers*, ed. Stevan Harrell (Seattle: University of Washington Press, 1995), 3–36.

6. For an analysis of comparative law as an ideology of governance—rather than merely disinterested scholarly study—see David Kennedy, "The Methods and the Politics," in *Comparative Legal Studies: Traditions and Transitions*, ed. Pierre Legrand and Roderick Munday (Cambridge: Cambridge University Press, 2003), 345–433.

7. In attempting a "global history of China," I draw inspiration from Timothy Brook's *Vermeer's Hat: The Seventeenth Century and the Dawn of the Global World* (New York: Bloomsbury Press, 2008).

8. The references to Persia and Peru are significant, given a history of Chinese diplomatic contacts with both, and of Chinese mass migration to the latter. See, for example, Adam McKeown, *Chinese Migrant Networks and Cultural Change: Peru, Chicago, Hawaii, 1900–1936* (Chicago: University of Chicago Press, 2001). On the history of anti-Chinese legislation in Mexico, see Robert Chao Romero, *The Chinese in Mexico 1882–1940* (Tucson: University of Arizona Press, 2010), 145–190.

9. Jonas Grimheden, *Themis v.* Xiezhi: *Assessing Judicial Independence in the People's Republic of China under International Human Rights Law* (Lund, Sweden: Lund University Press, 2004), 12.

10. Ernest Alabaster, preface to *Notes and Commentaries on Chinese Criminal Law, and Cognate Topics: With Special Relation to Ruling Cases; Together with a Brief Excursus on the Law of Property, Chiefly Founded on the Writings of the Late Sir Chaloner Alabaster* (London: Luzac, 1899), v.

11. As Granet observes, "La notion chinoise de l'*Ordre* exclut, sous tous ses aspects, l'idée de Loi." Marcel Granet, *La Pensée Chinoise* (Paris: La Renaissance du Livre, 1934), 590. As Jérôme Bourgon shows, the influential French legal scholar Jean Escarra in turn relied on Granet in his analysis of Chinese law. Jérôme Bourgon, "Aspects of Chinese Legal Culture (Part One)," *International Journal of Asian Studies* 4, no. 2 (2007): 243–245.

12. William P. Alford, "Law, Law, What Law? Why Western Scholars of China Have Not Had More to Say about Its Law," in *The Limits of the Rule of Law in China*, ed. Karen G. Turner, James V. Feinerman and R. Kent Guy (Seattle: University of Washington Press, 2000), 45.

13. See Max Weber, *The Religion of China: Confucianism and Taoism*, trans. and ed. Hans H. Gerth (Glencoe, IL: Free Press, 1951), 102, 148–150. See also Anthony T. Kronman, *Max Weber* (Stanford, CA: Stanford University Press, 1983).

14. Thomas B. Stephens, *Order and Discipline in China: The Shanghai Mixed Court, 1911–27* (Seattle: University of Washington Press, 1992), 115. John King Fairbank is perhaps the best-known advocate of the thesis that China lacks both a tradition of private law and a system of rule-of-law in general. See Fairbank, *China: A New History* (Cambridge, MA: Belknap Press of Harvard University Press, 1992), 185–186. Fairbank's lifelong theme of Chinese lawlessness already permeates much of his masterly *Trade and Diplomacy on the China Coast: The Opening of the Treaty Ports, 1842–1854* (Cambridge, MA: Harvard University Press, 1953). As Tani Barlow incisively analyzes in *Trade and Diplomacy on the China Coast*, "What the West 'had' that China did not, what in the end seduced China into passive acquiescence (made it Other) was Law. Or, to put it slightly differently, the universalist Law of treaty, human rights, science, and so on clarified the difference between China and the West as a relation of absence and presence, by pointing out the anarchic, ever multiplying, seething differences *within* China; China, alas, stood to Western Law as the particular stands to the Universal. And, I would hazard, that is why the theme of 'lawfulness' takes on such epic proportions in Fairbank's text." Tani E. Barlow, "Colonialism's Career in Postwar China Studies," in *Formations of Colonial Modernity in East Asia*, ed. Tani E. Barlow (Durham, NC: Duke University Press, 1997), 389–390.

15. On the rise of twinned discourses of rule-of-law and human rights in the post–Cold War world, see, for example, Yves Dezalay and Bryant G. Garth, eds., *Lawyers and the Rule of Law in an Era of Globalization* (Abingdon, Oxon; New York:

Routledge, 2011); Yves Dezalay and Bryant G. Garth, eds., *Global Prescriptions: The Production, Exportation, and Importation of a New Legal Orthodoxy* (Ann Arbor: University of Michigan Press, 2002); Samuel Moyn, *The Last Utopia: Human Rights in History* (Cambridge, MA: Belknap Press of Harvard University Press, 2010).

16. The most notorious, and polemical, statement is in Francis Fukuyama, *The End of History and the Last Man* (New York: Free Press, 1992).

17. See, for example, Randall Peerenboom, "Ruling the Country in Accordance with Law: Reflections on the Rule and Role of Law in Contemporary China," *Cultural Dynamics* 11, no. 3 (November 1999): 315–351; Margaret Jane Radin, "Reconsidering the Rule of Law," *Boston University Law Review* 69, no. 4 (July 1989): 783–791. For a thorough theoretical analysis of the multiple meanings of the term, see Brian Z. Tamanaha, *On the Rule of Law: History, Politics, Theory* (Cambridge: Cambridge University Press, 2004). On rule-of-law in authoritarian regimes, see Tom Ginsburg and Tamir Moustafa, eds., *Rule by Law: The Politics of Courts in Authoritarian Regimes* (Cambridge: Cambridge University Press, 2008).

18. For a classic statement of the self-evident desirability of rule-of-law, see, for example, Owen M. Fiss, "Against Settlement," *Yale Law Journal* 93, no. 6 (May 1984): 1073–1090. See also Morton J. Horwitz, "The Rule of Law: An Unqualified Human Good?," *Yale Law Journal* 86, no. 3 (January 1977): 565.

19. For a study of Chinese understandings of democracy, see Andrew J. Nathan, *Chinese Democracy* (New York: Knopf, 1985).

20. As Thomas Carothers notes, "despite the close ties of the rule of law to democracy and capitalism, it stands apart as a nonideological, even technical, solution." Thomas Carothers, "The Rule of Law Revival," *Foreign Affairs* 77, no. 2 (March/April 1998): 99. For one famous reduction of the rule-of-law to a system of rules, see Antonin Scalia, "The Rule of Law as a Law of Rules," *University of Chicago Law Review* 56, no. 4 (Fall 1989): 1175–1188.

21. The phrase is from Paul W. Kahn, *The Cultural Study of Law: Reconstructing Legal Scholarship* (Chicago: University of Chicago Press, 1999), 36. As Kahn elaborates, "to live under the rule of law is to maintain a set of beliefs about the self and community, time and space, authority and representation." Ibid., 36.

22. On being in the world, see generally Martin Heidegger, *Being and Time*, trans. Joan Stambaugh, rev. ed. (Albany: State University of New York Press, 2010).

23. Marbury v. Madison, 5 U.S. (1 Cranch) 137, 163 (1803).

24. Kahn, *Cultural Study of Law*, 67.

25. As David Hall and Roger Ames put it in their study of Chinese democracy, "Westerners cannot think of the 'rule of man' as anything other than an invitation to despotism." David L. Hall and Roger T. Ames, *The Democracy of the Dead: Dewey, Confucius, and the Hope for Democracy in China* (Chicago: Open Court Press, 1999), 216. For an interpretation of the Chinese political tradition as a system of rule-of-law, see Qiang Fang and Roger des Forges, "Were Chinese Rulers

above the Law? Toward a Theory of the Rule of Law in China from Early Times to 1949 CE," *Stanford Journal of International Law* 44 (2008): 101–146.

26. To be sure, in Canada indigenous peoples are in fact identified as "First Nations," recognizing the priority of their historical claim.

27. Dipesh Chakrabarty, *Provincializing Europe: Postcolonial Thought and Historical Difference* (Princeton, NJ: Princeton University Press, 2000), 16.

28. See Ran Hirschl, *Towards Juristocracy: The Origins and Consequences of the New Constitutionalism* (Cambridge, MA: Harvard University Press, 2004).

29. See, for example, Stanley Lubman's analysis of congressional debates on China-related issues, including human rights. Stanley Lubman, "The Dragon as Demon: Images of China on Capitol Hill," *Journal of Contemporary China* 13 (2004), 541–565.

30. Peter Fitzpatrick, *The Mythology of Modern Law* (London: Routledge, 1992).

31. Montesquieu, *The Spirit of the Laws,* trans. and ed. Anne M. Cohler, Basia Carolyn Miller, and Harold Samuel Stone (Cambridge: Cambridge University Press, 1989). As defined by Montesquieu, "monarchical government is that in which one alone governs, but by fixed and established laws; whereas, in despotic government, one alone, without law and without rule, draws everything along by his will and his caprices." Ibid., 10. For a more extended genealogy of Oriental despotism, especially in relation to European travel writings, see Joan-Pau Rubiés, "Oriental Despotism and European Orientalism: Botero to Montesquieu," *Journal of Early Modern History* 9 (2005): 109–180. For a historical critique of the notion of Oriental despotism and a genealogy of its reception in China, see Hou Xudong 侯旭东, "Zhongguo gudai zhuanzhi shuo de zhishi kaogu" 中国古代专制说的知识考古 [The theory of ancient Chinese despotism: An archaelogy of knowledge], *Jindaishi yanjiu* 近代史研究 [Modern Chinese history studies] (2008): 4–28.

32. See, for example, Madeline Yuan-yin Hsu, *Dreaming of Gold, Dreaming of Home: Transnationalism and Migration between the United States and South China, 1882–1943* (Stanford, CA: Stanford University Press, 2000); McKeown, *Chinese Migrant Networks;* Aihwa Ong, *Flexible Citizenship: The Cultural Logics of Transnationality* (Durham, NC: Duke University Press, 1999); Philip A. Kuhn, *Chinese among Others: Emigration in Modern Times* (Lanham, MD: Rowman & Littlefield, 2008). For an analysis of the limits of diaspora as a methodological concept, see Shu-mei Shih, *Visuality and Identity: Sinophone Articulations across the Pacific* (Berkeley: University of California Press, 2007).

33. Alford, "Law, Law, What Law?"

34. Kathryn Bernhardt and Philip C. C. Huang, eds., *Civil Law in Qing and Republican China* (Stanford, CA: Stanford University Press, 1994); Philip C. C. Huang, *Civil Justice in China: Representation and Practice in the Qing* (Stanford, CA: Stanford University Press, 1996); Matthew H. Sommer, *Sex, Law, and Society in Late Imperial China* (Stanford, CA: Stanford University Press, 2000).

35. Paul A. Cohen, *Discovering History in China: American Historical Writing on the Recent Chinese Past* (New York: Columbia University Press, 1984), 6.

36. Lucy E. Salyer, *Laws Harsh as Tigers: Chinese Immigrants and the Shaping of Modern Immigration Law* (Chapel Hill: University of North Carolina Press, 1995); Charles J. McClain, *In Search of Equality: The Chinese Struggle against Discrimination in Nineteenth-Century America* (Berkeley: University of California Press, 1994).

37. Hsu, *Dreaming of Gold*, is exemplary in the transnational mode of its analysis.

38. For an important, and early, exception to such intellectual segregation, see Delber L. McKee, *Chinese Exclusion versus the Open Door Policy, 1900–1906: Clashes over China Policy in the Roosevelt Era* (Detroit, MI: Wayne State University Press, 1977).

39. Studies of (semi)colonialism in China include James Hevia, *English Lessons: The Pedagogy of Imperialism in Nineteenth-Century China* (Durham, NC: Duke University Press; Hong Kong: Hong Kong University Press, 2003); Bryna Goodman and David S. G. Goodman, eds., *Twentieth-Century Colonialism: Localities, the Everyday, and the World* (Abingdon, Oxon: Routledge, 2012).

40. See, for example, Jodi Kim, *Ends of Empire, Asian American Critique and the Cold War* (Minneapolis: University of Minnesota Press, 2010).

41. For leading U.S., and more generally Anglophone, studies of the Chinese legal system, see, for example, Randall Peerenboom, *China's Long March toward Rule of Law* (Cambridge: Cambridge University Press, 2002); Stanley B. Lubman, *Bird in a Cage: Legal Reform in China after Mao* (Stanford, CA: Stanford University Press, 1999); Derk Bodde and Clarence Morris, *Law in Imperial China: Exemplified by 190 Ch'ing Dynasty Cases, Translated from the Hsing-an hui-lan, with Historical, Social, and Juridical Commentaries* (Cambridge, MA: Harvard University Press, 1967); Albert Hung-yee Chen, *An Introduction to the Legal System of the People's Republic of China*, 3rd ed. (Hong Kong: LexisNexis, 2004); Jianfu Chen, *Chinese Law: Context and Transformation* (Leiden, Netherlands: Martinus Nijhoff, 1998).

42. See, for example, Harold J. Berman, *Justice in the U.S.S.R.: An Interpretation of Soviet Law*, rev. ed. (Cambridge, MA: Harvard University Press, 1963); W. E. Butler, *Soviet Law*, 2nd ed. (Stoneham, MA: Butterworths, 1988); and more recently, Inga Markovits, *Justice in Lüritz: Experiencing Socialist Law in East Germany* (Princeton, NJ: Princeton University Press, 2010).

43. See, for example, Ritu Birla, *Stages of Capital: Law, Culture, and Market Governance in Late Colonial India* (Durham, NC: Duke University Press, 2009); Nasser Hussain, *The Jurisprudence of Emergency: Colonialism and the Rule of Law* (Ann Arbor: University of Michigan Press, 2003); Radhika Singha, *A Despotism of Law: Crime and Justice in Early Colonial India* (Delhi: Oxford University Press, 1998); Upendra Baxi, "'The State's Emissary': The Place of Law in Subaltern Studies," in *Subaltern Studies: Writings on South Asian History and Society*, ed. Partha Chatterjee and Gyanendra Pandey, vol. 7 (Delhi: Oxford University Press,

1992), 247–264; Antony Anghie, *Imperialism, Sovereignty and the Making of International Law* (Cambridge: Cambridge University Press, 2007); Martti Koskenniemi, *The Gentle Civilizer of Nations: The Rise and Fall of International Law, 1870–1960* (Cambridge: Cambridge University Press, 2004); Lauren Benton, *Law and Colonial Cultures: Legal Regimes in World History, 1400–1900* (New York: Cambridge University Press, 2002); Eve Darian-Smith and Peter Fitzpatrick, eds., *Laws of the Postcolonial* (Ann Arbor: University of Michigan Press, 1999); Jean Comaroff and John L. Comaroff, eds., *Law and Disorder in the Postcolony* (Chicago: University of Chicago Press, 2006).

44. This point is made forcefully by Eric Hayot, who refers to China's not being colonized as "a crucial event in the history of colonialism. . . . It is precisely by virtue of being on the margins of the postcolonial that China can contribute to the historical and theoretical work in the field." See Eric Hayot, *The Hypothetical Mandarin: Sympathy, Modernity, and Chinese Pain* (New York: Oxford University Press, 2009), 10.

45. See, for example, Sally Engle Merry, *Colonizing Hawai'i: The Cultural Power of Law* (Princeton, NJ: Princeton University Press, 2000); Winfred Lee Thompson, *The Introduction of American Law in the Philippines and Puerto Rico, 1898–1905* (Fayetteville: University of Arkansas Press, 1989).

46. However, there are studies of the dissemination of U.S. legal thought and legal ideology more generally, especially in Latin America. See, for example, Yves Dezalay and Bryant G. Garth, *The Internationalization of Palace Wars: Lawyers, Economists, and the Contest to Transform Latin American States* (Chicago: University of Chicago Press, 2002); James A. Gardner, *Legal Imperialism: American Lawyers and Foreign Aid in Latin America* (Madison: University of Wisconsin Press, 1980).

47. Paul Gewirtz, "The U.S.-China Rule of Law Initiative," *William & Mary Bill of Rights Journal* 11, no. 2 (February 2003): 619. Gewirtz directs the China Law Center at Yale Law School. Another major U.S. law reformer is Jerome Cohen, a groundbreaking scholar of Chinese law and director of the U.S. Law-Asia Institute at New York University. A longtime critic of China's record on criminal rights, Cohen has studied PRC criminal justice since the 1960s. See Jerome Alan Cohen, *The Criminal Process in the People's Republic of China, 1949–1963: An Introduction* (Cambridge, MA: Harvard University Press, 1968).

48. Mirjan R. Damaška, *The Faces of Justice and State Authority: A Comparative Approach to the Legal Process* (New Haven, CT: Yale University Press, 1986), 199.

49. I sketch this analogy in "The East Asian Legal Tradition," in *Cambridge Companion to Comparative Law*, ed. Mauro Bussani and Ugo Mattei (Cambridge: Cambridge University Press, 2012), 257.

50. Gayatri Chakravorty Spivak, *A Critique of Postcolonial Reason: Toward a History of the Vanishing Present* (Cambridge, MA: Harvard University Press, 1999), 37.

2. MAKING LEGAL AND UNLEGAL SUBJECTS IN HISTORY

1. Michel Foucault, *The Order of Things: An Archaeology of the Human Sciences* (1971; repr., New York: Vintage, 1994), xv.

2. Montesquieu, *The Spirit of the Laws*, trans. and ed. Anne M. Cohler, Basia Carolyn Miller, and Harold Samuel Stone (Cambridge: Cambridge University Press, 1989).

3. Foucault does not provide a citation to Borges's story, although he does (correctly) identify Borges as the author. See Jorge Luis Borges, "The Analytical Language of John Wilkins," in *Other Inquisitions, 1937–1952*, trans. Ruth L. C. Simms (Austin: University of Texas Press, 1964), 103.

4. Indeed, despite some effort to maintain distance to Borges's outrageous "Chinese encyclopaedia," Foucault ends up sounding utterly patronizing when he patiently suggests that we cannot dismiss "with complete certainty" the validity of the "Chinese" classification of animals into "tame" and "embalmed," for instance. See Foucault, *Order of Things*, xix.

5. Hans-Georg Gadamer, *Truth and Method*, ed. Joel Weinsheimer and Donald G. Marshall, 2nd ed. (New York: Crossroad, 1989), 295.

6. William P. Alford, "Law, Law, What Law? Why Western Scholars of China Have Not Had More to Say about Its Law," in *The Limits of the Rule of Law in China*, ed. Karen G. Turner, James V. Feinerman, and R. Kent Guy (Seattle: University of Washington Press, 2000), 45.

7. Whether we consciously reject or embrace that tradition, it provides the context against which any contemporary statement about Chinese law is made, understood, and misunderstood. Put differently, insofar as prejudice relies on unstated "truths," it need not even be communicated directly: "if the message is already waiting at the receiver's end, it doesn't even need to be sent; it just needs to be activated." David M. Halperin, *Saint Foucault: Towards a Gay Hagiography* (New York: Oxford University Press, 1995), 13.

8. That is, I am not rejecting functionalism in all forms and for all purposes. Indeed, if "function" is conceived broadly enough, the label "functionalism" can subsume almost any methodology. Even laws that seem to serve no function other than that of making an ideological statement (or, less tendentiously, expressing a collective value judgment) can be analyzed as serving an ideological (or expressive) function. However, I am not invested—either positively or negatively—in the label itself, and my goal here is simply to examine the limits of a particular mode of analysis that is conventionally associated with that label, namely, sociological functionalism.

9. For a classic statement of sociological functionalism, see Talcott Parsons, *The Social System* (Glencoe, IL: Free Press, 1951). The appeal of functionalism is by no means limited to comparative law. It animates much of law-and-society scholarship and legal history as well, where it implies an evolutionary paradigm for

the understanding of legal change. On the role of functionalism (or "adaptation-ism," as Gordon calls it) in legal history, see generally Robert W. Gordon, "Histori-cism in Legal Scholarship," *Yale Law Journal* 90, no. 5 (April 1981): 1017–1056. See also Ralf Michaels, "The Functional Method of Comparative Law," in *The Oxford Handbook of Comparative Law*, ed. Mathias Reimann and Reinhard Zimmermann (Oxford: Oxford University Press, 2006), 309–382.

10. See, for example, Sybille van der Sprenkel, *Legal Institutions in Manchu China: A Sociological Analysis* (London: University of London, Athlone Press, 1962), 80–96. Here, as elsewhere, I use the adjective "traditional" only provisionally. In the division of Chinese history into "traditional" and "modern," the latter term "usually refer[s] to the period of significant contact with the modern West." See Paul A. Cohen, *Discovering History in China: American Historical Writing on the Recent Chinese Past* (New York: Columbia University Press, 1984), 58. I use the phrase "traditional China" simply to denote a certain historical period, without implying a particular normative vision of history.

11. See, for example, Joseph Needham, *Science and Civilisation in China*, vol. 2 (Cambridge: Cambridge University Press, 1956), 518–583; Hu Shih, "The Natural Law in the Chinese Tradition," *University of Notre Dame Natural Law Institute Proceedings* 5 (1953): 117–163. Unless otherwise indicated, in the remainder of this book I use the terms "Confucian" and "Confucianism" to refer to the state ideology perpetuated by the imperial civil service examination system, with full awareness that this definition does not exhaust alternative meanings. On the one hand, this orthodox Confucianism, which grew increasingly rigid over time, stood in contrast to the philosophical Confucianisms in which it originated. On the other hand, it was also distinct from the Confucian officialdom's actual policies and administra-tive practices, which did not necessarily conform to the state's professed ideals.

12. Bernard S. Cohn, *Colonialism and Its Forms of Knowledge: The British in India* (Princeton, NJ: Princeton University Press, 1996), 57–75.

13. Ibid., 71.

14. Hugh T. Scogin Jr., "Between Heaven and Man: Contract and the State in Han Dynasty China," *Southern California Law Review* 63, no. 5 (July 1990): 1326.

15. Janet E. Ainsworth, "Categories and Culture: On the 'Rectification of Names' in Comparative Law," *Cornell Law Review* 82, no. 1 (November 1996): 19–20.

16. Max Gluckman, *The Judicial Process among the Barotse of Northern Rhodesia* (Manchester, UK: Manchester University Press, 1955), 271.

17. John Henry Merryman, "Comparative Law and Scientific Explanation," in *Law in the United States of America in Social and Technological Revolution: Reports from the United States of America on Topics of Major Concern as Established for the IX Congress of the International Academy of Comparative Law*, ed. John N. Hazard and Wenceslas J. Wagner (Brussels, Belgium: Émile Bruylant, 1974), 81–82.

18. Robert M. Cover, "Violence and the Word," *Yale Law Journal* 95, no. 8 (July 1986): 1601–1630. For a Marxist analysis of the materiality of ideology and its embeddedness in material practices of the state, see Louis Althusser, "Ideology and Ideological State Apparatuses (Notes toward an Investigation)," in *Lenin and Philosophy and Other Essays*, trans. Ben Brewster (New York: Monthly Review Press, 2001), 166.

19. On the necessarily global nature of legal theorizing, see William Twining, *Globalisation & Legal Theory* (London: Butterworths, 2000). Like Twining, Brian Tamanaha is notable in attempting a genuinely global theoretical account of law. See Brian Z. Tamanaha, *A General Jurisprudence of Law and Society* (Oxford: Oxford University Press, 2001).

20. On the politics of using the translation "barbarian," see Lydia Liu, *The Clash of Empires* (Cambridge, MA: Harvard University Press, 2004).

21. Stated simply, the objects of Orientalist knowledge fulfill its prophecies by embracing it. As Said observes, "the modern Orient, in short, participates in its own Orientalizing." Edward W. Said, *Orientalism* (New York: Pantheon Books, 1978), 325.

22. Boaventura de Sousa Santos, *Toward a New Common Sense: Law, Science, and Politics in the Paradigmatic Transition* (New York: Routledge, 1995), 472–473. To be sure, like much of the literature that takes globalization as its reference point, Santos envisions his "interlegality" as a largely new, peculiarly postmodern form of legality, but the phenomenon is hardly new, although it is perhaps more pronounced today. Harold Berman observes that possibly "the most distinctive feature of the Western legal tradition is the coexistence and competition within the same community of diverse jurisdictions and diverse legal systems." See Harold J. Berman, *Law and Revolution: The Formation of the Western Legal Tradition* (Cambridge, MA: Harvard University Press, 1983), 10. For an emphatic challenge to the conventional view that China and, by implication, Chinese law exist in millennial isolation from the rest of the world, see Joanna Waley-Cohen, *The Sextants of Beijing: Global Currents in Chinese History* (New York: Norton, 1999). Lionel Jensen argues that what we understand as "Confucianism" today is in fact a joint Sino-Western invention. See Lionel M. Jensen, *Manufacturing Confucianism: Chinese Traditions and Universal Civilization* (Durham, NC: Duke University Press, 1997).

23. For accounts of the Confucianization of Chinese law, see Derk Bodde and Clarence Morris, *Law in Imperial China: Exemplified by 190 Ch'ing Dynasty Cases; Translated from the Hsing-an hui-lan, with Historical, Social, and Juridical Commentaries* (Cambridge, MA: Harvard University Press, 1967); T'ung-tsu Ch'ü, *Law and Society in Traditional China* (Paris: Mouton, 1961).

24. See Alford, "Law, Law, What Law?," 48.

25. Robert W. Gordon, "Critical Legal Histories," *Stanford Law Review* 36, nos. 1 & 2 (January 1984): 109.

26. Ibid.

27. For a constitutive account of law, see Alan Hunt, *Explorations in Law and Society: Toward a Constitutive Theory of Law* (New York: Routledge, 1993).

28. Needham, *Science and Civilisation,* 575. Compare William Ewald, "Comparative Jurisprudence (I): What Was It Like to Try a Rat?," *University of Pennsylvania Law Review* 143, no. 6 (June 1995): 2111.

29. Montesquieu, *Spirit of the Laws,* bk. 1, chaps. 3, 8.

30. Pierre Legrand, in particular, has long insisted on the ontological nature of legal comparison, and of legal interpretation more generally. See, for example, Pierre Legrand, "Word/World (of Primordial Issues for Comparative Legal Studies)," in *Paradoxes of European Legal Integration,* ed. Hanne Petersen et al. (Aldershot, UK: Ashgate, 2008), 185–234; Legrand, "Paradoxically, Derrida: For a Comparative Legal Studies," *Cardozo Law Review* 27, no. 2 (November 2005): 631–717.

31. Performativity, as popularized by Judith Butler's analysis of sex and gender, is likely the most important postmodern analytic in understanding how the discourses of race, gender, and sexuality constitute us as subjects. It is noteworthy that Butler draws expressly on Austin's theory of "performative utterances," the key illustrations of which are legal statements. Law is perhaps not only incidentally but paradigmatically performative. See generally J. L. Austin, *How to Do Things with Words* (Oxford: Clarendon Press, 1962); J. L. Austin, "Performative Utterances," in *Philosophical Papers,* ed. J. O. Urmson and G. J. Warnock (Oxford: Clarendon Press, 1961), 220–239.

32. To be sure, law is only one discourse, in the Foucaultian sense, among many. From a broader perspective, Foucault's oeuvre is a study of the ways in which human beings have become subjects of various modern discourses, such as law, medicine, and science. As Foucault observes in *Discipline and Punish,* the "soul," or subjectivity, that we believe to inhabit the body is in fact "the effect and instrument of a political anatomy; the soul is the prison of the body." See Michel Foucault, *Discipline and Punish: The Birth of the Prison,* trans. Alan Sheridan (New York: Vintage Books, 1977), 30. While I read Foucault's history of the emergence of modern penal institutions as a legal analysis, Foucault himself at times adopts a narrower, positivist conception of law where law seems to constitute little more than the express command (or, more frequently, prohibition) of the sovereign. As Duncan Kennedy observes, Foucault often opposes this narrowly operating "juridical power" to "disciplinary power," viewing juridical power as " 'only the terminal form' or 'crystallization' of processes of power that take place at a distance from legal institutions." See Duncan Kennedy, "The Stakes of Law, or Hale and Foucault!," in *Sexy Dressing Etc.* (Cambridge, MA: Harvard University Press, 1993), 120. On Foucault's tendency toward legal positivism, see Hugh Baxter, "Bringing Foucault into Law and Law into Foucault," *Stanford Law Review* 48, no. 2 (January 1996): 449–479. In any event, from the perspective of Foucault's larger enterprise, it seems more accurate to view law as one of several modern disciplinary discourses rather than merely the express command of the state.

33. Althusser, "Ideology," 170, 172–173. In Althusser's view, the seeming obviousness of the "you and I are subjects" is the very effect of ideology, so that the notion of an "ideological subject" is itself "a tautological proposition." Ibid., 171. Turning "concrete individuals" into subjects is what ideology does. By comparing Foucault's "discourse" to Althusser's "ideology," I am not implying an identity between the two concepts. Indeed, Foucault intends his notion of "discourse" to complicate a simple Marxist dichotomy between a material base and ideology.

34. Ibid., 174.

35. This gloss on Althusser is from Judith Butler, *The Psychic Life of Power: Theories in Subjection* (Stanford, CA: Stanford University Press, 1997), 5.

36. Althusser, "Ideology," 176.

37. For an account of the deep embeddedness of U.S. family law in a capitalist political economy and its assumptions about the autonomy of legal subjects, see Martha Albertson Fineman, *The Neutered Mother, the Sexual Family, and Other Twentieth Century Tragedies* (New York: Routledge, 1995).

38. See Oliver Wendell Holmes, "The Path of the Law," *Harvard Law Review* 10, no. 8 (March 1897): 459.

39. Benedict Anderson, *Imagined Communities: Reflections on the Origin and Spread of Nationalism*, rev. ed. (London: Verso, 1991).

40. Alexis de Tocqueville, *Democracy in America*, ed. Phillips Bradley, vol. 1 (New York: Vintage, 1990), 280.

41. The characterization of Douglass' constitutional faith is from Robert M. Cover, "The Supreme Court, 1982 Term—Foreword: *Nomos* and Narrative," *Harvard Law Review* 97, no. 1 (November 1983): 30. In Douglass's own words, "I was conducted to the conclusion that the Constitution of the United States— inaugurated to 'form a more perfect union, establish justice, insure domestic tranquility, provide for the common defense, promote the general welfare, and secure the blessings of liberty'–could not well have been designed at the same time to maintain and perpetuate a system of rapine and murder like slavery, especially as not one word can be found in the Constitution to authorize such a belief." Frederick Douglass, *The Life and Times of Frederick Douglass: His Early Life as a Slave, His Escape from Bondage, and His Complete History* (1892; repr., New York: Collier Books, 1962), 261–262. Indeed, Douglass's identification with law has in turn become part of American cultural identity. See Priscilla Wald, "Neither Citizen nor Alien: National Narratives, Frederick Douglass, and the Politics of Self-Determination," in *Constituting Americans: Cultural Anxiety and Narrative Form* (Durham, NC: Duke University Press, 1995), 14–105.

42. David J. Langum, *Law and Community on the Mexican California Frontier: Anglo-American Expatriates and the Clash of Legal Traditions, 1821–1846* (Norman: University of Oklahoma Press, 1987), 163–186.

43. Ibid., 186.

44. The expatriate traders were exceedingly self-conscious as well as self-righteous about how their attachment to law set them apart from, and above, the native Californios. The fact that alcaldes, the local Mexican officials, roughly analogous to justices of the peace, performed a combination of judicial as well as administrative functions occasioned American cries of the violation of separation of powers. Ibid., 51.

45. Marc Galanter, "Reading the Landscape of Disputes: What We Know and Don't Know (and Think We Know) about Our Allegedly Contentious and Litigious Society," *UCLA Law Review* 31, no. 1 (October 1983): 64.

46. Learned Hand, "The Deficiencies of Trials to Reach the Heart of the Matter," in *Lectures on Legal Topics, 1921–1922*, by James N. Rosenberg et al., *Lectures Delivered before the Association of the Bar of the City of New York* 3 (New York: Macmillan, 1926), 105.

47. See, for example, M. P. Baumgartner, *The Moral Order of a Suburb* (New York: Oxford University Press, 1988), 127–128, which argues that "evidence from the suburbs suggests . . . that the penetration of law into American life has been considerably more limited in its range and effect than is commonly believed." Also see Robert C. Ellickson, *Order without Law: How Neighbors Settle Disputes* (Cambridge, MA: Harvard University Press, 1991).

48. Carol J. Greenhouse, "Interpreting American Litigiousness," in *History and Power in the Study of Law: New Directions in Legal Anthropology*, ed. June Starr and Jane F. Collier (Ithaca, NY: Cornell University Press, 1989), 252.

49. In a similar spirit, Gayatri Spivak elaborates a deconstructionist politics of reading whose challenge "is not to excuse, but to suspend accusation to examine with painstaking care if the protocols of the text contains a moment that can produce something that will generate a new and useful reading." See Gayatri Chakravorty Spivak, *A Critique of Postcolonial Reason: Toward a History of the Vanishing Present* (Cambridge, MA: Harvard University Press, 1999), 97–98.

50. Georg Wilhelm Friedrich Hegel, *The Philosophy of History*, trans. J. Sibree (New York: Dover, 1956), 103.

51. Ibid., 105–106.

52. Ibid., 116.

53. Shlomo Avineri, ed., *Karl Marx on Colonialism and Modernization: His Despatches and Other Writings on China, India, Mexico, the Middle East and North Africa* (Garden City, NY: Doubleday, 1968), 323; see also Karl Marx, *Marx on China, 1853–1860: Articles from The New York Daily Tribune*, with an introduction by Dona Torr (London: Lawrence & Wishart, 1951).

54. Foucault, *Order of Things*, xix.

55. Hegel, *Philosophy of History*, 105, 113.

56. Ibid., 121.

57. Ibid., 111.

58. Haun Saussy, *The Problem of a Chinese Aesthetic* (Stanford, CA: Stanford University Press, 1993), 161.

59. To be sure, in Marx's case even the modern Western legal civilization may ultimately be destined to wither away together with the state, but as the penultimate way station to utopia it certainly represents a higher stage in the development of historical materialism than the despotic law of Oriental civilizations. As Marx states unequivocally, colonial rule in Asia had a dual mission, "one destructive, the other regenerating—the annihilation of old Asiatic society, and the laying of the material foundations of Western society in Asia." See Karl Marx, "The Future Results of British Rule in India," in *The Marx-Engels Reader*, ed. Robert C. Tucker, 2nd ed. (New York: Norton, 1978), 659.

60. Jefferson to G. K. van Hogendorp, 13 October 1785, in *The Papers of Thomas Jefferson*, vol. 8: 25 February to 31 October 1785, ed. Julian P. Boyd (Princeton, NJ: Princeton University Press, 1953), 633; "Letter from Dr. Franklin to the Rev. Mr. George Whitefield," *The Evangelical Magazine* 11 (1803): 27–28.

61. See "From the Morals of *Confucius*," *The Pennsylvania Gazette*, February 28–March 7, 1737, describing Confucius' plan for "Order and Justice" in government; "Continuation of the Morals of *Confucius*," *The Pennsylvania Gazette*, March 14–21, 1737, extolling "the extraordinary Precautions which the Judges took before any Cause was brought before their Tribunal."

62. A. Owen Aldridge, *The Dragon and the Eagle: The Presence of China in the American Enlightenment* (Detroit, MI: Wayne State University Press, 1993), 91.

63. Consequa v. Fanning, 3 Johns. Ch. 587, 607 (N.Y. Ch. 1818). Pan Zhangyao, identified as "Consequa" in court records, ended up in litigation after he sold tea to U.S. merchants on credit and the buyers used complaints about the quality of tea as an excuse not to pay. His inability to collect in U.S. courts led directly to his ultimate bankruptcy. See Frederic D. Grant, Jr., "Failure of the Li-Ch'uan Hong: Litigation as a Hazard of Nineteenth Century Foreign Trade," *American Neptune* 48, no. 4 (1988): 243.

64. Stuart Creighton Miller, *The Unwelcome Immigrant: The American Image of the Chinese, 1785–1882* (Berkeley: University of California Press, 1969), 27–28. See also Milton R. Konvitz, *The Alien and the Asiatic in American Law* (Ithaca, NY: Cornell University Press, 1946).

65. California State Senate, Special Committee on Chinese Immigration, *Chinese Immigration: Its Social, Moral, and Political Effect: Report to the California State Senate of Its Special Committee on Chinese Immigration* (Sacramento: State Printing Office, 1878), 47, quoted in Tomás Almaguer, *Racial Fault Lines: The Historical Origins of White Supremacy in California* (Berkeley: University of California Press, 1994), 174. These conclusions were foreshadowed by a joint special committee of the U.S. Congress: "To admit these vast numbers of aliens to citizenship and the ballot would practically destroy republican institutions on the

Pacific coast, for the Chinese have no comprehension of any form of government but despotism, and have not the words in their own language to describe intelligibly the principles of our representative system." Report of the Joint Special Committee to Investigate Chinese Immigration, S. Rep. No. 44–689 (1877), quoted in Leti Volpp, " 'Obnoxious to Their Very Nature': Asian Americans and Constitutional Citizenship," *Citizenship Studies* 5, no. 1 (February 2001): 63.

66. Terrace v. Thompson, 274 F. 841, 849 (W.D. Wash. 1921), *aff'd*, 263 U.S. 197 (1923).

67. Ibid., observing, "It is obvious that the objection on the part of Congress is not due to color, as color, but only to color as an evidence of a type of civilization which it characterizes."

68. As David Porter's study of the changing image of China in England shows, over time it was transformed from a symbol of linguistic and philosophical legitimacy to one of religious, aesthetic, and ultimately commercial illegitimacy. See David Porter, *Ideographia: The Chinese Cipher in Early Modern Europe* (Stanford, CA: Stanford University Press, 2001).

69. Jacques Derrida, *Of Grammatology*, trans. Gayatri Chakravorty Spivak (Baltimore, MD: Johns Hopkins University Press, 1976), 80.

70. See Friedrich Nietzsche, *The Gay Science: With a Prelude in Rhymes and an Appendix of Songs*, trans. Walter Kaufmann (New York: Vintage, 1974).

71. Hegel, *Philosophy of History*, 175.

72. See generally Basil Guy, *The French Image of China before and after Voltaire*, Studies on Voltaire and the Eighteenth Century 21 (Geneva: Institut et Musée Voltaire, 1963), 261, observing, for example, Voltaire's high regard for what he viewed as the Chinese "cult of justice" and "the absence of fanaticism or religious prejudice."

73. John Henry Wigmore, *A Panorama of the World's Legal Systems*, vol. 1 (St. Paul, MN: West Publishing, 1928), 178, quoting a Spanish missionary; see also Matteo Ricci, *China in the Sixteenth Century: The Journals of Matthew Ricci, 1583–1610*, trans. Louis J. Gallagher (New York: Random House, 1953), 43, where Ricci finds Chinese law predictable and nonarbitrary, noting with approval that a code, once promulgated by the founder of a dynasty, "cannot be changed without good reason."

74. Derrida, *Of Grammatology*, 79. Ironically, the engagement of Derrida himself with China is not necessarily much deeper: "the *East* is never seriously studied or deconstructed in the Derridean text." See Gayatri Chakravorty Spivak, translator's preface to *Of Grammatology*, lxxxii.

75. Wigmore, *Panorama*, vol. 1, 155, quoting a Portuguese merchant.

76. See, for example, D. E. Mungello, *The Great Encounter of China and the West, 1500–1800* (Lanham, MD: Rowman & Littlefield, 1999).

77. Hegel, *Philosophy of History*, 134–135. For a more extensive analysis of Hegel's (mis)understanding of the Chinese language, see Jacques Derrida, "The Pit

and the Pyramid: Introduction to Hegel's Semiology," in *Margins of Philosophy*, trans. Alan Bass (Chicago: University of Chicago Press, 1982), 69–108.

78. Max Weber, *The Religion of China: Confucianism and Taoism*, trans. and ed. Hans H. Gerth (Glencoe, IL: Free Press, 1951), 125, 127.

79. See Olivier Roy, "Leibniz et le Chinois comme langue universelle" in *Leibniz et la Chine* (Paris: Librairie Philosophique J. Vrin, 1972), 135–140.

80. George Thomas Staunton, trans., preface to *Ta Tsing Leu Lee; Being Fundamental Laws, and a Selection from the Supplementary Statutes, of the Penal Code of China* (London: T. Cadwell and W. Davies, 1810), xiii.

81. Hosea Ballou Morse, *The Chronicles of the East India Company Trading in China, 1635–1834*, vol. 1 (Cambridge, MA: Harvard University Press; Oxford: Clarendon Press, 1926), 168. It is noteworthy that although Western images of Chinese law have never been monolithic, Jesuits' and other early modern observers' accounts were predominantly positive. However, as traders replaced missionaries as the dominant group of Westerners in China, the perceptions of Chinese law grew increasingly dim. See Gregory Blue, "China and Western Social Thought in the Modern Period," in *China and Historical Capitalism: Genealogies of Sinological Knowledge*, ed. Timothy Brook and Gregory Blue, Studies in Modern Capitalism (Cambridge: Cambridge University Press, 1999), 57–109.

82. Joseph Needham, "The Translation of Old Chinese Scientific and Technical Texts," in *Aspects of Translation*, ed. A. H. Smith, Studies in Communication 2 (London: Secker and Warburg, 1958), 87. For a review of the terms of this debate, see Derek Roebuck and King-kui Sin, "The Ego and I and Ngo: Theoretical Problems in the Translation of the Common Law into Chinese," in *Hong Kong, China and 1997: Essays in Legal Theory*, ed. Raymond Wacks (Hong Kong: Hong Kong University Press, 1993), 185–210. Kwai Hang Ng has found that the use of Cantonese as a spoken language does in fact make a difference in court room dynamics. See Kwai Hang Ng, *The Common Law in Two Voices: Language, Law, & the Post-Colonial Predicament in Hong Kong* (Stanford, CA: Stanford University Press, 2009).

83. Roger North, *A Discourse on the Study of the Laws* (London: Charles Baldwyn, 1824), 13, quoted in Roebuck and Sin, "Ego," 193. Of course, once the English did establish their language as a "legal" one, it was used to maintain their identity as a "rational" people by having parliamentary committees make "findings" about the neighboring linguistic communities—such as, "the Welsh language . . . distorts the truth, favours fraud and abets perjury." See Reginald Coupland, *Welsh and Scottish Nationalism: A Study* (London: Collins, 1954), 186, quoting education commissioners for the House of Commons in 1846. The Irish received similar treatment as subjects of language and law: "The English regarded traditional Irish culture—and its most impressive achievement, the Brehon laws—with the utmost disdain, as the work of mere barbarians. Gaelic, like Welsh, was not conducive to rational expression." See Michael Hechter, *Internal Colonialism: The Celtic Fringe in*

British National Development, 1536–1966 (Berkeley: University of California Press, 1975), 77 (citation omitted).

84. Karl A. Wittfogel, *Oriental Despotism: A Comparative Study of Total Power* (New Haven, CT: Yale University Press, 1957).

85. Mary L. Dudziak, *Cold War Civil Rights: Race and the Image of American Democracy* (Princeton, NJ: Princeton University Press, 2000); John Quigley, *Soviet Legal Innovation and the Law of the Western World* (Cambridge: Cambridge University Press, 2007), 96; Alford, "Law, Law, What Law?," 52.

86. See Robert S. Chang, *Disoriented: Asian Americans, Law, and the Nation-State* (New York: New York University Press, 1999), 53–58. That is, Asian Americans as a group are perceived to be diligent, well-educated, and economically successful—a Model Minority. Although the Model Minority myth has been debunked repeatedly, it retains its dual appeal: it generates and maintains an image of "bad" minorities, and at the same time it masks the ways in which Asian Americans in fact remain socially and economically marginalized. See Bob H. Suzuki, "Education and the Socialization of Asian Americans: A Revisionist Analysis of the 'Model Minority' Thesis," *Amerasia Journal* 4, no. 2 (1977): 23–51.

87. For an analysis of Asian Americans' ineligibility for full political citizenship, see generally Volpp, "Obnoxious," 63.

88. See L. Ling-chi Wang, "Race, Class, Citizenship and Extraterritoriality: Asian Americans and the 1996 Campaign Finance Scandal," *Amerasia Journal* 24, no. 1 (1998): 1–21; Wen Ho Lee, *My Country versus Me: The First-Hand Account by the Los Alamos Scientist Who Was Falsely Accused of Being a Spy* (New York: Hyperion, 2001); Neil Gotanda, "Comparative Racialization: Racial Profiling and the Case of Wen Ho Lee," *UCLA Law Review* 47, no. 6 (August 2000): 1689–1703. To be sure, in light of the Supreme Court's decision in Citizens United v. Federal Election Commission in 2010, concerns about campaign contributions by Chinese Americans seem ironic, given the subsequent legalization of corporate contributions. See 558 U.S. 310 (2010).

89. See Christian G. Fritz, "A Nineteenth Century 'Habeas Corpus Mill': The Chinese before the Federal Courts in California," *American Journal of Legal History* 32, no. 4 (October 1988): 347–372.

90. See Timothy Brook, Jérôme Bourgon, and Gregory Blue, *Death by a Thousand Cuts* (Cambridge, MA: Harvard University Press, 2008).

91. For comparative observations, see Li Chen, "Law, Empire, and Historiography of Modern Sino-Western Relations: A Case Study of the *Lady Hughes* Controversy in 1784," *Law and History Review* 27, no. 1 (2009): 1–54. Indeed, in the preface to his bilingual volume of plates illustrating Chinese punishments, George Mason, in 1801, introduces the Chinese penal code with a favorable comparison to England: "The wisdom of the Chinese Legislature is nowhere more conspicuous than in its treatment of robbers, no person being doomed to suffer death for having merely deprived another of some temporal property, provided he neither uses, nor

carries, any offensive weapon." George Henry Mason, *The Punishments of China, Illustrated by Twenty-Two Engravings: With Explanations in English and French* (London: W. Bulmer, 1801). While Mason does in fact find many Chinese punishments "cruel," there is much less balance to be found in the observations by Peter Auber in 1834, who announces that "The Government is China is despotic" and its subjects therefore are deficient in "all those faculties which distinguish men from the herd that grazes," while the British constitution is "the best form established." Peter Auber, *China: An Outline of the Government, Laws, and Policy* (London: Parbury, Allen, 1834), 51–52. On the reception of Mason's popular volume, see Brook et al., *Death by a Thousand Cuts,* 170–174, and Eric Hayot, *The Hypothetical Mandarin: Sympathy, Modernity, and Chinese Pain* (Oxford: Oxford University Press, 2009), 66–79.

92. Brook et al., *Death by a Thousand Cuts,* 86–95.

93. Ibid., 27.

94. Saussy, *Problem of a Chinese Aesthetic,* 151.

95. Gadamer, *Truth and Method,* 270.

96. As Philip Huang concludes, "The Qing legal system . . . embodied the practical reality of civil law and property rights without their representational realities." Philip Huang, *Civil Justice in China: Representation and Practice in the Qing* (Stanford, CA: Stanford University Press, 1992), 220.

97. See *The Analects,* trans. D. C. Lau (Harmondsworth, UK: Penguin, 1979), bk. 7, chap. 1, 86, quoting Confucius: "I transmit but do not innovate; I am truthful in what I say and devoted to antiquity."

98. That is, at least until recently. Remarkably, the recent official discourse of "harmonious society" draws (at least implicitly, if not expressly) on the Confucian tradition. See Chapter 6.

99. See Arif Dirlik, *Revolution and History: The Origins of Marxist Historiography in China, 1919–1937* (Berkeley: University of California Press, 1978).

100. Jing Junjian, "Legislation Related to the Civil Economy in the Qing Dynasty," trans. Matthew H. Sommer, in *Civil Law in Qing and Republican China,* ed. Kathryn Bernhardt and Philip C. C. Huang (Stanford, CA: Stanford University Press, 1994), 82.

101. For accounts of the debate, see, for example, Michael C. Davis, "Constitutionalism and Political Culture: The Debate over Human Rights and Asian Values," *Harvard Human Rights Journal* 11 (Spring 1998): 109–147; Karen Engle, "Culture and Human Rights: The Asian Values Debate in Context," *New York University Journal of International Law and Politics* 32, no. 2 (Winter 2000): 291–333; Randall Peerenboom, "Beyond Universalism and Relativism: The Evolving Debates about 'Values in Asia,'" *Indiana International & Comparative Law Review* 14, no. 1 (2003): 1–85.

102. These values were expressed at the 1993 Bangkok Declaration made at the Asian Regional Meeting in preparation for the World Conference on Human

Rights in Vienna later that year. The claims were prefigured in provocative statements made by Lee Kuan Yew and Mahathir Mohamad as well as China's White Paper on Human Rights in 1991.

103. Carl Schmitt, *The Concept of the Political*, trans. George Schwab (Chicago: University of Chicago Press, 1996), 54.

104. I analyze the Asian Values debate further in Teemu Ruskola, "Where Is Asia? When Is Asia? Theorizing Comparative Law and International Law," *U.C. Davis Law Review* 44, no. 3 (February 2011): 879–896. On the multiplicity of Asias, see Gayatri Chakravorty Spivak, *Other Asias* (Malden, MA: Blackwell, 2008).

105. This strategy is by no means novel. As Stefan Tanaka observes in his study of the invention of history as a modern discipline in post-Meiji Japan, Japan's claims to historic uniqueness "incorporated many elements used by Westerners to explain Oriental inferiority but turned them into positive characteristics that accounted for Japan's development." See Stefan Tanaka, *Japan's Orient: Rendering Pasts into History* (Berkeley: University of California Press, 1993), 274.

106. Cohen, *Discovering History*, 6.

107. To be sure, the Constitution has been amended several times, but at least in the popular view Americans continue to live under the "same" Constitution. This view is not necessarily shared by constitutional theorists. See, for example, Bruce Ackerman, *We the People*, vol. 1: Foundations (Cambridge, MA: Belknap Press of Harvard University Press, 1991). For an anti-essentialist theory of constitutional continuity over time, see Jed Rubenfeld, *Freedom and Time: A Theory of Constitutional Self-Government* (New Haven, CT: Yale University Press, 2001).

108. As another example of Confucian-like self-projection into tradition, consider Western appeals to an idealized "classical antiquity" (to be strictly distinguished from Eastern-influenced Hellenism) and the need to "preserve[] it within Western culture as the heritage of the past." See Gadamer, *Truth and Method*, 288. Reminding us that Orientalist discourses are constitutive not only of the Oriental as an object but also of the Western subject, James Carrier uses the term "Occidentalism" in a similar fashion to describe the ways in which anthropological studies of "the Orient" have contributed to the idealization of "the West." See James G. Carrier, "Occidentalism: The World Turned Upside-Down," *American Ethnologist* 19, no. 2 (May 1992): 195–212.

109. To quote Charles Taylor, "other-understanding is always in a sense comparative." Charles Taylor, *Philosophical Arguments* (Cambridge, MA: Harvard University Press, 1995), 150.

110. Gadamer, *Truth and Method*, 295.

111. Dipesh Chakrabarty, *Provincializing Europe: Postcolonial Thought and Historical Difference* (Princeton, NJ: Princeton University Press, 2000), 4.

112. There is a large, and growing, literature on the subject. See, for example, James A. Millward, *Beyond the Pass: Economy, Ethnicity, and Empire in Qing Central Asia, 1759–1864* (Stanford, CA: Stanford University Press, 1998); Peter C. Perdue,

China Marches West: The Qing Conquest of Central Eurasia (Cambridge, MA: Belknap Press of Harvard University Press, 2005); Laura Hostetler, *Qing Colonial Enterprise: Ethnography and Cartography in Early Modern China* (Chicago: University of Chicago Press, 2005).

113. Anderson, *Imagined Communities*, 86.

114. For analyses of Chinese influence in Latin America and Africa, see, for example, Carmen G. Gonzalez, "China's Engagement with Latin America: Partnership or Plunder?," in *Natural Resources and the Green Economy: Redefining the Challenges for People, States, and Corporations*, ed. Elena Blanco and Jona Razzaque (London: Brill, forthcoming); Timothy Webster, "China's Human Rights Footprint in Africa," *Columbia Journal of Transnational Law* 50 (forthcoming).

115. See, for example, John Fitzgerald, *Awakening China: Politics, Culture, and Class in the Nationalist Revolution* (Stanford, CA: Stanford University Press, 1996).

116. Michael Dowdle, "Heretical Laments: China and the Fallacies of 'Rule of Law,'" *Cultural Dynamics* 11, no. 3 (November 1999): 287. In this context, consider also the heated debates about the significance of judicial independence. Judicial independence may be a desirable goal, but, like rule-of-law itself, it is ultimately only an instrumental value, not an end in itself. As J. Mark Ramseyer observes, "Basic comparative research shows that independent judiciaries . . . are *not* common to freedom-loving nations everywhere." J. Mark Ramseyer, "The Puzzling (In) Dependence of Courts: A Comparative Approach," *Journal of Legal Studies* 23, no. 2 (June 1994): 721–722. Moreover, judicial independence does not exist in unqualified form even in its contemporary variant, nor has it had a stable historical meaning even in the United States. See, for example, Christine A. Desan, "Remaking Constitutional Tradition at the Margin of the Empire: The Creation of Legislative Adjudication in Colonial New York," *Law and History Review* 16, no. 2 (Summer 1998): 316, calling for a recognition that the colonial system of "legislative adjudication"—judicial decision making by legislatures—constitutes an integral part of the history of "American legality." For a recent interdisciplinary examination of judicial independence in the PRC, see Randall Peerenboom, ed., *Judicial Independence in China: Lessons for Global Rule of Law Promotion* (Cambridge: Cambridge University Press, 2010).

117. J. M. Balkin, "Understanding Legal Understanding: The Legal Subject and the Problem of Legal Coherence," *Yale Law Journal* 103, no. 1 (October 1993): 163.

3. TELLING STORIES ABOUT CORPORATIONS AND KINSHIP

1. See Zhonghua Renmin Gongheguo Gongsifa 中华人民共和国公司法 [PRC Company Law] (promulgated by Standing Committee of National People's Congress, Dec. 29, 1993, effective July 1, 1994). The law was amended in 2005. See Zhonghua Renmin Gongheguo Gongsi Fa 2005 Xiuding 中华人民共和国公司法

2005修订 [PRC Company Law 2005 Revision] (promulgated by Standing Committee of National People's Congress, Oct. 27, 2005, effective Jan. 2006).

2. Henry Hansmann and Reinier Kraakman, "The End of History for Corporate Law," *Georgetown Law Journal* 89, no. 2 (January 2001): 439–468.

3. Two caveats are in order. The overall goal of this chapter is to reconstruct the broad outlines of "corporation law" in the late imperial era (generally mid-to-late Qing [1644–1912 c.e.]). The view that emerges is consequently a relatively synchronic one. However, the last thing I wish to do is perpetuate the Hegelian notion of China as static and unchanging. A similar caveat applies to geographic generalization. Except where otherwise indicated, I have not pursued variations between different locales. However, as several commentators emphasize, Chinese customary law often varied by region. See, for example, D. E. Greenfield, "Marriage by Chinese Law and Custom in Hong Kong," *International and Comparative Law Quarterly* 7, no. 3 (July 1958): 442–443, stating, "By the nineteenth century . . . the variations in customary law had become localised." Also see Harald Kirfel, "Das Gewohnheitsrecht in China," *Sinologica* 3 (1953): 59–60, contrasting customary law of North and South China. It is noteworthy that much of the evidence of "clan corporations" comes from Southeast China, which has been (and still is) more commercialized than other parts of the country and thus appears to have had a more developed body of "corporation law."

4. Max Weber, *The Religion of China: Confucianism and Taoism*, trans. and ed. Hans H. Gerth (Glencoe, IL: Free Press, 1951), 85. As Weber elaborates elsewhere:

> A conception of the state as independent of the private person of the Emperor did not exist any more than a law of private corporations or voluntary associations. . . . The concept of juristic personality in the sense of the law of Antiquity is completely absent. . . . In spite of the *de facto* use of such institutions as the firm name, they never reached the point of becoming definite legal types as they did in Europe. . . . This underdeveloped state of the Chinese law of private associations and business organizations was caused by the continuing significance of the kinship group, within which all economic association is taking place.

Max Rheinstein, ed., *Max Weber on Law in Economy and Society*, trans. Edward Shils and Max Rheinstein (Cambridge, MA: Harvard University Press, 1954), 184–186.

5. John King Fairbank, *China: A New History* (Cambridge, MA: Belknap Press of Harvard University Press, 1992), 185–186.

6. See, for example, William C. Jones, ed., *Basic Principles of Civil Law in China* (Armonk, NY: M. E. Sharpe, 1989); Hu Kangshen 胡康申, "Wo guo de faren zhidu" 我国的法人制度 [Institution of legal personality in China], *Zhongguo faxue* 中国法学 [Chinese jurisprudence] no. 4 (1986): 7; Chen Qizhong 陈企中, "Shangpin

jingji he qiye faren" 商品经济和企业法人 [Commodity economy and enterprise legal persons], *Zhengzhi yu falü* 政治与法律 [Political science and law] no. 4 (1985): 7; Bai Youzhong, "Shilun faren de tezheng ji youlai" 试论法人的特征及由来 [On the characteristics and origins of legal personality], *Faxue yanjiu* 法学研究 [Studies in law] no. 3 (1983): 60.

To be sure, there are Chinese scholars who are mindful of the fact that many traditional collective entities functioned much like legal persons. For example, a study of the history of civil law in imperial China notes that households and clans traditionally constituted "basic production units." See Li Zhimin 李志敏, *Zhongguo gudai minfa* 中国古代民法 [Ancient Chinese civil law] (Beijing: Falü chubanshe 法律出版社, 1988), 23–24. However, the study does not focus on this insight, nor does it expressly analyze the phenomenon in terms of legal personality.

7. See Hill Gates, *China's Motor: A Thousand Years of Petty Capitalism* (Ithaca, NY: Cornell University Press, 1996), 84–120, describing commercially oriented clans, which she terms "patricorporations."

8. Bayless Manning, "The Shareholder's Appraisal Remedy: An Essay for Frank Coker," *Yale Law Journal* 72, no. 2 (December 1962): 245.

9. In the Confucian four-tier hierarchy, the *literati* occupied the top tier, peasants the second tier, artisans ranked third, and merchants came in last. The ideological explanation for merchants' low ranking was their lack of "productivity": unlike peasants and artisans who actually *produced* something, merchants simply lived parasitically by buying and selling what others had produced. To be sure, this conventional view is an oversimplification. Thomas Metzger, for instance, observes that the state's attitude to commerce "amount[ed] to a complex spectrum of opinion rather than a simple, consistent doctrine." Thomas A. Metzger, "The State and Commerce in Imperial China," *Asian & African Studies* 6 (1970): 25. In a similar vein, Timothy Brook notes the amenability of Confucian economic discourse "to a considerable play of interpretation," although always within "a cultural framework that preferred to praise moral reciprocity over profit taking" and tended "to see in each the diminution of the other." Timothy Brook, "Profit and Righteousness in Chinese Economic Culture," in *Culture and Economy: The Shaping of Capitalism in Eastern Asia,* ed. Timothy Brook and Hy V. Luong (Ann Arbor: University of Michigan Press, 1999), 28–32.

10. For a classic statement, see Georg Wilhelm Friedrich Hegel, *The Philosophy of History*, trans. J. Sibree (New York: Dover, 1956), 121, stating, "*Family.* On this form of moral union alone rests the Chinese State, and it is objective Family Piety that characterizes it." Also see Montesquieu, *The Spirit of the Laws*, trans. and ed. Anne M. Cohler, Basia Carolyn Miller, and Harold Samuel Stone (Cambridge: Cambridge University Press, 1989), 320, stating, "This empire is formed on the idea of family government"; Rheinstein, *Max Weber on Law*, 263, describing the patriarchal administration of justice as "a transposition of the intrafamilial mode of settling conflicts into the political body."

11. George Thomas Staunton, trans., preface to *Ta Tsing Leu Lee; Being Fundamental Laws, and a Selection from the Supplementary Statutes, of the Penal Code of China* (London: T. Cadwell and W. Davies, 1810), xviii.

12. Henry Sumner Maine, *Ancient Law: Its Connections with the Early History of Society, and Its Relations to Modern Ideas* (London: John Murray, 1861), describing the movement of "progressive" societies as one from "*Status*" to "*Contract*."

13. Corporate metaphysics was one of the main targets in Felix Cohen's manifesto. See Felix S. Cohen, "Transcendental Nonsense and the Functional Approach," *Columbia Law Review* 35, no. 6 (June 1935): 809–849.

14. See Robert Charles Clark, "Dominance of the Corporate Form of Organization," § 1.2.4 in *Corporate Law* (Boston, MA: Little, Brown, 1986). Clark himself is certainly aware of the culturally and socially contingent nature of this definition. As he explains, "What accounts for the corporation's success as a form of organization are its characteristics and a social environment that makes these characteristics useful." Ibid., §1.1.

15. See generally Adolf A. Berle Jr. and Gardiner C. Means, *The Modern Corporation and Private Property* (New York: Macmillan, 1933).

16. For the notion of a reversible analogy, see Kaja Silverman, *Flesh of My Flesh* (Stanford, CA: Stanford University Press, 2009). For a more detailed analysis of this comparative move, see Teemu Ruskola, "Raping Like a State," *UCLA Law Review* 57, no. 5 (June 2010): 1531–1533.

17. James Legge, trans. and ed., *The Shoo King*, in *The Chinese Classics*, 2nd ed. (Oxford: Clarendon Press, 1939), 333. Confucius himself did not expressly compare the ruler to a parent. His follower Mencius, however, did—and, significantly enough, it was Mencius's interpretation of the Master that ultimately became the foundation for the Neo-Confucian orthodoxy. See D. C. Lau, trans., *Mencius* (Harmondsworth, UK: Penguin, 1970), bk. 1, pt. A, 4; bk. 3, pt. A, 3.

18. T'ung-tsu Ch'ü, *Local Government in China under the Ch'ing* (Cambridge, MA: Harvard University Press, 1962), 14; John R. Watt, *The District Magistrate in Late Imperial China* (New York: Columbia University Press, 1972), 90.

19. In contravention of current anthropological usage, I refer to Chinese lineage organizations as "clans" or "clan corporations." By using the term "clan" generically, I hope to avoid getting embroiled in the more technical debates regarding Chinese kinship organization. Furthermore, as an increasing number of anthropologists and historians have observed, even the Chinese themselves do not use the kinship terms of their own language particularly consistently. See, for example, Ng Chin-Keong, *Trade and Society: The Amoy Network on the China Coast, 1683–1735* (Singapore: Singapore University Press, National University of Singapore, 1983), 30, stating, "Sources show that the usage of lineage (tsu) and surname (hsing), and sometimes even family (chia), could be interchangeable." Also see James L. Watson, "Chinese Kinship Reconsidered: Anthropological Perspectives on Historical Research," *China Quarterly* 1982, no. 92 (March 1982): 589, 592,

stating, "The Chinese have never been consistent in their use of these terms"; Denis
Twitchett, "Comment on J. L. Watson's Article," *China Quarterly* 1982, no. 92
(December 1982): 623, stating, "All these [kinship] terms 'xing' 'zu' 'shi' 'zong,' etc.,
only had one important meaning. . . . 'Those whom we care to consider as part of
us' in contradiction to the world outside." In fact, as this chapter suggests, many of
the analytical distinctions made traditionally by both anthropologists and the
Chinese themselves simply do not map onto the reality of Chinese kinship practices.

20. Maine, *Ancient Law*, 126.

21. Lau, *Mencius*, bk. 4, pt. B, 13. Compare Confucius, *The Analects*, trans.
D. C. Lau (Harmondsworth, UK: Penguin 1979), bk. 4, 20, lauding as truly filial a
son who during the three years of mourning after his father's death manages to
carry on the will of his father.

22. See Fung Yu-lan, *A History of Chinese Philosophy*, trans. Derk Bodde, vol. 1
(Princeton, NJ: Princeton University Press, 1952), 361, quoting *The Classic of Filial
Piety*; Francis L. K. Hsu, *Under the Ancestor's Shadow: Kinship, Personality and Social
Mobility in China* (1948; repr., Stanford, CA: Stanford University Press, 1971), 240.

23. See R. F. Johnston, *Lion and Dragon in Northern China* (London: John
Murray, 1910), 138, noting that under custom a man is liable for his ancestor's
debts even when they outweigh his assets.

24. For particularly striking examples of readings of *patria potestas* into 孝, see
P. G. von Möllendorf, *The Family Law of the Chinese* (Shanghai: Kelly & Walsh,
1896), 41, stating, "The [Chinese father's] *patria potestas* over children, whether
legitimate or adopted, is unlimited." Also see E. H. Parker, "Comparative Chinese
Family Law," *China Review, or Notes & Queries on the Far East* 8, no. 2 (1879): 68,
stating, "Fundamental principles . . . such as the Patriarchal Principle . . . pervade
the Law and Customs of the Chinese as completely and tenaciously as the *Patria
Potestas* ever did the Jurisprudence of Rome"; Ernest Alabaster, "Analogy between
the Chinese and Other Systems—Especially as Regards Roman Law," in *Notes and
Commentaries on Chinese Criminal Law, and Cognate Topics: With Special Relation
to Ruling Cases; Together with a Brief Excursus on the Law of Property, Chiefly
Founded on the Writings of the Late Sir Chaloner Alabaster* (London: Luzac, 1899),
615. In theory at least, *patria potestas* entailed the "power of life and death." See
Jane F. Gardner, *Family and* Familia *in Roman Law and Life* (Oxford: Clarendon
Press; New York: Oxford University Press, 1998), 2.

25. Tu Wei-ming, *Centrality and Commonality: An Essay on Chung-yung*,
Monograph of the Society for Asian and Comparative Philosophy 3 (Honolulu:
University Press of Hawaii, 1976), 67, 81.

26. Needless to add, this is the strictly formal Confucian view; in practice,
women constructed space for themselves in what Margery Wolf calls "uterine
families," composed of children and grandchildren. In contrast to the ritual
patrilineal family, the uterine family was founded on affection and personal

attachments. See Margery Wolf, *Women and the Family in Rural Taiwan* (Stanford, CA: Stanford University Press, 1972), 37.

27. Shiga Shuzo, "Family Property and the Law of Inheritance in Traditional China," in *Chinese Family Law and Social Change in Historical and Comparative Perspective*, ed. David C. Buxbaum, Asian Law Series 3 (Seattle: University of Washington Press, 1978), 109, 119–120.

28. Le P. Guy Boulais, trans., *Manuel du Code Chinois* (1924; repr., Taipei, Taiwan: Ch'eng Wen, 1966), 415. The provision dates back to the Tang (618–907 c.e.) dynasty. See Wallace Johnson, trans., *The T'ang Code*, vol. 2 (Princeton, NJ: Princeton University Press, 1997), art. 162.2. The Qing provision in question is contained in the first substatute under statute number 88. The Qing Code consists of statutes and substatutes. The latter, less than 500 in number, provided the basic legal principles and were modified, deleted, or added relatively infrequently, while the more detailed and more numerous substatutes contained rules modifying or applying the statutes to special situations. William C. Jones, trans., *The Great Qing Code* (Oxford: Clarendon Press; New York: Oxford University Press, 1994), is an excellent recent English translation that, however, contains only the statutes in the code. Therefore, for citations to European-language translations of substatutes I refer to Guy Boulais's French translation, *Manuel du Code Chinois*, which (though still incomplete) includes both statutes and substatutes. Staunton's earlier English translation, commendable though it is as a pioneer effort, is both inaccurate and incomplete. See Staunton, *Ta Tsing Leu Lee*.

29. See generally David Wakefield, *Fenjia: Household Division and Inheritance in Qing and Republican China* (Honolulu: University of Hawaii Press, 1998).

30. Santaro Okamatsu, *Provisional Report on Investigations of Laws and Customs in the Island of Formosa* (Kobe, Japan: Kobe Herald, 1902), xxv.

31. See Benjamin A. Elman, *Classicism, Politics, and Kinship: The Ch'ang-chou School of New Text Confucianism in Late Imperial China* (Berkeley: University of California Press, 1990), 40–42, 50–52.

32. Hui-chen Wang Liu, *The Traditional Chinese Clan Rules* (Locust Valley, NY: J. J. Augustin, 1959), 106.

33. It is important to note some additional caveats. I wish to suggest neither that all clan associations were de facto business corporations nor that the clan association was the only corporate form of business organization. Not only did many lineages—especially the humbler ones—not form clan associations, but even among clans that did do so, some perpetuated themselves by investing in various forms of cultural, rather than specifically economic, capital; witness a clan studied by Susan Naquin that relied on its specialized sectarian skills. See Susan Naquin, "Two Descent Groups in North China: The Wangs of Yung-p'ing Prefecture, 1500–1800," in *Kinship Organization in Late Imperial China, 1000–1940*, ed. Patricia Buckley Ebrey and James L. Watson (Berkeley: University of California Press, 1986), 210,

211–212. Benjamin Elman has detailed the history of a more conventional form of "cultural capitalism." Clans with histories of success in the civil service examinations devised strategies to maintain the ownership of their traditions of Confucian learning within the kinship group. See Elman, *Classicism, Politics, and Kinship*, 1–73. I also do not mean to imply that all clans were necessarily mere facades for nonkinship-related pursuits; no doubt many were focused on the celebration of Confucian kinship ideology for its own rewards (although in practice it may be difficult to separate their interest in its material rewards to those who ranked high in a hierarchical lineage structure based on sex, seniority, and scholarly status).

At the same time I do not mean to imply that clan corporations were the sole entities that functioned, in important ways, like modern business corporations. Other candidates for prototypes of the business corporation include guilds and monasteries. I have nevertheless chosen not to pursue an analysis of guilds and monasteries. Based on currently available evidence, guilds played a more restrictive economic role than clan corporations did, and the economic influence of monasteries decreased, rather than increased, over time. Although guilds seem to have been run largely on the management model of the modern business corporation (a two-tier board-management structure overseen by regular "shareholder" meetings), their property holdings were typically modest, as they functioned primarily as trade regulators rather than entrepreneurs. A key analytical reason for the kinship focus is the clan corporation's specifically legal relevance: as compared to the competing organizational forms, it enjoyed the greatest legal recognition.

34. David Faure, "The Lineage as a Business Company: Patronage versus Law in the Development of Chinese Business," in *The Second Conference on Modern Chinese Economic History, January 5–7, 1989* (Taipei, Taiwan: Institute of Economics, Academia Sinica, 1989), 350–352.

35. Ibid., 351–352.

36. See Rubie S. Watson, *Inequality among Brothers: Class and Kinship in South China* (Cambridge: Cambridge University Press, 1985), 32–34. For another contemporary account of lineages where membership is defined by monetary contribution, see Myron L. Cohen, "Agnatic Kinship in South Taiwan," *Ethnology* 8, no. 2 (April 1969): 180–181.

37. Johanna M. Meskill, "The Chinese Genealogy as a Research Source," in *Family and Kinship in Chinese Society*, ed. Maurice Freedman (Stanford, CA: Stanford University Press, 1970), 141–142.

38. See Kung-chuan Hsiao, *Rural China: Imperial Control in the Nineteenth Century* (Seattle: University of Washington Press, 1960), 353.

39. Ng Chin-Keong, *Trade and Society*, 31. On the falsification of surnames to "create" new kinship relations, see also Kai-wing Chow, *The Rise of Confucian Ritualism in Late Imperial China: Ethics, Classics, and Lineage Discourse* (Stanford, CA: Stanford University Press, 1994), 253 n. 29.

40. Ng Chin-Keong, *Trade and Society*, 31; Hsiao, *Rural China*, 353. See also Jacques Amyot, *The Manila Chinese: Familism in the Philippine Environment*, 2nd ed. (Quezon City: Institute of Philippine Culture, Ateneo de Manila University, 1973), 27–28, describing clan formation across surname lines among overseas Chinese in the Philippines.

41. Ann Waltner, *Getting an Heir: Adoption and the Construction of Kinship in Late Imperial China* (Honolulu: University of Hawaii Press, 1990), 90.

42. *Xiaojing Zhushu* [Commentary on the Classic of Filial Piety], 6.2A, quoted in T'ung-tsu Ch'ü, *Law and Society in Traditional China* (Paris: Mouton, 1965), 42.

43. See Arthur P. Wolf and Chieh-shan Huang, *Marriage and Adoption in China, 1845–1945* (Stanford, CA: Stanford University Press, 1980), 108; Hsien Chin Hu, *The Common Descent Group in China and Its Functions*, ed. Ralph Linton (New York: Viking Fund, 1948), 139.

44. Waltner, *Getting an Heir*, 48.

45. James L. Watson, "Transactions in People: The Chinese Market in Slaves, Servants, and Heirs," in *Asian and African Systems of Slavery*, ed. James L. Watson (Berkeley: University of California Press, 1980), 229.

46. Min-shang-shih hsi-kuan tiao-ch'a pao-kao-lu [Report on the Enquiry into Civil and Commercial Customs], 1465–1466, quoted in Wolf and Huang, *Marriage and Adoption*, 12.

47. For a sample contract, see Mui Tsai Commission, *Mui Tsai in Hong Kong and Malaya: Report of Commission*, Colonial 125 (London: H. M. Stationery Office, 1937) (photo. reprint 1879) (slightly edited for clarity). See also Watson, "Transactions in People," 234–235 (edited version of same agreement).

48. Wolf and Huang, *Marriage and Adoption*, 233. These contracts were much like those for boys. For an example, see Fu-mei Chang Chen and Ramon H. Myers, "Customary Law and the Economic Growth of China during the Ch'ing Period (I)," *Ch'ing-shih wen-t'i* 3, no. 5 (November 1976): 26. On the adoption of girls as future daughters-in-law in Taiwan, see also Chiyen Chen, "The Foster Daughter-in-Law System in Formosa," *American Journal of Comparative Law* 6 (1957): 302–314.

49. Wolf and Huang, *Marriage and Adoption*, 204.

50. Gates, *China's Motor*, 122. For examples of contracts for the sale of a concubine, see Chen and Myers, "Customary Law (I)," 26, 31.

51. Gates, *China's Motor*, 123–124.

52. *"Mui tsai"* is the commonly used transliteration of the Cantonese pronunciation (Mandarin *mei zai*). Since the *mui tsai* were the most common in South China and their study has focused on Canton and Hong Kong, most English-language studies retain the word in its Cantonese form. On mui-tsai as "chattels," see Watson, "Transactions in People," 243. For translated sample deeds of sale, see Maria Jaschok, *Concubines and Bondservants: A Social History* (London: Zed Books, 1988), 146–149. On their absorption into the idiom of kinship, see *Mui Tsai in*

Hong Kong and Malaya, 22, stating, "Chinese custom has always regarded a mui tsai as a member of the family which a paid domestic servant is not."

53. See generally Mi Chu Wiens, "Kinship Extended: The Tenant/Servants of Hui-chou," in *Orthodoxy in Late Imperial China*, ed. Kwang-ching Liu (Berkeley: University of California Press, 1990), 231, analyzing tenant/servant and tenant contracts in the late imperial period. For three translated tenant/servant contracts, see ibid., 242–243.

54. Ibid., 246–249. See also Hilary J. Beattie, *Land and Lineage in China: A Study of T'ung-ch'eng County, Anhwei, in the Ming and Ch'ing Dynasties* (Cambridge: Cambridge University Press, 1979), 14, observing that "in ideal circumstances [tenant/servants] could actually benefit from [the landlord's] exercise of Confucian paternalism."

55. On slaves' relative productivity, see James L. Watson, "Chattel Slavery in Chinese Peasant Society: A Comparative Analysis," *Ethnology* 15, no. 4 (October 1976): 361–375. As Watson notes, a relative lack of productivity does not make this form of slavery unique. As to white and red contracts, the latter provided greater security for the buyer, as it was marked by the magistrate's red stamp of approval. See Marinus J. Meijer, "Slavery at the End of the Ch'ing Dynasty," in *Essays on China's Legal Tradition*, ed. Jerome Alan Cohen, R. Randle Edwards, and Fu-mei Chang Cheng, Studies in East Asian Law (Princeton, NJ: Princeton University Press, 1980), 329–330. On slaves' disobedience as unfilial behavior, see Meijer, "Slavery," 331–332.

56. Watson, *Inequality among Brothers*, 35.

57. Morton H. Fried, *Fabric of Chinese Society: A Study of the Social Life of a Chinese County Seat* (New York: Praeger, 1953), 161.

58. Hu, *Common Descent Group*, 67.

59. Committee on Chinese Law and Custom in Hong Kong, *Chinese Law and Custom in Hong Kong: Report of a Committee Appointed by the Governor in October, 1948* (Hong Kong: Government Printer, 1953), 62.

60. G. Jamieson, *Chinese Family and Commercial Law* (Shanghai: Kelly and Walsh, 1921), 30. Compare Johnston, *Lion and Dragon*, 144, stating, "[In a] Chinese deed of sale . . . the reason why the seller is disposing of his land must always be stated. The theory seems to be that he should not want to sell his land, and that this desire to do so is highly regrettable if not reprehensible."

61. *Chinese Law and Custom*, 35.

62. Watson, "Chinese Kinship Reconsidered," 602.

63. See Mark A. Allee, *Law and Local Society in Late Imperial China: Northern Taiwan in the Nineteenth Century* (Stanford, CA: Stanford University Press, 1994), 93.

64. See Philip C. C. Huang, *The Peasant Family and Rural Development in the Yangzi Delta, 1350–1988* (Stanford, CA: Stanford University Press, 1990), 44.

65. Kang Chao, *Man and Land in Chinese History: An Economic Analysis* (Stanford, CA: Stanford University Press, 1986), 193.

66. See Ramon H. Myers and Yeh-chien Wang, "Economic Developments, 1644–1800," in *The Cambridge History of China*, vol. 9: Part One: The Ch'ing Dynasty to 1800, ed. Willard J. Peterson (Cambridge: Cambridge University Press, 2002), 57–66.

67. See Chung-li Chang, *The Income of the Chinese Gentry* (Seattle: Washington University Press, 1962), 197.

68. See Johanna Menzel Meskill, *A Chinese Pioneer Family: The Lins of Wu-feng Taiwan, 1729–1895* (Princeton, NJ: Princeton University Press, 1979), 239, 242, 253.

69. See Gates, *China's Motor*, 26; R. Keith Schoppa, *Xiang Lake: Nine Centuries of Chinese Life* (New Haven, CT: Yale University Press, 1989), 70, 77.

70. See Jack M. Potter, "Land and Lineage in Traditional China," in *Family and Kinship in Chinese Society*, 128.

71. The manager, in turn, was entitled to accept money contributions from the public. See Chen and Myers, "Customary Law (I)," 1, 11.

72. Susan Mann, *Local Merchants and the Chinese Bureaucracy, 1750–1950* (Stanford, CA: Stanford University Press, 1987), 23.

73. Meskill, "Chinese Genealogy," 143.

74. Hsu, *Under the Ancestor's Shadow*, 236.

75. Mann, *Local Merchants*, 90.

76. See Hui-chen Wang Liu, "An Analysis of Chinese Clan Rules: Confucian Theories in Action," in *Confucianism and Chinese Civilization*, ed. Arthur F. Wright (1964; repr., Stanford, CA: Stanford University Press, 1975), 41 (hereinafter "Analysis of Chinese Clan Rules I").

77. See D. C. Twitchett, "Documents on Clan Administration: I, The Rules of Administration of the Charitable Estate of the Fan Clan; Annotated Translation of the *I-chuang kuei-chü*," *Asia Major*, n.s., 8, no. 1 (1960): 13.

78. See, for example, Watson, *Inequality among Brothers*, 3, describing a large Hong Kong lineage "dominated by a small group of wealthy men"; Hu, *Common Descent Group*, 82, 84, describing the system of "management in turn" by the representatives of several fang; Twitchett, *Documents*, 30. On variations in management structures, see Liu, *Traditional Chinese Clan Rules*, 104–105.

79. See Liu, *Traditional Chinese Clan Rules*, 116.

80. Ibid., 103.

81. On "direct democracy," see Hsiao, *Rural China*, 332. The management structure and its problems have remained largely unchanged in the still-surviving clans in Hong Kong's outlying New Territories. Belinda Wong Sheung-yu describes "a split between nominal and real authority in the [clan] leadership" and membership meetings in which "the managers are decided upon by 'co-option and consensus rather than by election.'" See Belinda Wong Sheung-yu, "Chinese Customary Law: An Examination of *Tsos* and Family *Tongs*," *Hong Kong Law*

Journal 20, no. 1 (January 1990): 19–20. The manipulation of the membership's decision also occurs, of course, in shareholder meetings of many American corporations; indeed, it gives poignant new meaning to the notion of "corporate ritual." See generally Terrence E. Deal and Allan A. Kennedy, *Corporate Cultures: The Rites and Rituals of Corporate Life* (Reading, MA: Addison-Wesley, 1982), emphasizing the importance of ritual in a robust corporate culture.

82. See, for example, Hu, *Common Descent Group*, 124–125, noting a clan rule providing that only wealthy men hold the office of manager of the ancestral hall.

83. See Liu, "Analysis of Chinese Clan Rules I," 84, 106, 148. A number of clans prohibited even renting clan lands to relatives and making loans to them. These rules are complex to interpret. On the one hand, the fiduciary logic of kinship might be seen to require that clan lands not be used to make loans to relatives, given the evident dangers of favoritism. On the other hand, insofar as kin relations are viewed as properly a domain of heartfelt care and concern for others, assistance to needy kin ought to be provided altruistically and for free; to monetize a family relationship is to destroy it—witness customary prohibitions against any sales between family. Yet in many, if not most, cases the prohibitions seem to have been inspired not by concern for Confucian familism as much as by a recognition that because of the Confucian familist rhetoric espoused by clan rules, the collection of rents and loans from family members could be a very delicate affair.

84. Weber does note that trust land under collective ownership operated "under a special common name, as if designating a common firm for all holdings." See Weber, *Religion of China*, 82 (citation omitted). However, he imputes no particular significance to the fact and pursues the analogy no further.

85. See Allee, *Law and Local Society*, 166–169, on clans as litigants; compare Liu-hung Huang, *A Complete Book Concerning Happiness and Benevolence: A Manual for Local Magistrates in Seventeenth-Century China*, trans. and ed. Djang Chu (Tucson: University of Arizona Press, 1984), 253, advising magistrates to ensure that complaints filed by families include the name of the clan head. Denis Twitchett also observes that, even in the Song, the Fan clan was officially recognized by imperial edicts. See Twitchett, *Documents*, 33. In the case of propertied clans with ancestral clan halls, the hall was a visible symbol of corporate personality, and actions taken by the clan were said to be those of the "ancestral hall." See Hu, *Common Descent Group*, 64. Indeed, often the name of the ancestor whom a particular trust commemorated stood metonymically for the clan corporation as a whole: for example, a clan purchasing new land for the trust would buy land and pay land taxes in the name of the deceased ancestor. See *Chinese Law and Custom*, 207.

86. See generally John Dewey, "The Historic Background of Corporate Legal Personality," *Yale Law Journal* 35, no. 6 (April 1926): 655–673, ascribing the

source of this legal fiction, in part, to the fact that it emerged from an "individual-istic" age.

87. See Max Radin, "The Endless Problem of Corporate Personality," *Columbia Law Review* 32, no. 4 (April 1932): 643–667.

88. See R. Randle Edwards, "Ch'ing Legal Jurisdiction over Foreigners," in *Essays on China's Legal Tradition*, 257–258, stating, "The principal offender . . . was sentenced to death by slicing (*ling-ch'ih*), since the Ch'ing Penal Code provides that penalty for the offense of killing more than three or four persons from one family."

89. See Derk Bodde and Clarence Morris, *Law in Imperial China: Exemplified by 190 Ch'ing Dynasty Cases, Translated from the Hsing-an hui-lan, with Historical, Social, and Juridical Commentaries* (Cambridge, MA: Harvard University Press, 1967), 193–194, noting that the governor-general's decision that their familial relation was too distant to be considered a common family was overturned because they were traveling together and their joint property was stolen.

90. See Sue Gronewold, *Beautiful Merchandise: Prostitution in China, 1860–1936* (New York: Harrington Park Press, 1985), 38–40; Gail Hershatter, "Prostitu-tion and the Market in Women in Early Twentieth-Century Shanghai," in *Marriage and Inequality in Chinese Society*, ed. Rubie S. Watson and Patricia Buckley Ebrey, Studies on China 12 (Berkeley: University of California Press, 1991), 269; von Möllendorf, *Family Law*, 13–14. See also Dr. Jacobus X, *Documents on Medical Anthropology (Untrodden Fields of Anthropology)*, 2nd ed., vol. 1 (1898; repr., Huntington, NY: R. E. Krieger, 1972), 63–64, noting the use of familial terms of address—mother, sister, aunt, and so on—in Chinese brothels.

91. See Hu, *Common Descent Group*, 51–52, providing penalties for "irrespon-sible members who sell their genealogy, or copy the original to deceive the *tsu* [clan] and obtain profit for themselves, causing the forgery to become mixed up with the genuine genealogy"; Myron L. Cohen, "Cultural and Political Inventions in Modern China: The Case of the Chinese 'Peasant,'" *Daedalus* 122, no. 2 (Spring 1993): 163, stating, "Some [Chinese kinship] corporations did allow for the sale of shares"; Faure, "Lineage as a Business," 353; David Faure, "The Lineage as a Cultural Invention: The Case of the Pearl River Delta," *Modern China* 15, no. 1 (January 1989): 27–28, stating, "Shares might be created among groups that were not necessarily associated by descent." Of course, one is well advised to keep in mind that, much as they may offend purists, transfer restrictions are permissible and common in close corporations even in the United States today.

92. To be sure, one should note again that the promise of limited liability is rather illusory for undercapitalized modern business corporations as well. See Clark, *Corporate Law*, § 1.3.

93. According to the early Confucian classic *Li Ji* 禮記 [Record of Rites], children may not possess any property of their own during their parents' lifetime. See James Legge, trans. and ed., *Texts of Confucianism*, in *The Chinese Classics*, 2nd ed., vol.

3 (Oxford: Clarendon Press, 1939), 67. Okamatsu similarly reports that in a Taiwanese household, "the members have no right to own any property, and what they gain goes into the possession of the house head." See Okamatsu, *Laws and Customs*, xxi.

94. Wolf and Huang, *Marriage and Adoption*, 60. Nevertheless, in practice, individually held property seems to have been negligible. See Wakefield, *Fenjia*, 56, stating, "While individual property was theoretically possible within the property system, the amounts tended to be small."

95. See Jamieson, *Family and Commercial Law*, 129; see also *Chinese Law and Custom*, 12.

96. In the words of one of the leading English-language studies, Chinese clans exercised "considerable autonomy in the legal sense . . . at the expense of the authority of the state." Indeed, "the central authority has always entrusted the family and the *tsu* with the moral education and disciplining of its members, and the civil code remained underdeveloped." See Hu, *Common Descent Group*, 53.

97. T'ung-tsu Ch'ü, for example, speaks of "the almost abject obedience" commanded by clan heads. See Ch'ü, *Law and Society*, 40. See also Joseph W. Rice, "Family Safeguards of a Semi-Barbarous Code," *Law Notes* 12 (May 1908): 29–32, stating, "The reverence due to [Chinese] family elders, and the patriarchal power they possess over their wives and children, is so nearly boundless as to seem grotesque to the Occidental."

98. See Kathryn Bernhardt and Philip C. C. Huang, eds., *Civil Law in Qing and Republican China* (Stanford, CA: Stanford University Press, 1994), 1.

99. Confucius, *Confucian Analects*, in *The Chinese Classics*, trans. and ed. James Legge, 3rd ed. (1893; repr., Hong Kong: Hong Kong University Press, 1960), bk. 12, chap. 13, 257 (emphasis omitted). See also ibid., bk. 12, chap. 12, 257, stating, "The Master said, 'Ah! It is Yû, who could with half a word settle litigations!'"

100. Philip C. C. Huang, *Civil Justice in China: Representation and Practice in the Qing* (Stanford, CA: Stanford University Press, 1996), 220.

101. Madeleine Zelin, "The Rights of Tenants in Mid-Qing Sichuan: A Study of Land-Related Lawsuits in the Baxian Archives," *Journal of Asian Studies* 45, no. 3 (May 1986): 523.

102. See, for example, Hu, *Common Descent Group*, 85, noting that in the Qing, regulations for the management of clan lands used to be registered with state officials.

103. Alabaster, *Notes and Commentaries*, lvi (emphasis omitted). On the notion of family authority as an official delegation, see Sybille van der Sprenkel, *Legal Institutions in Manchu China: A Sociological Analysis* (London: University of London, Athlone Press, 1962), 96, 112, arguing that official enforcement of familial obligations had the effect of extending the jurisdiction of the state's legal machinery, and William P. Alford, *To Steal a Book is an Elegant Offense: Intellectual Property Law in Chinese Civilization* (Stanford, CA: Stanford University Press, 1995), 11, noting that state reliance on family, village, and guild leaders to adminis-

ter local customary rules "allowed the state's influence to reach far further than would otherwise have been the case."

104. Hui-chen Wang Liu, "An Analysis of Chinese Clan Rules: Confucian Theories in Action," in *Confucianism in Action*, ed. David S. Nivison and Arthur F. Wright (Stanford, CA: Stanford University Press, 1959), 94 (hereinafter "Analysis of Chinese Clan Rules II").

105. Hu, *Common Descent Group*, 133.

106. John Austin, *The Province of Jurisprudence Determined: Being the First Part of a Series of Lectures on Jurisprudence, or, the Philosophy of Positive Law*, 2nd ed., vol. 1 (London: John Murray, 1861), 58.

107. Henry Sumner Maine, *Village-Communities in the East and West*, 2nd ed. (London: J. Murray, 1872), 39.

108. See Twitchett, "Comment," 624, stating, "They rarely started from scratch, especially if there was an authoritative model available. All the family/lineage rules tend to be derivative"; Liu, *Traditional Chinese Clan Rules*, 21, stating, "There is a standard form [of clan rules], the one used most frequently." In Hong Kong, for example, even fairly large clan corporations did not necessarily have written clan rules. Written regulations may well have been less necessary there than in some other parts of the country because of the relatively large number of clan corporations in the Pearl River delta and the resulting richness of customary norms in the area. See Stephen Selby, "Everything You Wanted to Know about Chinese Customary Law (But Were Afraid to Ask)," *Hong Kong Law Journal* 21, no. 1 (January 1991): 55, stating, "There are few written statements of the terms of [ancestral trusts], so it must be assumed that for most clans, the terms were a matter of customary knowledge." Some commentators on Hong Kong customary law even suggest that some aspects of clan law were mandatory local custom. See Greenfield, "Marriage by Chinese Law," 443, stating, "It was not the [clan] council's *own* views of right and wrong that it enforced, but the customary law of the locality in which it lived."

109. See Olga Lang, *Chinese Family and Society* (New Haven, CT: Yale University Press, 1946), distinguishing between "clan elders" and "clan executives."

110. See Hu, *Common Descent Group*, 21, stating, "The work may be shared, . . . or, more frequently, it is performed in rotation, each head of a *fang* taking over for one year."

111. Liu, "Analysis of Chinese Clan Rules II," 66; Faure, "Lineage as a Cultural Invention," 8, stating, "By the Qing, a common ritual language had developed in relation to lineage practices that was used throughout China and that was not restricted to any particular social class."

112. See Hu, *Common Descent Group*, 189.

113. Hsiao, *Rural China*, 349.

114. Hu, *Common Descent Group*, 61, 187–188, translating a 1764 "Memorial Regarding the Abuses of the Ancestral Halls in Kiangsi."

115. See Hsiao, *Rural China*, 352.

116. See ibid., 355.

117. The provision is contained in a substatute of the 1842 edition of the Qing Code. None of the available Western language editions of the Code contains this substatute. For an English translation, see Hugh D. R. Baker, appendix III, in *Chinese Family and Kinship* (New York: Columbia University Press, 1979). As early as 1766, the Qianlong emperor referred in an edict to the possibility of breaking up lineages that got into trouble. See Hsiao, *Rural China*, 355.

118. See, for example, Johnston, *Lion and Dragon*, 155, asserting that the clan villages of Weihaiwei, "so far as their domestic affairs are concerned, are somewhat like so many little self-contained republics"; von Möllendorf, *Family Law*, 41, describing a system of "*imperium in imperio*," in which "officials hardly ever interfere with clan decisions"; G. Jamieson, "The History of Adoption and Its Relation to Modern Wills," *The China Review, or Notes & Queries on the Far East* 18, no. 3 (1889): 140, stating, "Each family constitutes a sort of petty kingdom, within which the father or senior male descendant is supreme head."

119. Yongzheng's edict is translated in Mann, *Local Merchants*, 17–18.

120. See, for example, Ng Chin-Keong, *Trade and Society*, 93–94, recounting eighteenth-century Amoy merchants' positive responses to local authorities' appeals to provide aid to public works as well as "to give relief to the unfortunate." Of course not all contributions were necessarily motivated by charity; some may have been the result of more or less overt blackmail by officials, others voluntary but calculated to incur official goodwill, while still others may have been genuinely charitable—and many probably inspired by a mixture of motives.

121. See van der Sprenkel, *Legal Institutions*, 96, 112, stating, "The *tsu* [clan] and guild tribunals may perhaps be thought of as subsidiaries of the official courts, exercising delegated powers"; Alford, *To Steal a Book*, 11, stating, "The state's reliance on family heads, village elders, and guild leaders to apply local custom . . . should instead be seen as akin to controlled delegation of authority."

122. See Hsiao, *Rural China*, 5, estimating the average population per magistrate in 1819.

123. Twitchett, for instance, argues that, at least in the Song, permitting clans to register their regulations with the imperial bureaucracy was "a rare privilege." See Denis Twitchett, "The Fan Clan's Charitable Estate, 1050–1760," in *Confucianism in Action,* 102, 109, describing a propertied clan as "a perpetual corporation." Over time, however, official recognition seems to have lost much of its privileged character. According to David Faure, initially only lineages that had produced ranking officials were permitted to establish large ancestral trusts, but "in time, the rule was circumvented by lineages tracing their descent from an ancestor, actual or imagined, who had achieved the official status before the Ming." See Faure, "Lineage as a Business," 8.

124. See Faure, "Lineage as a Business," 11–14.

125. The observation is from the long-reigning Kangxi emperor's 1722 valedictory edict. For a translation of the edict, see Jonathan D. Spence, *Emperor of China: Self-Portrait of K'ang-hsi* (New York: Knopf, 1974), 169.

126. The statute in question (No. 93) is translated into English in Jones, *The Great Qing Code*, 117. Unfortunately, Jones's translation of *The Great Qing Code* does not include substatutes. The substatute in question is translated into French in Boulais, *Manuel du Code Chinois*, 243.

127. For accounts of suits where clan members relied on the substatute for protection of clan property, see, for example, Mark A. Allee, "Code, Culture, and Custom: Foundations of Civil Case Verdicts in a Nineteenth-Century County Court," in *Civil Law in Qing and Republican China*, 126, describing an 1877–1878 dispute over ritual clan land in which the court held that "sacrificial property may not be mortgaged or sold"; Philip C. C. Huang, "Codified Law and Magisterial Adjudication in the Qing," in *Civil Law in Qing and Republican China*, 146, describing a 1769 suit over expropriation of timber on a lineage gravesite.

128. Johnston, *Lion and Dragon*, 112.

129. Jonathan K. Ocko, "Hierarchy and Harmony: Family Conflict as Seen in Ch'ing Legal Cases," in *Orthodoxy in Late Imperial China*, 227.

130. See Jones, *The Great Qing Code*, 322–324, stating, "Every child . . . who brings an accusation against his paternal grandparents or parents . . . (*even if it is true*) will receive 100 strokes of the heavy bamboo and penal servitude of three years"; see also Boulais, *Manuel du Code Chinois*, 644–645.

131. See Ocko, "Hierarchy and Harmony," 227, noting that "suits by junior relatives against seniors serving as trustees for their property" were "one instance in which the prohibition of suits against senior relatives was waived."

132. Allee, *Law and Local Society*, 134.

133. Alabaster, *Notes and Commentaries*, 593–595. Alabaster's transcription refers only to management by "each in turn," but, in accordance with custom, this unspecified "each" almost certainly refers to the different segments, or fang, of the family.

134. Ibid., 595–597.

135. See Fu-mei Chang Chen, "Provincial Documents of Laws and Regulations in the Ch'ing Period," *Ch'ing-shih wen-t'i* 3, no. 6 (December 1976): 40–45, describing the multistaged editing process of cases included in the compilation *Xing'an Huilan*.

136. Watson, *Inequality among Brothers*, 3.

137. Twitchett, "Fan Clan's Charitable Estate," 132.

138. See Edward Kroker, "The Concept of Property in Chinese Customary Law," *Transactions of the Asiatic Society of Japan*, 3rd ser., 7 (November 1959): 140–141.

139. Zelin, "Rights of Tenants," 513.

140. Watson, *Inequality among Brothers*.

141. Hu, *Common Descent Group*, 37.

142. Liu, "Analysis of Chinese Clan Rules II," 88.

143. See Hu, *Common Descent Group*, 18.

144. Compare Marc Galanter, "Why the 'Haves' Come Out Ahead: Speculations on the Limits of Legal Change," *Law & Society Review* 9, no. 1 (Autumn 1974): 149.

145. See Wang Yang-ming, "Inquiry on the *Great Learning*," in *Instructions for Practical Living and Other Neo-Confucian Writings*, trans. Wing-tsit Chan (New York: Columbia University Press, 1963), 271, 272.

146. See William Blackstone, *Commentaries on the Laws of England*, vol. 1 (Oxford: Clarendon Press, 1765), 430; United States v. Yazell, 382 U.S. 341, 361 (1966) (Black, J., dissenting).

147. This is de Bary's characterization of Zhu Xi's notion of the person, which he also describes as a "concept of the person as most truly itself when most fully in communion with other selves." See Wm. Theodore de Bary, *The Liberal Tradition in China* (Hong Kong: Chinese University Press; New York: Columbia University Press, 1983), 27.

148. Ibid., 24.

149. Tu Wei-ming, *Centrality and Commonality*, 77.

150. Alabaster, *Notes and Commentaries*, 594.

151. John Maynard Keynes, *A Tract on Monetary Reform* (London: Macmillan, 1923), 80.

152. Choa Choon Neoh v. Spottiswoode, [1896] 1 Kyshe 216, 220 (Sing.).

153. Ibid., 221–222. In contrast to their Singapore counterparts, clan corporations have survived in Hong Kong until late because of special legislation providing that ancestral lands in the colony's New Territories be governed solely by Chinese law and custom and hence remain exempt from the Rule Against Perpetuities. See New Territories Ordinance, (1953) Cap. 97, §1 (H.K.), reprinted in Hong Kong, *The Laws of Hong Kong*, rev. ed. (Hong Kong: Government Printer, 1984).

154. Gates, *China's Motor*, 45.

155. See Jamieson, *Family and Commercial Law*, 29.

156. Duncan Kennedy, "Distributive and Paternalist Motives in Contract and Tort Law, with Special Reference to Compulsory Terms and Unequal Bargaining Power," *Maryland Law Review* 41, no. 4 (1982): 638.

157. Melissa Macauley, *Social Power and Legal Culture: Litigation Masters in Late Imperial China* (Stanford, CA: Stanford University Press, 1998), 258.

158. Paul H. Ch'en, "Disloyalty to the State in Late Imperial China," in *State and Law in East Asia: Festschrift Karl Bünger*, ed. Dieter Eikemeier and Herbert Franke (Wiesbaden, Germany: Harrassowitz, 1981), 173.

159. Zhu Xi, *Xiao Xue Jizhu*, ed. Sibu Beiyao, 5:8a, quoted in Hsü Dau-lin, "The Myth of the 'Five Human Relations' of Confucius," *Monumenta Serica* 29 (1970–

1971): 35, stating, "There are no fathers and mothers in the world who (in the dealings with their children) are not right."

160. Gerald E. Frug, "The Ideology of Bureaucracy in American Law," *Harvard Law Review* 97, no. 6 (April 1984): 1308.

161. Blackstone, *Commentaries*, 465 (attributing the statement to Sir Edward Coke). Compare Tipling v. Pexall, [1614] 80 Eng. Rep. 1085 (P.C.): "None can create soules but God, but the King creates them, and therefore they have no soules."

162. Thomas Hobbes, *Leviathan*, ed. C. B. Macpherson (Harmondsworth, UK: Penguin, 1968), 375.

163. Blackstone, *Commentaries*, 455.

164. Cnty. of Santa Clara v. S. Pac. R. Co., 118 U.S. 394 (1886).

165. For statements of nonfictional character of corporations, see, for example, Ernst Freund, *The Legal Nature of Corporations* (Chicago: University of Chicago Press, 1897); Harold J. Laski, "The Personality of Associations," *Harvard Law Review* 29, no. 4 (February 1916): 416–423. A fervent believer in the creative power of *Genossenschaft*, or fellowship, Otto von Gierke was the most prominent proponent of the reality of "group persons" on the continent. See Otto von Gierke, *Community in Historical Perspective: A Translation of Selections from* Das deutsche Genossen-schaftsrect (The German Law of Fellowship), ed. Antony Black, trans. Mary Fischer (Cambridge: Cambridge University Press, 1990); Gierke, *Natural Law and the Theory of Society: 1500 to 1800; With a Lecture on the Ideas of Natural Law and Humanity by Ernst Troeltsch*, trans. Ernest Barker (Boston, MA: Beacon Press, 1957); Gierke, *Political Theories of the Middle Age*, trans. Frederic William Maitland (Cambridge: Cambridge University Press, 1958). A translator of Gierke, Frederic Maitland absorbed some of Gierke's ideas into his own writings as well.

166. See Radin, "Endless Problem," 643, 667.

167. Michael C. Jensen and William H. Meckling, "Theory of the Firm: Managerial Behavior, Agency Costs and Ownership Structure," *Journal of Financial Economics* 3, no. 4 (October 1976): 310–311.

168. See, for example, Frank H. Easterbrook and Daniel R. Fischel, *The Economic Structure of Corporate Law* (Cambridge, MA: Harvard University Press, 1991), 15, arguing that contemporary corporation law "almost always" conforms to the contractarian model.

169. Laski, "Personality of Associations," 420.

170. Lawrence E. Mitchell, "The Death of the Fiduciary Duty in Close Corporations," *University of Pennsylvania Law Review* 138, no. 6 (June 1990): 1729.

171. Jensen and Meckling, "Theory of the Firm," 307.

172. Frank H. Easterbrook and Daniel R. Fischel, "Contract and Fiduciary Duty," *Journal of Law & Economics* 36, no. 1 (April 1993): 427.

173. Easterbrook and Fischel, *Economic Structure*, 34. A "defining characteristic" of fiduciary duties is that they arise in situations with "impossibly high transactions

costs," according to Easterbrook and Fischel, "Contract and Fiduciary Duty," 444. When a contract contemplates the parties' entering into a long-term relation, it simply cannot foresee all possible contingencies and provide for them ex ante. "The only promise that makes sense in such an open-ended relation is to work hard and honestly." See Easterbrook and Fischel, *Economic Structure*, 91.

174. Ronald Dworkin, *Taking Rights Seriously* (London: Duckworth; Cambridge, MA: Harvard University Press, 1977), 151.

175. Easterbrook and Fischel, "Contract and Fiduciary Duty," 446.

176. Robert C. Clark, "Agency Costs versus Fiduciary Duties," in *Principals and Agents: The Structure of Business*, ed. John W. Pratt and Richard J. Zeckhauser (Boston, MA: Harvard Business School Press, 1985), 68.

177. Robert Charles Clark, "The Soundness of Financial Intermediaries," *Yale Law Journal* 86, no. 1 (November 1976): 19–20.

178. For communitarian stories, see, for example, Lawrence E. Mitchell, ed., *Progressive Corporate Law* (Boulder, CO: Westview Press, 1995); Margaret M. Blair and Lynn A. Stout, "Team Production in Business Organizations: An Introduction," *Journal of Corporation Law* 24, no. 4 (Summer 1999): 743–750. For a story of the corporation as a "citizen," with attendant civic duties, see James Boyd White, "How Should We Talk about Corporations? The Languages of Economics and of Citizenship," *Yale Law Journal* 94, no. 6 (May 1985): 1417–1425. This lack of agreement about the role of corporations and the nature of corporate governance is nothing new: when the American Law Institute formulated its code of corporate fiduciary duties in 1992, it observed that "no consensus existed in the legal community as to why corporate law imposes fiduciary duties or what the operative 'principles' of corporate fiduciary law ought to be." See William W. Bratton, "Self-Regulation, Normative Choice, and the Structure of Corporate Fiduciary Law," *George Washington Law Review* 61, no. 4 (April 1993): 1084.

179. Utilizing Becker's economic analysis of the family, I sketch such a reading in an essay entitled "Home Economics: What Is the Difference between a Family and a Corporation?," in *Rethinking Commodification: Cases and Readings in Law and Culture*, ed. Martha M. Ertman and Joan C. Williams (New York: New York University Press, 2005), 324–344.

180. William P. Alford, "The Inscrutable Occidental? Implications of Roberto Unger's Uses and Abuses of the Chinese Past," *Texas Law Review* 64, no. 5 (February 1986): 955.

181. Waltner, *Getting an Heir*, 90. It was no doubt for precisely this reason that south Fujianese maritime traders preferred to send adoptive sons, rather than their biological offspring, on perilous commercial voyages overseas. See Ng Chin-Keong, *Trade and Society*, 29.

182. Tomás Almaguer, *Racial Fault Lines: The Historical Origins of White Supremacy in California* (Berkeley: University of California Press, 1994), 50,

quoting an interview in 1844 with a prominent rancher that appeared in Hubert Bancroft's *History of California*.

183. See, for example, Elizabeth Fox-Genovese, *Within the Plantation Household: Black and White Women of the South* (Chapel Hill: University of North Carolina Press, 1988), 133, observing slave owners' construction of "our family white and black"; Emily Field van Tassell, " 'Only the Law Would Rule between Us': Antimiscegenation, the Moral Economy of Dependency, and the Debate over Rights after the Civil War," *Chicago-Kent Law Review* 70, no. 3 (1995): 884–890, describing the rhetorical assimilation of slaves into "family" and "household."

184. For an analysis of the historical rise of an ideological opposition, not just between the family and the corporation, but between the family and the market more generally, see the family law symposium introduced by Janet Halley and Kerry Rittich, "Critical Directions in Comparative Family Law: Genealogies and Contemporary Studies of Family Law Exceptionalism," *American Journal of Comparative Law* 58, no. 4 (Fall 2010): 753–776. In addition to investigating the contours of what the editors call "the economic family," hidden by the ideology of the sentimental family, the symposium examines the globalization of the market/family distinction as part of European colonialism.

185. See Lydia H. Liu, *The Clash of Empires: The Invention of China in Modern World Making* (Cambridge, MA: Harvard University Press, 2004), 85; see also, for example, Frederick Foo Chien, *The Opening of Korea: A Study of Chinese Diplomacy, 1876–1885* (Hamden, CT: Shoe String Press, 1967), 66; John King Fairbank, *Trade and Diplomacy on the China Coast: The Opening of the Treaty Ports, 1842–1854* (Cambridge, MA: Harvard University Press, 1953), 27; Maung Maung, *Burma in the Family of Nations* (New York: Institute of Pacific Relations, 1956), 38; Wang Gungwu, "The Rhetoric of a Lesser Empire: Early Sung Relations with Its Neighbors," in *China among Equals: The Middle Kingdom and Its Neighbors, 10th–14th Centuries*, ed. Morris Rossabi (Berkeley: University of California Press, 1983), 55.

4. CANTON IS NOT BOSTON

1. Robert M. Cover, "The Folktales of Justice: Tales of Jurisdiction," *Capital University Law Review* 14, no. 2 (1985): 179–204.

2. Both the English and Chinese texts of the treaty, with background notes, can be found in Hunter Miller, ed., *Treaties and Other International Acts of the United States of America*, vol. 4 (Washington, DC: Government Printing Office, 1934), 559.

3. Tyler Dennett, *Americans in Eastern Asia: A Critical Study of the Policy of the United States with Reference to China, Japan and Korea in the 19th Century* (New York: Macmillan, 1922), 288. For details, see Message of the President of the United States, Communicating, in Compliance with a Report of the Senate,

the Correspondence of Messrs. McLane and Parker, Late Commissioners to China, S. Exec. Doc. No. 35–22, pt. 2, at 1083, 1148 (2nd Sess. 1858).

4. S Exec. Doc. No. 35–22, at 1204.

5. See Thomas J. McCormick, *China Market: America's Quest for Informal Empire, 1893–1901* (Chicago: Quadrangle Books, 1967), 168–175.

6. Downes v. Bidwell, 182 U.S. 244, 374 (1901).

7. A. M. Latter, "The Government of the Foreigners in China," *Law Quarterly Review* 19 (1903): 316.

8. David J. Bederman, "Extraterritorial Domicile and the Constitution," *Virginia Journal of International Law* 28, no. 2 (Winter 1988): 465.

9. Schooner Exch. v. McFaddon, 11 U.S. (7 Cranch) 116, 136–137 (1812).

10. John Gallagher and Ronald Robinson, "The Imperialism of Free Trade," *Economic History Review* 6, no. 1 (1953): 1.

11. Ibid., 11.

12. Donald E. Pease, "US Imperialism: Global Dominance without Colonies," in *A Companion to Postcolonial Studies*, ed. Henry Schwarz and Sangeeta Ray (Malden, MA: Blackwell, 2000), 203.

13. See, for example, McCormick, *China Market*.

14. Johnson v. McIntosh, 21 U.S. 543 (1823).

15. See, for example, W. Ross Johnston, *Sovereignty and Protection: A Study of British Jurisdictional Imperialism in the Late Nineteenth Century*, Commonwealth Studies Center, no. 41 (Durham, NC: Duke University Press, 1973).

16. See, for example, L. Oppenheim, *International Law: A Treatise*, vol. 1: Peace (London: Longmans, Green, 1905), 60–61.

17. See Carl Schmitt, *The* Nomos *of the Earth in the International Law of the* Jus Publicum Europaeum, trans. G. L. Ulmen (New York: Telos Press, 2003). See also Antony Anghie, "Finding the Peripheries: Sovereignty and Colonialism in Nineteenth-Century International Law," *Harvard International Law Journal* 40, no. 1 (Winter 1999): 1.

18. John Locke, *Two Treatises of Government*, ed. Peter Laslett (Cambridge: Cambridge University Press, 1988), 301.

19. Cherokee Nation v. Georgia, 30 U.S. 1, 17 (1831).

20. Nevertheless, it was not a foregone conclusion as to just when, and to what extent, European sovereigns would recognize the United States. Indeed, while the U.S. Constitution is conventionally understood as concerned primarily with establishing popular sovereignty within the United States, its framers were equally keen to design a system of government that would meet the European standard of civilization. See David M. Golove and Daniel J. Hulsebosch, "A Civilized Nation: The Early American Constitution, the Law of Nations, and the Pursuit of International Recognition," *New York University Law Review* 85, no. 4 (October 2010): 932–1066. On the larger international audience for the Declaration of Indepen-

dence, see David Armitage, *The Declaration of Independence: A Global History* (Cambridge, MA: Harvard University Press, 2007).

21. I borrow the term from Robert A. Williams Jr., *The American Indian in Western Legal Thought: The Discourses of Conquest* (New York: Oxford University Press, 1990), 326.

22. See Amy Kaplan, *The Anarchy of Empire in the Making of U.S. Culture* (Cambridge, MA: Harvard University Press, 2002).

23. See Travers Twiss, *The Law of Nations Considered as Independent Political Communities: On the Rights and Duties of Nations in Time of Peace* (Oxford: Clarendon Press, 1884), 267; Francis Wharton, ed., *A Digest of the International Law of the United States, Taken from Documents Issued by Presidents and Secretaries of States, and from Decisions of Federal Courts and Opinions of Attorneys-General*, 2nd ed., vol. 1 (Washington, DC: Government Printing Office, 1887), 801–812.

24. For an analysis of China's ambiguous international legal status in colonial international law, see Teemu Ruskola, "Raping Like a State," *UCLA Law Review* 57, no. 5 (June 2010): 1477–1536.

25. Philip Chadwick Foster Smith, *The Empress of China* (Philadelphia, PA: Philadelphia Maritime Museum, 1984), 8.

26. James Morton Callahan, *American Relations in the Pacific and the Far East, 1784–1900*, Johns Hopkins University Studies in Historical and Political Science 19, nos. 1–3 (Baltimore, MD: Johns Hopkins University Press, 1901), 14, 84.

27. John W. Foster, *American Diplomacy in the Orient* (Boston, MA: Houghton Mifflin, 1903), 43.

28. Dennett, *Americans in Eastern Asia*, 7.

29. See R. Randle Edwards, "Ch'ing Legal Jurisdiction over Foreigners," in *Essays on China's Legal Tradition*, ed. Jerome Alan Cohen, R. Randle Edwards, and Fu-mei Chang Chen, Studies in East Asian Law (Princeton, NJ: Princeton University Press, 1980), 222–269.

30. Jonathan Goldstein, *Philadelphia and the China Trade, 1682–1846: Commercial, Cultural, and Attitudinal Effects* (University Park: Pennsylvania State University Press, 1978), 61.

31. Dennett, *Americans in Eastern Asia*, 87.

32. Edwards, "Ch'ing Legal Jurisdiction," 249.

33. Dennett, *Americans in Eastern Asia*, 84.

34. Ibid.

35. Message from the President of the United States, Transmitting a Report from the Secretary of State, Trade with China, H.R. Doc. No. 26–119, at 68 (1st Sess. 1840) ("Mr. Snow to the Secretary of State: Canton, August 29, 1839").

36. Dennett, *Americans in Eastern Asia*, 88.

37. Treaty of Amity and Commerce, U.S.-Siam, art. 9, Mar. 20, 1833, in Miller, *Treaties*, vol. 3 (1933), 757.

38. John Kuo Wei Tchen, *New York before Chinatown: Orientalism and the Shaping of American Culture, 1776–1882* (Baltimore, MD: Johns Hopkins University Press, 1999), 41–42. See also Dennett, *Americans in Eastern Asia*, 77; A. Owen Aldridge, *The Dragon and the Eagle: The Presence of China in the American Enlightenment* (Detroit, MI: Wayne State University Press, 1993), 96. It should be noted that the "mandarin" in question was a fake, employed by Astor to gain exemption from the embargo. However, insofar as Jefferson did believe him to be a genuine representative of the Chinese government, his actions suggest his evident regard for Chinese sovereignty.

39. The conventional reference—now under critique—for a description of the "tributary system" in East Asia is John King Fairbank, ed., *The Chinese World Order: Traditional China's Foreign Relations* (Cambridge, MA: Harvard University Press, 1968). For critical assessments of the tributary paradigm, mounted by a growing number of "new" Qing historians, see, for example, James L. Hevia, *Cherishing Men from Afar: Qing Guest Ritual and the Macartney Embassy of 1793* (Durham, NC: Duke University Press, 1995); Lydia H. Liu, *The Clash of Empires: The Invention of China in Modern World Making* (Cambridge, MA: Harvard University Press, 2004).

40. The literature on the Macartney embassy is far too large to cite in a single note. See generally Hevia, *Cherishing Men from Afar*, and the sources cited therein.

41. Ibid., 238.

42. J. L. Cranmer-Byng, ed., *An Embassy to China: Being the Journal Kept by Lord Macartney during His Embassy to the Emperor Ch'ien-lung, 1793–1794* (London: Longmans, 1962), 225–226.

43. Marshall Sahlins, "Cosmologies of Capitalism: The Trans-Pacific Sector of 'The World System,'" *Proceedings of the British Academy* 74 (1988): 13.

44. See Ssu-yü Teng and John K. Fairbank, *China's Response to the West: A Documentary Survey, 1839–1923* (Cambridge, MA: Harvard University Press, 1954), 24–28.

45. The Sino-British story has been told well by James Hevia and Lydia Liu. See Hevia, *Cherishing Men from Afar;* Hevia, *English Lessons: The Pedagogy of Imperialism in Nineteenth-Century China* (Durham, NC: Duke University Press; Hong Kong: Hong Kong University Press, 2003); Liu, *The Clash of Empires*.

46. See, for example, Michael H. Hunt, *The Making of a Special Relationship: The United States and China to 1914* (New York: Columbia University Press, 1983).

47. Daniel Webster, "Intercourse with China," in *The Works of Daniel Webster*, vol. 6 (Boston: Little and Brown, 1851), 469.

48. For the full language of the letters, see Message from the President Communicating (in Compliance with a Resolution of the Senate) Copies of the Instructions Given to the Late Commissioner to China, S. Doc. No. 28–138, at 8–9 (2nd Sess. 1845).

49. Jack Beeching, *The Chinese Opium Wars* (New York: Harcourt Brace Jovanovich, 1975), 173.

50. Claude M. Fuess, *The Life of Caleb Cushing*, vol. 1 (New York: Harcourt, Brace, 1923), 423.

51. Dennett, *Americans in Eastern Asia*, 143.

52. See Jerry Israel, *Progressivism and the Open Door: America and China, 1905–1921* (Pittsburgh, PA: University of Pittsburgh Press, 1971), 4–6.

53. "American Leadership in China," *The Nation* 72, no. 1871 (May 9, 1901): 369.

54. John Quincy Adams, "J. Q. Adams on the Opium War," *Proceedings of the Massachusetts Historical Society*, 3rd ser., 43 (February 1910): 324; John Quincy Adams, *Memoirs of John Quincy Adams: Comprising Portions of His Diary from 1795 to 1848*, ed. Charles Francis Adams, vol. 11 (Philadelphia: J. B. Lippincott, 1876), 31.

55. Dennett, *Americans in Eastern Asia*, 105 (quoting Freeman Hunt, *Hunt's Merchants' Magazine and Commercial Review*, March 1843, 205); W. C. Hunter, *The 'Fan Kwae' at Canton before Treaty Days: 1825–1844* (Taipei, Taiwan: Ch'eng-Wen, 1965), 154.

56. "Adams on the Opium War," 314.

57. John W. Edmonds, *Origin and Progress of the War between England and China: A Lecture; Delivered before the Newburgh Lyceum, Dec. 11, 1841* (New York: Narine & Co's Print, 1841), 3, 4, 6, 12, 24.

58. Message from the President of the United States, Transmitting an Abstract of the Treaty between the United States and the Chinese Empire, H.R. Doc. No. 28–69, at 1 (2nd Sess. 1845).

59. See United States Judicial Authority in China, 7 Op. Att'y Gen. 495, 503 (1855).

60. S. Doc. No. 28–138, at 8.

61. Dennett, *Americans in Eastern Asia*, 104.

62. Fuess, *Life of Caleb Cushing*, vol. 2, 230–231.

63. Message from the President of the United States, Transmitting a Treaty between the United States of America, and the Ta Tsing Empire, S. Doc. No. 28–67, at 12 (2nd Sess. 1845).

64. Ibid.

65. Ibid., at 16, 19 (emphasis added); Fuess, *Life of Caleb Cushing*, vol. 1, 430.

66. S. Doc. No. 28–67, at 18.

67. H.R. Doc. No. 28–69, at 5 (includes transcript of Cushing's letter to Calhoun, September 29, 1844).

68. Ibid., at 10.

69. Ibid., at 8.

70. Ibid., at 10.

71. Ibid.

72. Ibid., at 11.

73. Ibid., at 11–12.

74. Ibid., at 12.

75. In Hinckley's view, in these treaties extraterritoriality "appears not to have been thought exceptionally important," and the provisions regarding extraterritoriality were copied from earlier French and Dutch treaties, which were available to the American negotiators. See Frank E. Hinckley, *American Consular Jurisdiction in the Orient* (Washington, DC: W. H. Lowdermilk, 1906), 19.

76. See, for example, Treaty of Peace, U.S.-Algiers, June 30 and July 3, 1815, in Miller, *Treaties*, vol. 2 (1931), 585. The other treaties on which Cushing relied—namely, "the Porte," that is, the Ottoman Empire (1830), and Muscat (1833)—provided also for extraterritorial jurisdiction only in disputes among U.S. citizens, not disputes between U.S. citizens and natives. See, respectively, Treaty of Commerce and Navigation, U.S.-Turk., art. 4, May 7, 1830, in Miller, *Treaties*, vol. 3, 542–543, and Treaty of Amity and Commerce, U.S.-Oman, art. 9, Sept. 21, 1833, in Miller, *Treaties*, vol. 3, 801.

77. The extraterritoriality provisions of the U.S. treaties with Morocco (1786), Algiers (1795), and Tunis (1797–1799), for example, were limited primarily to civil disputes and, moreover, only to disputes among U.S. citizens. (Unlike the prior treaties, the treaty with Tripoli, 1796–1797, did not specify the extent of American extraterritorial jurisdiction, referring instead only to an unspecified—but reciprocal—"right of establishing consuls in each country." See Treaty of Peace and Friendship, U.S.-Tripoli, art. 9, Nov. 4, 1796, and Jan. 3, 1797, in Miller, *Treaties*, vol. 2, 365.) Hence, Americans did not enjoy extraterritorial protection even in their civil—let alone criminal—disputes with the natives of those states. For the treaty with Morocco, see Treaty of Peace and Friendship, U.S.-Morocco, arts. 20 and 21, June 28 and July 15, 1786, in Miller, *Treaties*, vol. 2, 216; for the treaty with Algiers, Treaty of Peace and Amity, U.S.-Algiers, arts. 15 and 16, Sept. 5, 1795, in Miller, *Treaties*, vol. 2, 302; and for the treaty with Tunis, see Treaty of Peace and Friendship, U.S.-Tunis, arts. 20 and 21, Aug. 28, 1797, and Mar. 26, 1799, in Miller, *Treaties*, vol. 2, 412. Only in subsequent treaties with the Barbary States did extraterritorial jurisdiction extend to criminal matters as well and, again, even then only to criminal matters that did not involve disputes between Americans and the natives. See, for example, Treaty of Peace, U.S.-Algiers, arts. 19 and 20, June 30 and July 3, 1815, in Miller, *Treaties*, vol. 2, 590.

78. Treaty of Peace and Friendship, U.S.-Tripoli, art. 9, Nov. 4, 1796, and Jan. 3, 1797, in Miller, *Treaties*, vol. 2, 365; see also, Treaty of Peace and Amity, U.S.-Tripoli, June 4, 1805, in Miller, *Treaties*, vol. 2, 529–556; Treaty of Peace, U.S.-Algiers, June 30 and July 3, 1815, in Miller, *Treaties*, vol. 2, 585–594; Treaty of Peace and Amity, U.S.-Algiers, Dec. 22 and 23, 1816, in Miller, *Treaties*, vol. 2,

617–644. The treaties with Algiers declare that the United States indeed "has no character of enmity against the laws, religion, or tranquility of any nation," not just those of "Musselmen." Treaty of Peace, U.S.-Algiers, art. 15, June 30 and July 3, 1815, in Miller, *Treaties*, vol. 2, 588–589. To be sure, whatever language the United States inserts into its treaties may or may not be an accurate statement of its actual policies, but surely such language is at least relevant in determining those policies.

79. See Articles of Arrangement with the King of the Sandwich Islands, U.S.-Hawaii, Dec. 23, 1826, in Miller, *Treaties*, vol. 3, 269–281; Commercial Regulations, U.S.-Samoa, Nov. 5, 1839, in Miller, *Treaties*, vol. 4, 241–256; Agreement Made by the Sultan of Sulu at Sooung, U.S.-Sulu, Feb. 5, 1842, in Miller, *Treaties*, vol. 4, 349–361. In fact, when Captain Jones arrived in Honolulu in 1826 to negotiate a Treaty of Commerce and Navigation for the United States, he expressed dismay, and even disbelief, at the demands for extraterritoriality expressed by other Westerners in Oahu. ("Such were the judicial views of the foreign residents and traders at Woahoo when [we] arrived!!") See Miller, Articles of Arrangement with the King of the Sandwich Islands, U.S.-Hawaii, Dec. 23, 1826, in Miller, *Treaties*, vol. 3, 277 (quoting Captain Jones's report).

80. Articles of Arrangement with the King of the Sandwich Islands, U.S.-Hawaii, Dec. 23, 1826, in Miller, *Treaties*, vol. 3, 270. Admittedly, for his purposes Cushing could easily—though not very convincingly—have distinguished the case of Hawaii on the grounds that it was in principle a "Christian" state, with at least a semblance (if little more than that) of Western-style political institutions. See Sally Engle Merry, *Colonizing Hawai'i: The Cultural Power of Law* (Princeton, NJ: Princeton University Press, 2000). Yet significantly Captain Jones did not ask for extraterritoriality when negotiating the U.S. treaty with Tahiti, during the same expedition, even though Tahiti was neither Christian nor politically Westernized (even superficially) like Hawaii.

81. H.R. Doc. No. 28–69, at 14.

82. Ibid., at 13.

83. See Treaty of Peace, Amity, and Commerce, U.S.-China, art. 19, July 3, 1844, in Miller, *Treaties*, vol. 4, 565.

84. To be sure, this was an unmistakably Protestant translation of an originally Catholic notion, which was harnessed here to support the imperial extension of power by a secular sovereign of the West. For all his invocations of Christianity, Cushing by no means intended to imply that American jurisdiction in China might be subject to, or overlap with, the jurisdictional claims of the pope.

85. Edward V. Gulick, *Peter Parker and the Opening of China* (Cambridge, MA: Harvard University Press, 1973), 114.

86. Dennett, *Americans in Eastern Asia*, 577.

87. See Treaty of Peace, Friendship, Commerce, and Navigation, U.S.-Brunei, June 23, 1850, in Miller, *Treaties*, vol. 5 (1936), 819–843.

88. He had been provided with a copy of the Treaty of Wanghia so that he could use it "to a certain extent . . . as precedent." Treaty of Peace and Amity, U.S.-Japan, Mar. 31, 1854, in Miller, *Treaties*, vol. 6 (1942), 516 [hereinafter Perry's Treaty] (quoting Perry's instructions). However the best he was able to obtain in terms of extraterritoriality was a general clause providing that "Shipwrecked persons and other Citizens of the United States shall be free as in other Countries, and not subjected to confinement, but shall be amenable to just laws." Perry's Treaty, 441. In his notes explaining the treaty, Perry acknowledges encountering "great difficulties" in obtaining immunities for Americans, but he makes it clear that he did intend the shipwreck provision to function as a general exemption for Americans from Japanese jurisdiction. (Perry explained, "The meaning intended to be conveyed by the words 'just laws' is that Americans shall not be subject to the exclusive laws and customs of Japan but to laws based upon justice and humanity. This understanding to continue until further negotiation upon the subject and the appointment of a Consular Agent." Perry's Treaty, 633.) Perry's understanding was confirmed conclusively in 1857 with an agreement on Further Regulation of U.S. Citizens in Japan, which provided that Americans in Japan were to be "tried by the American Consul General or Consul, and shall be punished, according to American Laws." See Convention for Further Regulating the Intercourse of American Citizens within the Empire of Japan, U.S.-Japan, art. 4, June 17, 1857, in Miller, *Treaties*, vol. 7 (1942), 597. The extraterritoriality provisions were further elaborated in the 1858–1859 treaty revision. See Treaty of Amity and Commerce, U.S.-Japan, arts. 6 and 9, July 29, 1858, and Mar. 19, 1859, in Miller, *Treaties*, vol. 7, 955–956, 958.

89. Treaty of Amity and Commerce, with General Regulations and Tariff of Export and Inland Duties, U.S.-Siam, May 29, 1856, in Miller, *Treaties*, vol. 7, 329–400.

90. For these treaties, see, respectively, Treaty of Friendship and Commerce, U.S.-Samoa, Jan. 17, 1878, in William M. Malloy, comp., *Treaties, Conventions, International Acts, Protocols and Agreements between the United States of America and Other Powers, 1776–1909*, vol. 2 (Washington, DC: Government Printing Office, 1910), 1574; Treaty of Peace, Amity, Commerce and Navigation, U.S.-Kor., May 22, 1883, in Malloy, *Treaties*, vol. 1, 334; Treaty of Amity, Commerce, and Navigation, U.S.-Tonga, Oct. 2, 1886, in Malloy, *Treaties*, vol. 2, 1781.

91. Treaty of Amity, Commerce, and Navigation, U.S.-Tonga, art. 12, Oct. 2, 1886, in Malloy, *Treaties*, vol. 2, 1781.

92. See Act of Aug. 11, 1848, ch. 150, 9 Stat. 276 (1848), effecting certain treaty provisions between the United States and China and the Ottoman Porte, and giving powers to ministers and consuls. The act was revised over time, mostly to extend its geographic coverage as the United States entered into new extraterritoriality treaties. See Act of June 22, 1860, ch. 179, 12 Stat. 72, effecting treaty

provisions between the United States, China, Japan, Siam, Persia, and other countries; Act of July 1, 1870, ch. 194, 16 Stat. 183, amending Act of June 22, 1860.

93. Act of June 22, 1860, ch. 179, s. 30, 12 Stat. at 78. The act was not repealed until August 1, 1956. S.J. Res. 165, 84th Cong., 70 Stat. 773 (1956). It empowered U.S. consuls and commercial agents "at islands or in countries not inhabited by any civilized people, or recognized by any treaty with the United States" to hear all civil cases involving sums less than a thousand dollars "in the same manner as justices of the peace are now authorized and empowered where the United States have exclusive jurisdiction." With regard to other civil cases and all criminal ones, they exercised the same jurisdiction as U.S. consular judges in China and in other extraterritorial jurisdictions established by treaty. 12 Stat. at 78.

94. The origins of this provision are highly obscure. There is no legislative history on it, and there appears to have been only one prosecution under it. In 1885, a request was made to the State Department for the prosecution of a U.S. trader on the island of "Gnap," for torturing a local youth whom he accused of "stealing." See Consular Jurisdiction, 18 Op. Att'y Gen. 219 (1885). The Attorney General authorized the sending of a commercial agent to bring the accused to justice, referring to "the well-received doctrine of international law, that consuls in barbarous or semi barbarous states are to be regarded as investing with extraterritoriality the place where their flag is planted, and if justice is to be administered at all, so far as concerns civilized foreigners visiting such states, it must be by tribunals" such as Congress had provided for in its 1860 enactment. Ibid., 220. "Gnap" apparently referred to Yap, part of the Caroline Islands in the Western Pacific. The island's name was misspelled "Guap" in instructions for the U.S. legation in Madrid to inform the Spanish authorities that the United States had no territorial designs on the island—at the time the object of conflicting claims by Spain and Germany. See Wharton, *Digest*, 439.

95. The assessment is by Kenneth Scott Latourette, "The History of Early Relations between the United States and China, 1784–1844," *Transactions of the Connecticut Academy of Arts and Sciences* 22 (New Haven, CT: Yale University Press, 1917), 140–141.

96. Foster, *American Diplomacy*, 89–90.

97. Louis G. Perez, *Japan Comes of Age: Mutsu Munemitsu and the Revision of the Unequal Treaties* (Madison, NJ: Fairleigh Dickinson University Press; London: Associated University Presses, 1999), 51–52.

98. Ibid., 37, 39.

99. Henry H. Perritt, Jr., "Jurisdiction in Cyberspace," *Villanova Law Review* 41, no. 1 (1996): 1, 100.

100. See, for example, Travers Twiss, *The Law of Nations, Considered as Independent Political Communities*, vol. 1: On the Rights and Duties of Nations in

Time of Peace (Oxford: Oxford University Press, 1861), 268–269. Twiss describes the "exceptional position of Europeans whilst resident amongst Asiatics" and refers to extraterritoriality treaties as "in the highest degree exceptional." Ibid., 223–224. See also Oppenheim, *International Law: A Treatise*, vol. 1, 481, who likewise characterizes the existence of extraterritorial jurisdiction in "non-Christian states" as "in every point an exceptional one."

101. Although this analysis invokes Schmitt's notion of the sovereign as one who decides on the state of exception, the focus of his constitutional inquiry is a single state, not a community of states. See Schmitt, *Political Theology: Four Chapters on the Concept of Sovereignty*, trans. Georg Schwab (Chicago: University of Chicago Press, 1985). Schmitt makes the larger structural point about the nature of European sovereignty, in a different vocabulary, in *The* Nomos *of the Earth*.

102. People v. Hall, 4 Cal. 399, 401–402 (1854). See generally Charles J. McClain, *In Search of Equality: The Chinese Struggle against Discrimination in Nineteenth-Century America* (Berkeley: University of California Press, 1994).

103. Act of May 6, 1882, ch. 126, 22 Stat. 58. In fact, the prohibition of naturalization by the Chinese was largely redundant. Already in 1878 the Chinese had been found ineligible for naturalization, being neither "white persons" nor "persons of African descent." As Judge Sawyer put it forthrightly, U.S. naturalization laws were clearly "intended to exclude some classes, and as all white aliens and those of the African race are entitled to naturalization under other words, it is difficult to perceive whom it could exclude unless it be the Chinese." *In re* Ah Yup, 1 F. Cas. 223, 223–224 (C.C.D. Cal. 1878) (No. 104).

104. Act of Oct. 1, 1888, ch. 1064, 25 Stat. 504 (supplementing the Act of May 6, 1882).

105. See Kunal M. Parker, "From Poor Law to Immigration Law: Changing Visions of Territorial Community in Antebellum Massachusetts," *Historical Geography* 28 (2000): 61–85; Parker, "State, Citizenship, and Territory: The Legal Construction of Immigrants in Antebellum Massachusetts," *Law and History Review* 19, no. 3 (Fall 2001): 583–644; Parker, "Making Blacks Foreigners: The Legal Construction of Former Slaves in Post-Revolutionary Massachusetts," *Utah Law Review* no. 1 (2001): 75–124.

106. See generally Lucy E. Salyer, *Laws Harsh as Tigers: Chinese Immigrants and the Shaping of Modern Immigration Law* (Chapel Hill: University of North Carolina Press, 1995).

107. Chae Chan Ping v. United States, 130 U.S. 581, 604 (1889) (quoting Schooner Exch. v. McFaddon, 11 U.S. (7 Cranch) 116, 136 (1812)).

108. Ibid., 600.

109. Ibid., 609.

110. Ibid., 606.

111. Sarah H. Cleveland, "Powers Inherent in Sovereignty: Indians, Aliens, Territories, and the Nineteenth Century Origins of Plenary Power over Foreign Affairs," *Texas Law Review* 81, no. 1 (November 2002): 280.

112. Musgrove v. Chun Teong Toy, [1891] A.C. 272 (P.C.), an appeal from Victoria, cited the U.S. Supreme Court's decision in Chae Chan Ping v. United States. Subsequently, the U.S. Supreme Court cited *Musgrove* for support in Fong Yue Ting v. United States, 149 U.S. 698 (1893).

113. See "Geary on Exclusion: He Believes the Law Can Be Enforced," *San Francisco Chronicle*, Dec. 9, 1892, 2. Many thanks to Daniel Tu for bringing this article to my attention.

114. Aristide R. Zolberg, "The Great Wall against China: Responses to the First Immigration Crisis, 1885–1925," in *Migration, Migration History, History: Old Paradigms and New Perspectives*, ed. Jan Lucassen and Leo Lucassen (Bern, Switzerland: Peter Lang, 1997), 291–315.

115. Fong Yue Ting v. United States, 149 U.S. 698, 737, 756 (1893) (Brewer and Field, J.J., dissenting). The Court's extension of the principles of the *Chinese Exclusion Case* to deportation remains good law insofar as lawfully admitted long-term residents can be deported by the authority of the federal government. However, subsequently the Court held that in deportation there are procedural due process guarantees. See Yamataya v. Fisher, 189 U.S. 86 (1903). The holding of the *Chinese Exclusion Case*, in contrast, has not been similarly qualified with regard to those excluded from entering the United States.

116. As to the putative lawlessness of territorial populations, the question, again, is how one defines law. For a rich analysis of many kinds of legal institutions among the pioneer populations on the frontier, see John Philip Reid, *Law for the Elephant: Property and Social Behavior on the Overland Trail* (San Marino, CA: Huntington Library Press, 1996). For a constitutional and historical survey of the territorial expansion of the United States, see Gary Lawson and Guy Seidman, *The Constitution of Empire: Territorial Expansion and American Legal History* (New Haven, CT: Yale University Press, 2004); Arnold H. Leibowitz, *Defining Status: A Comprehensive Analysis of United States Territorial Relations* (Dordrecht, Netherlands: Martinus Nijhoff, 1989).

117. Winfred Lee Thompson, *The Introduction of American Law in the Philippines and Puerto Rico, 1898–1905* (Fayetteville: University of Arkansas Press, 1989), 21.

118. See Elk v. Wilkins, 112 U.S. 94, 98 (1884).

119. For an extensive analysis of the doctrine of plenary power, see generally T. Alexander Aleinikoff, *Semblances of Sovereignty: The Constitution, the State, and American Citizenship* (Cambridge, MA: Harvard University Press, 2002). For an account of U.S. constitutionalism's dependence on the perpetuation of forms of unfreedom based on European settlers' belief that "the preservation and enhancement

of their own democratic institutions required Indian dispossession and the coercive use of dependent groups," see Aziz Rana, *The Two Faces of American Freedom* (Cambridge, MA: Harvard University Press, 2010), 3. I borrow the notion of internal Orientalism from Louisa Schein, who uses it to refer to a nation's Others within. See Louisa Schein, *Minority Rules: The Miao and the Feminine in China's Cultural Politics* (Durham, NC: Duke University Press, 2000), 100–131. While Schein's specific focus is internal Orientalism in the PRC, the United States evidently has its own internal Orientals as well. While Chinese and U.S. internal Orientalisms are distinctive, they share a focus on sexuality as a crucial signifier of difference.

120. Christine Talbot, " 'Turkey Is in Our Midst': Orientalism and the Contagion in Nineteenth Century Anti-Mormonism," *Journal of Law & Family Studies* 8, no. 2 (2006): 372. The Orient of anti-Mormon Orientalism was predominantly, although not exclusively, a Muslim one. Ultimately, it referred to any place or any time that was associated with polygamy and/or political despotism (which were ultimately indissociable) seen as belonging "to the indolent and opium-eating Turks and Asiatics, the miserable Africans, the North American savages, and the Latter-Day Saints." See ibid., 378, quoting Benjamin G. Ferris, *Utah and the Mormons: The History, Government, Doctrines, Customs, and Prospects of the Latter-Day Saints; From Personal Observation During a Six Months' Residence at Great Salt Lake City* (New York: Harper & Brothers, 1854), 247. On associations between Chinese immigration and Mormon polygamy, see Sarah Barringer Gordon, *The Mormon Question: Polygamy and Constitutional Conflict in Nineteenth-Century America* (Chapel Hill: University of North Carolina Press, 2001), 192–195.

121. Late Corp. of the Church of Jesus Christ of Latter-Day Saints v. United States, 136 U.S. 1, 49–50 (1890).

122. Reynolds v. United States, 98 U.S. 145, 165–166 (1878). On the governance and racialization of another, non-white territorial population, namely that of the Territory of New Mexico, see Laura Gomez, *Manifest Destinies: The Making of the Mexican American Race* (New York: New York University Press, 2008). Regarding the circulation of persons and ideas in the United States' external and internal colonies, Gomez notes that Senator Beveridge, who in 1901 became Chair of the Senate's committee on U.S. territories, had formulated his ideas about territorial governance on his travels in the Philippines. Ibid., 74.

123. Dennett, *Americans in Eastern Asia*, 169.

124. Dred Scott v. Sandford, 60 U.S. 393, 421 (1856). Referring to Cushing's failure to land the position of Chief Justice on the U.S. Supreme Court, even his exceedingly uncritical biographer opines that if Chief Justice Roger Taney (who authored the majority opinion in *Dred Scott*), "as seemed likely at one time, had died in 1856 and Cushing had been appointed Chief Justice, the 'Dred Scott decision' would have been rendered in substantially the same spirit and language." Fuess, *Life of Caleb Cushing*, vol. 2, 155.

125. See Reginald Horsman, *Race and Manifest Destiny: The Origins of American Racial Anglo-Saxonism* (Cambridge, MA: Harvard University Press, 1981).

126. Ibid., 1, 297.

127. Goldstein, *Philadelphia and the China Trade*, 72, 81.

128. Horsman, *Race and Manifest Destiny*, 297–298.

129. Ibid., 287–288.

130. Stuart Creighton Miller, most notably, argues that the Sinophobia that came to prevail at the end of the nineteenth century had much longer historical roots. See Stuart Creighton Miller, *The Unwelcome Immigrant: The American Image of the Chinese, 1785–1882* (Berkeley: University of California Press, 1969). Nevertheless, during the first half of the nineteenth century negative attitudes were balanced by positive ones, and even outweighed by them, according to the dominant scholarly view. See generally Jonathan Goldstein, Jerry Israel, and Hilary Conroy, eds., *America Views China: American Images of China Then and Now* (Bethlehem, PA: Lehigh University Press, 1991).

131. P. J. Marshall, "Britain and China in the Late Eighteenth Century," in *Ritual and Diplomacy: The Macartney Mission to China, 1792–1794*, ed. Robert A. Bickers (London: British Association for Chinese Studies/Wellsweep, 1993), 12; Hannah Arendt, *The Origins of Totalitarianism* (New York: Harcourt, Brace & World, 1968), 206. See also Michael Keevak, *Becoming Yellow: A Short History of Racial Thinking* (Princeton, NJ: Princeton University Press, 2011).

132. Fuess, *Life of Caleb Cushing*, vol. 2, 233.

133. See Benedict Anderson, *Imagined Communities: Reflections on the Origin and Spread of Nationalism*, rev. ed. (London: Verso, 1991).

134. See generally Kal Raustiala, *Does the Constitution Follow the Flag?: The Evolution of Territoriality in American Law* (Oxford: Oxford University Press, 2009).

5. THE DISTRICT OF CHINA IS NOT THE DISTRICT OF COLUMBIA

1. Chambers of the Surrogate to Attorney General (forwarded to Department of State), Nov. 28, 1910; Doc. 172.1; Decimal Files, 1910–1929; General Records of the Department of State, Record Group 59; National Archives at College Park, MD.

2. The following states obtained extraterritorial privileges in China (and are listed here in the order in which they obtained those privileges): Great Britain, United States, France, Sweden, Norway, Russia, Germany, Denmark, the Netherlands, Spain, Belgium, Italy, Austria-Hungary, Peru, Brazil, Portugal, Japan, Mexico, and Switzerland. For a general discussion of the jurisdictional complexity in post-1911 Shanghai, see Tahirih V. Lee, "A Maze of Jurisdictional Walls: Conflict and Cooperation among the Courts in Republican-Era Shanghai," *Chinese*

Walls in Time and Space: A Multidisciplinary Perspective, ed. Roger Des Forges et al. (Ithaca, NY: Cornell East Asia Program, 2010), 139–171.

3. Tahirih Victoria Lee, "Law and Local Autonomy at the International Mixed Court of Shanghai" (PhD diss., Yale University, 1990), 108.

4. See generally Frederick Wakeman, Jr., *Policing Shanghai, 1927–1937* (Berkeley: University of California Press, 1995).

5. Norwood F. Allman, *Shanghai Lawyer* (New York: Whittlesey House, 1943), 115–116.

6. Although there was no unanimity about the nature and effect of these leases, most commentators agreed with Oppenheim's view that they were ultimately cessions in disguise. See Lassa Oppenheim, *International Law: A Treatise*, vol. 1: Peace (London: Longmans, Green, 1905), 221. Lauterpacht, representing the minority position, insisted that in the case of "political leases" (as he called them) the lessor state retained its sovereignty during the lease. See Hersch Lauterpacht, *Private Law Sources and Analogies of International Law (With Special Reference to International Arbitration)* (London: Longmans, Green, 1927), 184–185. Remarkably, the British even entertained both theories at the same time, viewing their lease of the New Territories of Hong Kong as a cession of sovereignty while conceding Chinese sovereignty during their lease of Weihaiwei. Compare Peter Wesley-Smith, *Unequal Treaty, 1898–1997: China, Great Britain and Hong Kong's New Territories* (Hong Kong: Oxford University Press, 1980), with Carol G. S. Tan, *British Rule in China: Law and Justice in Weihaiwei, 1898–1930* (London: Wildy, Simmonds and Hill, 2008), 71, 82, and Pamela Atwell, *British Mandarins and Chinese Reformers: The British Administration of Weihaiwei (1898–1930) and the Territory's Return to Chinese Rule* (Hong Kong: Oxford University Press, 1985).

7. For the text of the lease, see "Abkommen zwischen dem Deutschen Reich und der Qing-Dynastie," in Mechthild Leutner, ed., *"Musterkolonie Kiautschou": Die Expansion des Deutschen Reiches in China; Deutsch-chinesische Beziehungen 1897 bis 1914; Eine Quellensammlung* (Berlin: Akaedime Verlag, 1997), 164. Indeed, *Harper's* went further and referred to Germany's first "colony" in China, noting that by "enforcing a protectorate over the whole of Shan-tung, Germany has commenced the virtual partition of China." See Poultney Bigelow, "Germany's First Colony in China," *Harper's New Monthly Magazine* 100, no. 598 (March 1900): 589. See also John E. Schrecker, *Imperialism and Chinese Nationalism: Germany in Shantung* (Cambridge, MA: Harvard University Press, 1971), 60, stating that "even though the new territory was technically a leasehold, the Germans never considered its status to be different from that of the other German colonies."

8. See "Abkommen zwischen dem Deutschen Reich und der Qing-Dynastie," 166.

9. See, for example, Yoshihisa Tak Matsusaka, *The Making of Japanese Manchuria, 1904–1932* (Cambridge, MA: Harvard University Asia Center, 2001). On "road sovereignty," see Wakeman, *Policing Shanghai*.

10. On the history and administrative structure of Shanghai, see generally A. M. Kotenev, *Shanghai: Its Municipality and the Chinese* (Shanghai: North-China Daily News & Herald, 1927).

11. David H. Bailey to George F. Seward, 15 September 1879, in *Papers Relating to the Foreign Relations of the United States*, vol. 1 (Washington, DC: Government Printing Office, 1880), 231.

12. See generally Luke T. Lee, *Consular Law and Practice*, 2nd ed. (Oxford: Clarendon Press, 1991).

13. See Eileen P. Scully, *Bargaining with the State from Afar: American Citizenship in Treaty Port China, 1844–1942* (New York: Columbia University Press, 2001), 68.

14. Allman, *Shanghai Lawyer*, 97. In more diplomatic language, the Senate was told in 1850 that American consuls in China were "destitute of all legal requirements." See Message from the President of the United States, Communicating the Report of the Commissioner to China, Made in Pursuance of the Provisions of the Act to Carry into Effect Certain Provisions of the Treaties between the United States and China and the Ottoman-Porte, S. Exec. Doc. No. 31–72, at 72 (1st Sess. 1850).

15. See legislation cited in Chapter 4, n. 92.

16. United States Judicial Authority in China, 7 Op. Att'y Gen. 495 (1855).

17. 11 Cong. Rec. 410 (1881) (statement of Sen. Carpenter). The senator expressed considerable consternation at the legislation authorizing U.S. extraterritorial courts in China: "I must apologize to Senators who have charged me with having been on the Judiciary Committee for several years and with not having brought forward a bill for the repeal of these statutes. I must say, and I say truthfully, that until within two years I had no more idea that such a provision could be found on any statutes passed by Congress than I had that I should be hanged myself by the judgment of a lamp-lighter." Ibid., 415.

The senator's proposed remedy was not judicial withdrawal from China but, rather, the establishment of proper courts to exercise the United States' extraterritorial jurisdiction: "You should establish a court to try [Americans in China], according to the Constitution. You should have a judicial district and a judge, a law for subpoenaing a grand jury, and you should have attorneys, clerks, &c., as we do at home." Ibid., 413. It is notable that the Supreme Court of California had already considered the constitutionality of consular courts in China in 1859 and upheld them. See Forbes v. Scannell, 13 Cal. 242, 279 (1859). In 1875 the U.S. Supreme Court considered an appeal from an American consular court in Egypt and similarly rejected a constitutional challenge to it. See Dainese v. Hale, 91 U.S. 13 (1875).

18. See Message from the President of the United States, Transmitting a Report of the Secretary of State in Relation to the Necessity of Modifying the Present System of Consular Jurisdiction of the United States in the Countries of the East, S. Exec. Doc. No. 47–21, at 3–4, 6 (1st Sess. 1881).

19. Ibid., at 8.

20. See Ross v. McIntyre, 140 U.S. 453, 464–65 (1891).

21. See Marie-Claire Bergère, *The Golden Age of the Chinese Bourgeoisie 1911–1937*, trans. Janet Lloyd, Studies in Modern Capitalism (Cambridge: Cambridge University Press, 1989), 50. See also Dorothy J. Orchard, "China's Use of the Boycott as a Political Weapon," *Annals of the American Academy of Political and Social Science* 152 (November 1930): 252–261.

22. Delber L. McKee, *Chinese Exclusion versus the Open Door Policy, 1900–1906: Clashes over China Policy in the Roosevelt Era* (Detroit, MI: Wayne State University Press, 1977).

23. See generally Herbert H. D. Peirce, *Report on Inspection of United States Consulates in the Orient* (Washington, DC: Government Printing Office, 1906).

24. Act Creating a United States Court for China and Prescribing the Jurisdiction Thereof, Pub. L. No. 59–403, 34 Stat. 814 (1906).

25. The observation is by David Bederman, one of the few—and earliest—contemporary scholars of the court. See David J. Bederman, "Extraterritorial Domicile and the Constitution," *Virginia Journal of International Law* 28, no. 2 (Winter 1988): 452. To date, the most substantial scholarly treatment of the court is contained in Scully, *Bargaining with the State*. Scully's wide-ranging study is informative and important. However, writing as a historian rather than as a legal scholar, Scully's primary focus is the court's role as an intermediary between the U.S. government and American citizens in China, not the court's jurisprudence. The chief contemporary treatments of the court in the legal literature are contained in the above article by Bederman, which focuses on the history of the concept of extraterritorial domicile, and Tahirih V. Lee, "The United States Court for China: A Triumph of Local Law," *Buffalo Law Review* 52, no. 4 (Fall 2004): 923–1075, whose main focus is the procedure and evidence law applied by the court. Kal Raustiala takes note of the court briefly in the context of his discussion of the history of U.S. extraterritoriality in China. See Kal Raustiala, *Does the Constitution Follow the Flag? The Evolution of Territoriality in American Law* (Oxford: Oxford University Press, 2009).

26. On the operation and status of the *Cour mixte*, see Ch. B. Maybon and Jean Fredet, *Histoire de la concession française de Changhai* (Paris: Librairie Plon, 1929), 349–350; George Soulié de Morant, *Les droits conventionnels des étrangers en Chine* (Paris: L. Tenin, 1916), 88–114; Soulié de Morant, *Exterritorialité et intérêts étrangers en Chine* (Paris: Paul Geuthner, 1925), 187–213.

27. As Jerry Israel emphasizes, the champions of Progressivism at home and imperialism abroad saw no contradiction between the two: enacting economic and social reforms at home and taking democracy abroad constituted two sides of a single mission. Jerry Israel, *Progressivism and the Open Door: America and China, 1905–1921* (Pittsburgh, PA: University of Pittsburgh Press, 1971), xviii.

28. *United States Court for China: Decennial Anniversary Brochure,* Publications 1 (Shanghai: Far Eastern American Bar Association, 1916), 24, quoting ex-Congressman Denby's remarks.

29. *A Bill to Amend the Act Creating a United States Court for China: Hearing before the H. Comm. on Foreign Affairs on H.R. 7909,* 74th Cong. 10 (1935). See, for example, William S. Fleming, *The United States Court for China as an Institution,* Extraterritoriality in China 2 (Shanghai: 1921), 1, stating that "the establishment of judicial machinery by the United States and by other treaty powers with China is the result of obligations which we have undertaken in our treaties with the Chinese government."

30. *President's Annual Report for 1919,* Bulletin 3 (Shanghai: Far Eastern American Bar Association, 1920), 11.

31. "Judge Feetham Surveys Shanghai: A Digest," *Pacific Affairs* 4, no. 7 (July 1931): 609.

32. *Decennial Annniversary Brochure,* 5.

33. *President's Annual Report for 1919,* 2. One German observer compared the arrival of European law in China to "the 'reception' of Roman law of the 15th and 16th century in north European countries," thus subordinating Chinese law expressly to the inevitable progress of European legal civilization. See Werner Vogel, "Modern Chinese Law and Jurisdiction: Some Comments," *Pacific Affairs* 4, no. 11 (November 1931): 975. Missionaries took up the crusade for law reform as well, with the establishment of the Soochow Comparative Law School, run by the Methodist Episcopal Church in Shanghai. See Alison E. W. Conner, "Soochow Law School and the Shanghai Bar," *Hong Kong Law Journal* 23, no. 3 (November 1993): 397.

34. Antony Anghie, "Finding the Peripheries: Sovereignty and Colonialism in Nineteenth-Century International Law," *Harvard International Law Journal* 40, no. 1 (Winter 1999): 52.

35. In the post-Boxer Rebellion treaty revision, China expressed a desire to "reform" and the United States a willingness to "assist." See Treaty between the United States and China for the Extension of the Commercial Relations between Them, U.S.-China, art. 3, Oct. 8, 1903, 33 Stat. 2208.

36. Extraterritorial Remedial Code, Dec. 12, 1922; Doc. 171.2/19, § 15; General Records of the Department of State, Record Group 59; National Archives at College Park, MD.

37. Treaty of Wanghia, U.S.-China, art. 21, July 3, 1858, 8 Stat. 592; Treaty of Tientsin, U.S.-China, art. 11, June 18, 1858, 12 Stat. 1023; 34 Stat. 814.

38. *United States Court for China: Hearings before the H. Comm. on Foreign Affairs on S. 4014,* 64th Cong. 16 (1917).

39. See *President's Annual Report,* 6, stating, "The word 'state,' whenever used in this Constitution, shall be deemed to comprise . . . insular or other possession of the United States and places over which the United States exercises extraterritorial

jurisdiction." The Far Eastern American Bar Association was established in 1914 and became affiliated with the American Bar Association in 1915. It had three vice presidents—one each for North China, South China, and the Philippines—and in 1916 it had a total of forty-seven members. See *Decennial Anniversary Brochure*, 52–53.

40. Charles Sumner Lobingier, preface to *Extraterritorial Cases*, ed. Charles Sumner Lobingier, vol. 1 (Manila, Philippines: Bureau of Printing, 1920), iii.

41. Charles Sumner Lobingier, *American Courts in China* (Shanghai: Far Eastern Bar Association, 1919), 6–7. Compare *Decennial Anniversary Brochure*, 1.

42. 74th Cong. 13.

43. Ibid., 7.

44. 64th Cong. 3 (statement of Wilbur J. Carr, director of Consular Service, State Department). In fact, an early draft of the bill for the U.S. Court for China described the court expressly as a "district court"; however, this characterization was left out of the final bill. See Message from the President of the United States, District Court of the United States for China and Korea, S. Doc. No. 58–95, at 2 (3rd Sess. 1905).

45. *United States Court for China: Hearing before the H. Comm. on Foreign Affairs on H. R. 4281*, 65th Cong. 20 (1917).

46. China Trade Act, 1922, chap. 346, § 2d, 15 U.S.C. § 142 (2006).

47. Smith v. Am. Asiatic Underwriters, Fed., Inc., U.S.A., 127 F.2d 754, 755 (9th Cir. 1942). Compare United States v. Chapman, 14 F.2d 312 (W.D. Wash. 1926). The case considered the U.S. Court for China a district court for the purposes of removal of a criminal suspect for trial.

48. *In re* Corrigan's Estate, 1 Extraterritorial Cases 717, 721 (1918).

49. See Lobingier, *American Courts in China*, 11, complaining that federal law "deals with subjects (mostly of public law) not directly affecting the ordinary American citizen residing in this part of the world."

50. 34 Stat. at 815 (art. 4).

51. 7 Op. Att'y Gen. at 504.

52. United States v. Biddle, 1 Extraterritorial Cases 84, 87 (1907); Biddle v. United States, 156. F 759 (9th Cir. 1907), describing the common law applicable in the U.S. Court for China as "the common law in force in the several American colonies at the date of the separation from the mother country." Remarkably, the Supreme Court of the Territory of Wyoming had held similarly in 1879 that "the common law" in force in the Territory was "English common law proper" as it stood "at the date of the Declaration of Independence"—not a synthetic "compound of the law as it applied in the several states." See Ware v. Wanless, 2 Wyo. 144, 152–153 (1879).

53. Lobingier, *American Courts in China*, 17, quoting Stirling Fessenden's characterization of the court's jurisprudence. The strongest formulation of this view insisted that "there is no common law of the United States as distinguished from

(that of) the individual states." Ibid., 16. This was simply untrue. Under Swift v. Tyson, 41 U.S. (16 Pet.) 1 (1842), which would not be overruled until Erie Railroad Co. v. Tompkins, 304 U.S. 64 (1938), a body of federal common law did indeed exist, whether or not the U.S. Court for China took note of it. Some federal guidance in criminal matters arrived subsequently in the form of a federal criminal law when Congress enacted the Federal Penal Code. For application of the Federal Penal Code in China, see, for example, United States v. Diaz, 1 Extraterritorial Cases 784 (1918); United States v. LeClair, 1 Extraterritorial Cases 414 (1914). Yet the Code was far from comprehensive and, of course, did not apply to civil disputes.

54. See United States v. Biddle and Biddle v. U.S. Subsequently, the court extended this holding to cover civil matters as well. See Cavanagh v. Worden, 1 Extraterritorial Cases 317 (1914).

55. The court's position was in fact later validated by the U.S. Supreme Court. In 1915 the Supreme Court held that the Philippine Tariff Act of August 5, 1909, passed by Congress but applicable only to the Philippines, was "a statute of the United States." See Gsell v. Insular Collector of Customs, 239 U.S. 93, 95 (1915).

56. The solution provided by *Biddle* was perhaps necessary, yet legislative history indicates that Congress had in fact considered authorizing the application of D.C. laws in China before finally rejecting the idea. A 1905 draft bill for the U.S. Court for China directed the court to apply "the laws of the United States and the laws of the District of Columbia not in conflict therewith," with the evident implication that "the laws of the District of Columbia" were not encompassed in the phrase "the laws of the United States." See S. Doc. No. 58–95, at 3. The decision to drop the reference to D.C. laws from the final bill thus suggests that as a matter of legislative intent, D.C. laws were not meant to be included in the mandate of the U.S. Court for China.

57. United States v. Allen, 1 Extraterritorial Cases 308, 311 (1914).

58. Ibid. The sole qualifications for "laws of the United States" to be applicable in China were that they had to be both "necessary" for the exercise of the court's extraterritorial jurisdiction (which was the case with almost every law, at least in Judge Lobingier's opinion) as well as "suitable" for the conditions of China. Ibid. On their own terms, most laws were not suitable to China; for one thing, almost invariably they contained references to government organs and officials that did not even exist in the District of China. The court brushed such objections aside summarily. For example, where a statute might refer to a D.C. "workhouse," an institution absent in China, the court would simply substitute the Shanghai American "prison" as the most closely analogous institution. See United States v. Osman, 1 Extraterritorial Cases 540 (1916).

59. United States v. Osman, 544. Remarkably, the court's holding in *Biddle* was followed in other extraterritorial cases outside China as well. See *In re* Blanchard's Estate, 29 N.Y.S.2d 359, 361 (1941), holding, in appeal from the United States Consular Court at Cairo, Egypt, that "the law governing intestate

succession is found in the special acts of Congress providing for intestate succession in the District of Columbia." On the application of D.C. law to U.S. citizens in Egypt, see Jasper Yeates Brinton, *The Mixed Courts of Egypt*, rev. ed. (New Haven, CT: Yale University Press, 1968), 165–166.

60. *Decennial Anniversary Brochure*, 24.

61. 64th Cong. 10 (statement of Rep. Henry Cooper, Member, House Comm. on Foreign Affairs). The bill under consideration, which sought to codify the law applicable in the U.S. Court for China, was never passed.

62. "Judge Wilfley Before the New York Chamber of Commerce, March 5, 1908," *Journal of the American Asiatic Association* 8 (April 1908): 71.

63. *United States Court for China: Hearing before the H. Comm. on Foreign Affairs on H.R. 4281*, 65th Cong. 13 (1917) (statement of Charles Lobingier, Judge, United States Court for China).

64. Referring to his exceedingly broad interpretation of the *Biddle* doctrine—blessed by the Ninth Circuit—which opened the door for the application of even "special acts" of Congress in China, Judge Lobingier maintained that "there can be no half-way adoption of that doctrine; it includes all such laws or none. It cannot logically be restricted to any particular class of acts. It is just as applicable to civil laws as to criminal; just as 'necessary' in respect to corporations as to procedure." See United States *ex rel.* Raven v. McRae, 1 Extraterritorial Cases 655, 664 (1917).

65. See, for example, Cavanagh v. Worden, 371; Way Cheong & Co. v. Methodist Episcopal Church (South) Mission, 2 Extraterritorial Cases 490, 491 (1923); Ezra v. Merriman, 1 Extraterritorial Cases 809, 810 (1918).

66. 65th Cong. 55. Elsewhere, Judge Lobingier asserted his preference for the D.C. code thus: "As between the Alaskan and Columbian Codes, both enacted by the same Congress, the former, which is a few months the earlier, having been drafted for a sparsely settled, frontier community, is, on the whole, better suited to conditions in China than the latter, tho each contains desirable features not found in the other." Lobingier, *American Courts in China*, 14.

67. See "The United States Court for China," *Harvard Law Review* 49, no. 5 (March 1936): 794, stating that legislation "for the District of Columbia . . . now forms the principal source of law for the Court for China"; Crawford M. Bishop, "American Extraterritorial Jurisdiction in China," *American Journal of International Law* 20, no. 2 (April 1926): 297, claiming that "for all legal purposes [the] position [of an American citizen in China] is the same as though he were in the Federal District." Compare 65th Cong. 7, arguing that "not only the lawyers in the courts but business men [*sic*] and litigants—prospective litigants, at least—have settled down to the proposition that the[] Alaska laws are the principal ones"; Am. Trading Co. v. Steele, 274 F. 774, 780 (9th Cir. 1921), "conceding, without deciding, that the Alaska Code is controlling in the United States Court for China."

68. Cavanagh v. Worden, 371, states, "Of the two Acts of Congress . . . prescribing grounds for divorce, that relating to the District of Columbia, as the latest expression of legislative opinion, will naturally be applied here if the two are in conflict." The House Committee on Foreign Affairs was quite stunned by this:

> *Mr. Cooper:* You mean by that that [the judge] uses the code of Alaska, so far as the residence requirement is concerned, and then applies the code of the District of Columbia for the rest of it?
> *Mr. Holcomb:* That is very well known, sir.
> *Mr. Cooper:* It may well be known. You mean that the judge selects what he thinks is the best to be administered?
> *Mr. Holcomb:* That is all he has to go by.

64th Cong. 19.

69. Raven v. McRae, 656. Essentially the court argued that to hold otherwise would permit the citizens of Alaska to repeal legislation applicable to the District of China and thus, effectively, to legislate outside its territorial limits. While the U.S. Court for China might have been thought sympathetic to the possibility of extraterritorial legislation, in the case of Alaska it found it a "legal and political monstrosity" and, accordingly, held that Alaskans were empowered to repeal laws of the Territory of Alaska only insofar as those laws applied to them, not anyone else.

70. China Trade Act, 1922, Pub. L. No. 67–312, 42 Stat. 849.

71. Act to Amend the China Trade Act, 1922, Pub. L. No. 68–484, 43 Stat. 995, 997 (1925) (China Trade Act Amendments). In any event, the awareness of either D.C. or Alaska law remained quite elementary in the District of China—despite the court's boasts of being home to the most valuable library of federal legislation outside of the United States. Consider, for example, the following urgent query that the district attorney cabled to the State Department: "Please ask District Attorney, District [of] Columbia, and telegraph answer what provision of law available to prosecute for throwing rock and breaking window in private building." See District Attorney of U.S. Court for China to Secretary of State, June 29, 1926; Doc. 172.006/57; General Records of the Department of State, Record Group 59; National Archives at College Park, MD.

Apart from Congress's concern about out-of-control Alaskan law in China, there were several other attempts as well—all of them unsuccessful—to define more precisely just which "laws of the United States" the court was supposed to be applying. As early as 1908, Congress had considered improving "the code of laws governing the conduct of the United States Court for China" by directing it to apply the laws of California. See Committee on Foreign Affairs, United States Court for China, H.R. Rep. No. 60–1662, at 1 (1st Sess. 1908). Judge Lobingier himself pushed for a bill that would have codified his preferred (and ultimately discretionary) mix of laws: making Alaska the primary source of law in China, while the District of Columbia code would continue to apply in cases where the laws of Alaska were "deficient." See 65th Cong. 55.

72. United States v. Grimsinger, 1 Extraterritorial Cases 282, 285–286 (1912). Construing the language in the section of the Alaska statute that provided for an element of discretion in determining the penalty, the court not only forced a reading of the language that made the discretion limitless in the District of China but it then claimed that "this definite and specific language . . . disclos[ed] the intent of Congress that the fixing of penalties for the punishment of crimes in this extraterritorial jurisdiction should be at the discretion of the trial officer." Ibid., 285. The appeal to legislative intent is spurious, considering how implausible it is that any member of Congress would have foreseen that the code of Alaska would eventually be applied in China as well.

73. United States v. Furbush, 2 Extraterritorial Cases 74, 85 (1921).

74. Effectively, as Bederman states, "living in China was deemed to be American enough to permit an extraterritorial domicile, but not American enough to allow the Constitution to apply." See Bederman, "Extraterritorial Domicile," 474.

75. 74th Cong. 7 (statement of Chauncey Holcomb, district attorney for the District of China).

76. Ibid., 17.

77. See generally *The Third Attack on the United States Court for China: Press Comments on the Outcome*, Bulletin 8 (Shanghai: Far Eastern American Bar Association, 1923).

78. During the hearings for Judge Lobingier's removal, the American consul general described the conditions in Shanghai as "deplorable": "Creditors of American firms are unable to collect when suit is necessary. Business firms are not inclined to deal with American firms because of the absence of facilities for enforcing contracts should such be necessary." All in all, this was regarded as "a serious matter from a commercial standpoint." See Edwin S. Cunningham, American Consul General in Shanghai, to Wilbur J. Carr, Secretary of State, June 22, 1922; Doc. 172/684; General Records of the Department of State, Record Group 59; National Archives at College Park, MD.

79. Dorr v. United States, 195 U.S. 138 (1904).

80. Lebbeus R. Wilfley, "How Great Britain Governs Her Colonies," *Yale Law Journal* 9, no. 5 (March 1900): 207–214.

81. 65th Cong. 11.

82. See, for example, Fleming, *United States Court for China*, 3, 8.

83. *Chinese Court Bill: Hearings before the H. Comm. on Foreign Affairs on H.R. 17142*, 60th Cong. 11 (1908) (statement of Stirling Fessenden); Associated American Chambers of Commerce of China, *Report of the Annual Meeting* (Shanghai: Associated Chambers of Commerce of China, 1925), 13.

84. Consular Court Regulations for China, General, 1864. H.R. Exec. Doc. No. 39–1007, pt. 2, at 413–421 (1866). For further regulations promulgated in 1881 and 1897, see Frank E. Hinckley, *American Consular Jurisdiction in the Orient*

(Washington, DC: W. H. Lowdermilk, 1906). For a detailed discussion of the court's procedure, see also Lee, "Triumph of Local Law."

85. 34 Stat. at 816, stating, "The procedure of the said court shall be in accordance, so far as practicable, with the existing procedure prescribed for consular courts in China in accordance with the Revised Statutes of the United States."

86. 65th Cong. 16.

87. See Extraterritorial Remedial Code; Doc. 171.2/19; RG 59; NACP.

88. Am. Trading Co. v. Steele, 781.

89. See Scully, *Bargaining with the State*, 118–119.

90. In 1933, the court was finally placed under the purview of the Department of Justice. Exec. Order No. 6166 (June 10, 1933), § 6.

91. Lee S. Overman, Senator, to Fred K. Nielsen, Assistant Solicitor, State Department, Apr. 15, 1916; Doc. 172./644; General Records of the Department of State, Record Group 59; National Archives at College Park, MD. Senator Overman's query was motivated by an inquiry from a lawyer in Chapel Hill, North Carolina, who was about to graduate and was interested in pursuing a legal career in Shanghai. See R. T. Bryan, Jr., to Lee S. Overman, Senator, Apr. 12, 1916; Doc. 172./644; RG 59; NACP. Although neither the senator nor the State Department was able to provide him with the rules of procedure for the U.S. Court for China, the tenacious Mr. Bryan was apparently not deterred, for he was admitted to the Bar of the court in May the following year. See Charles Sumner Lobingier, ed., "Roll of Attorneys," in *Extraterritorial Cases*, vol. 1 (Manila: Bureau of Printing, 1920), ix–x.

92. State Department to Lee S. Overman, Senator, Apr. 18, 1916; Doc. 172./644; RG 59; NACP. The State Department kindly suggested writing directly to the court for details. An attorney who had tried—unsuccessfully—to obtain a certified copy of the Extraterritorial Remedial Code had subsequently been informed that "there is apparently no record in the Court that this code was duly adopted or promulgated, as by order of court." See Frank E. Hinckley to Secretary of State, Jan. 16, 1925; Doc. 172.6/369; General Records of the Department of State, Record Group 59; National Archives at College Park, MD. When he wrote to the State Department expressing his alarm, the Department simply sent a polite letter in acknowledgment: "The Department thanks you for bringing this matter to its attention." See J. V. A. MacMurray, Assistant Secretary of State, to Frank E. Hinckley, Feb. 13, 1925; Doc. 172.6/369; RG 59; NACP.

93. In an analysis where it refused to apply Chinese postal laws, the court reproduced in detail a set of 1887 guidelines by the State Department, in which the Department expressed its considered opinion that the municipal regulations of the International Settlement (unlike Chinese laws) could in fact be enforced against American citizens in consular courts. See Mr. Bayard, Secretary of State, to Mr. Denby, Minister to China, Mar. 7, 1887, in 4 MS. Inst. China 244; John Bassett

Moore, *A Digest of International Law*, vol. 2 (Washington, DC: Government Printing Office, 1906), 648–650, reprinted in United States v. Donohoe, 1 Extraterritorial Cases 347, 350 (1914).

94. Moore, *Digest of International Law*, 649.

95. See "Judge Feetham Surveys Shanghai," 592, explaining "a special doctrine of rights" justifying the unique position of the International Settlement; Robert Bickers, "Shanghailanders: The Formation and Identity of the British Settler Community in Shanghai, 1843–1937," *Past & Present* 159 (May 1998): 169; Kotenev, *Shanghai: Its Municipality*.

96. King Ping Kee v. Am. Food Mfg. Co., 1 Extraterritorial Cases 735, 736–737 (1918). United States v. Bascom, 1 Extraterritorial Cases 382, 389 (1914), citing Macdonald v. Anderson, H.B.M. Sup. Ct. Jan. 16, 1904 for the British practice of applying Chinese law to land in China.

97. Charles Sumner Lobingier, "Shall China Have an Uniform Legal System?," *China Law Review* 6 (1933): 327–334.

98. For a contemporary example of a similar effort to turn lawlessness into lawfulness, see Muneer Ahmad's haunting analysis of the operation of U.S. military commissions in Guantánamo—another extraterritorial space of U.S. law. Defense lawyers there found themselves in a space "with virtually no rules of evidence, no discovery rules, no rules of decision, and no rules regarding precedent": it was up to the commissions to develop their own rules. In Ahmad's words, it was "a common law system at time zero, boundless in its potential, but entirely bereft of guidance as to how the law might actually evolve." Remarkably, when Ahmad and his co-counsel filed a motion with a passing reference to the commission's "Alice in Wonderland quality," the filing was rejected as "patently disrespectful" and thus disregarded. "By uttering the words 'Alice in Wonderland,' we unwittingly had made the motion disappear," Ahmad states. Muneer I. Ahmad, "Resisting Guantánamo: Rights at the Brink of Dehumanization," *Northwestern University Law Review* 103, no. 4 (2009): 1722–1724.

99. I borrow the notion of "despotism of law" from Radhika Singha, *A Despotism of Law: Crime and Justice in Early Colonial India* (Delhi: Oxford University Press, 1998).

100. Upon visiting China, Bertrand Russell complained that all Americans there were missionaries, not of Christianity, but of "Americanism," the values of which he defined as "clean living, clean thinking, and pep." See Bertrand Russell, *The Problem of China* (New York: Century, 1922), 221.

101. See Jerry Israel, *Progressivism and the Open Door,* 101; Edgar Snow, "The Americans in Shanghai," *The American Mercury* 20, no. 80 (August 1930): 437.

102. Allman, "America in China," in *Shanghai Lawyer,* 83–97.

103. Treaty of Wanghia, 595–597 (arts. 6 and 21).

104. Other Treaty Powers' extraterritoriality provisions followed a similar pattern. See generally G. W. Keeton, *The Development of Extraterritoriality in China*, 2 vols. (London: Longmans, Greens, 1928); Wesley R. Fischel, *The End of Extraterritoriality in China* (Berkeley: University of California Press, 1952).

105. See the Asiatic Barred Zone Act, or Immigration Act of 1917, Feb. 5, 1917, chap. 29, 39 Stat. 874. See also Mae M. Ngai, *Impossible Subjects: Illegal Aliens and the Making of Modern America* (Princeton, NJ: Princeton University Press, 2004), 18.

106. *The Report of the Honorable Elihu Root, Secretary of State, on the Petition to the President of Representative George E. Waldo, of Brooklyn, N.Y., for the Removal from Office of L. R. Wilfley, Judge of the United States Court for China* (Washington, DC: 1908), 95–96, 106.

107. Ibid., 102. The Bar exam consisted of sections on criminal law, equity, evidence and pleading, torts, and contracts, as well as a special section on the organic act of the U.S. Court for China. For exam questions, see ibid., 19–24. The petition was rejected as a dishonorable attack on the "fearlessness and integrity with which [Wifley] has stamped out vice and crime in Shanghai," and Theodore Roosevelt declared the petition "a public scandal" that was "an impeachment of decency" and of Wilfley's "zeal for the public good." Ibid., 94.

108. Ibid., 105.

109. Ibid., 107; Israel, *Progressivism and the Open Door*, 58. Also see Eileen P. Scully, "Prostitution as Privilege: The 'American Girl' of Treaty-Port Shanghai, 1860–1937," *International History Review* 20, no. 4 (December 1998): 855–883; Allman, *Shanghai Lawyer*; Gail Hershatter, *Dangerous Pleasures: Prostitution and Modernity in Twentieth-Century Shanghai* (Berkeley: University of California Press, 1999).

110. See *Report of the Honorable Elihu Root*, 107; Allman, *Shanghai Lawyer*, 104.

111. Allman, *Shanghai Lawyer*, 104. On the racially inflected operation of derivative spousal citizenship, see Leti Volpp, "Divesting Citizenship: On Asian American History and the Loss of Citizenship through Marriage," *UCLA Law Review* 53, no. 2 (December 2005): 405–484.

112. David Arnold, "European Orphans and Vagrants in India in the Nineteenth Century," *Journal of Imperial and Commonwealth History* 7, no. 2 (1979): 124, quoted in Scully, *Bargaining with the State*, 12. On the racial anxieties of Americans in Treaty Port China, see also Herbert Day Lamson, "Sino-American Miscegenation in Shanghai," *Social Forces* 14, no. 4 (May 1936): 580, linking "the system of extraterritoriality and the sense of being culturally superior" to the racial hierarchy of Shanghai.

113. Snow, "The Americans in Shanghai," 441.

114. "Murmurs from Mean Streets," *North China Herald* (Shanghai), May 9, 1989, 789, quoted in Scully, *Bargaining with the State*, 89.

115. Chauncey P. Holcomb, district attorney of the U.S. Court for China, to Secretary of State, May 10, 1916; Doc. 172.6/169; General Records of the Department of State, Record Group 59; National Archives at College Park, MD.

116. Sexton v. United States, 1 Extraterritorial Cases 180, 194 (1909).

117. Holcomb to Secretary of State; Doc. 172.6/169; RG 59; NACP.

118. United States v. Osman, 543.

119. See Bilibid Prison at Manila, 30 Op. Att'y Gen. 462 (1915), designating Bilibid Prison for the confinement of long-term prisoners sentenced in the U.S. Court for China.

120. Juan R. Torruella, *The Supreme Court and Puerto Rico: The Doctrine of Separate and Unequal* (Río Piedras: University of Puerto Rico, 1985), 61.

121. Downes v. Bidwell, 182 U.S. 244, 341–342 (1901).

122. Christina Duffy Burnett, "'They Say I Am Not an American . . .': The Noncitizen National and the Law of American Empire," *Virginia Journal of International Law* 48, no. 4 (Summer 2008): 711. It is clear that as the U.S. Court went about expanding its jurisdiction over America's new "subjects," as it specifically referred to Filipinos and Guamanians, it was not acting simply carelessly. The U.S. Court for China as well as its supervising agency, the State Department, distinguished constantly between "citizens" and "subjects." "There are those like Filipinos and Porto [*sic*] Ricans who are not full citizens but still subject to American authority," the court stated in an opinion in which it took jurisdiction over a Filipino. See United States v. Scogin, 1 Extraterritorial Cases 376, 377 (1914). See also Order of the U.S. Court for China, June 30, 1914; Doc. 172.6/129; General Records of the Department of State, RG 59; National Archives at College Park, MD; United States v. A Juvenile Offender, 1 Extraterritorial Cases 687, 687 (1918) ("The accused . . . is an American subject, born in Shanghai of Filipino parentage"). For an instance of the court assuming jurisdiction over a defendant from Guam, see United States v. Osman, 49. Likewise, in a letter to the State Department regarding several prisoners in Shanghai, the court referred to one of them as an "American subject, a native of the Island of Guam," while the rest were described as "American citizens." See Holcomb to Secretary of State; Doc. 172.6/169; RG 59; NACP.

123. See Scully, *Bargaining with the State*.

124. Memorandum by Office of the Solicitor, "The Question of the Jurisdiction of the Chinese Courts and the United States District Court in China in Cases of Persons Born in the United States of Chinese Parents, Thus Having Dual Nationality," Oct. 9, 1929; Doc. 893.012/43, p. 8; General Records of the Department of State, Record Group 59; National Archives at College Park, MD.

125. *In re* Lee's Will, 1 Extraterritorial Cases 699, 699–700, 702–704 (1918).

126. Ibid., 704. While the State Department's concern with the clothing of Robert Lee's wife and children may seem fetishistic, it is noteworthy that the

benefits of extraterritoriality were often as much a sartorial as legal achievement. According to Bergère, Chinese merchants "abandoned their long blue silk robes for jackets and trousers whenever the latter, which were symbols of extraterritorial status, could enhance their prestige or afford them protection." See Bergère, *Golden Age*, 47. Likewise, Chinese government officials complained of U.S. and European missionaries who wore Chinese clothing yet wished to claim immunity from Chinese law. See Pär Cassell, *Grounds of Judgement: Extraterritoriality and Imperial Power in Nineteenth-Century China and Japan* (Oxford: Oxford University Press, 2012). Even the notorious sign in a Shanghai park that proclaimed "No Chinese or Dogs Allowed" exempted Chinese persons dressed in Western garb. See Leo Ou-fan Lee, *Shanghai Modern: The Flowering of a New Urban Culture in China, 1930–1945* (Cambridge, MA: Harvard University Press, 1999), 29. For a history of the cultural and political significance of clothing in China's modernization, see Antonia Finnane, *Changing Clothes in China: Fashion, History, Nation* (New York: Columbia University Press, 2008). On the performativity of racial identity in law see generally Ariela J. Gross, *What Blood Won't Tell: A History of Race on Trial in America* (Cambridge, MA: Harvard University Press, 2008).

127. *In re* Lee's Will, 703.

128. Ibid., 705.

129. Ibid., 710. Likewise, in a case involving a widowed woman who had acquired U.S. citizenship through her marriage to an American man, the court struggled to allow her to retain her citizenship after her husband's death. However, a 1907 law on marital derivative citizenship permitted her to retain her American citizenship only "if she continue[d] to reside in the United States." See Act of March 2, 1907, Pub. L. No. 59–193, 34 Stat. 1228, 1229, referencing the expatriation of citizens and their protection abroad. The court held simply that, for the purposes of the act, China was not "abroad," and residency in "the territory of China" was as good as residency in the United States. *In re* McGhee's Estate, 1 Extraterritorial Cases 418, 422 (1914).

130. Allman, *Shanghai Lawyer*, 141.

131. A. M. Latter, "The Government of the Foreigners in China," *Law Quarterly Review* 19 (1903): 322.

132. Ibid.

133. Allman, *Shanghai Lawyer*, 143.

134. Scully, *Bargaining with the State*, 95.

135. Keith and Sheely to Far Eastern Division, Department of State, Oct. 31, 1927; Doc. 172.1/86; General Records of the Department of State, Record Group 59; National Archives at College Park, MD.

136. Frank B. Kellogg, Department of State, to Keith and Sheely, Oct. 31, 1927; Doc. 172.1/86; General Records of the Department of State, Record Group 59; National Archives at College Park, MD.

137. Richards v. Richards, 1 Extraterritorial Cases 480, 482–483 (1915).

138. Again, the court noted that in an annulment action against a non-U.S. defendant it could not award relief "as to costs or otherwise." See Ross v. Ross, 1 Extraterritorial Cases 924, 926 (1919).

139. "United States Court for China," 793 n. 4.

140. Especially in the area of criminal law, the manipulation of citizenship was an acute concern. A case in point was Edward Ezra—an elusive character who at various times professed citizenships of Turkey, Persia, Spain, and the United States. For an appearance of Ezra as a U.S. citizen, see Ezra v. Am. Sales Corp., 1 Extraterritorial Cases 954 (1920); for more on Ezra, see Lee, "Law and Local Autonomy," 50. Another prime example of similar individuals was James "Tientsin" Brown, a man born in the United States but since moving to China a man of many nationalities as he operated on, and beyond, the legal fringes of extraterritoriality in China. See generally Scully, *Bargaining with the State*. When, once again, he was charged with gambling in a German consular court, he pleaded American citizenship as defense. Exasperated by the fact that Brown had earlier denied his American nationality twice before U.S. extraterritorial tribunals, the American vice consul general informed German authorities that he had "no objections to the trial of Mr. Brown being held in your Consular Court." See American Vice Consul General in Shanghai to Dr. Knappe, German Consul General in Shanghai, Jan. 3, 1905; Box 5, Doc. C 124; Shanghai, Criminal Court Case Files, 1879–1912; Records of the Foreign Service Posts of the Department of State, Record Group 84; National Archives at College Park, MD. Indeed, according to the American authorities in the Philippines, who were also familiar with him, "Brown appears to consider himself a citizen of the United States only when it suits his convenience." See American Vice Consul General to Dr. Knappe; Box 5, Doc. C 124; Case Files 1879–1912; RG 84; NACP.

141. *Report of the Honorable Elihu Root*, 105.

142. Ibid., 16 (emphasis added).

143. See Daniel Hulsebosch, *Constituting Empire: New York and the Transformation of Constitutionalism in the Atlantic World, 1664–1830* (Chapel Hill, NC: University of North Carolina Press, 2005), 20–22.

144. See Stuart Banner, *How the Indians Lost Their Land: Law and Power on the Frontier*, Cambridge, MA: Belknap Press of Harvard University, 2007). On the changing terms of the Euro-Indian encounter, see Daniel K. Richter, *Facing East from Indian Country: A Native History of Early America* (Cambridge, MA: Harvard University Press, 2003); Richard White, *The Middle Ground: Indians, Empires, and Republics in the Great Lakes Region, 1650–1815* (Cambridge: Cambridge University Press, 1991).

145. Philip P. Frickey, "A Common Law for Our Age of Colonialism: The Judicial Divestiture of Indian Tribal Authority over Nonmembers," *Yale Law Journal* 109, no. 1 (October 1999): 7, 36–37, 52.

146. For a comprehensive analysis of the legal status of U.S. territories, see Arnold H. Leibowitz, *Defining Status: A Comprehensive Analysis of United States Territorial Relations* (Dordrecht, Netherlands: Martinus Nijhoff, 1989). See also Gerald L. Neuman, "Anomalous Zones," *Stanford Law Review* 48, no. 5 (May 1996): 1197–1234.

147. McDonald v. Mabee, 243 U.S. 90, 91 (1917). For an analysis of the complex operation of extraterritoriality in the American borderlands, see Daniel S. Margolies, *Spaces of Law in American Foreign Relations: Extradition and Extraterritoriality in the Borderlands and Beyond, 1877–1898* (Athens: University of Georgia Press, 2011).

148. There have been other courts with similar names in semi-colonial settings, notably in Egypt and Siam. However, except for the fact that they had jurisdiction in disputes involving foreigners, the Mixed Courts of Egypt and International Courts in Siam were very different from both the International Mixed Court in Shanghai and from each other. See, for example, Nathan J. Brown, "The Precarious Life and Slow Death of the Mixed Courts of Egypt," *International Journal of Middle East Studies* 25, no. 1 (February 1993): 33–52; Akiko Iijima, "The 'International Court' System in the Colonial History of Siam," *Taiwan Journal of Southeast Asian Studies* 5, no. 1 (2008): 31–64. For a comparative study of how "mixed" disputes were adjudicated in China and Japan in the late nineteenth century, see Cassell, *Grounds of Judgment.*

149. Thomas B. Stephens, *Order and Discipline in China: The Shanghai Mixed Court, 1911–27* (Seattle: University of Washington Press, 1992), 71.

150. Ibid., 55.

151. Ibid., xi.

152. Lee, "Law and Local Autonomy," 122.

153. Ibid., 57.

154. Ibid., 290.

155. Ibid., 307.

156. Ibid., 219.

157. Ibid., 150.

158. Stephens, *Order and Discipline*, 70–72.

159. On the Land Regulations, see ibid., 85.

160. On the role of the Municipal Council, see ibid., 74.

161. R. S. Gundry, "The Status of the Shanghai Municipality," *Journal of Comparative Legislation and International Law*, 3rd ser., 2, no. 1 (1920): 51.

162. David Dudley Field, "De la possibilité d'appliquer le droit international européen aux nations orientales," *Revue de droit international et de législation comparée* 7 (1875): 659, 663. In his embellished account of Chinese justice, he claimed that the punishments in all Oriental nations were "strange and cruel" and included even "crucifixion"—a claim without factual justification regarding China. To be sure, reports of crucifixion were not uncommon in the nineteenth century, apparently

based on a misperception by observers who saw a criminal on a frame undergoing *lingchi*, a punishment not included in the penal code and often translated as "death by a thousand cuts." See Timothy Brook, Jérôme Bourgon and Gregory Blue, *Death by a Thousand Cuts* (Cambridge, MA: Harvard University Press, 2008), 204.

163. Stephens, *Order and Discipline*, 44. For a nuanced analysis of the genesis of the court, see Cassell, *Grounds of Judgement*. As Cassell explains, the Mixed Court did not originate as an inherently colonial institution, nor was it inevitable that it ultimately became one. The Qing government had a long tradition of a variety of institutional mechanisms for settling disputes involving parties of different ethnic backgrounds. From the Chinese perspective, the Mixed Court was a potentially useful means of incorporating foreigners in Shanghai into the Qing administrative structure. The foreign population of Shanghai of course held a different interpretation, but Chinese officials were not simply dupes in agreeing to a system of co-adjudication: they had a coherent vision of how the court should function within the larger context of Qing sovereignty, even if they ultimately lacked the power to enforce that vision.

164. Lee, "Law and Local Autonomy," 196.

165. Ibid., 231.

166. Ibid., 217.

167. Stephens, *Order and Discipline*, 13; "Law and Local Autonomy," 141, 308.

168. Lee, "Law and Local Autonomy," 290–291.

169. On the court's sources of law, see ibid., 289–312; Stephens, *Order and Discipline*, 85–94.

170. Lee, "Law and Local Autonomy," 292.

171. Ibid., 226.

172. Ibid., 122.

173. See generally Jonathan K. Ocko, "I'll Take It All the Way to Beijing: Capital Appeals in the Qing," *Journal of Asian Studies* 47, no. 2 (May 1988): 291–315.

174. Lee, "Law and Local Autonomy," 284.

175. Stephens, *Order and Discipline*, 67.

176. A. M. Kotenev, *Shanghai: Its Mixed Court and Council* (Shanghai: North-China Daily News & Herald, 1925), ix, xi, 276.

177. Much of this chapter draws on Tahirih Lee's 1990 PhD dissertation, which unfortunately has not been published to date. Indeed, Stephens's account remains the dominant story. For a partial account of the court's work, see Tahirih V. Lee, "Risky Business: Courts, Culture, and the Marketplace," *University of Miami Law Review* 47, no. 5 (May 1993): 1335–1414. Pär Cassell's comparative history of extraterritorial jurisdiction in China and Japan has an illuminating discussion of the International Mixed Court. See Cassell, *Grounds of Judgement*, 63–84.

178. Stephens, *Order and Discipline*, 35.

179. Ibid., 113.

180. Ibid., 85.

181. Ibid., 113.

182. Ibid., 99.

183. For a nuanced institutional analysis of late imperial justice as "a rather subtle mix of mediatory and legalistic elements," see Martin Shapiro, *Courts: A Comparative and Political Analysis* (Chicago: University of Chicago Press, 1981).

184. Stated in the jargon of German systems theory, "Th[e] 'legal reality' is to be understood in a strictly system-relative way as the construction of an internal model of the external world." Gunther Teubner, *Law as an Autopoietic System*, ed. Zenon Bankowski, trans. Annie Bankowska and Ruth Adler (Oxford: Blackwell, 1993), 70.

185. Frederic D. Grant, Jr., "The Failure of the Li-ch'uan Hong: Litigation as a Hazard of Nineteenth Century Foreign Trade," *American Neptune* 48 (1988): 243, 247. See also Grant, "Hong Merchant Litigation in American Courts," *Proceedings of the Massachusetts Historical Society* 99 (1987): 44–62.

6. EPILOGUE

1. The debate is no longer *whether* the Constitution applies extraterritorially but *to what extent*—hence the post 9/11 arguments about the constitutional effects of offshoring the War on Terror to the U.S. naval base in Guantanamo Bay, for example. See generally Kal Raustiala, *Does the Constitution Follow the Flag?: The Evolution of Territoriality in American Law* (Oxford: Oxford University Press, 2009).

2. See Natsu Taylor Saito, "The Enduring Effect of the Chinese Exclusion Cases: The 'Plenary Power' Justification for On-Going Human Rights Abuses," *Asian Law Journal* 10, no. 1 (May 2003): 13, observing, "Today, it is the plenary power doctrine articulated in [the Chinese exclusion cases of the late 1800s] which allows the Justice Department to engage in the highly troubling selective imprisonment and deportation of Muslim, Arab, and Middle Eastern immigrants." Tragically, the PRC has been quick to seize on the latest reorientation of American Orientalism, as it has trained its sights on its own "internal Orientals" of choice, represented by the Uighurs of Chinese Central Asia—a minority nationality of Turkic Muslims. Uighur resistance to Chinese state power has been cast conveniently as "terrorism," the suppression of which is in turn a legal obligation of civilized states. See, for example, Chien-peng Chung, "China's 'War on Terror': September 11 and Uighur Separatism," *Foreign Affairs* 81, no. 4 (July/August 2002): 8–12.

3. Mayfair Mei-hui Yang, "Postcoloniality and Religiosity in Modern China: The Disenchantments of Sovereignty," *Theory, Culture & Society* 29, no. 2 (March 2011): 3–45. The systematic project of disenchantment of Chinese life was not limited to the sphere of the state but extended to society as well. As Prasenjit Duara

has analyzed, the Guomindang engaged in a series of "anti-superstition" drives in order to separate "superstitions" from permissible observance of "religion." See Prasenjit Duara, "Knowledge and Power in the Discourse of Modernity: The Campaigns against Popular Religion in Early Twentieth-Century China," *Journal of Asian Studies* 50, no. 1 (February 1991): 78–79. From a larger perspective, Yunxiang Yan discerns a larger social process under socialism that has resulted in the "demystification" of traditional notions of filial piety even in the private sphere of the family. See Yunxian Yan, *Private Life under Socialism: Love, Intimacy, and Family Change in a Chinese Village, 1949–1999* (Stanford, CA: Stanford University Press, 2003), 189.

4. On the normalization of China as a subject of international law, see Teemu Ruskola, "Raping Like a State," *UCLA Law Review* 57, no. 5 (June 2010): 1477–1536.

5. Michael H. Hunt, *The Making of a Special Relationship: The United States and China to 1914* (New York: Columbia University Press, 1983), 217.

6. See Jedidiah Kroncke, "An Early Tragedy of Comparative Constitutionalism: Frank Goodnow and the Chinese Republic," *Pacific Rim Law & Policy Journal* 21, no. 3 (2012): 563, quoting Frank Goodnow to Nicholas Butler, 26 February 1914, in *Frank Johnson Goodnow Papers, 1880–1940* (Special Collection, Milton S. Eisenhower Library, Johns Hopkins University).

7. Pound reported on his observation in several publications; see Roscoe Pound, "Progress of Law in China," *Washington Law Review and State Bar Journal* 23, no. 4 (November 1948): 345–362; "Law and Courts in China: Progress in the Administration of Justice," *American Bar Association Journal* 34, no. 4 (April 1948): 273–276; "The Chinese Civil Code in Action," *Tulane Law Review* 29, no. 2 (February 1955): 288 (written originally in 1948). See generally Jedidiah Kroncke, "Roscoe Pound in China: A Lost Precedent for the Liabilities of American Legal Exceptionalism," *Brooklyn Journal of International Law* 37 (forthcoming). The legal contributions of France, similar to the United States in that it too has historically regarded itself as the very home of the universal, were typified in the person of Jean Escarra, a French scholar who was a legal consultant to the Nationalist government in the interwar years. See A. F. P. Hulsewé and M. H. van der Valk, "Jean Escarra," *T'oung Pao*, 2nd ser., 44, nos. 1–3 (1956): 304–310.

8. See Xiaoqun Xu, *Trial of Modernity: Judicial Reform in Early Twentieth-Century China, 1901–1937* (Stanford, CA: Stanford University Press, 2008). For an account of the modernization of the Chinese prison system, recounted from a comparative perspective as a "global history," see Frank Dikötter, *Crime, Punishment and the Prison in Modern China* (New York: Columbia University Press, 2002). For a more general history of the Chinese criminal justice system, see Klaus Mühlhahn, *Criminal Justice in China: A History* (Cambridge, MA: Harvard University Press, 2009).

9. See "The Common Program of the Chinese People's Political Consultative Conference," translated in Albert P. Blaustein, *Fundamental Legal Documents of Communist China* (South Hackensack, NJ: Fred B. Rothman, 1962), 41 (art. 17).

10. For a critical assessment of the 1950 Marriage Law, see, for example, Margery Wolf, *Revolution Postponed: Women in Contemporary China* (Stanford, CA: Stanford University Press, 1985). For a nuanced study of the Marriage Law that takes note also of its unintended consequences—frequently favorable for poor rural women—see Neil J. Diamant, *Revolutionizing the Family: Politics, Love, and Divorce in Urban and Rural China, 1949–1968* (Berkeley: University of California Press, 2000).

11. Evgeny B. Pashukanis, *Law and Marxism: A General Theory*, ed. Chris Arthur, trans. Barbara Einhorn (London: Pluto Press, 1989).

12. The Stalinist jurist Andrei Vyshinsky, displacing Pashukanis as the preeminent Soviet legal theorist, defined "Soviet socialist law" as "the totality of the rules of conduct, established in the form of legislation by authoritative power of the toilers and expressing their will." See Andrei Y. Vyshinsky, ed., *The Law of the Soviet State*, trans. Hugh W. Babb (New York: Macmillan, 1948), 74; see also Lon L. Fuller, "Pashukanis and Vyshinsky: A Study in the Development of Marxian Legal Theory," *Michigan Law Review* 47, no. 8 (June 1949): 1157–1166.

13. Cited in Albert Hung-yee Chen, *An Introduction to the Legal System of the People's Republic of China* (Singapore: Butterworth Asia, 1992), 32. I borrow the term "living *nomos*" from Flora Sapio, *Sovereign Power and the Law in China* (Leiden, Netherlands: Brill, 2010), 231.

14. See, for example, Jerome Alan Cohen, "China's Legal Reform at the Crossroads," *Far Eastern Economic Review* 169, no. 2 (March 2006): 24–25.

15. Mühlhahn, *Criminal Justice in China*, 295.

16. Zhonghua Renmin Gongheguo Xianfa 中华人民共和国宪法 [PRC Constitution] art. 33 (1982) (China); PRC State Council Information Office, China's Efforts and Achievements in Promoting the Rule of Law (Beijing: 2008), available at http://www.china.org.cn/government/news/2008-02/28/content _11025486.htm.

17. On the rise and fall of the global prestige of German legal science at the end of the nineteenth century, see Duncan Kennedy, "Three Globalizations of Law and Legal Thought: 1850–2000," in *The New Law and Economic Development: A Critical Appraisal*, ed. David M. Trubek and Alvaro Santos (Cambridge: Cambridge University Press, 2006), 19–73, and Mathias Reimann, *The Reception of Continental Ideas in the Common Law World, 1820–1920* (Berlin: Duncker & Humblot, 1993).

18. See William P. Alford, "Tasseled Loafers for Barefoot Lawyers: Transformation and Tension in the World of Chinese Legal Workers," *China Quarterly* no. 141 (1995): 38. See also Alford, ed., *Raising the Bar: The Emerging Legal Profession*

in East Asia (Cambridge, MA: East Asian Legal Studies, Harvard University, 2006).

19. The observation is by Wang Hui, *The End of the Revolution: China and the Limits of Modernity* (London: Verso, 2009), 43. Echoing Wang, the interdisciplinary legal scholar Deng Zhenglai believes that Western modernization theory dominates Chinese legal discourse, making it essentially more "legal" than "Chinese." See generally Deng Zhenglai 邓正来, Zhongguo faxue xiang hechu qu 中国法学向何处去 [Where is Chinese jurisprudence headed] (Beijing: Shangwu yin shuguan 商务印书馆, 2006).

20. Treaty for the Relinquishment of Extraterritorial Rights in China and the Regulation of Related Matters, U.S.-China, art. 1, Jan. 11, 1943, 57 Stat. 767. See Kurt H. Nadelmann, "American Consular Jurisdiction in Morocco and the Tangier International Jurisdiction," *American Journal of International Law* 49, no. 4 (October 1955): 506–517. Remarkably, in 1952 the United States insisted before the International Court of Justice on the right of extraterritorial jurisdiction in Morocco—a French protectorate—on the basis of its 1836 treaty with Morocco. See Rights of Nationals of the United States of America in Morocco (Fr. v. U.S.), 1952 I.C.J. 176 (August 27). Even after the abolition of U.S. extraterritorial jurisdiction in Morocco in 1956, the United States continued to have a nominal right to consular jurisdiction in Muscat, on the basis of the 1833 U.S.-Muscat Treaty. That right did not end formally until the signing of the U.S.-Muscat-Oman treaty on December 20, 1958. See Treaty of Amity, Economic Relations and Consular Rights, U.S.-Muscat-Oman, Dec. 20, 1958, 11 U.S.T. 1835 (entered into force June 11, 1960).

21. Kal Raustiala, "Empire and Extraterritoriality in Twentieth Century America," *Southwestern Law Review* 40, no. 4 (2011): 605–615.

22. Thomas Babington Macaulay, *The Works of Lord Macaulay Complete*, ed. Hannah Moore Macaulay Trevelyan, vol. 3 (London: Longmans, Green, 1866), 141.

23. Bertrand Russell, *The Problem of China* (New York: Century, 1922), 179–180. Indeed, it was evident to both critics and supporters of the Open Door that the primary beneficiary of the policy would be the United States. As *The Nation* observed in 1901, "We do not need to seek an unfair advantage. An open door and no favor infallibly means for the United States . . . the greater share and gain in the commercial exploitation of China." See "American Leadership in China," *The Nation* 72, no. 1871 (May 9, 1901): 369.

24. See Turan Kayaoğlu, *Legal Imperialism: Sovereignty and Extraterritoriality in Japan, the Ottoman Empire, and China* (Cambridge: Cambridge University Press, 2010); Raustiala, *Does the Constitution Follow the Flag?*

25. Kayaoğlu, *Legal Imperialism*, 197.

26. Along similar lines, Kevin Herrick observes, "The treaty port system with its most-favored-nation clause applied across a broad, multilateral, and truly global

group of states and represents a new type of legal institution characteristic of models of cooperative governance found in modern international law." Indeed, he believes that the system "may be seen as the first truly global institution of its kind whose heirs may include the League of Nations, the United Nations, and the World Trade Organization." See Kevin Herrick, "The Merger of Two Systems: Chinese Adoption and Western Adaptation in the Formation of Modern International Law," *Georgia Journal of International and Comparative Law* 33, no. 3 (2005): 686, 688. To be sure, in Herrick's view both the Treaty Port system and modern multilateral institutions are *positive* international legal developments. For a more critical argument about continuities between nineteenth-century consular jurisdiction more generally and structural adjustment policies promoted by the World Bank and the International Monetary Fund, see David P. Fidler, "A Kinder, Gentler System of Capitulations? International Law, Structural Adjustment Policies, and the Standard of Liberal, Globalized Civilization," *Texas International Law Journal* 35, no. 3 (Summer 2000): 387–414.

27. Julia Ya Qin, " 'WTO-Plus' Obligations and Their Implications for the World Trade Organization Legal System: An Appraisal of the China Accession Protocol," *Journal of World Trade* 37, no. 3 (June 2003): 483–522.

28. For a categorical indictment of the abuses of rule-of-law, see Ugo Mattei and Laura Nader, eds., *Plunder: When the Rule of Law Is Illegal* (Malden, MA: Blackwell, 2008).

29. See, for example, Anna M. Han, "China's Company Law: Practicing Capitalism in a Transitional Economy," *Pacific Rim Law & Policy Journal* 5, no. 3 (July 1996): 457–507; Bing Song, "Competition Policy in a Transitional Economy: The Case of China," *Stanford Journal of International Law* 31, no. 2 (Summer 1995): 387–422; Victor Nee, "The Emergence of a Market Society: Changing Mechanisms of Stratification in China," *American Journal of Sociology* 101, no. 4 (January 1996): 908–949. On transitologists, see John D. Haskell and Boris N. Mamlyuk, "Capitalism, Communism . . . and Colonialism? Revisiting 'Transitology' as the Ideology of Informal Empire," *Global Jurist* 9, no. 2 (April 2009): Article 7, doi: 10.2202/1934–2640.1293.

30. For an acute challenge to transition theories applied to China, see David L. Wank, *Commodifying Communism: Business, Trust, and Politics in a Chinese City* (Cambridge: Cambridge University Press, 2001).

31. As Amy Chua observes, "The thrust of international development policy today remains essentially what it was in the sixties and seventies: to export markets, democracy, and the rule of law to the developing world." See Amy L. Chua, "Markets, Democracy, and Ethnicity: Toward a New Paradigm for Law and Development," *Yale Law Journal* 108, no. 1 (October 1998): 14.

32. Haun Saussy, "Hegel's Chinese Imagination," in *The Problem of a Chinese Aesthetic* (Stanford, CA: Stanford University Press, 1993), 179.

33. Elizabeth J. Perry, "Chinese Conceptions of 'Rights': From Mencius to Mao—and Now," *Perspectives on Politics* 6, no. 1 (March 2008): 46.

34. For studies of the emergence of rights consciousness in China, see, for example, Merle Goldman, *From Comrade to Citizen: Struggle for Political Rights in China* (Cambridge, MA: Harvard University Press, 2007); Kevin J. O'Brien and Lianjiang Li, *Rightful Resistance in Rural China* (New York: Cambridge University Press, 2006); Ching Kwan Lee, *Against the Law: Labor Protests in China's Rustbelt and Sunbelt* (Berkeley: University of California Press, 2007); Neil Diamant, Stanley B. Lubman, and Kevin J. O'Brien, eds., *Engaging the Law in China: State, Society, and Possibilities for Justice* (Stanford, CA: Stanford University Press, 2010); Keith J. Hand, "Using Law for a Righteous Purpose: The Sun Zhigang Incident and Evolving Forms of Citizen Action in the People's Republic of China," *Columbia Journal of Transnational Law* 45, no. 1 (2006): 114–195.

35. Article 34, on citizenship, was amended to provide for the protection of human rights at the same time as the Constitution was amended to provide for the protection of private property as well. Zhonghua Renmin Gongheguo Xianfa 中华人民共和国宪法 [PRC Constitution] art. 34 (1982).

36. It bears emphasizing that in no way am I suggesting that the state and the individual are the only politically or sociologically important actors in society; I am only describing the relative poverty of *legal* categories. Moreover, while prevailing liberal accounts of modern law are focused predominantly on the individual and the state, there are of course other accounts as well, such as David Luban's "liberal communitarianism." See David Luban, *Legal Modernism* (Ann Arbor: University of Michigan Press, 1997).

37. Michael Dutton, *Streetlife China* (Cambridge: Cambridge University Press, 1998), 17.

38. See Gloria Davies, "*Homo Dissensum Significans*, or The Perils of Taking a Stand in China," *Social Text* 29, no. 4 (2011): 29–56.

39. Although I characterize the PRC as a "modern centralized state," it is important to recognize that the actual exercise of political authority in the PRC is in fact much more decentralized than many casual Western observers realize. The central government in Beijing often has great difficulty imposing its will on the wealthy provincial governments of China's coastal regions, for example. (That outside observers remain unaware of this reflects no doubt in part an uncritical assumption of overwhelming state power on the model of Oriental despotism.) It is nevertheless significant that the PRC Constitution provides for a highly centralized structure of political authority, with lower levels of government enjoying delegated powers only: the *form* of the Chinese state is that of a modern centralized one. Equally important, although the central government may not be all-powerful, even the authority exercised by strong provincial governments is a mode of *state* authority. While the PRC may seek to dominate society through many dispersed state organs, political power remains concentrated in the institutions of the state.

40. As Ellen Hertz observes in her ethnography of the opening of the Shanghai stock market, in the PRC even the stock market *can* be a counterhegemonic—albeit not democratic—force. See Ellen Hertz, *The Trading Crowd: An Ethnography of the Shanghai Stock Market* (Cambridge: Cambridge University Press, 1998).

41. See Hualing Fu and Richard Cullen, "Weiquan (Rights Protection) Lawyering in an Authoritarian State: Building a Culture of Public-Interest Lawyering," *The China Journal* 59 (January 2008): 111–127; Sida Liu and Terence C. Halliday, "Political Liberalism and Political Embeddedness: Understanding Politics in the Work of Chinese Criminal Lawyers," *Law & Society Review* 45, no. 4 (2011): 831–865.

42. See You-tien Hsing, *The Great Urban Transformation: Politics of Land and Property in China* (Oxford: Oxford University Press, 2010), 203–204. On possessive individualism, see C. B. Macpherson, *The Political Theory of Possessive Individualism: Hobbes to Locke* (Oxford: Clarendon Press, 1962). Matthew Erie characterizes the way in which nail-house owners have appropriated rights discourse as one of "legal surrealism," a process whereby they have taken on the interpretation of law in their own hands. See Matthew S. Erie, "Property Rights, Legal Consciousness and the New Media in China: The Hard Case of the 'Toughest Nail-House in History,'" *China Information* 26, no. 1 (March 2012): 35–59.

43. Anne Orford, "Biopolitics and the Tragic Subject of Human Rights," in *The Logics of Biopower and the War on Terror: Living, Dying, Surviving*, ed. Elizabeth Dauphinee and Cristina Masters (New York: Palgrave Macmillan, 2007), 205, 223. For a critique of human rights discourse, see also David Kennedy, *The Dark Sides of Virtue: Reassessing International Humanitarianism* (Princeton, NJ: Princeton University Press, 2004). For critical analyses of the "underside of legal reform" in China specifically, see William P. Alford, "Exporting 'The Pursuit of Happiness,'" *Harvard Law Review* 133, no. 7 (May 2000): 1708; Ethan Michelson, "The Practice of Law as an Obstacle to Justice: Chinese Lawyers at Work," *Law & Society Review* 40, no. 1 (March 2006): 1–38; Rebecca E. Karl, "The Flight to Rights: 1990s China and Beyond," *Telos* no. 151 (Summer 2010): 87–104.

44. Homi K. Bhabha, *The Location of Culture* (New York: Routledge, 1994), 89.

45. See Oliver E. Williamson, *Markets and Hierarchies: Analysis and Antitrust Implications* (New York: Free Press, 1983).

46. Citizens United v. Fed. Election Comm'n, 558 U.S. 50 (2010).

47. See Joseph Vining, "China, Business Law, and Finance—Accession to the World Trade Organization," University of Michigan Law & Economics, Olin Working Paper No. 08–105; University of Michigan Public Law Working Paper No. 123, University of Michigan, Ann Arbor, 2008, http://papers.ssrn.com/sol3 /papers.cfm?abstract_id=1276348.

48. Fang Liufang, "China's Corporatization Experiment," *Duke Journal of Comparative & International Law* 5, no. 2 (Spring 1995): 155 n. 13.

49. Donald C. Clarke, "Regulation and Its Discontents: Understanding Economic Law in China," *Stanford Journal of International Law* 28, no. 2 (Spring 1992): 293.

50. Christopher Engholm, *Doing Business in Asia's Booming "China Triangle"* (Englewood Cliffs, NJ: Prentice Hall, 1994), 256. The unit provides its members with a variety of goods and services, such as housing, education, and health care, and it can also intervene on members' behalf in their dealings with other authorities. See Andrew G. Walder, *Communist Neo-Traditionalism: Work and Authority in Chinese Industry* (Berkeley: University of California Press, 1986), 29. See also Xiaobo Lü and Elizabeth J. Perry, eds., *Danwei: The Changing Chinese Workplace in Historical and Comparative Perspective*, Socialism and Social Movements (Armonk, NY: M. E. Sharpe, 1997).

51. Engholm, *Doing Business*, 253.

52. On the continuing economic importance of the work-unit, see Yu Xie and Xiaogang Wu, "*Danwei* Profitablity and Earnings Inequality in Urban China," *China Quarterly* 195 (September 2008): 558–581. Historically, the family metaphor has had considerable material implications in the social world of the work unit. By the force of custom, if not enacted law, children have succeeded to their parents' jobs, for example. Such a "pattern of informal job inheritance" has not been limited to workers; managers too have successfully bequeathed control to their sons or other kin. See Engholm, *Doing Business*, 258. Much as in the traditional clan corporation, the family metaphor has its insidious side as well: a status hierarchy potentially justifying a clannish kleptocracy. The result is, in sociological terms, an enterprise made up of "several status groups, each of which has its own publicly defined rights to income, job tenure, social security, labor insurance, and housing and residence—each of which, in other words, is legally entitled to a distinctive style of life." Walder, *Communist Neo-Traditionalism*, 40.

53. See, for example, Barry Naughton, "State Enterprise Restructuring: Renegotiating the Social Compact in Urban China," in *China Today: Economic Reforms, Social Cohesion and Collective Identities*, ed. Taciana Fisac Badell and Leila Fernández-Stembridge (London: RoutledgeCurzon, 2003), 7.

54. Engholm, *Doing Business*, 237. See also Chun Chang and Yijiang Wang, "The Nature of the Township-Village Enterprise," *Journal of Comparative Economics* 19, no. 3 (December 1994): 435.

55. Jean C. Oi, "Fiscal Reform and the Economic Foundations of Local State Corporatism in China," *World Politics* 45, no. 1 (October 1992): 100. See also Andrew G. Walder, "Local Governments as Industrial Firms: An Organizational Analysis of China's Transitional Economy," *American Journal of Sociology* 101, no. 2 (September 1995): 263–301.

56. See Song Lina, "Convergence: A Comparison of Township Firms and Local State Enterprises," in *China's Rural Industry: Structure, Development, and*

Reform, ed. William A. Byrd and Lin Qinsong (Oxford: Oxford University Press, 1990), 396.

57. Jean C. Oi, "The Fate of the Collective after the Commune," in *Chinese Society on the Eve of Tiananmen: The Impact of Reform*, ed. Deborah Davis and Ezra F. Vogel (Cambridge, MA: Council on East Asian Studies, Harvard University, 1990), 35.

58. Ibid., 33–36. The critical legal theorist Roberto Unger, perhaps most notably, regards TVEs as avatars of a new, progressive economic system—a view shared by several Chinese New Left observers. See Roberto Mangabeira Unger, *Democracy Realized: The Progressive Alternative* (London: Verso, 1998). For a critique of Unger's understanding of the Chinese legal tradition, see William P. Alford, "The Inscrutable Occidental? Implications of Roberto Unger's Uses and Abuses of the Chinese Past," *Texas Law Review* 64, no. 5 (February 1986): 915–972.

59. See Xianfa 宪法 [PRC Constitution] art. 8 (1982); Zhonghua Renmin Gongheguo Tudi Guanli Fa 中华人民共和国土地官理法 [PRC Land Administration Law] (promulgated by Standing Committee of the National People's Congress, June 25, 1986, effective Jan. 1, 1999), arts. 8, 14. See also Tudi Guanli Fa Shishi Tiaoli 土地官理法实施条例 [Regulations on the Implementation of the Land Administration Law] (promulgated by State Council, Dec. 27, 1998, effective Jan. 1, 1999).

60. Lee, *Against the Law*, 259.

61. See Hsing, *Great Urban Transformation*, 122–151. Although both the village and the company exist, Hsing refers to both with fictitious names. On the ill-defined nature of shareholding cooperatives as legal entities, see Donald Clarke, "How Do We Know When an Enterprise Exists? Unanswerable Questions and Legal Polycentricity in China," *Columbia Journal of Asian Law* 19, no. 1 (Spring–Fall 2005): 50–71.

62. Less colloquially, the phenomenon is described in terms of "attached" or "affiliated" (*guakao*) enterprises. See Fang Liufang, "China's Corporatization Experiment," 205–206.

63. See Margaret M. Pearson, *China's New Business Elite: The Political Consequences of Economic Reform* (Berkeley: University of California Press, 1997), 112.

64. See Wank, *Commodifying Communism*.

65. William C. Jones, "Some Questions Regarding the Significance of the General Provisions of Civil Law of the People's Republic of China," *Harvard International Law Journal* 28, no. 2 (Spring 1987): 322.

66. See Zhonghua Renmin Gongheguo Gongsi Fa 2005 Xiuding 中华人民共和国公司法 2005 修订 [PRC Company Law 2005 Revision] art. 1 (promulgated by Standing Committee of National People's Congress, Oct. 27, 2005, effective Jan, 1, 2006).

67. On the idea of "a peasant clan writ large," see Peter L. Berger, "Is Asia's Success Transplantable?," *Asian Wall Street Journal*, April 20, 1994.

68. For an excellent study of the changing role of the family in the early phase of China's political and economic reforms, see Michael Dutton, *Policing and Punishment in China: From Patriarchy to 'the People'* (Cambridge: Cambridge University Press, 1992), 189–290. For an analysis of the continuing vitality of socialism in China today, see Lin Chun, *The Transformation of Chinese Socialism* (Durham, NC: Duke University Press, 2006).

69. See Douglas C. North, *Institutions, Institutional Change and Economic Performance: Political Economy of Institutions and Decisions* (Cambridge: Cambridge University Press, 1990).

70. See Wuquan Fa (物权法) [Property Law] (promulgated by the National People's Congress, Mar. 16, 2007, effective Oct. 1, 2007) (Lawinfochina) (China); see also Frank K. Upham, "From Demsetz to Deng: Speculations on the Implications of Chinese Growth for Law and Development Theory," *New York University Journal of International Law and Politics* 41, no. 3 (Spring 2009): 551–602; Upham, "Mythmaking in the Rule of Law Orthodoxy" (Carnegie Paper No. 30, Carnegie Endowment for International Peace, Washington, DC, 2002); Donald C. Clarke, "Economic Development and the Rights Hypothesis: The China Problem," *American Journal of Comparative Law* 51, no. 1 (Winter 2003): 89–112.

71. On the emergence and regulation of individual households, see Edward J. Epstein and Ye Lin, "Individual Enterprise in Contemporary Urban China: A Legal Analysis of Status and Regulation," *International Lawyer* 21, no. 2 (Spring 1987): 397–401.

72. See Alison W. Conner, "To Get Rich Is Precarious: Regulation of Private Enterprise in the People's Republic of China," *Journal of Chinese Law* 5, no. 1 (Spring 1991): 1, 6 & n. 27 and the sources cited therein.

73. When the permanent regulations for "real," i.e., non-family, private enterprises came out, they established a clear, if arbitrary, legal definition—an enterprise with fewer than eight employees constituted a "household," and one with more than eight a "private enterprise." See article 2 of Siying Qiye Zanxing Tiaoli 私营企业暂行条例 [Provisional Regulations on Private Enterprises] (promulgated by the State Council, June 25, 1988, effective July 1, 1988). What is the metaphysical significance of the number *eight*? Chinese legal scholars attribute the figure to a reference by Marx in *Das Kapital*. See Conner, "To Get Rich Is Precarious," 10 n. 53. Why no limit on the number of *family members*? Evidently, hiring labor is exploitative—putting one's family to work is not. The family, after all, is a community of solidarity, or so the regulations seem to assume, in a spirit decidedly more Confucian than Communist.

74. I borrow the suggestive, albeit rather naturalistic, DNA metaphor from James Q. Whitman, "Western Legal Imperialism: Thinking about the Deep Historical Roots," *Theoretical Inquiries in Law* 10, no. 2 (July 2009): 305–332.

75. See Clarke, "The China Problem."

76. See Jedidiah Kroncke, "Taming the Imagined Dragons: China, Missionaries, and Modern U.S. Legal Exceptionalism" (unpublished manuscript).

77. See, for example, Peter Stein, "The Attraction of the Civil Law in Post-Revolutionary America," *Virginia Law Review* 52, no. 3 (April 1966): 403–434, and Mathias Reimann, *The Reception of Continental Ideas*.

78. On the common law's openness to cosmopolitanism, see John Fabian Witt, *Patriots and Cosmopolitans: Hidden Histories of Law* (Cambridge, MA: Harvard University Press, 2007), and H. Patrick Glenn, *On Common Laws* (Oxford: Oxford University Press, 2007).

79. Remarkably, a recent Dutch rule-of-law program has invested in translating contemporary Chinese legal theory into English, in contrast to the more usual approach of translating Euro-American ideas into Chinese. Among other things, it funded the translation of Xia Yong 夏勇, *Zhongguo minquan zhexue* 中国民权哲学 (Beijing: Sanlian shudian 三联书店, 2004), published in English as Xia Yong, *The Philosophy of Civil Rights in the Context of China* (Leiden, Netherlands: Martinus Nijhoff, 2011).

80. On the popularity of references to Maine, see Albert H. Y. Chen, "The Developing Theory of Law and Market Economy in Contemporary China," in *Legal Developments in China: Market Economy and Law*, ed. Wang Guiguo and Wei Zhenying (Hong Kong: Sweet & Maxwell, 1996), 4, 9–10. For a historical analysis of Maine as a champion of "liberal imperialism," see Karuna Mantena, *Alibis of Empire: Henry Maine and the Ends of Liberal Imperialism* (Princeton, NJ: Princeton University Press, 2010).

81. See Zhang Kuan 张宽, "Oumeiren yanzhong de 'feiwo zulei'" 欧美人眼中的非我族类 ['Otherness' in the eyes of Europeans and Americans], *Dushu* 读书 9 (1993): 3–8. For Zhang Kuan's later account, see Zhang Kuan, "The Dilemma of Postcolonial Criticism in Contemporary China," *Ariel* 40, no. 1 (2009): 143–159.

82. See Wang Hui, "The 1989 Social Movement and the Historical Roots of China's Neoliberalism," in *China's New Order: Society, Politics, and Economy in Transition*, trans. and ed. Theodore Huters (Cambridge, MA: Harvard University Press, 2003), 41–138. As Wang observes in another essay, "There has not been a single Chinese postcolonial critique of Han centrism from the standpoint of peripheral culture. What is particularly amusing is that Chinese postmodernists turn the postmodernist critique of Eurocentrism on its head to argue for Chineseness and to search for the prospects for China repositioning itself as the center of the world." See Wang Hui, "Contemporary Chinese Thought and the Question of Modernity," in ibid., 170. For critical assessments of the Zhang Kuan controversy, see also Ben Xu, "The Postmodern-Postcolonial Stimulus and the Rise of Chinese Post-ist Theory," in *Disenchanted Democracy: Chinese Cultural Criticism after 1989* (Ann Arbor: University of Michigan Press, 1999), 88–128; Haun Saussy, "Postmodernism in China: A Sketch and Some Queries," in *Great Walls of Discourse*

and Other Adventures in Cultural China (Cambridge, MA: Harvard University Asia Center, 2001), 118–145.

83. Cui Zhiyuan is the most commonly cited instance of the influence of Critical Legal Studies in China, although he is a political scientist (trained at the University of Chicago) who became acquainted with Roberto Unger at Harvard Law School while teaching at the Massachusetts Institute of Technology. For his writing in English, see Zhiyuan Cui, "Whither China? The Discourse on Property Rights in the Chinese Reform Context," *Social Text* 55 (Summer 1998): 67–81. For an earlier call for Chinese intellectuals to heed the utility of Critical Legal Studies (among other fields), see Cui Zhi-yuan 崔之元, "Zhidu chuangxin yu di'erci sixiang jiefang" 制度創新與第二次思想解放 [Institutional innovation and a second liberation of thought], *Ershiyi Shiji* 二十一世紀 [Twenty-first century] 24 (August 1994): 5–16. On Cui's engagement with Unger, see Zhiyuan Cui, "Introduction," in Roberto Mangabeira Unger, *Politics: The Central Texts*, ed. Zhiyuan Cui (London: Verso, 1997), v–xvi. For a critical assessment of Cui Zhiyuan in New Left discourse, see Gloria Davies, *Worrying about China: The Language of Chinese Critical Inquiry* (Cambridge, MA: Harvard University Press, 2007), 72–76. In what is perhaps a sign of growing interest in postcolonial theory by PRC legal scholars, the *Chinese Social Science Quarterly* is publishing a translation of the article version of this book's theoretical argument. See Teemu Ruskola, "Falü dongfang xue" 法律东方学 [Legal Orientalism], *Zhongguo shehui kexue luncong* 中国社会科学论丛 [Chinese social science quarterly] 46 (forthcoming, Winter 2012–2013).

84. See Wang Shengjun's interview in Renminwang 人民网, "Kaizhan shehui zhuyi fazhi linian jiaoyu zaojiu gao suzhi zhengfa duiwu—fang zhongyang zhengfa wei mishuzhang Wang Shengjun" 开展社会主义法治理念教育 造就高素质政法队伍— 访中央政法委秘书长王胜俊 [Carry out education of the socialist rule of law conception and train high-quality political-legal ranks—Visiting Central Party Political and Legal Committee's Wang Shengjun], Aug. 3, 2008, http://legal.people .com.cn/GB/42735/4663959.html, quoted in Samuli Seppänen, "Ideological Conflict in the Chinese Rule of Law Discourse" (SJD thesis, Harvard University, 2012), 108. Elsewhere Wang insists that the judiciary is among the "most important ideological areas" where Chinese and foreign forces compete, urging vigilance toward hostile "forces" that seek to use China's courts to Westernize and divide the nation. See Benjamin L. Liebman, "A Return to Populist Legality? Historical Legacies and Legal Reform," in *Mao's Invisible Hand: The Political Foundations of Adaptive Governance in China*, ed. Sebastian Heilmann and Elizabeth J. Perry (Cambridge, MA: Harvard University Asia Center, 2011), 196–197.

85. See Seppänen, "Ideological Conflict."

86. Gaoju qizhi yushijujin nuli kaichuang renmin fayuan gongzuo xin jumian 高举旗帜 与时俱进 努力开创人民法院工作新局面, Wang Shengjun 王胜俊, Aug. 7, 2008, http://old.chinacourt.org/public/detail.php?id=316078.

87. Seppänen, "Ideological Conflict," 90–158.

88. He Weifang de bolaoge 賀衛方的博嘮閣, "'Sange zhishang' shei zishang" '三个至上'谁至上 [Which of the "three supremes" is supreme?], blog entry by He Weifang, Aug. 27, 2008, http://blog.sina.com.cn/s/blog_488663200100atga.html.

89. See Wang Xiaoming, "Toward a 'Great Unity': Theories of Subjectivity in China in the Early Decades of the Modern Era," trans. Darwin H. Tsen, *Social Text* 30, no. 1 (Spring 2012): 143–157.

90. For a Schmittian political analysis, see Michael Dutton, *Policing Chinese Politics: A History* (Durham, NC: Duke University Press, 2005). Remarkably, most studies of Chinese constitutional law have very little to say about the Party. For an exception, see Xin He, "The Party's Leadership as a Living Constitution in China," *Hong Kong Law Journal* 42, no. 1 (2012): 73–94. On the concept of the state of exception, see Carl Schmitt, *Political Theology: Four Chapters on the Concept of Sovereignty*, trans. George Schwab (Chicago: University of Chicago Press, 1985).

91. See Sapio, *Sovereign Power*. In a similar vein, Sarah Biddulph argues that while police powers in China have to a great extent been legalized and regularized, in practice there are few constraints on the scope of administrative detention. See Sarah Biddulph, *Legal Reform and Administrative Detention Powers in China* (Cambridge: Cambridge University Press, 2007).

92. See Liebman, "Return to Populist Legality?," 180, 186. Needless to add, Liebman is fully aware that the latest invocation of revolutionary ideals does not signal their return in full-fledged form. Ibid., 184. For an analysis of the role and uses of discretion in PRC adjudication, see Margaret Y. K. Woo, "Law and Discretion in the Contemporary Chinese Courts," *Pacific Rim Law & Policy Journal* 8, no. 3 (September 1999): 581–615.

93. See generally Sujian Guo and Baogang Guo, eds., *China in Search of a Harmonious Society* (Lanham, MD: Lexington Books, 2008). Seppänen links the discourse of harmonious society to what he calls Chinese neoconservatism. See Seppänen, "Ideological Conflict," 93–94.

94. See generally Su Li 苏力, *Fazhi jiqi bentu ziyuan* 法治及其本土资源 [Rule of law and its local resources] (Beijing: Zhengfa daxue chubanshe 政法大学出版社, 1996). On Suli, see also Albert H. Y. Chen, "Socio-legal Thought and Legal Modernization in Contemporary China: A Case Study of the Jurisprudence of Zhu Suli," in *Law, Legal Culture and Politics in the Twenty First Century*, ed. Guenther Doeker-Mach and Klaus A. Ziegert (Stuttgart, Germany: Franz Steiner Verlag, 2004), 227–249; Frank K. Upham, "Who Will Find the Defendant if He Stays with His Sheep? Justice in Rural China," *Yale Law Journal* 114, no. 7 (May 2005): 1675–1718. Suli's writings in English address the role of the Party in the Chinese legal system. See Zhu Suli, "Political Parties in China's Judiciary," *Duke Journal of Comparative & International Law* 17, no. 2 (Spring 2007): 533–560; Zhu Suli, "The Party and the Courts," in *Judicial Independence in China: Lessons for Global Rule of Law Promotion*, ed. Randall Peerenboom (Cambridge: Cambridge University Press, 2010), 52–68. Zhu's latest methodological turn is to law-and-literature. See Su Li 苏力,

Falü yu wenxue: yi zhongguo chuantong xiju wei cailiao 法律与文学: 以中国传统戏剧为材料 [Law and literature: traditional Chinese plays as materials] (Beijing: Sanlian shudian 三联书店, 2006).

95. See Su Li 苏 力, "Renzhen duidai renzhi 认真对待人治 [Taking rule of man seriously]," *Huadong zhengfa xueyuan xuebao* 华东政法学院学报 12 (1998): 18, reprinted in Su Li 苏力, *Zhidu shi ruhe xingcheng de* 制度是如何形成的 [How institutions are formed] (Beijing: Peking University Press, 2007), 210–221.

96. See Xia Yong, *Philosophy of Civil Rights*, 55.

97. See Jiang Qing 蒋庆, *Zhengzhi ruxue: Dangdai ruxue de zhuanxiang, tezhi yu fazhan* 政治儒学: 当代儒学的转向, 特质与发展 [Political Confucianism: the transformation, characteristics and development of contemporary Confucianism] (Beijing: Sanlian shudian 三联书店, 2003). For an English-language discussion of his evolving views, see Jiang Qing, *A Confucian Constitutional Order: How China's Ancient Past Can Shape Its Political Future*, ed. Daniel A. Bell and Ruiping Fan, trans. Edmund Ryden (Princeton, NJ: Princeton University Press, 2012). See also Ruiping Fan, ed., *The Renaissance of Confucianism in Contemporary China* (Dordrecht, Netherlands: Springer, 2011); Jiang Qing and Daniel A. Bell, "A Confucian Constitution for China," *New York Times*, July 11, 2012, A25; Dong Zhongshu, "The Way of the King Penetrates Three," in *Sources of Chinese Tradition*, vol. 1: From Earliest Times to 1600, comp. Wm. Theodore de Bary and Irene Bloom, 2nd ed. (New York: Columbia University Press, 1999), 300–301. It should be noted that the reconciliation of Confucianism with liberalism is a transnational enterprise. In the United States, it is associated most closely with Wm. Theodore de Bary. See, for example, Wm. Theodore de Bary, *The Liberal Tradition in China* (New York: Columbia University Press, 1983); de Bary, *Asian Values and Human Rights: A Confucian Communitarian Perspective* (Cambridge, MA: Harvard University Press, 1998); and Wm. Theodore de Bary and Tu Weiming, eds., *Confucianism and Human Rights* (New York: Columbia University Press, 1998).

98. See Daniel A. Bell, "Jiang Qing's *Political Confucianism*," in *China's New Confucianism: Politics and Everyday Life in a Changing Society* (Princeton, NJ: Princeton University Press, 2008), 175–191. To be sure, in the latest iteration of his evolving views, Jiang acknowledges this problem and proposes a mechanism for resolving stand-offs among the three legislative chambers. See Jiang, *A Confucian Constitutional Order*, 41–42.

99. See Seppänen, "Ideological Conflict," 323.

100. Zhu's doctoral dissertation, a comparative study of the concept of social control in China and the United States, poses an acute challenge to the epistemological foundations of Euro-American social theory. Zhu's concluding chapter draws expressly on Edward Said and Michel Foucault to develop a critique of "cultural imperialism." See Zhu Suli, "A Critique of Social Control in Cross-Cultural Studies" (PhD thesis, Arizona State University, 1992).

101. Xia Yong, *Philosophy of Civil Rights*, 6.

102. Ibid., 156.

103. See generally Louis Henkin, "The Constitution and United States Sovereignty: A Century of *Chinese Exclusion* and Its Progeny," *Harvard Law Review* 100, no. 4 (February 1987): 853–886.

104. T. Alexander Aleinikoff, *Semblances of Sovereignty: The Constitution, the State, and American Citizenship* (Cambridge, MA: Harvard University Press, 2002), 5.

105. Ibid., 155, 184.

106. See Gabriel J. Chin, "Regulating Race: Asian Exclusion and the Administrative State," *Harvard Civil Rights-Civil Liberties Law Review* 37, no. 1 (Winter 2002): 5; Leti Volpp, "The Citizen and the Terrorist," *UCLA Law Review* 49, no. 5 (June 2002): 1575–1600.

107. United States *ex rel.* Knauff v. Shaughnessy, 338 U.S. 537, 544 (1950). On the "obnoxious" Chinese, see Leti Volpp, " 'Obnoxious to Their Very Nature': Asian Americans and Constitutional Citizenship," *Citizenship Studies* 5, no. 1 (February 2001): 57–71.

108. The account below of this hidden legacy draws on Gabriel Chin's "Regulating Race."

109. Ibid., 4.

110. See Administrative Procedure Act, Pub. L. No. 79-404, 60 Stat. 237 (1946) (codified at 5 U.S.C. §§ 500–596 (2006)).

111. Roscoe Pound, "Justice According to Law (II)," *Columbia Law Review* 14, no. 1 (January 1914): 22.

112. The term "high-end administrative model" is Chin's. See "Regulating Race," 46.

113. David Kairys, "Searching for the Rule of Law," *Suffolk University Law Review* 36, no. 2 (2003): 319.

114. See Margaret Jane Radin, "Reconsidering the Rule of Law," *Boston University Law Review* 69, no. 4 (July 1989): 808.

115. See Antonio Gramsci, *Prison Notebooks*, ed. Joseph A. Buttigieg, trans. Joseph A. Buttigieg and Antonio Callari, 2 vols. (New York: Columbia University Press, 1992–1996). See also Ranajit Guha, *Dominance without Hegemony: History and Power in Colonial India* (Cambridge, MA: Harvard University Press, 1997).

116. On the multiplicity of concepts of freedom, and unfreedom, see, for example, David Kelly and Anthony Reid, eds., *Asian Freedoms: The Idea of Freedom in East and Southeast Asia* (Cambridge: Cambridge University Press, 1998); Robert H. Taylor, ed., *The Idea of Freedom in Asia and Africa* (Stanford, CA: Stanford University Press, 2002); Harri Englund, *Prisoners of Freedom: Human Rights and the African Poor* (Berkeley: University of California Press, 2006). Yves Dezalay and Bryant Garth chart the varied trajectories of law's rule in postcolonial Asia—emancipatory and otherwise—in *Asian Legal Revivals: Lawyers in the Shadow of Empire* (Chicago: University of Chicago Press, 2010).

Comment on Chinese Sources

In transliterating Chinese sources, I have generally used *pinyin*, except for proper nouns that have a conventional English rendering (e.g., Canton). When sources cited use other transliteration systems, I have left them unchanged. Somewhat unconventionally, I use both standard and simplified versions of Chinese characters in this book, depending on context. For example, when referring to classical Chinese thought, I use standard characters, but when analyzing socialist legal thought, I employ simplified characters. This strikes me as necessary in order to be faithful to the vernacular of specific times and places. For accessibility, when referring to foreign-language sources I have tried to identify published English-language translations whenever possible. Where none exist or I am not aware of them, I have provided my own translations.

Acknowledgments

Legal Orientalism is the synthesis of work I have done over a decade. It has benefited from countless conversations and debates I have had with many people who
have enriched not only this book but also my intellectual and personal life. Properly
acknowledging all the individuals, audiences, and institutions that have contributed to the final product would entail writing an intellectual autobiography that
far exceeds the space available here.

Over time the research for this book has been supported by two universities
that have been my primary institutional homes, Emory Law School—since 2007—
and the Washington College of Law at American University. I want to thank Dean
Robert Schapiro at Emory and Dean Claudio Grossman at American University for
their material and personal support. In addition, I have had the good fortune to be
a visitor at several institutions where I have benefited from wonderful colleagues
and many other kinds of academic resources as well. They include Columbia Law
School, Cornell Law School, Fordham Law School, Georgetown University Law
Center, the Woodrow Wilson School of Public and International Affairs at Princeton University, and the School of Oriental and African Studies at the University of
London.

In addition, three fellowships have provided me with the scarcest of all academic resources: time. I am deeply grateful for the support provided by the Institute for Advanced Study (Princeton, NJ), the Law and Public Affairs Program at Princeton University, and a Charles A. Ryskamp Research Fellowship awarded by the American Council of Learned Societies.

Numerous librarians have helped me tirelessly in the many places where I have worked on this book. I want to thank, especially, Terry Gordon, Kelly Parker, and Felicity Walsh at Emory Law School; Thanh Nguyen at Georgetown University Law Center; Adeen Postar at American University; and Marcia Tucker at the Institute for Advanced Study. Likewise, I owe many thanks to research assistants who have helped me at various stages, especially with the endnotes. They include Hyungi Ryu and Alex Shin at Emory, and Amy Ericksen and Michael McLellan at American University. Citations to legal materials in this book follow generally the *Bluebook* system of citations. Annie Chan worked exceptionally hard in the final stages to meld the *Bluebook* format with the standard conventions used by Harvard University Press for nonlegal soures.

Chapters 1, 3, 4, and 6 of this book draw on previously published articles, although in largely rewritten form. I am grateful for permission to use parts of the following publications: "Conceptualizing Corporations and Kinship: Comparative Law and Development Theory in a Chinese Perspective," *Stanford Law Review* 52, no. 6 (2000): 1599–1729; "Law without Law, or Is 'Chinese Law' an Oxymoron?," *William & Mary Bill of Rights Journal* 11, no. 2 (2003): 655–669; "Legal Orientalism," *Michigan Law Review* 101, no. 1 (2002): 179–234; "Canton Is Not Boston: The Invention of American Imperial Sovereignty," *American Quarterly* 57 (2005): 859–884; "Colonialism without Colonies: On the Extraterritorial Jurisprudence of the U.S. Court for China," *Law & Contemporary Problems* 71, no. 3 (2008): 217–242.

Almost every academic presentation I have made over the last several years has included some element that has found its way into this book. Although I cannot thank individual audience members, their questions have helped me immensely, even though I have not been able to answer all the queries they have raised. I extend my warmest thanks to the many people who generously invited me to present some of the material in *Legal Orientalism* (sometimes on multiple occasions): Lama Abu-Odeh, Padideh Ala'i, Bill Alford, Keith Aoki, Reuven Avi-Yonah, Sandy Bermann, Margaret Blair, Linda Bosniak, Rosa Brooks, Deborah Cao, Lan Cao, Pär Cassell, Anupam Chander, Albert Chen, Connie Chin, Leo Ching, Thomas Christensen, Jerry Cohen, Vivian Curran, Michael Davies, Thomas Duve, Jorge Esquirol, Bardo Fassbender, Shelley Fisher-Fishkin, Peter Fitzpatrick, Krista Forsgren, Katherine Franke, Mary Gallagher, Paul Gewirtz, Jonathan Goldberg, Whit Gray, Michele Graziadei, Ariela Gross, Thordur Gunnarsson, Christine Harrington, Lochlann Jain, Suvir Kaul, Jukka Kekkonen, David Kennedy, Amalia Kessler, Martti Koskenniemi, Charlotte Ku, Mitch Lasser, David Law, Eugenia Lean, Ching-Kwan Lee, Ben Liebman, Ania Loomba, Linda McClain, Sahlil Mehra, Naomi Mezey, Ralf Michaels, Larry Mitchell, Michael Moon, Fernanda Nicola, Kimmo Nuotio, Marleen O'Connor, Jean Oi, Roger O'Keefe, Anne Orford, Di Otto, Michael Palmer, Gyan Pandey, Penny Pether, Jim Pfander, Mark Ramseyer, Mathias Reimann, Annelise Riles, Kerry Rittich, Kim Scheppele, Mike Seidman, Nan Seuffert, Dan Shao, Gary Simpson, Clyde Spillenger, Nomi Stolzenberg, Lynn Stout, Madhavi Sunder, Carol Tan, Ruti Teitel, Kellye Testy, Rose Cuizon Villazor, Robert Wai, Wang Ban, David Wank, Robin West, and Jim Whitman.

I have also drawn support from the advice, conversations, and good cheer of a large community of friends and colleagues, including Padideh Ala'i, Hubert Allen, Ken Anderson, Tony Anghie, Abdullahi An-Na'im, Gary Bell, Mayling Birney, Susan Carle, Cathy Caruth, Chen Li, Chen Yifeng, Morgan Cloud, Alison Conner, Christina Crosby, Eve Darian-Smith, Cathy Davidson, Jacques deLisle, Michael Diamond, Anthony Dicks, Ben Elman, Christine Farley, Jim Feinerman, Shoshana Felman, Martin Flaherty, Stuart Freeman, Lewis Grossman, Shinhee Han, Keith Hand, Dirk Hartog, Eric Hayot, Doug Howland, Nico Howson, Janet Jakobsen, Amy Kaplan, Farhad Karim, Duncan Kennedy, Karen Knop, Prabha Kotiswaran, Jedidiah Kroncke, Tahirih Lee, Pierre Legrand, Lydia Liu, Sanda Lwin, Binny Miller, Susette Min, Ellen Mortensen, Aamer Mumtaz, David Nugent, Ann Pellegrini, Michael Perry, Nancy Polikoff, Jeff Prescott, Kal Raustiala, Camille Robcis, Lawrence Rosen, Hinrich Schütze, Joan Scott, Holli Semetko, Ann Shalleck, Shu-mei Shih, Reva Siegel, Kaja Silverman, Katherine Stone, Tim Webster, Franz Werro, Elizabeth Wilson, Ken Wissoker, Hiro Yoshikawa, Matti Zelin, and Zhu Sanzhu.

I want to thank, especially, those who have read and commented on all or part of the material in *Legal Orientalism*: Bruce Ackerman, Jack Balkin, Daniel Bell, Ritu Birla, Jamie Boyle, Tim Brook, Christina Burnett, Jack Chin, Don Clarke, Dick Craswell, Gloria Davies, Adrienne Davis, Gina Dent, Yves Dezalay, Mary Dudziak, Michael Dutton, Randy Edwards, Martha Ertman, Martha Fineman, Hill Gates, Janet Halley, Mark Jones, Dan Klerman, Susie Lee, Ben Liebman, Lisa Lowe, Stanley Lubman, Sally Merry, John Merryman, Kunal Parker, Randy Peerenboom, Julia Qin, Haun Saussy, Eileen Scully, Vicki Schultz, Samuli Seppänen, Gayatri Spivak, Leti Volpp, Priscilla Wald, Joan Williams, and Zhu Suli.

I owe special thanks to Muneer Ahmad, Ed Cohen, David Kazanjian, Mae Ngai, Josie Saldaña, and Shuang Shen for their enormously insightful feedback when I workshopped an early version of this project. I received very helpful comments also from the anonymous reviewers solicited by Harvard University Press.

Indeed, I want to thank Shan Wang, Lindsay Waters, and others at HUP for the professionalism and speed with which they turned a manuscript into a book.

Although it has been a quarter of a century, I want to acknowledge a group of extraordinary undergraduate teachers at Stanford, whose passion for scholarship continues to inspire me to this day: Helen Brooks, P.J. Ivanhoe, Hal Kahn, and Lyman Van Slyke. Thank you! And going down memory lane, I just might have given up on memorizing Chinese characters if it hadn't been for the company of Madeline Hsu, Andrea Worden, and Portia Wu at the Stanford language center in Taipei in the early 1990s.

Finally, I want to thank my mother, Liisa Sjöstedt, to whom this book is dedicated. And the greatest thank you of all goes to David L. Eng, for reading multiple drafts and making this a much, much better book—and for making life good. Really good.

Index